Vagabond Fictions

Vagabond Fictions

Gender and Experiment in British Women's Writing, 1945–1970

Carole Sweeney

EDINBURGH
University Press

Edinburgh University Press is one of the leading university presses in the UK. We publish academic books and journals in our selected subject areas across the humanities and social sciences, combining cutting-edge scholarship with high editorial and production values to produce academic works of lasting importance. For more information visit our website: edinburghuniversitypress.com

© Carole Sweeney, 2020, 2022

Edinburgh University Press Ltd
The Tun – Holyrood Road, 12(2f) Jackson's Entry, Edinburgh EH8 8PJ

First published in hardback by Edinburgh University Press 2020

Typeset in 10.5/13 Adobe Sabon by
Servis Filmsetting Ltd, Stockport, Cheshire

A CIP record for this book is available from the British Library

ISBN 978 1 4744 2617 6 (hardback)
ISBN 978 1 4744 2618 3 (paperback)
ISBN 978 1 4744 2619 0 (webready PDF)
ISBN 978 1 4744 2620 6 (epub)

The right of Carole Sweeney to be identified as the author of this work has been asserted in accordance with the Copyright, Designs and Patents Act 1988, and the Copyright and Related Rights Regulations 2003 (SI No. 2498).

Contents

Acknowledgements		vi
	Introduction: Angels and Tyrants	1
1.	Critical Terrains	9
2.	Anna Kavan: Glass Girls	31
3.	Brigid Brophy: A 'comet in her day'	73
4.	Christine Brooke-Rose: 'un écrivain dite éxperimentale'	118
5.	Eva Figes: 'there must be freedom to experiment'	162
6.	Ann Quin: Forms Forming Themselves	205
	Afterword: Evolution, Batons and Beaks	246
Bibliography		249
Index		280

Acknowledgements

I thank all my surpassingly obliging readers who helped me refine and, in some cases, rein in, my thinking and writing; Tim Parnell, Nonia Williams, Leigh Wilson and Johanna O'Shea, whose meticulous editing, reading and formatting skills cannot be highly enough praised.

I thank the group of scholars whose work on these five writers has been important in the evolution of this book: Natalie Ferris, Hannah Van Hove, Kaye Mitchell, Nonia Williams, Julia Jordan, Adam Guy, Leigh Wilson, Victoria Walker, Patrick Burley, Andrew Hodgson and Chris Clarke. And, of course, Richard Canning and Gerri Kimber too, for all things Brophy.

I also thank my colleagues in the English Department at Goldsmiths Maura Dooley, Abi Shinn and Nick Campbell for showing an interest in my work. No mean feat. Also thanks to Jo, Maria, Mary and Sarah for all the friendship.

I was supported in my research by two generous fellowships from the Harry Ransom Humanities Research Center in Austin, Texas and the Lilly Library's Everett Helm Fellowship for my archival work on Brooke-Rose and Ann Quin respectively.

I especially thank my husband, Tim Parnell, whose love of innovative writing via *Tristram Shandy* led to the formation of the Goldsmiths Prize that re-kindled my interest in all things experimental. This book is dedicated to him and to Pascale. And to Tom and Monique for all the lovely *séjours*. And to the other Tom for printer patience and quizzing.

I am grateful to the following for permitting me to use earlier versions of published material: 'Keeping the Ruins Private: Anna Kavan and Heroin Addiction', *Women: A Cultural Review* 28: 4 (2017); 'The Dissenting Feminist', in Richard Canning and Gerri Kimber (eds), *Brigid Brophy: Avant-Garde Writer, Critic, Activist* (Edinburgh University Press, 2020); 'Cadaverized Girls: The Writing of Anna Kavan', *Textual Practice*, 31: 2 (2017); '"Groping inside language": Translation,

Humour and Experiment in Christine Brooke-Rose's *Between* and Brigid Brophy's *In Transit*', *Textual Practice*, 32: 2 (2018).

Page numbers are unavailable for some of the press clippings from the archival material but full source details are given.

Introduction: Angels and Tyrants

> Have you ever tried to do something very difficult as well as you can over a long period, and found that nobody notices? (Christine Brooke-Rose, *Invisible Author*, p. 1)

This book is a work of critical recovery of five experimental women writers, Anna Kavan, Ann Quin, Christine Brooke-Rose, Eva Figes and Brigid Brophy, all of whom, in different ways, wrote beyond and against the aesthetic and thematic conventions of their times but whose work has been, for the most part, neglected in accounts of the development of postwar British literature. Filling in a blank spot in the history of twentieth-century women's writing, this study examines how, in broadly unrelated and distinctive ways, all five engaged in what Brooke-Rose called a 'good airing out' of the mid-century British novel and, in so doing, troubled the critical commonplace that suggests the British novel after 1945 was characterised by a wholesale return to the kind of realism associated with pre-modernism.[1] The aesthetic experiments of all five writers challenge what Virginia Woolf called conventional realism's 'powerful and unscrupulous tyrant' obliging writers to provide a narrative with a convincing 'air of probability embalming the whole'.[2]

In addition to formal experimentation, their writing also refuses the thematic strictures of the romantic marriage plot with its repression of female quest and the centrality of the Woolfian 'Angel in the House'; the model of self-effacing domestic femininity, so often the enemy of women's creativity.[3] Discarding this domestic angel as well as sending packing the tyrant of plot-driven narrative, these five writers are free to roam 'under every rock and cranny of the world' in their writing experiments.[4] Woolf's rejection of this domestic Angel resonates with her earlier observations in *A Room of One's Own* (1929) on the sense of an interloper consciousness, where she states that for women 'far from being a natural inheritor' of the public sphere, coming to writing can be accompanied by a 'sudden splitting off of consciousness' in which she finds herself quite 'alien and critical'.[5] Such a 'splitting' is not, I suggest, wholly negative, as it can facilitate a writer's productive estrangement from a sense of gendered 'naturalness' that has underwritten women's confinement to the private sphere, defined by what Brooke-Rose calls the 'constant pull' of domestic responsibility that interrupts and disperses woman's creativity and freedoms.[6] Much of the writing considered here exhibits a movement away from domestic space, or shows it to be creatively and intellectually limiting for women, and into states of transit, transformation and displacement, a movement I am calling vagabondage. This outwards narrative trajectory articulates what Karen Lawrence calls 'an *expansion* of women's sphere and *extension* of their itinerary'[7] after 1945 when a general relaxing of 'paternalistic Victorian controls' facilitated the enlargement of women's rights and liberties.[8] Although feminism was already accelerating in the 1960s, the writing considered here was produced before the formal establishment of the Women's Liberation Movement and the more concentrated feminist activism of the 1970s, already richly documented in feminist literary criticism. In this way, then, these writers were not influenced by the ideological and critical orthodoxies that later developed around both Anglo-American and French feminism, remaining broadly guarded, or at least agnostic, towards the feminist movement. When they do write about gender and being a 'woman writer' both in their creative and in critical work, as Figes, Brophy and Brooke-Rose all do, they approach the subject with a circumspection that displays what Patricia Waugh describes as a 'double-voicing'; a mode of women's writing that can be both affirmative and sceptical, concerned neither with the recovery and celebration of pure essence that speaks 'female' in some authentic way, nor with a notion of gender that is wholly separate and independent of the woman in the world.[9] I am interested here, then, in the kinds of experiments with form and ideas of gender taken by these writers in a pre-feminist period; that is, before later feminist debates around questions of biological essence and gender identity in the 1970s and 1980s. Thus, this study takes as its cut-off point the year 1970, just as the Equal Pay Act is enshrined in law and when two important feminist works, Germaine Greer's *Female Eunuch* and Figes's *Patriarchal Attitudes* are published.

'To be an experimental woman writer', observed Brooke-Rose, entails

> Three words, Three difficulties. *To be a woman*: vast and vastly written up. To be a woman writer: narrower but proportionately ditto [...] it is yet a third thing for a woman to be genuinely welcomed and attended to as an 'experimental' writer.[10]

For centuries, overdetermined as the object of writing, assuming authorship for women writers has often required a negotiation, or at least an acknowledgement, of their own 'vast' gender identity in ways that male writers have not experienced – their sex assumed naturally as the universal subject more than capable of making new forms. To be a woman writer comes with the burden of a systematic 'written up-ness' in history and culture that must be confronted and banished before women can begin to think freely about form and theme. To be a woman *experimental* writer entails yet another set of obstacles that have been difficult to overcome.

Ellen G. Friedman and Miriam Fuchs have suggested that there are very specific reasons as to why formally innovative writing by women has been neglected in literary history.[11] First, they note a tendency in earlier modernist studies to regard Virginia Woolf and Gertrude Stein, H.D., Mina Loy and Dorothy Richardson, as 'having been second', if not always 'secondary' to Joyce and Proust. They posit a second, significantly more compelling, reason for the neglect of women's experimental writing that they attribute, in part, to debates within feminist literary criticism itself. They argue that for decades feminist criticism has 'hunted subtexts and muted texts to uncover a feminine discourse while overlooking the texts by women experimentalists who may be writing that discourse in deliberate, open, and varied ways' (p. 6). Put otherwise, they believe that feminist literary criticism has been so preoccupied with retrieval, rehabilitation and the search for an authentically 'feminine' or female voice in writing that it has often overlooked questions of aesthetic form. My study, then, aims to overturn this neglect by focusing on the diversity of the aesthetic experiments of these five writers as well as on their negotiation of any 'feminine discourse'.

Despite the obvious formal aesthetic differences across their work, each of these writers deploy narrative techniques that eschew, or significantly modify, the conventions of classic realism – 'a single, authoritative storyteller; well-motivated characters interacting in recognizable social patterns [...] the movement to closure'.[12] However, their experiments with form cannot easily be accommodated into the reaction and counter-reaction model of literary history that insists upon the opposition of realism to experimentalism. As will be considered presently, literary production between 1945 and 1970 was more multifaceted than this model suggests. I am consciously, then, using the term experimental throughout this book as a deliberately less precise, more commodious, term than either late modernism, avant-gardism or postmodernism as it allows for a far less trammelled periodised consideration of the variety of writing by each of these writers. The term experimental avoids the inevitable 'sandwiching' effect that often bedevils critical examinations of the British novel at mid-century in which writing finds itself positioned between what Tyrus Miller calls the 'conceptual pigeonholes' of either 'the caged eagle of modernism' or 'the spangled parakeet of postmodernism'.[13] Avian metaphors aside, what we can say with certainty is that in terms of periodisation, these writers all come *after* modernism, occasionally, but not consistently, sharing some of its concerns regarding interiority and temporality, and *before* the metafictional self-reflexivity of postmodernism. As the editors of *The Routledge Companion to Experimental Literature* put it, the term experimentalism is 'irreducibly diverse' and might include '[u]nfettered improvisation and the rigorous application of rules, accidental composition and hyper-rational design, free invention and obsessively faithful duplication, extreme conceptualism and extreme materiality'.[14]

In this way, then, I consider the work of each writer in terms of its individual experimentalism in ways that do not seek to locate it either in modernism's longer *durée,* or as exemplary of a nascent postmodernism.[15] Crucially, these five writers experimented with language and narrative in ways that did not necessitate a polarisation between realism and, its putative opposite, experimentalism. Adapting and extending realism's boundaries and codes, these writers did not subscribe to what Brooke-Rose calls 'a great oversimplification' of how experimental texts function: 'There's always a representative function', she says, 'simply because language is representative [...] we've all become much more self-conscious about it, but I don't think we can actually get out of representation'.[16] Such an acknowledgement that language has an essentially representative relationship, however variable, with 'reality' avoids the need to wholly repudiate realism, which, in fact, as Peter Boxall points out is seldom 'really realism' at all.[17] Accordingly, as we shall see, the experimental techniques used by these writers are diverse, ranging from Kavan's 'strange, softly terrifying' psychological expressionism, to Brophy's archly rococo realism in *The Snow Ball* and *Flesh*, Quin's blackly comic reworking of the Oedipus myth to the poststructuralist concerns of Brooke-Rose's lipogrammatical *Between* and the scientific precision of *Out*.[18]

While I consider this study a work of feminist criticism in that it recovers lost female writers whose work deserves to be read, I do not propose that the various forms of textual experiments explored by these five writers are inherently ideologically subversive; that is, textual experiment is not the equivalent of progressive, or transgressive, thinking and, conversely, realism (however understood) is not assumed to be directly representative of a patriarchal system. Merely pitting experimentalism against realism in ideological terms simplifies the complexities of poetic practices and the diverse ways in which gender difference can be explored in experimental writing. In this way, then, my study stands in partial disagreement with the principal thesis of the ground-breaking work of Friedman and Fuchs's *Breaking the Sequence: Women's Experimental Fiction* (1989), in which they suggest that realism is an inherently conservative, masculine form of writing representing 'patriarchal mastery in Western culture' (p. 4), and that experimentalism is intrinsically and always politically subversive. Far from writing off earlier feminist thinking regarding the relationship between writing and gender, that is between textual and sexual politics, I have found this kind of discrepancy vitally constructive for the project of this book which understands contemporary feminist literary criticism to be sufficiently intellectually broad that it can allow many shades of discord and dissent, especially when looking back to writing that mostly pre-dates the flourishing of second-wave feminism in Britain. The various kinds of dissension with some of the tenets of this second wave will be discussed in detail in relation to Christine Brooke-Rose, Eva Figes and Brigid Brophy.

The designation 'British' in the book's title is a reasonably clear descriptor, but in fact out of the five writers only Ann Quin strictly conforms to this designation of nationality. With an Irish father and long periods spent in Ireland as a child, Brigid Brophy considered herself to be Anglo-Irish but lived and worked in England all her life. Born in Geneva to a British father and a Swiss-American mother, Christine Brooke-Rose was brought up in Brussels, educated at Oxford and London, lived in Britain until she was middle-aged and then in France for the rest of her life. Anna Kavan was born in Cannes and spent a peripatetic childhood shuttling between England, America and Europe, and lived and travelled in France, Burma and New Zealand before settling in London. A German-Jewish refugee from Nazi Germany, Eva Figes came to Britain at the age of seven where she lived for the remainder of her life. Britishness is thus understood expansively here to describe these writers who lived (mostly) in Britain but some of whom had lives marked by expatriation and transit.

It must be acknowledged, of course, these were not the only women writers engaged in such an aeration of prose in this period and one might reasonably enquire as to the whereabouts of the more renowned women experimenters such as Muriel Spark, Doris Lessing, Angela Carter, Ivy Compton-Burnett or even Elizabeth Bowen. The absence of Spark in particular might surprise some readers. How can one write a book about women's postwar experimental fiction without mentioning a writer who once declared, 'Fuck the general reader, the general reader does not exist', and who gave us the metafictional self-consciousness of *The Comforters* (1957)?[19] The simple answer, of course, is that there already exists a substantial body of critical work on Spark, whereas the five writers examined here have suffered from comparative critical neglect. The same can be said of Carter, whose work continues to enjoy significant critical attention. If Spark and Carter are absent because of their well-established reputations, other neglected mid-century British women experimenters such as Penelope Shuttle, Rosemary Tonkin, Maureen Duffy and Shena Mackay do not make it into this study as their *oeuvres* are slighter but might justifiably be next in line for critical recovery.

Aside from the idea of aesthetic and thematic vagabondage, I have avoided advancing any one overarching thesis or theoretical framework in my study. While drawing upon ideas of Kristevan abjection, the dead mother, female melancholia and, more broadly, on apposite feminist and queer theory, I do so only locally where individual texts require a more detailed engagement with specific critical concepts. This approach reduces the risk of excavating the work of individual writers in pursuit of textual evidence that might prove (or disprove) any one theoretical proposition and thus avoids rendering the varied textures and modes of writing to elucidatory units of relevance. In order to more fully counter the critical neglect of these five writers, I have given some attention to their individual biographies, in particular to the ways in which they came to experiment, sometimes after, in the case of Kavan and Brooke-Rose, beginning their careers as significantly more conventionally realist writers.

I begin, then, in Chapter 1 by surveying the critical debates on postwar British writing, questioning the view that in the two decades after the end of modernism British literature underwent a comprehensive return to social realism with an associated repudiation of formal experiment. I also discuss here what Rita Felski calls a 'feminine' writing practice, one that avoids any essentialising notions of the feminine/female/feminist suggested by the concept *of écriture féminine*.[20] The chapter begins with a brief adumbration of the extension of women's social and sexual freedoms in the years 1945–70. Chapter 2 examines the work of Anna Kavan whose career spanned fifty years in two distinct phases. Looking at *Sleep Has His House* (1948), *Asylum Piece* (1940) and *Ice* (1967) in particular, I consider how Kavan's writing works over the figure of the 'dead' mother, depression and the violence of sexual relationships. Also considered is Kavan's long-term addiction to heroin and the ways in which this has affected, and often limited, the critical reception of her work. Chapter 3 focuses on the work of Brigid Brophy whose work is extraordinary for its diversity, ranging from biographies of Ronald Firbank and Mozart to elegantly queer novels of elaborate artifice, and iconoclastic literary criticism. A prolific novelist, Brophy, wrote eleven works of fiction in her too-short lifetime. These included *The King of a Rainy Country* (1956), *In Transit* (1969) and *Flesh* (1962), each of which anticipates later feminist debates on essentialism and the cultural construction of gender. Brophy's novels are notable for their experiments within, around and against the conventions of novelistic realism.

Favouring play over plot, and multilingualism over monolingualism, Christine Brooke-Rose wrote 'metastories' with 'metacharacters'. Reading *Between* (1968), *Out* (1964) and *Such* (1966), as well as a selection of her critical writing, Chapter 4 examines how she developed the 'narratorless mode', OULIPO-style constraints and lipogrammatic forms in her work. The most theoretically informed writer of the five, much of Brooke-Rose's writing antedates Barthes's concept of the 'writerly' text. Perhaps best known for her 1970 feminist bestselling *Patriarchal Attitudes*, as well as her incisive journalism and non-fiction writing, Eva Figes wrote three novels between 1966 and 1969 – *Equinox* (1966), *Winter's Journey* (1967) and *Konek Landing* (1969), all of which are considered in Chapter 5. Figes was part of a loose group of British 'experimenters' in the 1960s whose mission it was to write prose that counteracted prevalent literary production that wrote as if '*Ulysses* had never been written'.[21] Ann Quin's work was only just gaining momentum when she died at the age of thirty-seven. Taking her artistic cues from the varied and stimulating influences in the 1960s countercultural *zeitgeist* – the *nouveau roman*, the Black Mountain poets, French cinema, the energies of pop art in visual culture, and from her extensive travels in the USA, Quin's work deploys a diversity of experimental techniques that are examined in Chapter 6 through readings of *Berg* (1964), *Three* (1966) and *Passages* (1969).

Notes

1. Christine Brooke-Rose, 'Samuel Beckett and The Anti-Novel', *The London Magazine, The London Magazine*, 5: 12 (December 1958), pp. 3–46 (p. 38).
2. Virginia Woolf, 'Modern Fiction', in Virginia Woolf, *The Common Reader: Volume 1*, rev. edn, ed. Andrew McNeillie (London: Vintage, 2003), pp. 146–54 (p. 149).
3. Virginia Woolf, 'Professions for Women', in *The Death of the Moth and Other Essays* (New York: Harcourt Brace Jovanovich, 1974), pp. 236–42 (p. 236).

4. Ibid., p. 240.
5. Virginia Woolf, *A Room of One's Own* (London: Hogarth Press, 1929), pp. 87–8.
6. Brooke-Rose, 'Conversation', interview with Friedman and Fuchs, p. 34. Tillie Olsen, 'One Out of Twelve: Writers Who are Women in Our Century', in *Silences* (New York: Feminist Press, 2003), pp. 22–46 (p. 34).
7. Karen R. Lawrence, *Penelope Voyages: Women and Travel in the British Literary Tradition* (Ithaca, NY: Cornell University Press, 1994), p. 18.
8. Arthur Marwick, *British Society Since 1945: The Penguin Social History of Britain*, 4th edn (London: Penguin, 2003), p. x.
9. Patricia Waugh, 'Feminism and Writing: The Politics of Culture', in Laura Marcus and Peter Nicholls (eds), *The Cambridge History of Twentieth Century Literature* (Cambridge: Cambridge: University Press, 2004), pp. 600–17 (p. 601).
10. Brooke-Rose, 'Illiterations', in G. N. Forester and M. J. Nicholls (eds), *Verbivoracious Festschrift Volume 1: Christine Brooke-Rose* (Great Britain and Glentrees, Singapore: Verbivoracious Press, 2014), pp. 41–59 (pp. 41–3).
11. Ellen G. Friedman and Miriam Fuchs (eds), *Breaking the Sequence: Women's Experimental Fiction* (Princeton, NJ: Princeton University Press, 1989), p. 6. Subsequent page references are given in the text in parentheses.
12. Ibid., p. 4.
13. Tyrus Miller, *Late Modernism: Politics, Fiction, and the Arts Between the World Wars* (Berkeley: University of California Press (1999), p. 24.
14. Joe Bray, Alison Gibbons and Brian McHale (eds), 'Introduction', in Joe Bray, Alison Gibbons and Brian McHale (eds), *Routledge Companion to Experimental Literature* (Abingdon, Oxon: Routledge, 2012), pp. 1–18 (p. 1).
15. See Douglas Mao and Rebecca Walkowitz, 'The New Modernist Studies', *PMLA*, 123: 3 (2008), pp. 737–48.
16. Brooke-Rose, 'Conversation', interview with Friedman and Fuchs, p. 37.
17. Peter Boxall, *The Value of the Novel* (Cambridge: Cambridge University Press, 2015), p. 48.
18. John Woodburn, *The Saturday Review*, 23 August 1947, Anna Kavan Papers, 1867–1991, McFarlin Library, The University of Tulsa.
19. Muriel Spark, *Loitering with Intent* (London: Bodley Head, 1981), p. 56; Spark, *The Comforters* (London: Macmillan, 1957).
20. Rita Felski, *Beyond Feminist Aesthetics: Feminist Literature and Social Change* (Cambridge, MA: Harvard University Press, 1989).
21. Alan Burns and Charles Sugnet (eds), *The Imagination on Trial: British and American Writers Discuss Their Working Methods* (London: Allison & Busby, 1981), pp. 2–3.

Chapter 1

Critical Terrains

'I grew up in the fifties [. . .] and, by god, I deserved what happened next'[1]

The five writers considered in this book lived and worked in the long postwar era – a period covering postwar reconstruction and repair, lingering economic austerity with the continuation of rationing until 1954, the technological advancements of the 'white heat of technology' and the liberalising legislations of the 1960s that culminated in the so-called 'permissive society'. While changes in social and sexual attitudes did not, of course, apply equally to all women of all ages and circumstances across the class spectrum, by the end of the 1960s most women's educational and employment prospects had expanded appreciably. As feminist historian Lynn Abrams notes: 'Women from across the middle and working classes [. . .] for whom the moral constraints concerning self-fashioning and sexual behaviour were being loosened, were able to construct a lifestyle and outlook very different from that of their mothers'.[2]

At the immediate end of the Second World War, the land girls, code-breakers, clippies and munitions workers as well as the Women's Auxiliary Air Force (WAAF) and the Women's Royal Navy Service (WRNS) found themselves unemployed and the first postwar decade saw high numbers of these formerly employed women returning to traditional domestic roles in the home.[3] The idea of the home at this time embodied, as Claire Langhamer notes, 'the symbolic, and actual, centre of post-war reconstruction'.[4] Rebuilding the economy and housing infrastructure were urgent priorities but the privations remained. It was, as Arthur Marwick notes, a 'crepuscular zone', full of the shadows of wartime but warmed just a little with the 'heartening hints' of a new dawn.[5] The narrow Labour victory of 1945 suggested an appetite for social change to address serious food and housing shortages and to equalise the vast socio-economic disparities between social classes.[6] Within two years the government had produced two major reports recommending comprehensive reforms in health, social welfare and education provisions in what has become known as the postwar consensus.

The later 1950s and into the 1960s have been described as a period of shared values, respect for authority, social cohesion, community, consensus, meat-and-two-veg suburbanism and, above all, 'happy families' and at the heart of this domestic scenario was the 'fully-made-up middle-class housewife in a shiny new kitchen'.[7] Historians have emphasised that this period was one in which 'the modern domestic ideal of an affluent nuclear family living in a home of their own and enjoying the benefits of leisurely home life took shape'.[8] While young women were being educated to university level in increasing numbers, marriage and children remained the principal goal of young women's intellectual activity, with few women continuing to work after marriage, and even fewer after having children.[9] Although some women did work outside of the home, especially after the age of forty, domesticity was still women's primary role and even young women who were educated to university level were expected to give up employment as soon as they married and achieve a seemly balance between their intellectual and domestic personae:[10] 'The educated wife of today [. . .] must not lean too far one way or the other'.[11] There were, according to Abrams, competing pressures and expectations placed on girls and women who came of age in the 1950s as they were growing up between, on the one hand, 'conservative discourses on womanhood' and, on the other, a 'social reality incorporating greater freedoms and opportunities'.[12]

The 1960s saw the introduction of a tranche of liberal legislation designed to give women more power over their reproductive, financial and labour rights. The introduction of the contraceptive pill in 1961 was almost immediately life-changing for many women and by the summer of 1962 150,000 women were taking it, increasing to almost half a million by 1964.[13] After thirteen years of Conservative rule, Harold Wilson's Labour Government came to power in 1964 with a slim majority and set about passing a series of liberal reforms.[14] A fundamental constituent of women's reproductive freedom, the Abortion Act came into effect on 27 April 1968, ending centuries of dangerous and degrading backstreet abortions. The Married Women's Property Act was revised in 1964, allowing women to keep half of their allowance from their husbands, a significant development for many women for whom everything they owned or earned became their husband's property on marriage. The Divorce Reform Act of 1969 recognised marital breakdown as a valid reason for divorce, effectively empowering woman to leave unhappy marriages.[15] Women's work was still paid significantly less than that of men, hence the demand for 'Equal pay for equal work', one of the four cornerstones of the first National Women's Liberation Conference in 1970.[16]

Postwar Writing: Backwards and Inwards?

The months and years after the end of hostilities in Europe on VE Day on 8 May 1945 saw a prolonged period of austerity in Britain, with rationing continuing until 1954. While death tolls and bomb damage were quantifiable, the damage inflicted on traumatised domestic psyches was mostly invisible and incalculable.[17] With repairs to make and resources to be replenished, this was inevitably a period, as Malcom Bradbury points out, 'less of major arts than of fundamental redirections'.[18] In the literary arts, a sense of discontinuity and of an artistic ending defined, said Rose Macaulay in 1946, the mood of the 'brittle time[s]'.[19] More pessimistically, the famously morose Cyril Connolly regarded the immediate postwar period as one of complete aesthetic exhaustion in which 'no new crop of novelists' was emerging.[20] The sense of moribundity was conspicuous in a 1954 series of articles on the novel in *The Observer* entitled 'Is the Novel Dead?' in which appeared the now-familiar lamentation over the death of the novel which seemed to be pottering, thought Giles Gordon, 'into near-extinction as a serious art form'.[21] In a piece entitled 'The Novel as a Takeover Bid', first broadcast for the BBC's Third Programme in 1963, Brigid Brophy looks back at this anxiety:

> To worry about the state of the novel – with its morals or intelligence or both – is as time-honoured as to worry about the state of the younger generation [...] Soon after the last war an extraordinary fashion broke out amongst literary public figures for pronouncing that the novel is dead.[22]

Declarations of enervation and expiration, especially regarding the novel, based as much on the idea of the death of modernism as on the continuing effects of war, rattled down the 1950s in many of the major magazines and newspapers.[23] As the last of modernism's little magazines disappeared, a sense of an aesthetic ending was prevalent, and by 1945 modernism seemed to have finally expired as Malcom Bradbury summarised:

> Modernism was over, even tainted: the deaths of Joyce, Woolf, Yeats and Freud had reinforced the feeling. In critical circles, it was already being historicized, defined, monumentalized, given its name and structures; it was no longer avant [...] but *arrière*.[24]

Finding new directions for postwar writing after modernism entailed, A.S. Byatt argued, finding the 'appropriate form' for the novel which necessitated decisions about 'the acceptance or rejection of appropriate or inappropriate models'.[25]

Such discussions about new forms and models for the novel after modernism have tended, as Alan Munton notes, to disappear into 'an Orwellian memory hole'.[26] Concurring with this, Bradbury described it as a 'vacancy in recent cultural history' – while the first forty years of twentieth-century British literature have been extensively documented, the following forty are less charted:[27] 'Critical records are slight, and our sense of the major directions at work uncertain'.[28] Despite the subsequent absence of critical attention to this period, a critical *ideé reçue* developed in the 1960s and 1970s suggesting that postwar British writing was definitively characterised by an unconditional retreat from aesthetic modernism and an associated return to realism. This narrative developed chiefly as a result of two works: Bernard Bergonzi's *The Situation of the Novel* (1970) and *The Reaction against Experiment in the English Novel 1950–1960* (1967) by Rubin Rabinowitz.[29] Both studies suggest that the end of modernism occurred in the 1930s, and was followed by a near-comprehensive return to social realism, a move regarded by Bergonzi as a return to a more formally 'traditional style' of writing, tending towards a thematic narrowness that was 'both backward and inward-looking'.[30] British literature in this period, he argued, showed little interest in the idea of the 'human condition' that was being explored in the European, particularly French, novel.[31] While this may be disputable in its particulars, Bergonzi's position that the postwar and mid-century British novel showed some 'inventiveness' but was broadly lacking in any of the 'sense of development and spectacular advance' of modernism is hard to refute.[32] Similarly, identifying the new crop of 'English novelists' as mainly 'focussed on contemporary social problems', Rabinowitz argued that they were less interested 'with the form and the style of their novels' and were writing as if 'the techniques of Joyce, Virginia Woolf and other experimental novelists' had never occurred. Most postwar writers, he concluded, 'conscientiously rejected experimental techniques in their fiction'.[33] This model of return and rejection continued into the 1950s and early 1960s. Writing in 1963, John Wain maintained that the experimental novel had 'died with Joyce' and, appearing to ignore *Finnegans Wake*, that after *Ulysses* 'there has been very little experimental-writing that strikes one as serious, or motivated by anything other than faddishness or the irritable search for new gimmicks'.[34] In the 1950s, the flight from modernism was exemplified by the flourishing of a new kind of social realism by the so-called

Angry Young Men, among them Kinsgsley Amis, John Braine and John Osborne.[35] Elsewhere, in poetry, The Movement poets (labelled as such in 1954 by *The Spectator*) were either indifferent or openly hostile to what they saw as 'modernist obfuscation', favouring in its place a commonsense 'progressive robustness'.[36] This position is nowhere more clear than in Amis's 1958 denunciation of experimental literature as inconsequential wordplay favouring formal innovation over meaningful content. 'Experiment', he grumbles, 'boils down pretty regularly' merely to a question of 'obtruded oddity':

> whether in construction – multiple viewpoints and such – or in style; it is not felt that adventurousness in subject matter or attitude or tone really counts. Shift from one scene to the next in midsentence, cut down on verbs or definite articles, and you are putting yourself right up in the forefront, at any rate in the eyes of those who were reared on Joyce and Virginia Woolf and take a jaundiced view of more recent developments.[37]

Others saw this purported backward turn as not only formal but also thematic, with many major novels of the period looking nostalgically back to a lost world of pre-war privilege, what Bergonzi calls 'a vanished phase of history',[38] in which the certainties of class and privilege seen in, for example, Evelyn Waugh's *Brideshead Revisited* (1945) and Anthony Powell's Proustian *A Dance to the Music of Time* (1951–75) are relatively intact.[39]

In the wake of modernism, then, it seemed as if the only way forward was rearward to what Raymond Williams referred to as older forms of writing, what he calls the 'realistic novel that articulates the substance and quality of a way of life' in two separate modes of the 'social' novel and the 'personal' novel.[40] But was the period 1945–70 really one in which all writers, to a man and woman, unvaryingly forgot all they knew of the Bergsonian *durée*, Proustian *mémoire involuntaire*, the Joycean epiphany and Woolfian 'moments of being'? The choice seemed to be between the communality of the social that was attached to realism or the putative solipsism of aesthetic experiment. Chris Baldick notes that such debates turn around the 'rival claims of artistic form or "pattern"' set against and in opposition to 'lived experience'.[41] He concludes that '[i]n one way or another, the various critical positions of this period arrive at a compromise settlement, formulating the novel's dual responsibilities to aesthetic form and to moral value, to Art and to Life'.[42]

By 1960, Malcom Bradbury began to suggest that the 'polar distinctions' between realist novels and those with a 'propensity toward form, fictionality, and reflexive self-examination' 'had been greatly shaken up',[43] and would later suggest that the novel was generally in a state of constant 'oscillation between two parts of its nature', what he terms its 'referential and discursive' versus its 'aesthetic function'.[44] In this way, then, a contrast becomes clear between writers who used language in a robustly plain-speaking way and those who tended towards the 'experimental', the 'fantastic' and the 'visionary'.[45] What is largely taken for granted in this debate, however is that the novel in Britain uniformly turned 'inwards', that is back to realism (which it had never fully dislodged in the ways it had, for example, in France). In actuality, postwar writing in Britain was, as Randall Stevenson notes, considerably 'more varied and extensive than is sometimes supposed' and a 'return to realism' is far from the whole picture.[46] Inevitably, there are pockets of artistic discord and innovation in any age or period. In the longer *durée* of the 'new' modernist studies which casts its net progressively wider in terms of its 'temporal, spatial, and vertical dimensions',[47] a new generation of critics have begun to reassess the variations in postwar writing.[48] This has resulted in a revivification of the study of mid-century British fiction by questioning some of the ossified critical debates around the 'return' to realism as a reaction against the formal excesses of modernism and, further, that this realism was always the antithesis of formal experimentalism.

Building on the earlier work of Andrzej Gąsiorek's *Post-War British Fiction: Realism and After* (1995), Marina MacKay and Lyndsey Stonebridge's *British Fiction after Modernism: The Novel at Mid-Century* (2007) revived critical debates around these questions, suggesting that 'mid-century fiction has a complex and under-thought relation to the history of which it was an uneasy part' and had to contend with not only the aftermath of war but the lingering traces of modernism and the changed postwar literary 'scene'.[49] *Contra* Bergonzi and Rabinowitz's rejection and return model, they argue that literary production has a significantly more uneven development than that suggested by this paradigm. More recently, David James has agreed that literary history does not proceed by 'neat portraits of affiliation or progression',[50] and that assertions about the backwards and inwards nature of British fiction after modernism insisting on its 'affinity with Victorian classic realism' in which a 'stylistic virtuosity' is relegated 'in favor of social commentary' require much closer examination.[51]

Any suggestion of breaks and boundaries between literary periods, styles and movements must, therefore, be more conditional than precise – there can be few pronouncements that sound anything like as decisive as Virginia Woolf's famously extravagant claim that 'on or about December 1910 human character changed'.[52] For writers working in modernism's wake, this period was characterised by an assortment of moods and aesthetic tones that saw both the continuation of pre-modernist traditions and conventions of realism as well as the survival of some of the anti-mimetic modes of the modernist novel.[53] For MacKay and Stonebridge, the return of realist writing was partly the result of the greatly altered contexts of the 'postwar consensus' in which 'there was no room', they argue, for 'the social and political isolation that had been so crucial [. . .] for the modernist novel'.[54] No longer a living movement, the long shadow cast by modernism nonetheless remained problematically present, argues Baldick, and in fact 'loomed large for post-war critics' and its defenders had to 'justify modernist methods in a changed cultural context, and against a background of some political suspicion'.[55]

Much depends, though, on how we view aesthetic modernism's relationship to the world and how it negotiated the tensions between 'Art and Life'. Rather than regarding it as formally innovative but apolitically impassive and its stylistic innovations as wholly autonomous from life, we might more usefully understand modernism as a variegated set of practices that, as Peter Nicholls notes in his bracing comparative study, *Modernisms* (1995), produced 'complex inscriptions of ideologies' across its various styles and modes.[56] This manifestly goes against the pronouncements of arch anti-modernist C. P. Snow, who blamed Joyce and Woolf for encouraging a kind of experimental writing that became 'totally meaningless in a very short time'.[57] Modernism, Snow argued, had killed off the general reader with 'mindless and unreadable novels of sensibility'.[58]

That the novel after modernism was offered two paths became, then, something of a critical sticking point, promulgating the idea of an essential tension between realism and experiment. As David James notes, 'bifurcations of realism and experimentation die hard in criticism on the period'[59] which were fixated on the vexatious opposition between the two. As we shall see, this opposition becomes even less secure and more complicated, as Laura Marcus has discussed, when questions of gender and the sexual politics of representation are incorporated into the debate.[60] Seeming to discount such issues, Iris Murdoch's 1961 essay, 'Against Dryness; A Polemical Sketch', argues that the choice for the postwar novelist was essentially between 'crystalline or journalistic' forms of writing.[61] Thus, a contrast becomes clear between the anti-modernists and the experimenters; that is, between those writers who use language in an ostensibly empirical way and those who use language in unfamiliar ways.

Experimental Realism

Realism has been understood both as an historical phenomenon chiefly of the nineteenth century and in formal terms as a narrative with a third-person omniscient narrator who invisibly directs and manipulates the reader into believing in the 'realness' of the linear plot and causality of events occurring in recognisable settings with psychologically complex characters. For Barthes, the distinction between a novel's realism and its realistic-ness is crucial; the 'most realistic narrative imaginable', he says, 'flows in an unrealistic manner' that is both 'fragmentary and erratic', finally producing the 'reality effect',[62] for which, says Nathalie Sarraute in *The Age of Suspicion*, readers have a 'natural penchant'.[63]

'In our great writers and painters', Malcolm Bradbury argues, 'realism has never simply been innocent, of an agreed and fixed nature, or exterior to artistic scepticism and enquiry'.[64] For David Lodge, mid-century fiction produced 'formal experiment and formal self-consciousness' not in 'the high modernist mode' but rather 'more in the tradition of Sterne, building into the structure of the novel itself an awareness of the problematics of fictional discourse'.[65] In such writing, he concludes, 'Realism is not rejected, but it is not employed naively and thus becomes a more heterogeneous mode'. Gąsiorek also makes a convincing case for dropping the rigid boundaries between realism and experimentalism in his discussion of how the 'conflict between realism and experimentalism' posits a false, purely formalist dichotomy.[66] Using Barthes's division of the *lisible* and the *scriptible*, he suggests a reconceptualisation of realism rather than an outright condemnation. Thus, realism becomes malleable and, as such, more than capable of being used experimentally. It can evolve to accommodate changing times and new speakers as testified by the proliferation of types of realism – post-realism, traumatic realism, and hysterical realism all offering varying degrees of Barthes's reality effect.[67] Thus, as Bertolt Brecht suggested, we can 'spring-clean' realism; renovate it periodically in order to allow each generation of writers to make free and 'lively use of all means, old and new, tried and untried, deriving from art and deriving from other sources'. Acknowledging that this constant overhaul might be a 'tall order', Brecht trusts artists to use their 'originality', their 'sense of humour' and 'power of invention' to continually create new versions of realism.[68]

Jed Esty holds that realism 'has been freed from some of its erstwhile antagonists (romanticism, modernism, the avant-garde)' and that it is now possible to 'talk about realist components of novels or realist novels without implying some kind of absolute divide from experimentalism'.[69] Christine Brooke-Rose recognises precisely this possibility in an interview in 1989 when asked why she chose to write experimental 'indeterminate' novels, she retorted, 'What a strange opposition. The realistic novel has its own indeterminacies'.[70] These indeterminacies, then, make any antithetical relationship with experimentalism insecure,[71] especially when we release postwar writing from the gravitational pull of modernism and accept the possibility that realism might be renewed, adapted and renovated rather than simply rejected, an especially important consideration when we come now to consider the question of the relationship of experimentalism to gender and sexual difference in women's writing.

To be an Experimental Woman Writer: 'Three words. Three difficulties'

Maria Lauret has argued that the use of realism in women's writing is very often distinct from more conventional realisms as it can be both subjective and polemic in its use of 'extraliterary feminist discourse'.[72] In *Changing the Story*, Gayle Greene proposes that feminist literature of the 1960s and 1970s, much of it apparently realist, should be considered a major literary movement as it combined the 'excitement and experimentation of Modernism with the social critique of the great age of realism'.[73] And yet in the 1980s it was common to see realism set up as the enemy of feminism and that women writers of realist fiction – 'female practitioners of a determinedly male' tradition – were betraying 'the cause initiated by Woolf' who had 'envisioned a remodelling of fiction to accommodate nonmale perspectives and experience'.[74] This reductive view persists, as we see more recently in *Women's Experimental Writing*, in which Ellen Berry talks of realism's 'easy pleasures' as coterminous with 'discursive structures that are inherently patriarchal'.[75]

This study, then, reads openly and widely around women's experiments with prose staying attentive not only to the differences between each writer's textual practices but also to questions of what is particularly female, feminine or feminist about their experimental writing. In this regard, Brooke-Rose's *résumé* of women's experimental writing is invaluable as an originating stimulus:

> Clearly the silencing of women critics and writers, and especially of women experimental writers, is true, is constant, and is done by ignoring them or, more often than might be supposed, by stealing from them without acknowledgement. I have experienced both myself and simply put up with it. Nevertheless I have always been deeply suspicious of all movements and

labels which create blind obsessions. A writer, man or woman, is essentially alone, and will be 'good' or 'bad' independently of sex or origin.[76]

I will combine this vigilance towards essentialism with an approach informed by Rita Felski's *Beyond Feminist Aesthetics: Feminist Literature and Social Change* (1989) in which she says that 'It is impossible to make a convincing case for the claim that that there is anything inherently feminine or feminist in experimental writing as such'.[77] While experimental writing might form an important part of the history of women's writing, there is, finally, no essential relationship between feminism and experimental form as the 'defamiliarizing capacity of literary language and form does not in itself bear any necessary relationship to the political and social goals of feminism'.[78] Felski says that foregrounding ideas of *jouissance*, rupture and fragmentation rather than cognition as 'privileged sites of resistance to patriarchal ideology by virtue of its subversion of the representational and instrumental function of language' relies on a 'theoretical sleight-of-hand' insisting that women's writing is best positioned outside of any (rational) symbolic order in a state of permanently 'marginalized dissidence'.[79] Hence, for Felski just as anti-realism is not always analogous with a progressive political stance, conventional realism is not understood as a 'vague homology' for patriarchal logic.[80] Judy Little wholly concurs: 'Even if we isolate a radically unique style as experimental [...] this does not necessarily write or invoke a revolutionary ideology'.[81] Thus, the refusal of narrative linearity in favour of textual fragmentation is not in itself demonstrative of an essentialist 'female' or 'feminine' schema and, as such, complicates, and in places, refuses, Hélène Cixous's concept of *écriture féminine* that suggests a direct and reductive relationship between non-linear writing, the feminine body and political subversion. In 'Le Rire de la Méduse' (1975), Cixous defines women's writing as one that 'cannot fail to be more than subversive' in its refusal of logic and linearity: it is 'volcanic, as it is written it brings about an upheaval of the old property crust, carrier of masculine investments'.[82] For Cixous, such writing is always self-consciously 'other' to patriarchal thinking that has imprisoned women in what Woolf calls the 'capricious and coloured light of the other sex'.[83]

With characteristic exactitude, Woolf insisted that women's 'tampering with the expected sequence' must be done 'not for the sake of breaking, but for the sake of creating'.[84] Crucially, for Woolf this textual tampering, breaking and smashing was intimately allied to her own creative and intellectual practice that allowed for a distinctive approach that, while acknowledging the various constraints on women's writing, avoided complying with any definitive idea of the female or feminine: 'I can take my way; experiment with my own imagination in my own way'.[85] The 'female imagination', if it exists at all, is as shifting and contingent as the male imagination but crucially, as Woolf insists, the real difference between them is the condition of non-freedom into which women writers and artists have been born. While men (of a certain class and ethnicity, to be sure) have had no restrictions placed on their education, socialisation and freedom of physical movement, girls and women have been taught to be 'ladies'; confined to the home and to the trifling pursuits of sewing, piano playing and conversing in decorous and polite ways. This state of women's non-freedom is, as Rachel Blau DuPlessis argues, fundamental to the romance or marriage plot in which the main female character is 'muffled', any desire to quest and explore is repressed and her ending always to be found in the stasis of the 'extreme sexual differences' enforced by marriage. For DuPlessis 'writing beyond the ending' of these plots involves a 'transgressive invention of narrative strategies' that express 'critical dissent from the dominant narrative'.[86]

What Rita Felski calls a 'feminine writing practice', allows for an intellectually expansive idea of women's writing that is sufficiently capacious to avoid any essentialising notions of the feminine and which accepts a diversity of creative and critical practices that cannot be contained by any aesthetic or intellectual imperative delineating the category of 'woman'. Felski insists upon the 'impossibility of a feminist aesthetic' and, further, that in the formal analysis of literary texts it is untenable to 'speak of "masculine" or "feminine" in any meaningful sense'. Trying to 'deduce an abstract literary theory of "masculine" or "feminine", "subversive", and "reactionary" forms in isolation from the social conditions of their production and reception' is inadequate, she says, and leads to closed readings that can inhibit interpretative richness.[87] The chimera of a 'feminist aesthetic' has tended to hinder any adequate assessment of both the value and limitations of contemporary feminist writing by measuring it against an aesthetic of a 'feminine' writing practice, which in recent years has been most frequently derived from an essentialist aesthetics of textuality. Elaine Showalter also famously argued against the notion of any discernibly 'female sensibility' or 'innate sexual attitude' that reveals itself in literary texts as a set of gendered imagery and in a 'form specific to women'.[88] This kind of thinking, she says, is not only essentialist but runs 'dangerously close to reiterating the familiar stereotypes' in which women are permanently attached to illogic and fragmentation and men to rationality and logic.[89] Angela Carter was similarly dismissive of any biological essentialism affixed to women's writing, proclaiming 'My anatomy is only part of an infinitely complex organisation, myself', accordingly marking herself her out as a dissident feminist in much the same way as Brigid Brophy.[90] Like them, Felski also insists that 'multiplicity, indeterminacy, or negativity are not in themselves specifically feminist, or indeed specifically anything'.[91]

Renovating Felski's thinking, Kaye Mitchell reassesses these debates on women's experimental writing and maintains that 'it is not requisite to insist either on the necessarily feminine nature' of women's experimental writing as this implies a kind of 'rootedness' in some type of 'troublesome biological femaleness' and on the unavoidably 'subversive nature' of experiment.[92] Mitchell agrees that what unites many women experimental writers is a *'repudiation* of narrative authority [. . .] in favour of apparently more "spontaneous," "unconscious," and "impressionistic" modes of writing' but that this exists alongside 'a quite deliberate (willed and authoritative) *manipulation* of linguistic and generic forms' that produces a variety of writing styles and modes that do not inevitably depend on the anti-symbolic energies of the Kristevan chora or the fluid pre-linguistic semiosis of *écriture féminine*.[93] This articulation carefully avoids an over-reductive approach to the question of what constitutes experimentalism in literature and suggests we examine the ways in which experimental women writers manipulate existing genres and narrative modes as much as focusing on female 'identity'. She also counsels an avoidance of catch-all formulations that conflate postmodernism and the avant-garde with experimentalism; these categories, she notes, do overlap but they 'are certainly not coterminous'.[94]

In 'Illiterations', Brooke-Rose remarked on women writers whose work did not conform to the feminist concerns of their times: the 'sisterhood', she argues was 'with some notable exceptions, generally too busy on feminist "themes" and on rediscovering or reinterpreting female authors of the past [. . .] that it has no time to notice or to make an effort to understand, let alone to back, an unfamiliar (experimental) woman writer who does not necessarily write on such themes'.[95] As practical and thought-provoking as *A Room of One's Own,* as eruditely rational as *The Second Sex* and as innovative as 'The Laugh of The Medusa', 'Illiterations' broaches many of the questions concerning women's experimental writing that are central to this book. Women's admission, Brooke-Rose says, into the literary arts has been a hard-won thing as the denial of education for girls and their sequestered roles as dutiful daughters, submissive wives and doting mothers is not conducive to any kind of intellectual work. For so long the object of writing and of the male gaze, women come to writing already knowing that their place is one of marginalisation. Serious women writers, she says, face three incrementally challenging hurdles. The first is the difficulty in simply getting into print; the second is the extremely infrequent acceptance of women writers into the canon – here she mentions Barbara Pym, Jean Rhys, Christina Stead, Ivy Compton-Burnett, Isak Dinesen and Nathalie Sarraute. The final challenge is to be accepted as an innovator and an 'experimental' writer such as Gertrude Stein and Djuna Barnes. Innovation depends on one's position to a given tradition; exclusion from a tradition and its institutional rules and practices provides a precarious platform for challenging and adapting what has gone before. But Brooke-Rose goes much further when she suggests that society continues to cling to a deep-rooted 'fear of women as memory, as birth, as death', and this thinking of woman as primal body and pre-linguistic chaos has led to her 'total occultation from the writing process', excluded from any 'possible posterity'. Women cannot write anything other than their lives, their bodies; they can only write 'disguised autobiography' and are therefore not considered properly creative.[96] I shall return to this question of biography in more detail in the chapters on Anna Kavan and Ann Quin. But for now, it is sufficient to note the historical obstacles that women writers have faced, both practical and psychological, but perhaps as importantly the invisible but powerful prohibitions around taking seriously women writers not just as participants in the canon but also as innovators and pioneers. Brooke-Rose concludes her essay on this with one final, and to my mind crucial, observation that 'One safe way not to recognize innovative women is to shove them under a label, and one such label is "woman writer"'.[97]

Questioning the label of 'woman writer' is necessary, Brooke-Rose says, not just because the description might be off-putting for those who will find any and every reason not to read women writers but also because the label has been indiscriminately appropriated by feminism. No enemy of feminism, Brooke-Rose was, however, aware of the orthodoxies and dogma that can grow up rapidly around a school of thought. As a former Bletchley code-breaker, her diagnostic acumen entailed a healthy scepticism towards labels, categories and encoding. For her, the quixotic discourse that built up around French feminism risked confining women in psychoanalytical categorical imperatives that seemed to repeat the kind of mythologising which Simone de Beauvoir condemned as the 'Eternal Feminine, unique and changeless', a static category of immutable essence that is the opposite of 'the dispersed, contingent, and multiple experiences of actual women'.[98] French feminism, or at least the version that became known as such, reinstated or reinscribed an essentialism and with that, a new orthodoxy positing the relationship between gender and writing; fragmentation, non-linearity and illogicality, it seemed, most represented the flow and chaos of women's writing bodies. Thus, writing becomes body in the most fundamental way. This, then, was feminine language; one that sought to break free from the supposed restrictions of patriarchal logic, hierarchy and linearity. This view, however, is refused by Janet Todd who asserts that

> Literary works gives images of women that are not absolutely identical, and the differences among them must be significant. Historical flux and change should not be prematurely ended in symbolic stasis so that women can suffer for once and for all an identity fixation on the level of style, releasing action only to the 'woman' of the semiotic.[99]

In other words, the semiotic and the pre-Oedipal are ascribed to an idea of femininity which is assumed to possess an inherent connection with some primitive or cosmic order that pre-exists the symbolic order and to which women, no matter who they are or in what material conditions they happen to find themselves, are permanently and irretrievably attached.[100] Elsewhere, Juliet Mitchell states that she does not believe that there is 'such a thing as female writing' or a 'woman's voice', following Kristeva's idea that women coming to writing can only really mimic masculine language and therefore can only possess a 'hysteric voice':

> There is the hysteric's voice which is the woman's masculine language (one has to speak masculinely in a phallocentric world) talking about feminine experience. It's both simultaneously the woman novelist's refusal of the woman's world [. . .] and her construction from within a masculine world of that woman's world.[101]

What feminist writers and critics want, by and large, is a rectification of the representational systems and to expose the concepts of nature and the natural that have kept women in their gendered place. What they have disagreed on, however, is the exact nature of the rectification and on the relationship between gender and writing. Feminist critical practice is, however, sufficiently inclusive to accommodate, as Felski notes in *Literature after Feminism* (2003), some 'serious conflicts of opinions' about this relationship.[102] Thus, as previously suggested, my position stands in partial disagreement with that of Friedman and Fuchs in their pioneering work, *Breaking the Sequence*, in which they argue that women writers who reject 'dominant forms [. . .] assail the social structure' in such a way that 'the rupturing of traditional forms becomes a political act, and the feminine narrative resulting from such rupture is allied with the feminist project'.[103] However, their assertion that experimental writers produce an 'alternative fictional space' is important for my own thinking here as, while it may not always and necessarily be female or feminist or politically subversive, it allows for, as Friedman later says, an 'anonymity, strangeness, orphanhood, nomadism, or madness' in women's writing.[104] This alternative space, then, is what I call vagabondage; an experimental aesthetic spirit that looks *outwards* and *away* from artistic convention, social custom and the space of the domestic in ways that do not conform easily to any fixed biological or political idea of either woman or women's writing.[105] I suggest, then, that experimentalism across these five writers is a composite of realism and anti-realism that complicates any idea of an essential female or feminine aesthetic and makes difficult any claim that there exists an unswerving equivalence between textual experiment and ideological subversion. Each writer considered here has a highly distinctive way of handling language, mood, genre, and theme, and therefore must be read on a case-by-case basis rather than by a limiting or prescriptive theory positing a reductively simple relationship between language, feminism and subversion. Even though many of them articulate robust views on women's role in society, Brophy, Figes and Brooke-Rose all express significant reservations about feminism. Kavan's expressionistic writing may be mostly about women and is experimental in its formal departure from the conventional realism and domestic novels of its time but one would be hard pressed to read it as explicitly feminist in any substantial way. So, while some of the writers considered here have an ambivalent relationship with feminism, I nonetheless regard this book as a work of feminist literary criticism, as I believe that feminist criticism is a sufficiently broad church with a capacious intellectual generosity that can accommodate non-conformism and dissension within women's writing and thus can acknowledge the significance of women writers who, while not always obviously feminist, can be fruitfully read to give us a wider and richer sense of literary and intellectual history and reinstate 'a female perspective by extending knowledge about women's experience and contributions to culture'.[106]

Finally, then, what is experimental writing? 'Is it a genre?', asks Brooke-Rose – 'People often talk as if it were, although most experiment either widens the concept of a particular genre or explodes the notion of genre altogether'.[107] Genre or no, the term or label experimentalism operates, for the most part, transhistorically insofar as it cannot be exclusively attached to the energies of the historical avant-garde of the early twentieth century nor to later literary movements of modernism or postmodernism. In short, as Natalia Cecire, observes, the term experimental has 'a very vexed relationship to historicization' and is often a label to which we turn when we want to circumvent historical confinement.[108] She notes the spaciousness of the term: 'there is no particular set of forms that can guarantee that a work will be received as experimental, which registers the necessity of an account of experimentalism that can accommodate enormous formal diversity'.[109] It is to this extensive formal diversity of experiment that I attend in the following chapters and it is my hope that my response to Brooke-Rose's 'three words' and three difficulties will become clear as the book progresses.

Notes

1. Angela Carter, 'Truly It Felt Like Year One', in Sara Maitland (ed.), *Very Heaven: Looking Back at the 1960s* (London: Virago, 1988), pp. 211–12 (p. 210).
2. Lynn Abrams, 'Liberating the Female Self: Epiphanies, Conflict and Coherence in the Life Stories of Post-War British Women', *Social History*, 39: 1 (2014), pp. 14–35 (p. 16).
3. See Helen McCarthy, 'Women, Marriage and Paid Work in Post-War Britain', *Women's History Review*, 26: 1 (2017), pp. 46–61.
4. Claire Langhamer, 'The Meanings of Home in Postwar Britain', *Journal of Contemporary History*, 40: 2 (2005), pp. 341–62 (p. 342). By 1957, 2.5 million flats and homes had been built, a large proportion of which was social housing. See John Burnett, *A Social History of Housing 1815–1985*, 2nd edn (London: Methuen, 1986), pp. 249, 286.
5. Marwick, *British Society*, p. 3.
6. Labour won 47.7% with significantly more women voting Labour than men. See Pat Thane, 'Women Since 1945', in Paul Johnson (ed.), *Twentieth-Century Britain: Economic, Social, and Cultural Change* (London: Longman, 1994), pp. 392–411 (p. 277).
7. Nick Thomas, 'Will the Real 1950s Please Stand Up? Views of a Contradictory Decade', *Cultural and Social History*, 5: 2 (2008), pp. 227–35 (p. 228).
8. Graham Crow, 'The Post-War Development of the Modern Domestic Ideal', ed. Graham Allan and Graham Crow, *Home and Family. Creating the Domestic Sphere* (Basingstoke: Palgrave Macmillan, 1989), pp. 14–32, 20.
9. This overall picture is more complicated, however, as the number of women in employment actually increased. See Stephen Brooke, 'Gender and Working Class Identity in Britain in the 1950s', *Journal of Social History*, 34: 4 (2001), pp. 773–95.
10. While some women attended college or university or went out to work, the importance of the stay-at-home mother in childrearing became a focus of public scrutiny as testified by the popularity of John Bowlby's *Child Care and the Growth of Love* (Harmondsworth: Penguin, 1953).
11. Judith Hubback, *Wives Who Went to College* (London: Heinemann, 1957), p. 159.
12. Abrams, 'Liberating', p. 16.
13. Access to the Pill in the 1960s was still tightly restricted by the medical profession and it was not freely available on the NHS until 1974.
14. The abolition of the death penalty in 1965; the partial decriminalisation of homosexuality in 1967; the legalisation of abortion in 1967; the end of

theatrical censorship in 1968 and the reformation of British divorce laws in 1969.
15. The Matrimonial Homes Act 1967 and Matrimonial Proceedings & Property Act 1970 expanded women's legal rights within marriage.
16. Two further demands, for equal education and training, and free 24-hour childcare were made. Later in the 1970s, a fifth demand, for women's financial and legal independence, was added: 850 women went on strike at the Ford Dagenham plant in Essex on 7 June 1968 against earning 15 per cent less than men for doing identical or similar work. Recently, BBC journalist Samira Ahmed referred to the Ford Dagenham strike as an example which is unfortunately still relevant.
17. On the influence of the Second World War on literary cultures in Britain, see Gill Plain's *Literature of the 1940s: War, Postwar and 'Peace'*; Jenny Hartley, *Millions Like Us: British Women's Fiction of the Second World War* (London: Virago, 1997); Marina MacKay, *Modernism and World War II* (Cambridge: Cambridge University Press, 2007); Lyndsey Stonebridge, *The Writing of Anxiety: Imagining Wartime in Mid-Century British Culture* (Basingstoke: Palgrave Macmillan, 2007); Leo Mellor, *Reading the Ruins: Modernism, Bombsites and British Culture* (Cambridge: Cambridge University Press, 2011) and Sara Wasson, *Urban Gothic of The Second World War: Dark London* (Basingstoke: Palgrave Macmillan, 2010).
18. Malcolm Bradbury, *No, Not Bloomsbury* (London: André Deutsch, 1987), p. 72.
19. Rose Macaulay, 'The Future of Fiction', in John Lehmann (ed.), *New Writing and Daylight*, 7 (London: Hogarth Press, 1946), pp. 71–5 (p. 72).
20. Cyril Connolly, 'Comment', in *Horizon: A Review of Literature and Art*, December 1944, p. 367. On the exhaustion following 'total war', see Gill Plain, *Literature of the 1940s*, pp. 1–35.
21. Giles Gordon, 'Diary: Experimental Slideshows', *London Review of Books*, 15: 19 (7 October 1993) <https://www.lrb.co.uk/the-paper/v15/n19/giles-gordon/diary> (accessed 20 July 2019).
22. Brigid Brophy, *Don't Never Forget: Collected Views and Reviews* (New York: Holt, Rinehart and Winston, 1966), p. 93. Bernard Bergonzi describes these debates over the death of the novel as 'critical apocalypticism' in *The Situation of the Novel* (London: Macmillan, 1970), p. 13. See also Lionel Trilling, *The Liberal Imagination: Essays on Literature and Society* (New York: Viking Press, 1950).
23. Namely, *The New Statesman*, *The Observer*, *Times Literary Supplement*, *Encounter*, *London Magazine*, and *The Spectator*. See Tracy Hargreaves and Alice Ferrebe, 'Introduction: Literature of the 1950s and 1960s', *The Yearbook of English Studies*, 42 (2012), pp. 1–12.
24. Malcolm Bradbury, *The Modern British Novel*, p. 268.
25. A. S. Byatt, 'People in Paper Houses: Attitudes to "Realism"' and "Experiment" in English Post-War Fiction', in *Passions of the Mind: Selected Writings*, pp. 165–88 (New York, Turtle Bay Books, 1992).
26. Alan Munton, *English Fiction of the Second World War* (London: Faber and Faber, 1989), p. 4.
27. Bradbury, *No, Not Bloomsbury*, p. 69.

28. Ibid., p. 88.
29. Bergonzi, *Situation*; Rubin Rabinowitz, *The Reaction against Experiment in the English Novel, 1950–60* (New York: Columbia University Press, 1967).
30. Bergonzi, *Situation*, p. 5.
31. Ibid., p. 56.
32. Ibid., p. 20.
33. Rabinowitz, *Reaction*, p. 2.
34. John Wain, cited in Rabinowitz, *Reaction*, p. 8.
35. See Kenneth Allsop, *The Angry Decade: A Survey of the Cultural Revolt of the 1950s* (London: Peter Owen, 1958); James Gindin, *Postwar British Fiction: New Accents and Attitudes* (Berkeley: California University Press, 1962) and William Van O'Connor, *The New University Wits and the End of Modernism* (Carbondale: Southern Illinois University Press, 1963). See also Shelagh Delaney's *A Taste of Honey* (1958) and parts of Doris Lessing's *The Golden Notebook* (1962).
36. Dominic Head, *The Cambridge Introduction to Modern British Fiction, 1950–2000* (Cambridge: Cambridge University Press, 2002), p. 50.
37. Kingsley Amis, review, 1958, cited in David Lodge, 'The Novelist at The Crossroads', in Malcolm Bradbury (ed.), *The Novel Today: Contemporary Writers on Modern Fiction* (Manchester: Manchester University Press/ Rowman & Littlefield, 1977), pp. 84–110 (p. 101).
38. Bergonzi, *Situation*, p. 186.
39. Evelyn Waugh, *Brideshead Revisited* (London: Chapman and Hall, 1945); Anthony Powell, *A Dance to the Music of Time* (London: Heinemann, 1951–75).
40. Raymond Williams, 'Realism and the Contemporary Novel', *Universities and Left Review*, 4, Summer 1948, pp. 22–4.
41. Chris Baldick, *Criticism and Literary Theory 1890 to the Present* (London: Routledge, 1996), p. 144.
42. Ibid., p. 144.
43. Bradbury, *The Novel Today*, pp. 8, 90.
44. Bradbury, *No, Not Bloomsbury*, p. 187.
45. Ibid., p. 177. Robert Scholes termed fabulation the difference between 'empirical' and 'fictional' modes of narrative. *The Fabulators* (New York: Oxford University Press, 1967), p. 84.
46. Randall Stevenson, *The British Novel Since the Thirties: An Introduction* (London: Batsford Ltd, 1986), p. 223.
47. Mao and Walkowitz, 'New Modernist Studies', p. 737.
48. New work includes Kaye Mitchell and Nonia Williams (eds), *British Avant-Garde Fiction of the 1960s* (Edinburgh: Edinburgh University Press, 2019); Kaye Mitchell, 'Post-War Fiction: Realism and Experimentation', in Clare Hanson and Susan Watkins (eds), *The History of British Women's Writing 1945–1975* (London: Macmillan, 2017), pp. 19–36; Richard Canning and Gerri Kimber (eds), *Brigid Brophy: Avant-Garde Writer, Critic, Activist* (Edinburgh: Edinburgh University Press, 2020).
49. Marina MacKay and Lyndsey Stonebridge (eds), *British Fiction After Modernism: The Novel at Mid-Century* (Basingstoke: Palgrave, 2007), p. 2.

50. David James, 'Introduction: Critical Constructions of British Fiction Since 1945', in David James (ed.) *Cambridge Companion to British Fiction Since 1945* (Cambridge University Press, 2015), pp. 1–12 (p. 1).
51. David James, 'Localizing Late Modernism: Interwar Regionalism and the Genesis of the "Micro Novel"', *Journal of Modern Literature*, 32: 4 (2009), pp. 43–64 (p. 43). See also his concept of late modernism in *The Legacies of Modernism: Historicising Postwar and Contemporary Fiction* (Cambridge: Cambridge University Press, 2012). See David Lodge, *The Novelist at the Crossroads and other Essays on Fiction and Criticism* (London: Routledge and Kegan Paul, 1971); D. J. Taylor, *After the War: The Novel and English Society Since 1945* (London: Chatto & Windus, 1993); Bradbury, *The Novel Today*.
52. Virginia Woolf, 'Mr. Bennett and Mrs. Brown', in *Collected Essays: Volume I*, ed. Leonard Woolf (London: Hogarth Press, 1966), pp. 319–37 (p. 320).
53. See Julia Jordan, 'Late Modernism and the Avant-Garde Renaissance', in James (ed.), *British Fiction Since 1945*, pp. 145–59.
54. MacKay and Stonebridge (eds), *British Fiction*, p. 1.
55. Baldick, *Criticism*, p. 117.
56. Peter Nicholls, *Modernisms: A Literary Guide* (London: Macmillan, 1995), p. xii.
57. C. P. Snow, interview with Frank Kermode, in Frank Kermode, 'The House of Fiction: Interviews with Seven Novelists', in Bradbury, *The Novel Today*, pp. 111–35 (pp. 128–9).
58. Cited in Rubin Rabinowitz, 'The Reaction against Modernism: Amis, Snow, Wilson', in John Richetti, John Bender, Deirdre David and Michael Seidel (eds), *The Columbia History of the British Novel* (New York: Columbia University Press, 1994), pp. 895–927 (p. 905).
59. James, 'Introduction', in James (ed.), *British Fiction*, p. 2.
60. See Laura Marcus, 'Feminist Aesthetics and the New Realism', in Isobel Armstrong (ed.), *New Feminist Discourses: Critical Essays on Theories and Texts, Volume 2* (London: Routledge, 1992), pp. 11–25 (p. 11). See also Matthew Beaumont's *Adventures in Realism* (Oxford: Blackwell, 2007).
61. Iris Murdoch, 'Against Dryness: A Polemical Sketch', in Bradbury, *The Novel Today*, pp. 23–31 (p. 28).
62. Roland Barthes, 'The Reality Effect', in Tzvetan Todorov (ed.), *French Literary Theory: A Reader*, trans. R. Carter (Cambridge: Cambridge University Press, 1982), pp. 11–17 (p. 16).
63. Nathalie Sarraute, *The Age of Suspicion: Essays on The Novel*, trans. Maria Jolas (New York: George Braziller, 1963), p. 110.
64. Bradbury, 'A Dog Engulfed in Sand: Character and Abstraction in Contemporary Writing and Painting', in Bradbury, *No, Not Bloomsbury*, p. 23.
65. David Lodge, 'The State of Fiction: A Symposium', *New Review*, 5: 1 (1978), pp. 14–76 (p. 50).
66. Andrzej Gąsiorek, *Post-War British Fiction: Realism and After* (London: Edward Arnold, 1995), p. v. See also Ronald Hayman, 'Realism and

Experiment are Not Antithetical', in Hayman, *The Novel Today: 1967–1975* (Longman for the British Council, 1976).
67. As we know from the quarrels between Sartre and Adorno, and Brecht and Lukács, legitimate claims can be made that realism might be progressive when seen in opposition to anti-representative form. Lukács was adamant that realism was the mode of the genuine literary avant-garde. György Lukács, 'Realism in the Balance' in *Aesthetics and Politics*, trans. Ronald Taylor (London: New Left, 1977), pp. 28–59.
68. Bertolt Brecht, 'From the Popular and the Realistic (1938)', in Richard Drain (ed.), *Twentieth Century Theatre: A Sourcebook* (London: Routledge, 1995), pp. 188–93 (p. 188). In his analysis of the Brecht/Lukács divide, Fredric Jameson argues that formal experimentalism can become subsumed into a new aesthetic orthodoxy whereby it ceases to be innovative. Jameson, 'Reflections in Conclusion', in *Aesthetics and Politics* (London: Verso, 2007), pp. 196–213 (p. 211).
69. Jed Esty, 'Realism Wars', *Novel: A Forum on Fiction*, 49: 2 (2016), pp. 316–42 (p. 319).
70. Brooke-Rose, 'A Conversation with Christine Brooke-Rose', interview with Ellen G. Friedman and Miriam Fuchs, *The Review of Contemporary Fiction*, 9: 3 (1989). Also in Ellen G. Friedman and Richard Martin (eds), *Utterly Other Discourse: The Texts of Christine Brooke-Rose* (Chicago: Dalkey Archive, 1950), pp. 29–37 (p. 30).
71. See Jordan, 'Late Modernism', p. 149.
72. Maria Lauret, *Liberating Literature: Feminist Fiction in America* (London: Routledge, 1994), p. 3.
73. Gayle Greene, *Changing the Story: Feminist Fiction and the Tradition* (Bloomington: Indiana University Press, 1991), p. 2.
74. Richard Bradford, *The Novel Now: Contemporary British Fiction* (Oxford: Blackwell, 2007), p. 188.
75. Ellen E. Berry, *Women's Experimental Writing: Negative Aesthetics and Feminist Critique* (London: Bloomsbury, 2016), pp. 5–6.
76. Brooke-Rose, 'A Womb of One's Own', in Brooke-Rose, *Stories, Theories and Things* (Cambridge: Cambridge University Press, 1991), pp. 223–36 (p. 225–6).
77. Felski, *Beyond Feminist Aesthetics*, p. 5.
78. Ibid., p. 6.
79. Ibid., pp. 4–5.
80. Ibid., p. 7.
81. Judy Little, *The Experimental Self: Dialogic Subjectivity in Woolf, Pym, and Brooke-Rose*, (Carbondale and Edwardsville: Southern Illinois University Press, 1996), p. 6.
82. Hélène Cixous, 'The Laugh of the Medusa', trans. Keith Cohen and Paula Cohen, *Signs*, 1: 4 (1976), pp. 875–93 (p. 888).
83. Woolf, *Room*, p. 88.
84. Ibid., p. 55.
85. Virginia Woolf, *A Writer's Diary: Being Extracts from the Diary of Virginia Woolf* (New York: Harcourt Brace Jovanovich, 1953), p. 292.
86. Rachel Blau DuPlessis, *Writing Beyond the Ending: Narrative Strategies*

of Twentieth-Century Women Writers (Bloomington: Indiana University Press, 1985), p. 5.
87. Felski, *Beyond Feminist Aesthetics*, p. 2. In addition to Felski, Friedman and Fuchs (1989), and Berry (2016), other important works include Susan Rubin Suleiman, *Subversive Intent: Gender, Politics, and the Avant-Garde* (Cambridge, MA: Harvard University Press, 1990); Marianne DeKoven, *A Different Language: Gertrude Stein's Experimental Writing* (Madison: University of Wisconsin Press, 1983); Laura Hinton and Cynthia Hogue (eds), *We Who Love to be Astonished: Experimental Women's Writing and Performance Poetics* (Tuscaloosa: University of Alabama Press, 2001).
88. Elaine Showalter, *A Literature of Their Own: British Women Novelists: From Bronte to Lessing*, rev. edn (Princeton, NJ: Princeton University Press, 1999), p. 12.
89. Ibid., p. 12.
90. Angela Carter, *The Sadeian Woman and the Ideology of Pornography* (London: Virago, 1979), p. 4. See also Edmund Gordon, *The Invention of Angela Carter: A Biography* (Oxford: Oxford University Press, 2017), p. 77.
91. Felski, *Beyond Feminist Aesthetics*, p. 7.
92. Kaye Mitchell, 'Introduction: The Gender Politics of Experiment', *Contemporary Women's Writing*, 9: 1 (2015), pp. 1–15 (p. 7).
93. Ibid., p. 3.
94. Ibid., p. 3. *The Routledge Companion to Experimental Literature* tends to use these terms interchangeably, with some notable exceptions. Joe Bray, Alison Gibbons and Brian McHale (eds) *The Routledge Companion to Experimental Literature* (Abingdon, Oxon: Routledge, 2012).
95. Brooke-Rose, 'Illiterations', in *Stories, Theories and Things*, pp. 250–64 (p. 264).
96. Ibid., p. 258.
97. Ibid., pp. 263–4.
98. Simone de Beauvoir, *The Second Sex*, trans. H. M. Parshley (London: Vintage, 1997), p. 283.
99. Janet Todd, *Feminist Literary History: A Defence* (Cambridge: Polity Press, 1988), p. 84.
100. Gayle Greene and Coppélia Kahn (eds), *Making a Difference: Feminist Literary Criticism* (London: Methuen, 1985), pp. 1–2.
101. Juliet Mitchell, *Women: The Longest Revolution: Essays in Feminism, Literature and Psychoanalysis* (London: Virago, 1984). pp. 289–90.
102. Rita Felski, *Literature After Feminism* (Chicago: University of Chicago Press, 2003) p. 5.
103. Friedman and Fuchs (eds), *Breaking the Sequence*, p. 4.
104. Ellen G. Friedman, 'Where are the Missing Contents? (Post)Modernism, Gender, and the Canon', *PMLA*, 108: 2 (1993), pp. 240–52, p. 245.
105. Referring more generally to the early twentieth century avant-garde, Felski notes that the question of form versus content often arises when one introduces gender into the equation: A 'feminist perspective [...] cannot help but influence the criteria by which sameness and difference are measured; what looks like formal innovations and representational

in the immanent logic of art history often turn out to be mired in an all-too-familiar ethos of oedipal rebellion and an avowed disdain for the feminine and the maternal'. See Jonathan P. Eburne and Rita Felski, 'What is an Avant-Garde? Introduction', *New Literary History*, 41: 4 (2010), pp. v–xv (p. viii).
106. Greene and Kahn (eds), *Making a Difference*, pp. 1–2.
107. Brooke-Rose, 'Illiterations', p. 259.
108. Natalia Cecire, 'Experimentalism by Contact', *Diacritics* 43: 1 (2015), pp. 6–35 (p. 13).
109. Ibid., p. 13.

Chapter 2

Anna Kavan: Glass Girls

It is conceivable that had it not been for the efforts of pioneering publisher Peter Owen who, despite increasingly poor commercial remuneration and diminishing critical appeal, indefatigably published her work until her death in 1968, Anna Kavan's *oeuvre* might well have fallen into complete obscurity. One of the 'neglected, the modern, the foreign, the difficult and the downright unpopular writers' championed by Owen in the postwar period,[1] his determination to keep Kavan's writing in circulation resulted in their translation into several languages. Introduced to her in 1956, Owen recalled that he had initially rejected Kavan's work as the 'stories' that she sent him from 'time to time' were at times 'brilliant' but at others 'fell below the high standard she had set herself'.[2] Such variation in quality notwithstanding, he would come to regard her as a writer 'whose vision transcends that of their contemporaries' but whose work often remains 'unappreciated in their own lifetime'.[3] 'Anna Kavan', Owen remarked in 2001, 'is only now achieving recognition as one of the most remarkable authors of her time'.[4]

With the exception of *Ice* (1967), her best-known and final work, Kavan's writing has, until recently, sustained longstanding critical neglect and, despite Owen's support, has occupied only a peripheral position in the history of mid-twentieth-century British literature; considered at length in only two monographs, Francis Booth's *Among Those Left: The British Experimental Novel 1940–1980* (2012) and Sara Wasson's *Urban Gothic of the Second World War* (2010).[5] Booth's study (usefully comprehensive but unwieldy and unscholarly) examines Kavan's work in the context of mid-century experimentalism alongside, among others, Christine Brooke-Rose, Rayner Heppenstall, Ann Quin, Eva Figes and B. S. Johnson. Wasson places Kavan's novels, in particular *I am Lazarus* (1945), alongside those of Henry Green and Elizabeth Bowen as part of a 'dark' literary wartime London; a bombed-out, postwar city grieving for its maimed and dead.[6] Kavan has been included, however, in several anthologies of twentieth-century writing, most notably *The Oxford Companion to Twentieth-Century Literature in English* (1996), Margaret Crosland's *Beyond The Lighthouse: English Women Novelists in the Twentieth Century* (1981) and Harry Blamires' *A Short History of English Literature* (1984).[7] Inclusion in literary surveys is not, of course, indicative of wider critical consequence, and it is not my intention here to rehabilitate Kavan as a major twentieth-century writer or to suggest unequivocally that her distinctive writing style was always successful in its experimentalism. In fact, her *oeuvre* is notable for its unevenness; at times, she writes with concision and psychological insight, at others, she fixatedly works over a series of repeated motifs that sometimes lack sufficient textual precision. Writing in 1997, Vivian Gornick positions Kavan in a 'tradition in Britain of "unstable" literary women that includes Antonia White, Anna Kavan, Jean Rhys, and Virginia Woolf', all of whom wrote 'a remarkably interior prose'; Woolf, she says, 'never began at less than transcendence' but Kavan, she concludes rather dismissively, 'never rose above obsession'.[8] Robert Nye's judicious evaluation of Kavan as 'lyricist and fantasist of importance' rather than a major writer, seems to me to capture the occasionally inconsistent quality of her *oeuvre* while acknowledging her significant contribution to mid-century British writing.[9]

Difficult to classify generically, Kavan's experimentalism has been described variously as modernist, science fiction, surrealist, expressionist, and as an example of the *nouveau roman*; 'the only group of writers to whom', according to her biographer David Callard, 'she ever expressed a partiality'.[10] However, the soubriquet that has clung most tenaciously to her work is Brian Aldiss's description of her as 'Kafka's sister', which is a rather lazy, even sub-standard, comparison, as her writing is a flatter, more affectively detached prose that increasingly pushes away from any 'real' world. But, 'Like Kafka', Aldiss maintained,

> Kavan seems as a child always to have felt herself in the wrong; and this feeling, as she reached adult years, also matured, into the prevailing sense that somehow her existence was unjustified, insubstantial. Like Kafka, she suffered in her struggle to come to terms with other people, and with herself.[11]

He also insists that the '"I" character' in her writing is unproblematically Kavan's 'mirror image' that always expresses 'the same gamut of anxiety'.[12] While some of Aldiss's assertions are valid, in particular the claim that Kavan might well be 'one of the few English symbolists',[13] what they miss, however, is a detailed consideration of the evidently different philosophical and intellectual contexts of each writer; a move that simply folds her particular type of expressionism into Kafka's own.

Given the scarcity of scholarly work on Kavan, it is striking that no fewer than three biographies exist, each broadly repeating the same handful of details of the little that is known of her life. While each varies slightly in focus, David Callard's *The Case of Anna Kavan* (1993), Jeremy Reed's *A Stranger on Earth: The Life and Work of Anna Kavan* (2006) and Jennifer Sturm's *Anna Kavan's New Zealand: A Pacific Interlude in a Turbulent Life* (2009) all provide some useful background knowledge but little in the way of rigorous critical evaluation. This situation changed in 2014 with the first Anna Kavan Symposium, followed by a 2017 special issue on Kavan in *Women: A Cultural Review*. In her introduction to this collection, Victoria Walker, whose work has been pivotal in a modest renaissance of Kavan scholarship, notes that Kavan's critical neglect and marginalisation is, perhaps, due less to her formal experimentation with non-linear narrative and her abandonment of 'plot and character development', than to her work's more general 'resistance to categorization'.[14] To be sure, Kavan's critical legacy is not helped by the fact that her *oeuvre* sits uneasily in any category or periodisation, not least as it is divided aesthetically between two distinctive phases of her writing; the conventional realism of the pre-war writing as Helen Ferguson and, after 1940, the experimental writing under the name Anna Kavan. In neither of these periods, however, has Kavan's writing found a secure critical position in the longer *durée* of modernism, whether early, high or late – a situation now starting to change as scholars begin to give her work more sustained critical attention.[15] The reasons for her exclusion from modernist studies are not my chief concern here, but it is likely due to the early critical work on her writing, in particular that of Booth, Callard and Reed, who gave limited attention to the aesthetics of Kavan's prose. While perhaps useful as points of departure, their work is so maladroitly psychopathographical in its mechanical use of her life, they provide only very slight critical readings lacking in interpretive complexity or apposite knowledge of psychoanalytical tools with which to approach the highly vexed question of biography, especially for women writers. In what follows, it will become clear that while a superficial biographic reading does little justice to Kavan's work, one simply cannot ignore the psychic traces of certain aspects of her life that undoubtedly, if obliquely, resonate in some of her best writing.

The novels she wrote as Helen Ferguson between 1929 and 1937 are, to all appearances, broadly realist, but this realism is mostly a surface effect beneath which already stalks undercurrents of subjective disintegration that characterise her postwar writing. After 1940, Kavan's writing is characterised by a sense of antagonistic affect that is projected outwardly onto objects, landscapes and climatic conditions. Her experimental prose charts the interior worlds of her fragile, psychologically beleaguered 'glass girls', on whom I will focus in this chapter. These girls exist in various states of rejection, accusation and persecution, often pursued by a series of tormentors in the shape of doctors, guards, benefactors, lovers, husbands, or parents turned jailers, who tyrannise the girls. Whatever their real biological age, the female protagonists in Kavan's fiction are always signified as 'girls' rather than women; her body, 'slight as a child's', fragile and thin, and lacking any of the fleshed out roundness of sexual maturity, is always on the edge of an endangered corporeality as the disturbed mind becomes separated from all physicality.[16] The focus of an indeterminate peril, Kavan's 'girls' are tormented, pursued and imprisoned and progressively removed from all networks of belonging and intimacy. Treated like baggage to be dutifully carted around the world, these girls are unloved outcasts who find themselves in increasingly incomprehensible surroundings. Subject to the inexplicably cruel whims of others, they inhabit indecipherable wastelands; by turns, the quasi-apocalyptic topography of *Ice*, the grotesquely weird dreamscape of *Sleep Has His House* (1948) or the stifling heat of 'Southern climes' in *A Scarcity of Love* (1956) – spaces where all bodily vitality is slowly extinguished. Permeated with a pervasive sense of psychological claustrophobia and encroaching menace, Kavan's narratives turn around a limited number of repeated scenes: the sudden and cataclysmic loss of signification and affect, a withdrawal from vitality, and the estrangement of a vulnerable 'girl' in menacing anthropomorphised settings. With 'no sun, no shadows, no life, a dead cold', the worlds in Kavan's writing comprise reiterated events of dispossession and maltreatment.[17] Described by J. G. Ballard as positioned somewhere 'between poetry and madness', in many of the works I examine here Kavan's language produces an incantatory repetition of scenarios of affective desolation, the result of what Julia Kristeva calls a 'symbolic abdication' in which the subject can only conceive of death as a solution to the 'void of the lost object'.[18] This void comes in many forms in Kavan's narratives as the girls move around a constricted circuit of traumatic events, held in thrall to unnamed devitalising, often highly menacing, forces under which language is experienced as estranged and nullifying – what Kavan calls a plasmatic 'dream screen'.[19] With their numbed dialogue, expressionistic landscapes and glacial maternal figures, Kavan's 'screens' exhibit a profound melancholia in which the subject turns away from vitality, and gradually succumbs to a life-in-death. Inhabiting worlds characterised by affective coldness and a catastrophic loss of signification, Kavan's girls always return to the site of an impossible mourning for childhood loss; they cannot help but look back at the 'nursery windows' in order to relive 'life's fear and pain'.[20]

Suggesting that the 'disjointed narratives' in *Sleep Has His House* (*The House of Sleep* in the US edition) can be read as a 'radical "feminine" aesthetic', Jane Garrity argues that they reveal a pre-Oedipal language that is semiotic, 'chaotic, open-ended, [. . .] often situated on the threshold between sense and nonsense'.[21] She further suggests that the fragmented texture of Kavan's writing can be read as a defiant feminist act against 'a literary tradition that demands order, coherence, linearity, and mastery'.[22] While it is certainly true that Kavan's writing sometimes borders on the edges of stylistic coherence, this cannot be wholly ascribed, I argue, to a defiance of patriarchal authority, textual or otherwise. It is, rather, Kavan's desire to articulate a strangeness, a sense of alienation and outsiderness, that defines all her protagonists, both male and female: 'Kavan's protagonist is typically not only an exile, an outcast; he or she is truly also a stranger to himself or herself. Her writing explores these liminal and borderline states in terms of psychological and social complication'.[23] In its pursuit of this 'strangeness', Kavan's writing defamiliarises and estranges all domestic space and relationships thereby rendering them as sites of persecution and catastrophic affective damage producing a prose style that commingles the subjective interior of the psyche and the external world until the two are indivisible.

Under the name Helen Ferguson, Kavan wrote six novels: *A Charmed Circle* (1929), *The Dark Sisters* (1930), *Let Me Alone* (1930), *A Stranger Still* (1935), *Goose Cross* (1936) and *Rich Get Rich* (1937), many of which prefigure some of the psychosexual preoccupations discernible in her later writing, in particular the brutal sexual struggle between man and woman, an obliteration of affect and a sense of unspecified persecution or rejection. Outwardly adhering to some sense of the realistic, these earlier novels have neat, if unsophisticated, plots, linear narrative structures and partially 'rounded' characterisation, but already, in the descriptions of tree-lined suburbs, country houses, interwar manufacturing towns and bourgeois domestic interiors, there is a sense of indeterminate menace shadowing these stories. Set on the boundaries of some ambiguously identifiably 'real' world, these novels present characters struggling to express any emotion in a permanently threatening atmosphere of abandonment and rejection; one that goes well beyond any romantic or sexual rejection. On the back cover of *A Charmed Circle*, Doris Lessing calls it a 'short, bleak and shocking' novel, inhabited by anxious women with 'dark, secret faces' who are often described as expressionless, like 'dull, dejected ghosts', women caught in a world where all choices seem to be negative: persecution over attachment and connection; abortion (still an extremely taboo subject) over reproduction; victimhood rather than mutuality; destructive obsession over empathy; betrayal over trust. Although they become, over the years, noticeably more psychologically claustrophobic in tone, the Helen Ferguson novels seem to resemble many middlebrow potboilers of the time with a veneer of realist verisimilitude holding together plots concerning romantic disappointment and bitter family rivalries. Disappearing with little trace, these early novels earned, Victoria Walker notes, neither 'effusive praise nor censure'.[24]

As noted, Kavan's writing career fell into two distinct parts, punctuated by the decisive year 1939–40, when, after repeated breakdowns and several suicide attempts, Helen Ferguson (*née* Woods) emerged from a Swiss sanatorium with her brown hair dyed a striking platinum blonde and calling herself Anna Kavan, the name of a character taken from two early Helen Ferguson novels, *Let Me Alone* and *A Stranger Still*. In the former, the character Anna Kavan, an introverted and fretful orphan, is based on the first year of Ferguson's disastrous marriage to Donald Ferguson and their time spent in Burma. Kavan emerged from her breakdown a wholly changed writer. A discernible transformation of style came with the publication of *Change the Name* (1941) under the name Anna Kavan (changed officially while she was living in New York) that discarded the earlier façade of narrative realism in favour of a more oneiric, expressionistic mode characterised, as Jennifer Sturm has noted, by a 'disturbing motif of unreality'.[25] Of her new writing style, Kavan notes:

> I wanted to abandon realistic writing insofar as it describes exclusively events in the physical environment, and to make the reader aware of the existence of the different, though just as real, 'reality' which lies just beyond the surface of ordinary daily life and the surface aspect of things. I am convinced that a vast, exciting new territory is waiting to be explored by the writer in that direction.[26]

Gone are descriptions of afternoon tennis and tense luncheons; in their place, enigmatic fabular narratives set in isolated castles surrounded by dense foliage and impenetrable woods or abandoned houses inexplicably encircled by flotillas of ice and snow or oppressive houses in the tropics subjected to suffocating heat. Any discernible external reality has metamorphosed into symbolic landscapes that assume a lurid anthropomorphism against which events appear like scenes in a 'grotesque nightmare film', and human figures lose any sense of particularity and definition, becoming stock or archetypical in ways that resemble the genre of the fairy tale.[27] This second period was described by Anaïs Nin as one of nocturnal worlds full of 'waking dreamers' who exist 'in solitude with their shadows, hallucinations, prophecies' that speak of 'fantasies, imagination and non-reason'.[28] Many of these novels are structured around narratives in which a malevolent figure is consumed by hatred for a weak girl who is cast out, sometimes literally, but more often figuratively by subjection to an excruciating emotional coldness.

Kavan's writing transmogrifies, then, from narratives set in small manufacturing towns in semi-suburban houses and structured around petty travails around inheritance or romance to hallucinatory settings using what she called her 'night-time language' that allows her to 'dive with extraordinary accuracy' into the 'night-plasma' of the psyche: 'Into the ephemeral image I dive, one after the other: sometimes one crystallizes into a brief sharpness – never to permanence'.[29] In a letter to Nin, novelist Elizabeth Moore notes how Kavan's writing shows its 'wounds' and is 'touched with neurosis' that possesses 'an extra dimensional perception', with 'the night's tangling images, half-thoughts, wheeling worlds'.[30] Poised on the porous border between dreams and reality, the 'wheeling worlds' of Kavan's fiction experiment with various modes of disconnection, isolation and disconsolation originating in, but *not*, I will argue, directly reflective of, sustained childhood neglect that, for complex, and finally unprovable, reasons related to her contact with psychoanalysis and drug therapy, allowed her to tap into a different stratum of affective content. In an article in 1946, Kavan describes this psychic space as 'that dangerous territory of dream symbolism where all laws are incomprehensible, all authorities incalculable; where the hidden threat feeds every rose and all simplicity hides the ominous complication'.[31] Kavan's writing demonstrates what Eva Figes believed to be the primary objectives of the experimental writer: 'What matters is the writer should shock into awareness, startle, above all, that he [sic] should not engage in the trade of reassurance'.[32] At its very best, Kavan's writing does all three.

A prolific writer over her lifetime, a single chapter cannot claim to do justice to the entirety of Kavan's *oeuvre*. Offered here then, are readings of a selection of some of her more important experimental writing, focusing on *I am Lazarus, Sleep Has His House, Who Are You?* (1963), *A Scarcity of Love, Ice*, and the posthumously published *Julia and the Bazooka* (1970), as well as *Asylum Piece and Other Stories* (1940).

The Problems of Biography

The 'facts' of Anna Kavan's life are not easy to recover. Unhappily for her biographers, Kavan very deliberately destroyed all her diaries with the exception of a 16-month period from July 1926 to November 1927, thus a degree of speculation is required in order to compile an even partially coherent narrative of her life. Aldiss described Kavan's fiction as one that 'remains at arm's length from the facts of life' and what emerges from her novels 'is part of an elaborate game of hide-and-seek which a writer plays, perhaps unconsciously, not necessarily with the reader but with himself or herself'.[33] Given the dearth of verifiable facts, it is no surprise then that each biography contains more than a little conjecture, as well as some questionable assertions regarding the connection between her life and her writing, resulting in two rather unreliable biographies that too crudely plot her life against her writing. As Walker notes, 'the tale of Kavan's life is a jumble of fact, fiction, exaggeration and omission, developed and perpetuated as it has passed from magazine article to fly-leaf, popular biography, book review and back again'.[34] Reinforcing the quasi-mythology of Kavan's life, her friend, Raymond Marriot, described Kavan as a mercurial figure: 'She cast doubts, she lied, she fabricated, she spoke the truth, she was most honest'.[35]

The hodge-podge of truth, half-remembered anecdotes, exaggeration and inference has tended to buttress much of the limited critical work on Kavan that has existed until recently, most of it drawn upon earlier material by Kavan's long-term friend, the Welsh writer Rhys Davies. Published shortly after her death, these pieces inaugurated what Walker describes as 'the myth of Kavan' that is the handful of facts and half-facts – her drug addiction, her uncaring mother, childhood neglect and her unconventional personality – sketched in Davies's article 'The Bazooka Girl',[36] and more fleshed out in his final novel, *Honeysuckle Girl* (1975).[37] The book, which is, it must be remembered, a fiction, states what is surely the most frequently reiterated fact about Kavan's life with the possible exception of her addiction to heroin and her name change; namely, the dramatic physical transformation that occurred when she changed her hair colour from brown to platinum blonde. This physical alteration is emphasised and stands, in Davies's view, in a causal relationship with the subsequent adoption of the name Anna Kavan taken from one of her characters in *Let Me Alone*. These two facts, however unverifiable they may be in their particulars, are *always* mentioned in criticism on Kavan (I, too, must admit guilt in this direction) as if this physical metamorphosis can unproblematically elucidate her writing. Janet Wilson, for example, argues that this name change was a way of keeping herself alive 'following severe depression, suicide attempts and prolonged psychiatric treatment, all of which had annulled her sense of self. It enabled her to distance herself from her previous life and literary persona, and make a new start'.[38] This view is borne out by Kavan's own admission that what she desired above all was an escape from her personae as Helen Ferguson/Edmonds: 'I want to get right away from Helen Edmonds and all her associations'.[39]

It is irrefutable that certain details of Kavan's personal life stand in a complicated relationship to her artistic practice, but it is, I think, a relationship that suggests proximity and association rather than replication or reflection. The issue of Kavan's life, or more precisely the relationship of her life to her writing, remains challenging for her critics. A writer's life, indeed any life, is inevitably lived in a variety of ways; eventfully or uneventfully, disgracefully or modestly; in short, human lives are simply lived. But for writers and artists this simple fact becomes discernibly more complex, both at the time of writing and thereafter, as artists are regarded, to varying degrees, to be wrangling with psychic material for the content of their work. I will address this question of psychic wrangling in more detail presently, but for now suffice to say that I do not believe that writers can be so categorically detached from the material that filters down, either directly or obliquely, reliably or uncertainly, from their lives into their writing. All writers, to a greater or lesser degree to be sure, mould some of this material into imaginative shapes that might be part-refraction, part-reflection, part-rejection of their actual lives worked over by intellectual labour and poetic imagination to produce writing that both *is* and *is not* in a correlative relationship to 'real life'. For women writers and artists, this wrangling has historically assumed a more loaded signification because of the ways in which women have been deprived, says Monique Wittig, 'of the authority of speech', which has kept them from 'any claim to the abstract, philosophical, political discourses that give shape to the social body'.[40] In this way, the poetics of women's writing is vulnerable to straightforward biographical criticism, their art functioning in a disproportionately revelatory way as a spyhole into their lives. There is, then, no easy and direct equivalence to be drawn between Kavan's life and artistic expression, as the ways in which life affects art (and vice versa) exist in an unstable relationship, but that is not say, however, the one exists wholly independently from the other. Kavan's writing, I suggest, stands in an oblique relationship to her psyche and to some pivotal moments in her life that shaped or affected her personality; yet this in no way diminishes or reduces the former at the expense of the latter. This is not the same as simply reading off her life from her work but rather allowing that a certain remoteness of tone and affect discernible in her writing might be read through a psychoanalytic lens as a creative working through of complex issues arising from her relationship to early experiences of emotional scarcity. Aldiss, as noted above, recognises the complex inscription of the facts of Kavan's life into her writing, noting that what 'arises from the printed page' must be approached with interpretative caution.[41]

Much of Kavan's writing registers the complex psychic traces resulting from events in her life, and marshals this into aesthetic form that is not reducible to simple biography but forms, rather, a complex writerly concatenation. Rather than reading off life from art, Jacqueline Rose says that we need to remember that 'for the writer, the lived life was the point of departure rather than, as it is for the biographer, the place at which there is a desperate need to arrive'.[42] Plotting her life directly onto her writing with a perfunctory logic of equivalence reduces Kavan's talent to little more than an inadvertent side effect of her experiences of depression and addiction, both of which were powerfully present in her life but neither of which definitely explain or define her writing. To propose otherwise suggests that her art is simply an annex to her life; an approach that has been applied more habitually to women writers who have been allocated their pathologised place in literary history as mad, tragic, or suicidal, their talent merely an accidental by-product of their disturbed psyches: 'don't think that this life, for all your efforts, will ever be anything other than the thing you truly are'.[43] A crudely biographical reading devalues, Garrity says, Kavan's complex writing to 'autobiographical evidence of her mental illness and drug-addiction; within this context her disjointed narratives, otherworldly settings and fixated characters are assumed to result from her unstable psyche, rather than from any literary aptitude'.[44]

Rhys Davies claimed that Kavan was 'writing in a mirror' which 'simply imprisoned her'.[45] But Kavan once said that she lived always with *two* mirrors; one offering a direct reflection using good, strong light to expose the truth of the physical self; the other, a less straightforwardly reflective surface that might be used, as she noted, 'somewhat more leniently'.[46] Two mirrors that simultaneously reflect and refract serve here as an apposite structuring analogy for approaching Kavan's work; surfaces that take their material from the events of life but distort these in intentionally manipulated perspectives.[47] Kavan investigates these complex distortions in her writing in ways that experiment with physic material.

Vivian Gornick argues that Kavan's writing is 'drawn exclusively and repeatedly' from her own life 'in a way that recalls not so much a writer drawing legitimately on intimate experience as a talented analytic patient who, despairing of release, repeats in poetic fever a description of the events that captures the shape of original damage'.[48] While I do not agree that Kavan was merely a 'talented patient', an accidental writer who managed to make something out of her 'madness', her experiments with disintegrating the boundaries between subjective interiority and exteriority form part of a complex working through, via those 'double mirrors', of an enduring melancholy for the lost maternal body. Thus, Kavan's writing exists in a deflected but fundamental relationship to her life; her writing is not an equivalent correspondence to her experience of narcosis, depression and affective deprivation, but is rather a delayed, refracted register of these and in particular of a primary loss of maternal warmth. The Kavan 'girl' is confined on the boundaries between life and death and exists in the depressive aura of what Julia Kristeva calls the 'black sun' of melancholia. Condemned to a devitalised existence, the inert girls in Kavan's writing are always ready 'for a plunge into death'.[49] The enervating rays of this black sun inundate much of Kavan's later writing with its succession of deadened, entombed 'girls' who are progressively excluded from any intelligible representational order which points to a severely damaged bond with the maternal figure and a problematic relationship with the symbolic order. Kristeva has argued that in order to successfully take up a position in the symbolic, 'matricide is our vital necessity, the *sina qua non* of individuation'.[50] This metaphorical killing of the mother is an imperative act for the subject who, in order to achieve healthy psychological incorporation, must move away from the chaos of the maternal semiotic. But the killing of the mother is not realised in Kavan's writing, a situation further complicated by the fact that there was no meaningful attachment to the maternal chora in the first place. Early and ongoing detachment between mother and child leads to the child's disturbed relationship to the semiotic chora that subsequently hinders, or prevents, the child's entry into the symbolic order. Drawing on what we know of serious emotional neglect in Kavan's early childhood and the ways in which this slowly works through her writing; first in a rather oblique, even subterranean, manner only to emerge more fully after 1940, I examine, what Valentine Cunningham calls the fundamental 'unconsolation' of Kavan's writing and its 'enclosingly anguished world of mirrors and fish-bowls'.[51] This world is created out of an expressionism in which subjective states are projected onto an exterior world that becomes a phantasmagoric screen externalising the girl's perturbed state of mind. For her part, Kavan regarded her work as more than simply reporting her own life and considered her writing style to be experimental. In correspondence with George Bullock, she writes: 'An experimental book always needs a certain build up [. . .] not only booksellers but critics have to be given a lead, otherwise they feel confused and antagonised by something they can't fit into a convenient pigeonhole'.[52]

Attempting to avoid a reductive biographical approach, then, I suggest that there is a way of approaching Kavan's writing in relation to some of her early life events – what Gornick calls its 'original damage' – that allows for a critically productive interpretation of her writing. Thus, I draw upon what (little) we know of serious emotional neglect in Kavan's early childhood and suggest that this formative deprivation of emotional warmth infuses her work; first, in a rather oblique, even subterranean manner only to emerge more fully after 1940, when her writing eschews chronologically linear narratives and neatly crafted plotting fundamental to conventional realism. In order to make this case for a psychoanalytically inflected reading, some reference to crucial moments in Kavan's life is required.

Woods/Ferguson/Kavan

Born in Cannes to Helen Bright and Claude Woods, in 1901, Anna Kavan began life as Helen Emily Woods. Her early childhood does not appear to have been especially stable, loving or happy. Handed over to a succession of nannies and wet nurses, the infant Helen was permitted to see her mother only briefly each day. What little is known of Kavan's early upbringing reveals events that can only be regarded as damaging to the emotional development of an infant and young child who seems to have been unwanted and unloved. Kavan's mother, an inveterate socialite, flitted from one glittering event to another across Europe and America. The day after she was born, the baby Helen was sent away to live with a wet nurse and her family, not an exceptionally unusual practice for this social class. Her mother retrieved her some time later, bringing her to live in a lavishly appointed house in West London. Although she was permitted only to see her mother for ten minutes each day, just before dinner, the young Helen, Kavan's diary tells us, was on the whole, relatively happy. This happiness, however, was short-lived. Her parents left for America, leaving their young daughter to another nurse, Sammy, who took her to live with her family in London. During this period of separation from her parents and with a new family structure to assimilate, Helen had an appendix operation, a frightening experience for a young child and one sure to have left its mark on her after waking up alone in hospital with no family present.

Her father returned to England and then took her and Sammy to live first in New York, then in California. At six years old, Kavan writes that she was 'betrayed' again by her parents who simply seemed to 'disappear' after her arrival and she was subsequently sent to a series of different boarding schools in America until she was thirteen. The isolation of the abandoned child is prevalent throughout *Sleep Has His House*: 'At school and at home it was the same; I was alone [. . .] There was no place for me in the day world. My home was in darkness and my companions were shadows beckoning from a glass'.[53] She was never to see her father again, as he allegedly fell overboard on a ship in Tuxpan Harbour, Mexico. Whether this was suicide or accident was never determined; either way, Kavan did not learn of his death until some years later. Kavan's mother remarried Joseph White but he soon died, after which, in 1934, she married a wealthy South African, Hugh Tevis, who was almost twenty years younger and openly homosexual. For the rest of her life, Kavan's mother lived in South Africa, where Kavan visited her on occasion, but after her mother's death she found herself cut out of her expected inheritance.

After her father's death, Kavan was sent to Lausanne to boarding school, then to Parson Mead School in Surrey, then Malvern Girls College, and she was eventually offered a place at Oxford. Although she was given £600 a year allowance (about £37, 000 in 2020 terms) by her mother, this did not seem to enable any chance of a higher education and she never took up her offer. In 1920, she married Donald Ferguson, thirty years old to her nineteen, who would later appear as Matthew Kavan in *Let Me Alone* and then partially rewritten in *Who Are You?* (1963).[54] With Ferguson, Kavan travelled to Burma where she gave birth to a son, Bryan, in 1922.[55] In 1923, both she and the baby returned, without Ferguson, to Britain and the couple subsequently divorced in 1927. Little is known of her life after this divorce, but the surviving diary from the year July 1926 to November 1927 records her first foray into heroin use – 'The H makes one's eyes beautiful'[56] – as well as her enrolment at the London Central School of Arts and Crafts where she studied painting.[57] Around this time she began an affair with a painter called Stuart Edmonds, who she would marry in 1928. She gave birth to a daughter called Margaret in 1935 who died in infancy, and later adopted another daughter called Susanna. As with Bryan, Kavan appears to have had very limited contact with this child after her split from Edmonds, who seems to have opposed her custody of the child, but these are not fully verifiable facts and we can only work with supposition to fill in the gaps. After some visits to Susanna, Kavan stops mentioning her name in her letters and by 1944, as Walker notes, 'both Bryan and

Susanna were lost to her'.[58] In the space of just a few years, then, Kavan had married twice and lost three children. Perhaps no wonder then that in 1938, she was admitted to a sanatorium in Switzerland after a severe breakdown.

Between 1939 and 1943 Kavan fled the deprivations of wartime Britain and travelled extensively. In late 1939, she went to New Zealand with Ian Hamilton, and they also travelled together to Norway, to North and Central America, living in La Joya California for six months before they separated – Hamilton returned to New Zealand and Kavan sailed to South Africa to join her mother. On her way, she had yet another change of romantic fortune when she met Charles Fairchild Fuller, a wealthy, well-connected American architect with whom she engaged in a passionate but short-lived affair. In October 1940, they travelled to New York together where Kavan became acquainted with a bohemian circle including Walker Evans and James Agee. According to Hugh Davis, Agee acted as what he called an 'amateur agent' for Kavan, forwarding her manuscript to an editor, Robert Lindscott, at Houghton Mifflin.[59] Nothing came of this, but Kavan was to be connected to Agee once again in her review of *Let Us Now Praise Famous Men* when she worked for *Horizon* after the war. Unable to secure a visa, Kavan had to leave America and from there travelled back to New Zealand from February 1941 to November 1942. This period brought another set of changed circumstances and relations and has been documented by both Jennifer Sturm and Janet Wilson.[60]

Returning to Britain in late 1942, Kavan met a new group of friends that included Kay Dick (who was also an acquaintance of Brigid Brophy's) and through this circle met Cyril Connolly, joining, albeit for a brief period, the staff of his *Horizon* magazine.[61] Not long after, there was another stay in a Swiss clinic where she met Dr Karl Bluth through whom she was introduced to the so-called 'existential' psychiatry of Ludwig Binswanger.[62] In 1943, Kavan was offered a job working with soldiers suffering from what is now called post-traumatic stress disorder, at the Mill Hill Emergency Hospital with Dr Maxwell Jones. In a letter to Hamilton she describes the position: 'My main job is interviewing the patients one at a time and putting them through a sort of questionnaire which is designed to bring out a general impression of personality and to trace the development of effort syndrome'.[63] As Walker notes, Kavan's experiences at Mill Hill were formative and along with her 'experiences of progressive psychiatric treatment', her work there would 'profoundly alter her understanding of her own mental difficulties and her relationship to the psychiatric profession'.[64] This time produced her second collection of stories *I am Lazarus*, an important stage in Kavan's thinking not only about the long-term effects of mental illness but also about how one might shape language in order to articulate the traumatised mind.[65] Reviewing this work in 1946, Leo Lerman said: 'I hesitate to classify her pieces as stories, for she is less concerned with formal story structure – plot, characterization, time, place, personality – than she is with communicating the integral essence of mental upheaval'.[66]

The Wounded Child

Writing in *Horizon* in 1944, Kavan expresses an interest in what she calls, rather inexpertly, the 'subconscious', expressing a belief in why the relationship between the 'psychological reactions of human beings to their environment' is finally of more 'vital interest than the environment itself':

> Even in stories of action employing a realist technique, the source of genuine interest springs from an understanding of the fundamentals of human personality. It is the interpretation of complexes, together with their sequence of inevitable events, which gives to any book the truly satisfactory rhythmic progression of music.[67]

In this second stage of her career, Kavan's writing draws away from what Woolf called the 'narrative business' of 'getting from lunch to dinner',[68] to show the existence of what she calls 'a sub-life, contemporaneous with but completely independent of the main current of one's existence'.[69] Kavan's attitude to character and narrative is, in some ways, reminiscent of Woolf's interest in creating 'characters without any features at all'. We must be, Woolf says, tolerant of the chaos that might come from this sub-life: the 'truth itself is bound to reach us in rather an exhausted and chaotic condition' and therefore the writer (and reader) of such 'truth' must 'tolerate the obscure, the fragmentary, the failure'.[70] For Woolf, writing was recuperative; her prose a vivacious inquiry into the multiple possibilities of language and subjectivity. For Kavan however, language moves in the opposite direction; it closes down and retracts, diminishing, rather than enlarging, communicative vivacity. In much of her writing, there is a deep-seated disconnection of the psyche from the lucid, external world; any sense of sustained signification, and of rational meaning, becomes dissociated from experience, feeling and sensation until all that remains is a narrow range of automated responses that renders the subject a mechanical rather than human figure.

In what exists of the diaries in the period before the metamorphosis of Helen Ferguson into Anna Kavan, we read that the young Helen regarded 'real life as a hateful and tiresome dream'. The tedium of life, she wrote, was only alleviated by her secretive faculty for self-analysis that manifests in her writing as abstracted dream language, the sort that Kavan praises in her *Horizon* review of Woolf's *A Haunted House*, whose stories possess, she notes, the 'prosaic substance of everyday woven into the lovely, fragile mysteriousness of a dream'.[71] It is such a transfiguration of the commonplace into the strange and the fantastic upon which Kavan's writing turns but for her the dream world is not 'lovely', more a nightmarish shrinking back of symbolism that creates an inscrutable and deadened world.[72] The isolation of the abandoned child is prevalent in many passages of *Sleep*: 'At school and at home it was the same I was alone [. . .] There was no place for me in the day world. My home was in darkness and my companions were shadows beckoning from a glass'.[73] Imbued with an atmosphere of 'cold, loneliness' and 'eternal fog', *Asylum Piece* expresses intensely painful isolation.[74] In 'Piece 11', Kavan writes of the disappearance of love that leaves everything 'the same but not the same': 'No hand enfolded mine in the clasp of love. My thoughts were again solitary, disintegrate, disharmonious – the music gone'.[75] Cleary, then, this writing process was not a Woolfian 'digging out of beautiful caves' but a movement to interiority shaped by a powerful decathexis; that is, the removal of affective or libidinal attachment, attributable, as I will argue, to a disruption of maternal affect. An exhausting procedure says Freud ('Mourning and Melancholia', p. 154), decathexis is undertaken at 'great expense of time and cathectic energy, while all the time the existence of the object is continued in the mind. The process of decathexis alters the presentation of reality, resulting in the emptying out of recognisable human forms into dummies and mannequins, the transmogrification of the natural world into expressionist dreamscapes with 'huge lurid sunsets' and menacing light that threatens to drown the world with its garish intensity, then finally the separation of the protagonists from the rituals of any 'real', external world.[76] The fable-like tales depict the separation, mostly forced but occasionally voluntary, of the subject from an embodied attachment to the world. Both *Asylum Piece*, described by Joyce Carol Oates as replete with 'passages of startling poignancy and radiance', and the half-memoir, semi-dream chronicle, *Sleep Has His House* are marked by decathecting and devitalising energies that push the 'girls' increasingly further away from any lucid meaning or symbolism.[77]

Inhabited by emaciated girls who move through oppressive landscapes of either bitter coldness or stultifying heat, Kavan's 'girls' are engulfed by a sense of persecution and are repeatedly subjected to, as one reviewer put it, a 'fresh kind of peril'.[78] Her characters exist in a nightmarish version of reality often reminiscent of the dreamlike topography of surrealism where events occur in a 'murky inferno' of 'blind and mad armour-plated monsters', roaming through a remote, 'semi-demolished wilderness' of 'chaos and despair'.[79] Pursued and imprisoned by nameless gaolers, immobilised by heat or cold, a pervasive sense of enmity and antagonism infiltrates all of Kavan's writing: 'Somewhere in the world', she writes, 'I have an implacable enemy although I do not know his name'.[80] In various ways, the childlike protagonists have all been psychically wounded and forsaken; estranged from the lucid, rational world of the everyday, they are compelled to live in recurring states of nameless dread which is 'like hearing the same story repeated again and again, recasting familiar situations and characters in tones that grow more nightmarish as the years pass'.[81]

The nightmarish quality of Kavan's expressionistic writing centres on the paralysis of both body and mind, followed by some kind of incarceration where the girl passively awaits her fate with a mixture of terror and guilt. As in Kafka, to whom she has been compared,[82] the knock on the door in Kavan's fiction is a harbinger of imminent persecution and often imprisonment in a world that is at once unreadable and frightening. Nin describes Kavan's *Asylum Piece* as Kafkaesque stories in which the 'nonrational human being is caught in a web of unreality'.[83] Persecution is not a minor chord in Kavan's writing, rather, as she herself noted, it '*is* the book'.[84] In Kafka, it is the shadow of the censorious father who looms large, while in Kavan it is the pitiless mother who is the threatening presence for her wounded girls. This mother figure takes many forms; a partial absence in a house, radiating remoteness and disapproval from a distance or, more obliquely, she is represented as a jailor, a medical official and even as a sexually brutish husband.

A collection of enigmatic, imploded fables suffused with a sense of indeterminate and sadistic menace, *Asylum Piece* was the first work published under the name Anna Kavan. Each piece in the collection leads inexorably to the eponymous asylum; they can hardly be called 'stories' in any conventional sense, but possess, nonetheless, a sense of belonging to a narrative cycle rather than a miscellany of prose fragments. Running through much of this collection is the sense of punishment that is meted out on the girl; she knows that it is coming but does not know when or how it will happen. The punishment is arbitrary and inexplicable; possibly for some unspecified rebellion or betrayal in the past, possibly for nothing at all. In *Asylum Piece*, the girl has Patrons who are displeased with her behaviour and send her back to her room down in the gloom and the fog where she must remain sad and alone.[85]

Rejected and despondent, the girl craves 'sunshine and warmth', even if the sunshine is entirely artificial and, at times, stifling it is preferable to the freezing fog below.[86] A spectral presence, the girl lives in the shadow of these intimidating figures, 'always moving in her own little circle of dissociation [. . .] as if her real self were elsewhere'.[87]

One of the early stories, 'The Birthmark', begins with a nameless girl in a state of parental abandonment as her mother has decided to go abroad for reason of the father's ill health. Not quite making friends with H (like Kafka, Kavan is fond of giving only initials for characters' names), another pupil in the boarding school to which she is sent, the narrator notes the 'strange sense of nullification' surrounding this other girl who reacts to events with 'resignation combined with dread'.[88] H possesses a rather extraordinary birthmark on her upper arm, a mark that is a peculiar combination of the organic and the machine, reminiscent perhaps of the inscriptions of the punishment machine of *In the Penal Colony*. The birthmark is a combination of deadly sharp angles, a 'toothed' circle with sharp points in which is contained a more recognisably organically structure; perhaps a rose, a 'tiny shape very soft and tender' (p. 13). A relationship fails to develop out of a peculiar encounter in which H shows the mark to the narrator and the piece jumps forward a number of years to an unstipulated time and place to a town with a castle in a nameless 'foreign country'. In the castle, there is a prison which houses, as the 'unaccountably depressed' narrator learns, 'offenders of a certain type' (p. 15). Peering through the weeds and cracks in the flagstones, she sees an underground cell in which a 'shrouded form' appears to be lying on a bier, the mark on her 'almost transparent flesh' surely the same spike-encircled rose (p. 17). Why H is imprisoned here is never explained. The narrator is challenged to produce her papers by the prison guards brandishing their truncheons and revolvers. This time she escapes imprisonment, but the narrator of 'The Enemy' is not so fortunate and finally is carried away by 'three men in uniform, or white jackets, one of them carrying a syringe. All will be done in a quiet and orderly manner' (pp. 33–4).

A generalised feeling of helplessness is reiterated in 'Asylum Piece':

> If only one knew of what and by whom one were accused, when, where, and by what laws one were to be judged [. . .] but as it is one hears nothing but conflicting rumours, everything is hidden and uncertain, liable to change at a moment's notice or without any notice at all. (p. 44)

Hearing nothing that might shed light on her imminent fate, the perilous world of the Kavan girl is an unfathomable space of existence in which life, death, or happiness depends wholly upon the whim and decree of others.

The Dead Mother

In Kavan's writing, all human affect is progressively reduced to a frozen, un-vital inwardness, the result of an 'impossible mourning' for the 'dead' mother. Kristeva's ideas on female depression and melancholia in *Black Sun* and André Green's concept of the 'dead' mother might be drawn on productively here in order to read the catastrophic loss of affect in Kavan's writing that revolves around the 'unsymbolizable' loss of the dead mother. In repeated scenarios of stultification and detachment, rejection and punishment, Kavan's writing works over a failure to mourn this loss of a mother who has *always* been dead to the child. Like a dummy or a marionette, this figure possesses the outward appearance of a human presence but is devoid of any animation and affect, thus unable to provide any vital embodiment for the child for whom 'it becomes forbidden ... to be'.[89] Melancholia, the failure to mourn the loss of the mother, turns in on the child and 'cadaverizes' the subject, in whom all life is gradually 'slowed down or interrupted [...] absorbed into sorrow'.[90]

The wounds of childhood neglect mark Kavan's writing with an atmosphere of paralysis and emotional fixation consistent with the narcissistic melancholia that develops around the hatred for the child's lost love object, expressed by Kristeva as an '*impossible mourning for the maternal object*' (p. 9) As stated, in order to enter into the symbolic order, the child *must* dissolve the bond with the mother in a crucial act of matricide. If this negation is not achieved the child cannot learn to repress the trauma of this memory of negation – a process that is painful but, when well executed, allows the child to achieve a healthy separation from the mother. If this does not happen, then the child becomes trapped in the semiotic chora, destined to work over repeatedly the same imagery and symbols of that failure of negation and its traumatic content. This negation, according to Kristeva, necessitates a period of mourning for the loss of the mother, the 'indispensable object', and this is crucial for the child who must learn to separate from the maternal. Thus, emotions formerly associated with and addressed to the mother have to find alternative expression in the 'imaginary or symbolic level' (p. 40). Those who do not achieve this negation become overwhelmed by melancholia, as they cannot 'cancel it out, suspend it, and nostalgically fall back on the real object (the Thing) of their loss, which is just what they do not manage to lose, and to which they remain painfully riveted' (p. 43). Any ongoing enthralment to the maternal produces a deep asymbolia as the 'weight of the primal Thing prevails, and all translatability become impossible', and emotional paralysis is the result (p. 42). The necessary act of matricide that allows the child to be a healthy, separate subject has not been achieved and the narratives become congested around this point. For men, the inverse of this matricidal impulse is expressed as misogyny but for women it is fundamentally more self-destructive; directed inwards against the self rather than outwards towards the world, it is not so much a hatred, says Kristeva, but 'an implosive mood that walls itself in and kills me secretly, very slowly, through permanent bitterness, bouts of sadness' (p. 29). A woman's feelings are directed inwards and against the body of the reviled, motherless self, forcing the subject either into the semantic emptiness of asymbolia where nothing can be properly attached to meaning or, conversely, to over-investment in the cognitive excesses of a chaotic universe. Either way, the maternal figure always assumes 'a sinister sort of significance' in Kavan's narratives.[91]

While the paralysis demonstrable in Kavan's writing is often agonising for her characters, for Kavan as a writer, the recognition of this melancholia and paralysis (possibly achieved, in part, through her long periods of psychoanalysis) was creatively productive. The writer calling herself Anna Kavan who emerges from the sanatorium in 1940, begins to work over the experience of an absent or 'dead' mother in an altered mode of experimental writing. Signs become continually introjected as the Kavan 'girls' all gradually disappear in spirals of self-annihilation, what Kristeva calls the 'putting to death of the self'.[92] Many of the girls desire to turn to stone, to petrify themselves with the horror of living, or else to fall into the spaces between the clouds. At other times, they want to become like the disembodied summits of mountains with their 'terrible great ghost-shapes of luminous pallor floating on the dark sky', to sink into 'black gaps of shadow', to be at one with the 'fearful cold otherness of the non-human world'.[93] The withdrawal from the world is nowhere more apparent than in *Asylum Piece*, where the nameless girl lives in a permanent condition of isolation and affective deprivation: 'I am alone forever in this room where the light burns all night long and the professional faces of strangers, without warmth or pity, glance at me through the half open door'. Immobile and deathly in appearance, she is in 'a state of complete quiescence' with 'unfocused eyes wide open' like those of a 'lost person' (pp. 131, 157).

As noted, Kavan's early life was marked by emotional neglect. The serious disruption of the mother–child dyad, in some ways not untypical for that generation of children raised by wealthy parents, inhibits the flow of warm, synergetic affect and libidinal energy, causing the neglected child to actively embrace her own solitude. As André Green notes, 'The subject nestles into it. He [sic] becomes his own mother'. These children, then, learn to regard solitude as their only destiny: 'Arrested in their capacity to love, subjects who are under the empire of the dead mother can only aspire to autonomy. Sharing remains forbidden to them'.[94] Permeated by an atmosphere of 'cold, loneliness' and 'eternal fog', *Asylum Piece* expresses intensely painful isolation. In 'Piece 11', Kavan writes of the disappearance of love that leaves everything 'the same but not the same': 'No hand enfolded mine in the clasp of love. My thoughts were again solitary, disintegrate, disharmonious – the music gone' (p. 129).

In particular, language struggles to find words to represent the maternal figure: 'It is not easy to describe my mother. Remote and starry, her sad stranger's grace did not concern the landscape of the day. Should I say that she was beautiful or did not love me?'[95] In *A Scarcity of Love*, we learn that the ice-queen mother, Regina, has 'cold eyes', a 'narrow mouth' that is 'thin with menace', 'slender white snake-arm[s]' and is possessed of a venomous temperament, the sinister castle in the forest in which she dwells is remote and impenetrable.[96] She hates her child from conception and as soon as her baby, Gerda, is born she sends her away to a wet-nurse to live in the mountains for many years until she is summoned to join her and her new husband in an itinerant, impersonal life of hotels and parties. Gerda is showered with gifts by her mother, 'she'd been given the gold sandals, more beautiful than anything she'd possessed' (p. 81), but is emotionally neglected – 'nobody in the world seemed to want her; there was no-one to whom she could speak to about herself' (p. 92). She grows increasingly wretched; an evanescent 'moon girl' who is lost to the world:

> The sun disappeared. Instantly there was a chill in the air. With uncanny speed the world began to turn hostile and dark and cold. Between one stone and the next, all colour was expunged [. . .] She could feel the alien country, hostile and savage and huge, the endless lifeless hills crowding behind one another like the waves of some monstrous sea [. . .] She was lost, utterly, hopelessly lost, out of her world. (p. 175)

The sense of alienation that overtakes Gerda here is noted in one of Kavan's diary entries. After visiting her mother in South Africa at her opulent but inhospitable house in Monterey, a 'dry plateau of semi-desert', Kavan writes: 'I'm really terrified in a childish way of getting stuck out here, unable to move, and petrified forever in a repetition of my childhood isolation'. She goes on: 'It must be bad for me to stay so long in the neighbourhood of my mother. All the old frustration paralysis feeling comes over me. I feel less and less able to work or have any independent existence – less and less like a real person'.[97] The words that stand out here are 'petrified', 'repetition', 'terrified', 'paralysis' and 'isolation', all of which she suggests were the motifs of her childhood in the presence of an emotionally remote and demanding mother who transmits a fatally devitalising energy to her daughter. The spurned Gerda is similarly alone. Desperate to please an indifferent mother, she is neglected, isolated from the world, and 'deprived of the things that other children enjoyed – home, affection, companions'. When her mother tells her how very unwanted she was, this produces not righteous anger, but a profound sense of guilt and a feeling of being 'subservient and inferior', alone in her total 'separateness' from her family and the world (*Scarcity*, p. 82). Initially happy in her marriage, Gerda's life soon goes inexplicably and catastrophically wrong after her stay in a fever hospital and she rapidly loses any vitality in a downward spiral leading to her madness and death; 'Nobody in the world seemed to want her . . . no place where she mattered, belonged' (p. 84).

Another rejected, desolate girl is at the centre of 'Annunciation', a story taken from *A Bright Green Field and Other Stories* (1958). Mary is confined to a room in a large house as a punishment for first, bed-wetting and, later, the onset of menstruation. Her maturing body is smothered in a tight-fitting dress and underwear to conceal her sexual development, her changing emotions disallowed by all around her. The only way Mary can experience any feelings is through the body of a wounded bird, a baby pigeon that has been pecked nearly to death after being put back in the wrong nest. Mary's body is denied, concealed and made to feel wholly alien. For Kristeva, it is the body that 'bears witness to the affect – to sadness as imprint of separation and beginning of the symbol's sway', and any 'experience of reality' must, then, be tied to the body.[98] The bodies of Kavan's girls are figured as on the side of death rather than life. Pale, exhausted, thin and preternaturally frail, they are permanently victims, doomed to enact the repetition of melancholic depression and to struggle against 'symbolic abdication'.

The 'abdication' of which Kristeva speaks is also known as asymbolia – a catastrophic loss of meaning that inhabits so many of Kavan's characters, originating from what Garrity calls a 'subversive engagement with the maternal'.[99] The 'impossible mourning' for the maternal imprisons the melancholic subject in a world with a 'morbid lining',[100] and involves the transformation of the maternal figure into what Green calls the 'dead mother' – the absent or depressive mother who is an imago for the child: 'a distant figure, toneless, practically inanimate'.[101] As noted,

Kristeva's notions of matricide and melancholia closely correspond to Green's 'dead mother' complex where the mother, due to depression or illness, is physically available but emotionally dead and thus inaccessible to the child, existing only as a figure lacking any animation and tonicity in body, speech and emotions. A zombie-like figure, the mother is un-dead, and thus cannot be 'killed' in the necessary act of matricide, so she lives on as the 'necessary, tyrannical judge' to accuse, punish and deaden her child.[102] The child of an emotionally dead, depressive mother, says Green, is destined to seek a kind of death in life, which takes the form of emotional and bodily disavowal as well as a longing for intense solitude: 'The mother's blank mourning induces blank mourning in the infant, burying a part of his ego in the maternal necropolis'.[103] Following periods of depression (understood very broadly) in which the mother, often unconsciously, withdraws love for her child, the figure of the unreachable mother becomes 'an imago' in the 'child's mind, brutally transforming a living object, which was a source of vitality for the child, into a distant figure', and this can deeply permeate 'the cathexes of certain patients', damaging their chances of a healthy 'object-libidinal and narcissistic future'.[104] This loss of animation and bodily warmth is often represented in Kavan's writing by de-animated figures such as dummies, mannequins or dolls that are coded as maternal. In *Sleep* this is nightmarishly played out in a 'gruesome travesty of mother and child' where a 'brass-like' woman, garishly made up with scarlet lipstick around 'her raw red mouth' suggestive of a fancified genital organ breast-feeds from a 'long rubbery phallus-shaped nipple' that she inserts into the waiting mouth of a wooden manikin that grows monstrously:

> In a series of brisk efficient motions she approaches the cot; lets down the side (with harsh buzz-saw rasp); bends stiff from the waist [. . .] With her hard hands she reaches inside the wool-white, lambs-wool coverings [. . .] and grasps firmly, lifting out a manikin.[105]

The grotesque doll figure stands in for the loss of the mother, which, despite its obvious lifelessness, remains the only provider of sustenance.[106] Such nullified detachment and deanimation of the human is also discernible throughout *Julia and the Bazooka* (1970). The characteristically nameless protagonist is arrested by an inspector (of what, we are never told), detained in a 'small, cold, brightly lit room' and interrogated – the inspector gradually becoming like an inanimate dummy or a *papier mâché* mask.[107]

The withdrawal of maternal affection comes as a shock to the child who experiences this loss of affective warmth as a cataclysmic event, one that forces a self-destructive movement away from the erotic towards

Thanatos. The child becomes, through no fault of its own, the victim of a sudden emotional detachment, and such rapid affective loss carries in its wake a profound loss of meaning, as the child has no explanation for why her world has radically transformed. Crucially, this mother appears to be alive but is effectively dead to the child. An emotionally blank figure for the child, she exhibits no signs of an inner life, like Regina, the countess in *Scarcity*, who is 'like a machine' (*Scarcity*, p. 105). Here, Kavan demonstrates what happens to the child's affective schema when the mother has *never* been emotionally present to represent the semiotic chora for the child – a mother who has always been dead for the child. The compulsion to write the 'dead mother' produces a fixation on scenarios of devastation and punishment and a loss of subject–object lucidity, one that slowly immobilises the Kavan girls into states of affective deprivation in which any sense of an outside is reduced to 'psychical holes'.[108] A passage in *Sleep* describes this:

> What a fearful thing it can be to wake suddenly in the deepest hour of the night. Blackness all around; everything formless, the dark pressing against the eyeballs; the darkness a black thumb pressed to the staring eyeballs distended with dread [...] At first I don't know what I am to become. I am like an embryo prematurely expelled from the womb. I remember nothing, know nothing I haven't the least idea what is making me tremble all over like a person suffering the effect of shock.[109]

Agonisingly attached to both maternal loss and a failed matricide, the 'glass girls' in Kavan's writing drift between life and death in a limbo of affective deprivation. Unlike men's experience of maternal loss, women cannot find a substitute for the mother in heterosexual relations and are thus more deeply wounded by melancholia, often condemned to chase after 'continuously disappointing adventures and loves' or else to retreat from the world, 'disconsolate and aphasic, alone with the unnamed Thing'.[110] Kavan's writing might be read as 'a disaster of words in the face of the unnamable affect'.[111] Caught up in the disaster of the (un)dead mother, Kavan's girls languish in the debilitating corona of the black sun of melancholia around which they continually orbit, vainly seeking either compensation or substitution. The failed mother–child dyad produces the distorted subjectivity of the unloved, solitary girl who, in turn, projects her 'ill-being' onto an external reality so intensely that the inside–outside distinction dissolves in a catastrophe of affect in which all interiority is rendered as external event or metaphor, often directed towards a cataclysmic *dénouement*, exemplified by the ending of *Ice*: '[a] terrible cold world of ice and death had replaced the living world we had always known'.[112]

A Clean White Powder

It is probable that Kavan first tried heroin in the 1920s when the upper-class 'fast' set in London had relatively easy access to both morphine and cocaine.[113] While the precise details are difficult to verify factually, around 1926–7 Kavan was probably given heroin for the first time, referred to as 'H' in her diaries and letters, as a painkiller, to alleviate severe, often suicidal, depression and then administered it by syringe for the rest of her adult life. Around 1939–40, after several serious breakdowns and suicide attempts, she left a Swiss sanatorium habitually using heroin that had probably been therapeutically prescribed for sleeping disorders and severe depression. From that point onwards, until her death in 1968, when she was found collapsed over a box of heroin in her Kensington flat, she had an intermittent, but intense, relationship with the drug. If heroin was essential to Kavan's life, though, it was not central to her writing. But this has not deterred many critics and biographers from 'explaining' her writing as a side-effect of drug use. In his impressionistic study, 'Planet Heroin: Women and Drugs', Lawrence Driscoll describes Kavan as a 'heroin addict and writer', as if these were comparable occupations.[114] The prominence given to heroin addiction in both Callard and Reed's biographies offers some often rather dubious interpretations of her drug use. For example, Callard writes, 'It was deep-rooted nihilism and a sense that life is given meaning only by constant danger which drew her to both racing drivers and heroin use'.[115] Kavan's 'nihilism' was probably severe clinical depression; it is highly likely, therefore, that her use of heroin was less a flirtation with danger than a form of self-medication that, along with periods of psychoanalysis, kept this depression at bay. Acknowledging the importance of heroin in Kavan's life is not to reduce her creativity to pathology whereby her work is entirely subsumed into her construction as an 'addict writer'. It is possible, but by no means certain or verifiable in any definitive way, that for Kavan, heroin was an analgesic that assuaged what is described in 'The Zebra Struck' in *Julia and the Bazooka* as a 'metaphysical horror': 'living in chaos' against 'a background of black isolation' and 'terrifying utter loneliness'.[116]

That Kavan was addicted to heroin is irrefutable; that her writing can be read *solely* as a straightforward *product* of addiction is far less evident. Heroin users are not, contrary to some popular accounts, permanently in the grip of a hallucinatory phantasmagoria. Anaïs Nin's praise for Kavan's *Asylum Piece* erroneously refers to Kavan's use of 'hallucinatory drugs', suggesting that heroin functioned for her as it did for Jean Genet, Lautréamont and Rimbaud.[117] The effects of heroin use on Kavan's writing must, necessarily, remain hypothetical but this has not discouraged critics and reviewers from declaring Kavan's work to be semi, or even wholly, documentary chronicles of addiction. In 1970, Clive Jordan in *The Telegraph* pointed out the 'unmistakable mark' of heroin on Kavan's writing that produced, he claimed, 'a concentration on certain images in the writing [. . .] Buried, crumbling cities, staircases stretching to infinity, gloomy walls relentlessly closing in, breakneck journeys, hideous faces, shapeshifting, jungle creatures and, above all, cold, snow and ice'.[118] Jordan reads Kavan's protagonists as addicts in 'search and flight across a freezing world', which is, he says, 'a brilliant metaphor for addiction. The icy world mirrors the despairing loneliness of addiction and emotional solitude'.[119] It is not clear that there is such a thing as an 'unmistakable' signifier of heroin; however, we might assert that Kavan's writing is not *produced* by drug use but facilitated by narcosis insofar as it allowed her to alter her relationship to her imagination and to experiment with different levels of consciousness. Arguing that Kavan's 'fantasies' had 'their root in drug addiction', Robert Nye believed that her imagination, like that of Coleridge and De Quincey, found 'an emblem and idiom in drugs'. Nye concedes that Rhys Davies's introduction to the posthumously published *Julia and the Bazooka* is correct to examine Kavan's 'art' with 'some straightforward acknowledgement of her drug use' but points out that her drug use cannot solely account for the 'febrile and highly colored brilliance of some of her texts'.[120]

For Elizabeth Young, heroin is everywhere in the psychic topography of Kavan's 'chilly emotional landscape'.[121] It is true that, after 1940, Kavan's work is indisputably infiltrated by an atmosphere of intensity; of either perishing coldness or stifling heat as well as recurring images of towering glacial mountains, emaciated girls, blinding white fogs, a disgust of intimacy and of the flesh, disassociation and detachment. Unrelentingly desolate, the psychic topography of her writing is 'stark, barren, bone-dry, colorless', the atmosphere so glacial that it is impervious to warming by even the most of blazing suns (*Scarcity*, p. 139). Characters in her fiction habitually endure torment, suffering and incarceration and are 'haunted by demons, automata and split personalities'.[122] The imagery that characterizes much of her writing is that of a petrified, pitiless world lacking in any warmth, with an atmosphere of 'monstrous god-like indifference' exemplified in *A Scarcity of Love*:

> She looked up at the now disembodied summits, terrible great ghost-shapes of luminous pallor floating on the dark sky [. . .] Deliberately she identified

herself with their inhumanity and utter loneliness – with the fearful coldness of the non-human world [...] She drew the horror and awe and loneliness of the mountains into herself; willing it to freeze her into some substance so rocklike that it could never melt, never be broken, harder than stone and colder than ice; so that no one should ever again have the power to hurt her, or even come near her. (pp. 49–50)

While one cannot deny the presence of this affective 'petrification' in Kavan's writing, it is highly likely that this emotional frigidity was already there, before the heroin, and before the suicide attempts and the hospitalisation in Switzerland. We might think, then, of the relationship between addiction and writing as a process similar to psychoanalysis; it is possible that the experience of heroin use permitted Kavan richer access to certain pre-existing, affective states that then became the material on which her imagination worked and her writing experimented. Thus, as Gornick says, Kavan's relationship to narcosis may be regarded as one permitting her to capture 'the shape of original damage' in a 'poetic fever'.[123]

While it may provoke a sensitive dreamlike state for a short period, heroin does not, as noted, effect a dramatic transformation on human character; rather, it augments what is already present in the disposition of the user and habitually repressed by habit or necessity. As Thomas De Quincey said, 'If a man whose talk is of oxen should become an opium-eater, the probability is, that (if he is not too dull to dream at all) he will dream about oxen'.[124] In Kavan's writing there is none of Coleridge's 'honey dew' and 'milk of paradise' from 'Kubla Khan' (ll: 53–4), but rather wastelands of 'loveless oblivion' and the 'negation of life' in a 'clean, cold, hard, detached' world'.[125] Heroin allowed Kavan a conduit to some of the psychic material already set in motion by occasional periods of psychoanalysis. Her writing, then, is the expressionistic extension of affective states that are intensified rather than created by narcosis.

By 1910, the 'disease model' of opioids had developed in response to concerns over dependency resulting in the Dangerous Drugs Act of 1920, ushering in what became known as the Rolleston Era. Between 1926 and 1966, what became known as the 'British system' was adopted for the prescription and administration of heroin to registered patients. It worked exceptionally well and lasted until the Brain Committee Reports of 1961 and 1965 and the subsequent establishment of the Clinic System in 1968, whereby doctors in Britain could only legally prescribe heroin or morphine according to two criteria, one of which was to 'Those who are capable of leading a fairly normal and useful life'.[126] Under this system, doctors were permitted to define addiction as an illness and to prescribe both heroin and morphine intravenously to patients in order to manage their addiction.

Although at certain points in her life a daily user, heroin seemed not to be gravely injurious to Anna Kavan's health. For almost forty years, she led a relatively 'normal', if unconventional, life intermittently but intimately attached to her syringe, nicknamed her bazooka, and to her psychiatrist, Dr Karl Theodor Bluth, who not only supplied the drug but also had a commanding influence on Kavan's views on psychoanalysis and psychiatry. Until his death in 1964, Kavan obtained high-grade, clean heroin freely and legally from Bluth. Distraught by his death, she was equally distressed at the thought of being ordered to go to a clinic where her drug use, hitherto a discreetly private affair between herself and Bluth, would be bureaucratically regulated and she would be publicly defined as an 'addict'; her private, cherished habit now made a concern of the state. Making her addiction visible was precisely what Kavan did not do. For her, using heroin was a wholly personal matter, as natural and necessary as eating or sleeping, allowing her to pursue a 'useful and normal life' in the world. As the narrator of 'High in the Mountains' says of the 'evils of drug taking' and her own addiction to the 'clean white powder': 'What I do never affects anyone else. I don't behave in an embarrassing way'.[127] For Kavan, behaving in such a way would be to expose her addiction and, worse, permanently define her as an addict whose work and personality would always be read through the lens of addiction. Although she did, as Walker has noted, periodically attempt to 'kick the habit', undergoing several periods of withdrawal, Kavan settled comfortably into a regular dosage of heroin provided by Bluth.[128]

As Elizabeth Young notes, 'Kavan rarely wrote directly about her addiction, but indirectly she rarely wrote about anything else'.[129] Jane Garrity considers that Kavan's best writing has often been 'pathologized as the autobiographical result of a drug-induced nightmare'.[130] This nightmarish quality is described by Victoria Nelson as 'psychotopographic literature', wherein feelings and sensations are projected onto the external world which becomes an expressionistic screen for the psyche.[131] To be sure, the verifiable phenomenal world is unmoored from its solid foundations and becomes indistinguishable from internal affective processes that in turn produces a *weirdness* in which the protagonists are permanently strangers. As we shall see, *Ice* has much of this alienating, screen-like phantasmagoria; the setting reminiscent of 'a discarded film set', with 'no solidity', 'made of mist and nylon, with nothing behind'.[132]

Julia and the Bazooka is the only piece of Kavan's work that explicitly addresses drug dependency and the distress associated with withdrawal. For Julia, heroin is as 'essential to her as insulin to a diabetic';

it is crucial for psychological equilibrium and with 'its support she is conscientious and energetic' able to live a 'normal existence [. . .] most unlike the popular notion of a drug addict'.[133] Offering physical comfort, heroin also functions as an affective maternal and paternal surrogate, enveloping Julia in the softest of blankets and allowing her to feel at home in the world: she 'hardly remembered how sad and lonely she used to feel before she had the syringe' (p. 153). The doctor who gives Julia her bazooka is depicted as benevolently paternal; he is 'understanding and kind like the father she has imaged but has never known' (p. 153). Julia is in need of heroin's therapeutic effects as her 'personality has been damaged by a complete absence of love in childhood so that she cannot make contact or feel at home in the world'. Recognising the life-saving properties of her 'bazooka', Julia's doctor 'does not want to take the syringe away', telling her 'you've used it for years already and you're none the worse. In fact you'd be far worse off without it' (p. 153).

In 'The Old Address', one of the most apparently confessional stories in this collection, Kavan details the pains of heroin withdrawal and the attendant return of depression, both of which transform the world into a 'hell of hallucination and horror'; a 'nightmare of violence, isolation and cruelty' is created by the perceiving mind of the addicted protagonist who is overcome with feelings of demented disgust (pp. 13, 18). The unnamed girl's attempts at withdrawal are disastrous and very graphically detailed in the title story: 'Each time the horror of returning to consciousness had made it impossible ever to try again. Except that the other horror was so much greater' (pp. 15–16). The only escape from the suffocating depression that produces in her feelings of intense misanthropy, the 'abominable, disgusting world' and claustrophobia is to take a taxi to the 'old address' where she can obtain drugs: 'There's only one way of escape that I've ever discovered' (p. 18). The recognition and acceptance of addiction in this short piece, not expressed so directly anywhere else in Kavan's writing, is amplified in the last story of the collection where the syringe, 'worn away by continuous use' is like an amulet against the world; 'Nothing can frighten her while she has the syringe' (p. 152). Later, the reasons for Julia's addiction are presented as straightforward – she had 'no love in childhood' and 'can't make contact with people or feel at home in the world. Heroin attenuates this damage, comforting her as a loving parent might, and without it 'she could not lead a normal existence, her life would be a shambles' (p. 153).

Heroin was, Aldiss says, Kavan's 'accomplice' and her 'truce with reality'. Crucially, it was a wholly private matter for Kavan; 'neither in appearance nor in behaviour', he continues, 'did she reveal her incurable heroin addiction'.¹³⁴ She did not conform to the idea of the drug-user as a spectacle of fallen humanity whose surrender to compulsion separates him or her from others. For women, drug addiction has been depicted in the cultural imagination as a particularly wretched slide into self-destruction involving vagrancy, disease, sexual recklessness and even prostitution. In a potted, somewhat anecdotal survey of Kavan's life in the preface to the collection of stories, *Julia and the Bazooka*, Virginia Ironside is at pains to stress that, even in the throes of her heroin addiction Kavan 'never let herself go'; she was always 'dressed immaculately, her platinum hair beautifully set'.¹³⁵ To be sure, in all existing photographs of Kavan she is well groomed, sartorially pristine and staring down the camera with confident self-possession; the arresting thinness of her physique, characteristic of many heroin users, only adding to the overall impression of studied elegance. The protagonist of 'Julia and the Bazooka' complains bitterly about the hackneyed representation of drug users: 'it is ridiculous to say all drug addicts are alike, all liars, all vicious, all psychopaths or delinquents just out for kicks' (*Julia*, p. 153). Many users can continue to function (within reason) in everyday life with few external symptoms of addiction. Kavan went to great pains to conceal the visible effects of her addiction. Young notes that all her friends and acquaintances made 'considerable efforts to dispel such feelings of uncase [sic] by stressing how smart and cheerful she was, how little her drug addiction appeared to affect her'. She goes on to suggest, however, that any attempts

> to distance Kavan from her drug habit, although well-meaning, are misleading. She was one of those rare writers who did not publish at all until she was an addict. Heroin was central to her existence, her lover, her religion, her salvation, and almost all her later work charts the processes of addiction [. . .] using again and again images – of cold, of ice, of forbidding landscapes [. . .] in a manner that should be familiar to us from any study of the great De Quincey and other addict writers of the Romantic period.¹³⁶

While the hyperbole of Young's assessment is questionable, the claim that heroin was central to Kavan's life is true insofar as it allowed her to live a mostly industrious existence as long as she had access to a regular supply and was not compelled to endure the agonies of withdrawal. Whether heroin is central to understanding Kavan's writing is quite another question.

By the time of Bluth's death in 1964, there was a significant change in the attitude towards heroin addiction in Britain and it became increasingly difficult for Kavan to obtain clean needles with which to administer her dose. In 1968, she was assigned to a Drug Dependency Unit in

Charing Cross Hospital under the care of Doctor Gisella Oppenheim, described by Kavan as a 'briskly sensible psychiatrist' who had a distinctly less lenient attitude to heroin use than Bluth. Now required by law to make her 'ruins' public, Kavan had to attend the clinic in order to get her supply, complaining bitterly that the 'entire supply and demand business has gone mad regarding drugs'.[137] Although she continued to use heroin regularly, those close to Kavan at this time 'commented on her frequently wilful and erratic behaviour'. Increasingly unhappy, Kavan was still writing but, as she told her publisher, Peter Owen, she was really 'only waiting for death'.[138]

In 'The Rhetoric of Drugs', Derrida contemplates the collective aversion to the idea of the drug addict, regarded as someone who inevitably relies on an 'experience without truth', selfishly indulging in 'the rhetoric of fantasy'.[139] While it is true that Kavan may not have been in touch with city or community life, she was far from exiling herself from reality and lived a productive life in her adult years. As well as writing and painting, Kavan travelled extensively, once noting that she had 'travelled about 25,000 miles, about the circumference of the world' between 1929 and 1967, living briefly in the United States and New Zealand, and with sojourns in Indonesia, South Africa, and Fiji.[140] After Bluth's death, however, she became increasingly reclusive, retreating into smaller daily routines. Constantly worried about her drug supply, she began to stockpile heroin around her flat. When Kavan died in 1968, the police allegedly, and perhaps apocryphally, found enough heroin in her flat to kill the whole street.

Ice: 'something in her demanded victimization'

Described by Doris Lessing as a phantasmagoric 'rollercoaster ride to death',[141] *Ice* is Kavan's best-known work, and has been something of a cult favourite since its publication in 1967. In a letter to Peter Owen, Kavan notes her pleasure at the first reader's report that described the novel, that she considered 'a sort of present day fable', as 'a mixture of Kafka and the Avengers'.[142] More fabular than sci-fi, it was nonetheless awarded the best Science Fiction novel of 1967 by Brain Aldiss, whose introduction to the American edition of *Ice* notes that it possessed 'all the virtues and very few of the vices – the pretension or the obscurity' of a 'high-SF novel'.[143] Despite some negative contemporary reviews, *Ice* found an appreciative reading public who perhaps saw its supra-reality as resonant with the contemporary psychedelic cultures of the late 1960s.

Like Brooke-Rose's *Out*, Alan Burns's *Europe After the Rain*, and J. G. Ballard's *The Crystal World*, *Ice* might be said to bear the traces of its anxious times – the Cuban Missile Crisis of 1962, the French atomic bomb test at Mururoa Atoll in 1966 and the various intrigues of the ongoing Cold War.[144] Depicting a world that has undergone an unidentified catastrophe in which civilisation has disintegrated and the landscape has been laid to waste, the novel recounts the triangulated sado-masochistic pursuit of another of Kavan's brittle 'glass girls' with 'pale, almost transparent skin' who is obsessively, often aggressively, stalked by two men, each transposable in terms of characterisation, across a frigid, devastated landscape: 'Not a building intact. Wreckage heaped in blank spaces where houses had been. Walls had crumbled; steps ascended and stooped in mid-air; arches opened onto deep craters'.[145] These images are also, of course, consistent with the wartime damage that Kavan would have witnessed upon her return to London after the end of the War:

> the empty lanes silent between shapeless shapes of decay, the ruined forts jutting out into the greengage sea, the huge steps of a giant's staircase where the great wall had fallen, subsiding in fallen sections. Everywhere the ubiquitous ruins, decayed fortifications, evidence of a warlike bloodthirsty past. (p. 34)

The pervasive emotional and sexual catastrophe and intense victimisation of the archetypical Kavan 'glass girl' in *Ice* continues many of the themes of earlier work, albeit set against a significantly larger canvas of meteorological disaster in a world on the verge of being engulfed in ice. The ice is literal but can be read as an extended metaphor for the affective calamity that freezes up all warm life forms and is, in many ways, the culmination of what Kristeva describes as a psychic process wherein life is gradually 'slowed down or interrupted [...] absorbed into sorrow',[146] into a 'collective death-wish, driven by the fatal impulse of self-destruction' (p. 123). An uneasy absorption and commingling of exteriority and interiority, familiar from the oneiric expressionism of *Sleep Has His House* and *A Scarcity of Love*, characterises the atmosphere of *Ice*. From the outset, we learn that the strangeness of the 'outer world' is 'an extension' of the narrator's 'own disturbed state of mind' (pp. 60–1), possibly produced by drugs, and that the boundaries between the two states are porous and engender a sense of delusion of 'horrible dreams, in which she always appeared as a helpless victim' (pp. 8–9). The text evacuates any idea of agency and intention in the narrative, replacing them with only doubt and unreality in the accounts of the narrator: '[i]n a peculiar way, the un-reality of the outer world appeared to be an extension of my own disturbed state' (pp. 60–1) – the boundaries between these two states are porous, and produce a strong sense of nightmare. Indeed, the pervasive, at times overwhelming, sense of non-reality is so strong in *Ice* that the text has the impression of incessantly closing in on itself, the claustrophobic tightness of its repetition and circularity almost cancelling out its own narrative at times. These repetitive returns to original scenes of oppression and damage in *Ice* reach back as far as the girl's childhood, evident in specific phrases and formulations, and generate a complicating sense of narrative focus: 'I had a curious feeling that I was living on several planes simultaneously; the overlapping of these planes was confusing' (p. 52).

Ice did not altogether impress the critics, such as one in the *London Magazine* who regarded it as fundamentally second-rate, derivative of the techniques of better-known experimental writers and texts – 'As if Beckett had cut up Henry James, as if Kerouac had written *Ulysses*, as if Kafka had scripted *Marienbad*'. The aesthetic muddle-headedness implicit here is characteristic of the critical reception of some of Kavan's work that was regarded as either imitative or, as Leigh Wilson has insightfully pointed up, in some way *sui generis*, her experimentalism the result of being 'a kind of idiot savant'.[147] Of course, these are two quite divergent receptions which, on the one hand, suggest that Kavan can only impersonate other experimental writers, designated by the same reviewer as 'the determined literariness, of the productions, words nurtured on words, silences bred of libraries'. And on the other, the same reviewer claims that Kavan's work does not participate in or show knowledge of wider literary traditions and that after reading the 'hysterical recoil' manifest in *Ice* one is left only 'with hard objects like pebbles or shells, that are in fact words, to sift through and from which to try to assemble a meaning, a pattern, a diagram, anything' (p. 95).

Narrated by an obsessive, unnamed male, who is as untrustworthy an ominiscient narrator as one can possibly get in that he is given powers to recount events that are beyond his knowledge and geography, *Ice* recounts the compulsively sadistic pursuit of a 'girl', a quarry who is frail, silent and as transparently fragile as 'moonlight venetian glass'; above all she is physically brittle and psychologically blank, a natural victim who invites her own persecution – the 'irreparable damage inflicted had long ago rendered her fate inevitable' (*Ice*, p. 5) and as a result 'something in her demanded victimization' (p. 73). Conditioned by the 'systematic oppression' and 'bullying' of her past, the girl has a perpetual 'victim's look', ready to be pursued, beaten and raped by her pursuers. In this appalling pursuit, which may or may not be 'real', the girl is devoid of all agency; she is a petrified repository of the 'injuries she had received in childhood' (pp. 16–17); her 'fragile body' is 'broken and bruised', and her 'personality' damaged by a sadistic mother who kept her in a permanent state of frightened subjection' (p. 8).

The patterns of sexual pursuit and violation in *Ice* repeat a dynamic in Kavan's work in which a passive girl is at the mercy of a series of oppressors; here, it is a sadistic narrator-voyeur-protagonist and a brutish husband, who morphs into a warden, who fantasise about, and finally enact, sexual violence upon her. At every turn, the narrative emphasises female passivity and victimhood – the girl is so blank she believes she is merging with her oppressor – a common feeling in abusive relationships; 'we were like halves of one being, joined in some mysterious symbiosis' (p. 98). The depiction of rape is highly disconcerting:

> He approached the bed with unhurried steps. She did not move until he bent over her, when she twisted away abruptly, as if trying to escape, buried her face in the pillow. His hand reached out, slid over her shoulder, strong fingers feeling along her jawbone, gripping, tilting, forcing her head up. She resisted violently, in sudden terror, twisting and turning wildly, struggling against his strength. He did nothing at all, let her go on fighting. Her feeble struggles amused him, he knew they would not last long. He looked on in silence, in half-smiling amusement, always tilting her face with slight but inescapable pressure, while she exhausted herself. (pp. 36)

In the moments after the rape, the girl appears dead: she 'gave no indication of life, lying exposed on the ruined bed as on a slab in a mortuary'. Her body is contorted by the force of the attack – 'the neck slightly twisted in a way that suggested violence' (p. 37). Later, the girl's beaten body is described in graphic detail by the abuser who feels no pity when he sees her lifeless body but rather is overcome with a sense of being 'defrauded' because he himself had not inflicted the final wounds upon her with 'tender love':

> A little blood had trickled out of her mouth. Her neck had an unnatural twist; a living girl could not have turned her head at that angle: the neck was broken. She had been dragged by the hair, hands which had twisted it into a sort of rope had dulled its silvery brightness. On her back blood was still fresh in places, wet and bright red; in other places it had caked black on the white flesh. I looked particularly at one arm, on which the circular marks of teeth stood out clearly. The bones of the forearm were broken, the sharp pointed ends of bone projected at the wrist through the torn tissue. (p. 54)

However one reads these descriptions of the violated female body, it is extremely challenging to salvage the sexual violence in *Ice* for any kind of feminist reading and I will not attempt to do so here.[148] Unlike some critics, I cannot wholly concur that the 'threateningly lethal sexual objectification of Woman' is marshalled in *Ice* to illuminate either the 'political violence of the Cold War' or, more broadly, to offer a critique of systemic patriarchal violence.[149] Indeed, I do not agree that one should insist on rescuing the graphic sexual violence in *Ice* for an empowered feminist reading as to do so would be conspicuously out of step with Kavan's *oeuvre*. If one reads *Ice* against *Who Are You?*, the violence in the former does not come altogether as a shock. In the latter, Mr Dog Head is possessed by a fierce, almost insane antagonism, and 'the lust to conquer'[150] the vulnerable girl who during the act of the rape feels like 'she's dying [. . .] being horribly murdered' (*Who*, p. 71).

The pursuit of the girl occurs in an apocalyptic landscape, again unnamed – it 'could have been any town, in any country' (*Ice*, p. 104) – in which an indeterminate ecological catastrophe has occurred that has laid the world to waste resulting in a state of permanent emergency with food shortages and burgeoning black-shirted, jackbooted fascism, and over which a fatal deep freeze is setting:

> Global conditions were worsening. There was no sign of destruction coming to a halt, and its inexorable progress induced general demoralization. It was more impossible than ever to find out what was really happening, impossible to know what to believe. (p. 100)

Menace, paranoia, and repetition define every contour of the novel as the triangle of characters are enmeshed in a sadistic, voyeuristic *danse macabre* devoid of desire or any intention other than domination and possession. The girl feels no separation between herself and her attacker; she is wholly subsumed, reduced to absolute zero:

> In an indescribable way our looks tangled together. I seemed to be looking at my own reflection. Suddenly I was entangled in utmost confusion, not sure which of us was which [. . .] I fought to retain my identity, but all my efforts failed to keep us apart. I continually found I was not myself, but him. [. . .] I fled from the room in utter confusion: afterwards did not know what had happened, or if anything had. (p. 98)

The imperilled state of the girl led a reviewer in *The Observer* to describe *Ice* as 'a series of linked nightmares featuring standard dream situations', but the reviewer conceded that the novel was 'written compulsively enough to take you inside the dream, if not to relate it to the outer world'.[151] Like the blankness itself, time and climatic conditions have ceased to be reliable markers for humanity: 'The past had vanished and become nothing; the future was the inconceivable nothingness of annihilation. All that was left was the ceaselessly shrinking fragment of time called "now"' (p. 153). *Ice* transmutes the affective catastrophe of Kavan's earlier work onto a broader narrative *mise-en-scène* in which no less than global time is devastated.

Notes

1. Anon., 'Peter Owen, Publisher – Obituary', *The Telegraph*, 16 May 2016 <https://www.telegraph.co.uk/obituaries/2016/05/31/peter-owen-publisher--obituary> (accessed 25 November 2019).
2. Peter Owen, 'Introduction', in Anna Kavan, *Asylum Piece and Other Stories* (London: Peter Owen, 2001), p. 3.
3. Ibid., p. 4.
4. From my own unpublished interview with Owen.
5. Francis Booth, *Amongst Those Left: The British Experimental Novel 1940–1980* (e-print: Lulu Press, 2012); Sara Wasson, *Urban Gothic of The Second World War: Dark London* (Basingstoke: Palgrave Macmillan, 2010). See also Geoff Ward, 'The Wibberlee Wobberlee Walk: Lowry, Hamilton, Kavan and the Addictions of 1940s Fiction', in Rod Mengham and N. H. Reeve (eds), *The Fiction of the 1940s: Stories of Survival* (Basingstoke: Palgrave Macmillan, 2001), pp. 26–45. In 2017, a special issue of *Women: A Cultural Review* was devoted to Kavan.
6. Wasson, *Urban Gothic*. Elsewhere, Kavan's work has been regarded as 'slipstream' fiction. Originally coined by science fiction writer Bruce Sterling in the 1980s, the term denotes a loosely defined category of genre fiction and has been applied to a diverse group of writers including J. G. Ballard, Borges, Beckett, Sebald, Paul Auster and Angela Carter. See Gary K. Wolfe, *Evaporating Genres: Essays on Fantastic Literature* (Middletown, CT: Wesleyan University Press, 2011).
7. Jenny Stringer (ed.), *The Oxford Companion of Twentieth-Century Literature in English* (Oxford: Oxford University Press, 1996); Margaret Crosland, *Beyond the Lighthouse: English Women Novelists in the Twentieth Century* (London: Constable, 1981); Harry Blamires, *A Short History of English Literature*, 2nd edn (London: Methuen, 1984). See also doctoral theses: Priscilla Diaz-Dorr, 'Anna Kavan: A Critical Introduction' (1988); Jennifer Sturm, 'Fictionalising the Facts: An Exploration of the "Place" of Aotearoa/ New Zealand in the Post-War Autobiographical Fiction of Anna Kavan' (2006) and Victoria Walker, 'The Fiction of Anna Kavan (1901-1968)' (2012). Jeremy Reed, *A Stranger on Earth: The Life and Work of Anna Kavan* (London: Peter Owen, 2006); David Callard, *The Case of Anna Kavan* (London: Peter Owen, 1993).
8. Vivian Gornick, *The End of the Novel of Love* (London: Virago, 1999 (Boston, MA: Beacon Press, 1997)), pp. 62–3.
9. Robert Nye, 'Anna Kavan', in George Woodcock (ed.), *Twentieth-Century Fiction* (London: Macmillan, 1983), pp. 346–8 (p. 348).
10. Callard, *Anna Kavan*, p. 141.
11. This term was first mentioned in Brian Aldiss in the introduction to *My Madness: The Selected Writings of Anna Kavan* (London: Picador London 1990). It was republished as 'Kafka's Sister', *Journal of the Fantastic in the Arts*, 3: 2.10 (1991), pp. 14–21 (from which this quotation is drawn), and in *The Detached Retina: Aspects of SF and Fantasy* (Liverpool: Liverpool University Press, 1995), pp. 137–44 (p. 143).
12. Aldiss, 'Kafka's Sister', p. 14.

13. Ibid., p. 19.
14. Victoria Walker, 'An Introduction to Anna Kavan: New Readings', *Women: A Cultural Review*, 28: 4 (2017), p. 285.
15. In addition to Walker, recent Kavan scholars include Hanna van Hove, Leigh Wilson and Natalie Ferris. In *Modernism and the Machinery of Madness* (Cambridge: Cambridge University Press, 2017), Andrew Gaedtze compares Kavan to Mina Loy, Beckett and other modernist writers.
16. Anna Kavan, *Ice* (London: Peter Owen, 2006), pp. 7–8. My focus here is on Kavan's 'glass girls' but Leigh Wilson reminded me that there are also persecuted men in *Asylum Piece* and *I am Lazarus*.
17. Ibid., p. 13.
18. Julia Kristeva, *Black Sun: Depression and Melancholia*, trans. Leon S. Roudiez (New York: Columbia University Press, 1989), p. 9.
19. Anna Kavan, *Sleep Has His House* (London: Peter Owen, 1973), p. 82. Hereafter, page references are given in the text in parentheses.
20. Callard, *Anna Kavan*, p. 65.
21. Jane Garrity, 'Nocturnal Transgressions in *The House of Sleep*: Anna Kavan's Maternal Registers', *Modern Fiction Studies*, 40: 2 (1994), pp. 253–77 (pp. 254–5, 258).
22. Ibid., p. 255.
23. Eleonora Rao, '"The Black Sun": Anna Kavan's Narratives of Abjection', *Textus*, 4 (1991), pp. 119–46 (p. 131).
24. Walker, 'The Fiction', p. 9.
25. Jennifer Sturm, 'Introduction', in Anna Kavan, *Guilty* (London: Peter Owen, 2007), p. 9.
26. Cited in Callard, *Anna Kavan*, p. 122.
27. Anna Kavan, *A Scarcity of Love* (London: Peter Owen, 1971), p. 42. Hereafter, page references given in the text in parentheses.
28. Anaïs Nin, *The Novel of the Future* (New York: Macmillan, 1986), p. 171.
29. Kavan, *Sleep*, p. 8.
30. Elizabeth Moore, Letter to Anaïs Nin, in *The Diary of Anaïs Nin: Volume VI, 1955–1966*, ed. Gunther Stuhlmann (New York: Harcourt Brace Jovanovich, 1976), p. 183.
31. Anna Kavan, 'Selected Notices: Back to Victoria', in Anna Kavan, *Machines in the Head: Selected Short Writing*, ed. Victoria Walker (London: Peter Owen, 2019), p. 221.
32. Eva Figes, 'Note', in *Beyond the Words: Eleven Writers in Search of a New Fiction*, ed. Giles Gordon (London: Hutchison, 1975), pp. 113–14 (p. 113).
33. Aldiss, 'Kafka's Sister', p. 138.
34. Walker, 'The Fiction', p. 8.
35. See Emma Garman, 'Feminize Your Canon: Anna Kavan', *the Paris Review*, 10 December 2018 <https://www.theparisreview.org/blog/2018/12/10/feminize-your-canon-anna-kavan> (accessed December 2018). See also Vivian Gornick, 'The Great Depression of Anna Kavan', *Village Voice*, 26: 49 (2–8 December 1981), pp. 49–51; and Clive Jordan, 'Icy Heroin'.

36. Rhys Davies, 'The Bazooka Girl: A Note on Anna Kavan', *London Magazine*, February 1970, pp. 13–15.
37. Rhys Davies, *Honeysuckle Girl* (London: Heinemann, 1975).
38. Janet Wilson, 'A Pacific Sojourn: Anna Kavan and the New Zealand Connection, 1941–2', *Women: A Cultural Review*, 28: 4 (2017), pp. 343–57 (p. 344).
39. Anna Kavan, letter to Ian Hamilton, 20 February 1943, Walter Ian Hamilton Papers, Alexander Turnbull Library, National Library of New Zealand, Wellington. The name change came into official use at the end of 1940.
40. Monique Wittig, 'The Mark of Gender', in Nancy K. Miller (ed.), *The Poetics of Gender* (New York: Columbia University Press, 1986), pp. 63–73 (p. 67).
41. Aldiss, 'Introduction', in Anna Kavan, *My Madness*, p. viii.
42. Jacqueline Rose, 'This is not a Biography', *London Review of Books*, 24: 16 (22 August 2002), pp. 12–15 <https://www.lrb.co.uk/v24/n16/jacqueline-rose/this-is-not-a-biography> (accessed 12 April 2019).
43. Ibid., pp. 12–15. See Carole Sweeney, '"Keeping the ruins private": Anna Kavan and Heroin Addiction', *Women: A Cultural Review*, 28: 4 (2017), pp. 312–26.
44. Garrity, 'Nocturnal Transgressions', p. 253.
45. Davies, 'The Bazooka Girl' p. 13.
46. Reed, *Stranger*, p. 57.
47. This is examined in relation to Kavan's art in Natalie Ferris, 'The Double Play of Mirrors: Anna Kavan, Autobiography and Self-Portraiture', *Women: A Cultural Review*, 28: 4 (2017), pp. 391–409.
48. Gornick, 'The Great Depression', p. 49.
49. Kristeva, *Black Sun*, p. 4.
50. Ibid., p. 27.
51. Valentine Cunningham, *New Statesman*, 28 March 1975, p. 424.
52. See unpublished correspondence between Anna Kavan and George Bullock, 1947–8, Anna Kavan Papers, 1867-1991, McFarlin Library, The University of Tulsa, Series III, Box 1, Folder 6. Also cited in Garrity, 'Nocturnal Transgressions', p. 274.
53. Kavan, *Sleep*, p. 101.
54. See Walker, 'The Fiction'. In *Let Me Alone*, the character Anna Kavan, an introverted and fretful orphan, is made to relinquish her Oxford place and forced to marry a brutish, much older husband by her domineering aunt.
55. Bryan Ferguson had a short life, dying in the war in the Second World War 1944 as a Black Watch Royal Highlanders. He seems rarely to have seen Kavan after her return to England from Burma.
56. Callard, *Anna Kavan*, p. 33.
57. The Anna Kavan archive at the McFarlin Library at the University of Tulsa houses what remains of her artwork.
58. Walker, 'The Fiction', p. 21.
59. Hugh Davies, *The Making of James Agee* (Knoxville: University of Tennessee Press, 2008).
60. See Jennifer Sturm (ed.), *Anna Kavan's New Zealand: A Pacific Interlude*

in a Turbulent Life (Auckland: Vintage, 2009); and Wilson, 'A Pacific Sojourn'.
61. Overseen by Connolly, *Horizon* ran for nine years. The journal counted among its contributors Stephen Spender, Andre Gide, T. S. Eliot, Paul Eluard, Virginia Woolf, Louis Aragon and W. H. Auden, and battled against the 'grand slaughter' of the little magazines'. Michael Shelden, *Friends of Promise: Cyril Connolly and the World of Horizon* (London: Hamish Hamilton, 1989), p. 11.
62. See Walker, 'The Fiction', pp. 113 and 172.
63. Anna Kavan, letter to Ian Hamilton, 23 June 1943, Walter Ian Hamilton Papers, Alexander Turnbull Library, National Library of New Zealand, Wellington.
64. Walker, 'The Fiction, p, 101.
65. Anna Kavan, *I am Lazarus* (London: Jonathan Cape, 1945).
66. Leo Lerman, *The Saturday Review*, 10 August 1946, pp. 9–10.
67. Anna Kavan, *Horizon*, 'Selected Notices', *Horizon*, November 1944, pp. 359–61 (p. 359).
68. Virginia Woolf, *The Diary of Virginia Woolf: Volume 3, 1925-1930*, ed. Anne Olivier Bell and Andrew McNeillie (London: Hogarth Press, 1980), p. 209.
69. Kavan, *Lazarus*, p. 8.
70. Virginia Woolf, 'Mr Bennett and Mrs Brown', in *Collected Essays: Volume I*, ed. Leonard Woolf (London: Hogarth Press, 1966), pp. 319–37 (p. 337).
71. Anna Kavan, 'Review: *A Haunted House, and Other Short Stories*, by Virginia Woolf', *Horizon*, April 1944, pp. 283–5 (p. 284) <http://www.unz.org/Pub/Horizon-1944apr-00283> (accessed 26 January 2015).
72. Callard, *Anna Kavan*, p. 122.
73. Kavan, *Sleep*, p. 101.
74. Kavan, *Asylum Piece*, p. 21.
75. Ibid., p. 129.
76. Kavan, *Scarcity*, p. 22.
77. Joyce Carol Oates, 'Book Review', review of *Asylum Piece* and *Sleep Has His House*, *New York Times*, 1 June 1980, p. 14.
78. Jill Robinson, 'Anna Kavan Transformed Her Pain to Art', *New York Times Book Review*, 11 May 1975, pp. 47–8.
79. Kavan, *Sleep*, p. 173.
80. Kavan, 'The Enemy', in *Asylum Piece*, p. 31.
81. Kate Zambreno, 'Anna Kavan: Context No. 18', Dakleyarchive.com <http://www.dalkeyarchive.com/anna-kavan> (accessed 11 June 2014).
82. See Aldiss, 'Kafka's Sister'.
83. Anaïs Nin, *Novel of the Future*, p. 171.
84. Anna Kavan, letter to Peter Owen, cited in Callard, *Anna Kavan*, p. 138.
85. Kavan, *Asylum Piece*, p. 26.
86. Ibid., p. 24.
87. Kavan, *Scarcity*, p. 106.
88. Kavan, 'The Birthmark', in *Asylum Piece*, p. 11. Subsequent page references will be given in the text in parentheses.

89. André Green, 'The Dead Mother', in *On Private Madness* (London: Hogarth Press, 1986), pp. 142–73 (p. 152).
90. Kristeva, *Black Sun*, p. 4. Subsequent page references given in the text in parentheses.
91. Kavan, *Scarcity*, p. 106.
92. Ibid., p. 28.
93. Ibid., p. 49.
94. Green, 'The Dead Mother', pp. 156–7.
95. Kavan, *Sleep*, p. 7.
96. Kavan, *Scarcity*, p. 85. Subsequent page references will be given in parentheses.
97. Callard, *Anna Kavan*, p. 94.
98. Kristeva, *Black Sun*, p. 22.
99. Garrity, 'Nocturnal Transgressions', p. 258.
100. Kristeva, *Black Sun*, pp. 9, 257.
101. Green, 'The Dead Mother', p. 142.
102. Kristeva, *Black Sun*, p. 11.
103. Green, 'The Dead Mother', p. 195.
104. Ibid., p. 142.
105. Kavan, *Sleep*, pp. 149–51.
106. Julia Jordan examines the figure of the automaton in late modernist writing in 'Autonomous Automata: Opacity and the Fugitive Character in the Modernist Novel and After', in David James (ed.), *The Legacies of Modernism: Historicising Postwar and Contemporary Fiction* (Cambridge: Cambridge University Press, 2011), pp. 96–113. See also Victoria Nelson, *The Secret Life of Puppets* (London: Harvard University Press, 2001).
107. Anna Kavan, 'Fog', in Kavan, *Julia and the Bazooka* (London: Peter Owen, 2009), pp. 28–36 (p. 31).
108. Green, 'The Dead Mother', p. 146.
109. Kavan, *Sleep*, p. 8.
110. Kristeva, *Black Sun*, p. 13.
111. Ibid., p. 258.
112. Kavan, *Ice*, p. 158.
113. A popular morphine product, Omnophon came with its own syringe. See Royal Pharmaceutical Society Museum, 'Drugs for Pleasure, Drugs for Pain? Developing Treatments with Controlled Drugs Part Two: Opium, Morphine, & Heroin', 2011.
114. Lawrence Driscoll, 'Planet Heroin: Women and Drugs', in Lawrence Driscoll, *Reconsidering Drugs: Mapping Victorian and Modern Drug Discourses* (London: Palgrave, 2000), pp. 101–27 (p. 120).
115. Callard, *Anna Kavan*, p. 31.
116. Kavan, 'The Zebra Struck', in *Julia*, pp. 114–35 (p. 116).
117. Nin, *Novel of the Future*, p. 13. Nin's view is mistaken as heroin itself is not hallucinogenic.
118. Clive Jordan, 'Among the Lost Things', *Daily Telegraph*, 25 February 1972, pp. 39–46. See also Clive Jordan, 'Icy Heroin', *New Statesman*, 6 March 1970, pp. 333–4.
119. Jordan, 'Among the Lost Things'.
120. Nye, 'Anna Kavan', pp. 347–8.

121. Elizabeth Young, *Pandora's Handbag: Adventures in the Book World – Selected Prose Past and Present* (London: Serpent's Tail, 2001), p. 187.
122. Walker, 'The Fiction', p. 46.
123. Gornick, 'The Great Depression', p. 49.
124. Thomas De Quincey, 'Confessions of an English Opium-Eater', in De Quincey, *Confessions of an English Opium-Eater and Other Writings* ed. Robert Morrison (Oxford: Oxford World's Classics, 2008), pp. 3–80 (p. 6).
125. Kavan, 'High in the Mountains', in *Julia*, pp. 99–106 (pp. 101, 106).
126. *Rolleston Report*, Ministry of Health, Departmental Committee on Morphine and Heroin Addiction (London: HMSO, 1926), p. 18.
127. Kavan, 'High in the Mountains', in *Julia*, p. 101.
128. Walker, 'The Fiction', p. 58.
129. Young, *Pandora's Handbag*, p. 189.
130. Garrity, 'Nocturnal Transgressions', p. 255.
131. Victoria Nelson, 'Symmes Hole, or the South Polar Romance', *Raritan*, 17: 2 (1997), pp. 136–66 (p. 45).
132. Kavan, *Ice*, pp. 27, 31.
133. Kavan, 'Julia and the Bazooka', in *Julia*, pp. 150–3 (p. 153). Subsequent references are given in the text in parentheses.
134. Aldiss, 'Introduction', in Kavan, *My Madness*, p. xi.
135. Virginia Ironside, 'Preface', in *Julia*, p. 5.
136. Elizabeth Young, *Pandora's Handbag*, p. 185.
137. Callard, *Anna Kavan*, pp. 144, 146.
138. Ibid., p. 128.
139. Jacques Derrida, 'The Rhetoric of Drugs', trans. Michael Israel, in Jacques Derrida, *Points ... Interviews, 1974–1994*, ed. Elisabeth Weber, trans. Peggy Kamuf et al. (Stanford, CA: Stanford University Press, 1995), pp. 228–54 (p. 236).
140. Reed, *Stranger*, p. 72.
141. Introduction to *Ice*, p. 9.
142. Anna Kavan, Letters to Peter Owen, 24 March 1966 and 29 March 1966, Box 1, folder 18, Series I: Correspondence, 1977–2000, Peter Owen Ltd Records, Harry Ransom Humanities Research Center, University of Texas at Austin.
143. Brian Aldiss, 'Introduction', in Anna Kavan, *Ice* (London: Picador, 1973), pp. 14–21 (pp. 7–8).
144. See Walker on *Ice* as a working through of Cold War politics, 'The Fiction of Anna Kavan'.
145. Kavan, *Ice*, p. 31. All subsequent references to *Ice* will be given parenthetically.
146. Kristeva, *Black Sun*, p. 4.
147. Leigh Wilson, 'Anna Kavan's *Ice* and Alan Burns' *Europe After the Rain*: Repetition with a Difference', *Women: A Cultural Review*, 28: 4 (2017), pp. 327–42 (p. 328).
148. See Leigh Wilson's 'Anna Kavan's *Ice*' for a nuanced analysis of the 'problematic' sexual politics of *Ice*.
149. See Leigh Wilson, Victoria Walker, and also Timmel Duchamp's, 'What's the Story: Reading Anna Kavan's *Ice*', *LCRW*, 6 June 2001 <https://

smallbeerpress.com/free-stuff-to-read/2001/06/06/whats-the-story-reading-anna-kavans-ice> (accessed 15 April 2019).
150. Anna Kavan, *Who Are You?* (London: Peter Owen, 2002), pp. 100, 112. Subsequent references are given in the text in parentheses.
151. Irving Wardle, 'Twilight in St Petersburg', *The Observer*, 3 September 1967, p. 23.

Chapter 3

Brigid Brophy: A 'comet in her day'

People are a bit debased about what they expect in fiction. When it isn't there and so much is wittily left out, I think they get confused. (Brigid Brophy, *The Guardian*, 14 June 1989)

Introduction

Lounging across a zebra skin rug on a television studio floor, the TV presenter Jonathan King quizzes a group of Swinging London's most famous actresses, presenters and singers all of whom, according to King, are not only, 'lovely ladies' but also 'career girls'. However patronising they now sound to modern sensibilities, the questions King asks concerning romance and marriage reveal something of a shift, albeit slight, in attitudes towards women's social and cultural roles in 1967. Dianne Rigg, Adrienne Posta, Georgia Brown and Cathy McGowan, all prominent celebrities of the day, are vocal in their response to King's provocative statement and are joined by a quieter, more obviously unconventional, woman who, perched atop a tall stool, slowly smoking a cigarette, looks down at the reclining King with a sardonic mien. Brigid Brophy, for it is she, responds to King's increasingly inane questions on the affront to male chivalry posed by women's liberation, deadpanning, 'I am extremely chivalrous towards men', and goes on to extol the 'sheer sexiness' of the Poet Laureate, Cecil Day-Lewis, with what can only be described as mischievous insouciance.

For a writer to be included in this fashionable crowd of women on a TV programme such as *Good Evening* was testament to Brophy's fame in the 1960s, when she had a reputation not only as a 'daring writer who was impatient with conventions',[1] but also as 'one of the strangest and wittiest British writers of the past half century'.[2] Famous as a panellist, critic, essayist and novelist, Brophy became a familiar figure on TV and radio in the 1960s and 1970s. An unruffled presence on her stool in the TV studio, Brophy emanates an urbane nonchalance tinged with ironic, even camp, humour, a combination discernible in much of her writing. As well as being a novelist and essayist, Brophy wrote literary reviews for several newspapers and penned several influential pamphlets on atheism, animal rights, marriage, and vegetarianism. President of the first incarnation of the National Anti-Vivisection Society, Brophy was renowned for her crusading activism, not only for animal rights for which she changed the ethical landscape in Britain but also for her work with the Writers Action Group and for her role in the passing of the Public Lending Right Act in 1979. Unconventional and remarkably eclectic in genre, subject and style, Brophy's literary *oeuvre* followed no template and despite her commitment to challenging prevailing orthodoxies on marriage, monogamy and heterosexuality, all of which she saw as far more oppressive for women than men, she distanced herself from feminism.

Describing herself as a 'serenely married vegetarian sex-pacifist',[3] Brophy was, according to *People* magazine, 'the best prose writer of her generation' and in S. J. Newman's view was 'One of the oddest, most brilliant and most enduring of [...] 1960s symptoms'.[4] Certainly, her work remains both brilliant and odd, but not, as it has transpired, enduring as, despite the zest that it brought to the British literary scene in the 1950s and 1960s, Brophy's writing has struggled to find lasting critical attention. In her preface to *The Burglar*, which serves as both exegesis and apologia for her oeuvre and reputation, Brophy comments on the difficulty that her novels posed to a contemporary readership:

> Despite their invariably baroque designs, my novels are grossly dissimilar to one another in style and subject – which is a gross handicap on the commercial market, where readers who equate novels with quarter-pound boxes of chocolates prefer the author's brand name to assure them the packet won't contain any substance that [they] haven't digested before.[5]

In what seems seem like a paradigmatic 'Brophyian' incident, in a letter from an American editor at *The Atlantic Monthly Press* to Brophy's British publishers Macmillan, the sender notes the difficulty of publishing her book on Freud, *Black Ship to Hell*, with its 'Bropyhian argumentation at its most incisive'. Brophy returned by the manuscript to the editors unrepentantly unchanged in 'tone and temper'.[6] Her daughter, Kate Levey, explains this Brophyianism:

> she didn't have a recipe [...] She sashayed her way between fiction and non-fiction, polemics and practical campaigning, wrong footing many a critic and reader. She did not compromise [...] She would not spoon-feed her audience.

And yes, her vertiginous standards, her purist ideals, led some to experience her as a pain in the neck.[7]

After her death from multiple sclerosis in 1995, Brophy's literary agent, Giles Gordon, wrote a poignant obituary detailing the richness of her literary, cultural and political interests over three decades. She was an

> Atheist, vegetarian, socialist; novelist and short-story writer; humanist; biographer; playwright [. . .]; Freudian promoter of animal rights; children's author [. . .]; tennis fanatic [. . .] and, on television, football fancier; most loyal of friends; reverer of Jane Austen; lover of Italy; Mozart adorer [. . .]; disliker of 'Shakespeare in performance'; smoker of cigarettes in a chic holder and painter of her fingernails purple; mother, grandmother, wife; feminist; lover of men and women.[8]

But 'above all', Gordon concluded, Brophy was 'an intellectual'. At a time when to be even just clever was not much of a compliment for a woman, Brophy was regarded by Brooke-Rose as the 'brainiest woman in Britain',[9] and by Shena Mackay as 'the best brain of her generation'.[10] Indeed, contemporary reviewers of her work insisted on pointing up its 'braininess' and its tendency, as they saw it, to highbrow showing off, thus acquiring her, in her own words, a 'mantle of pugnacity.' This cleverness was regarded by many of her peers as the work of a show-off controversialist who was needlessly provocative, rendering her as 'monstrously pugnacious' in the public imagination.[11] As Irma Kurtz said:

> Many people find her essays opinionated [. . .] When we criticise her, however, not as an artist or as a thinker but as spokeswoman for her sex, the so-called gentle one, we are on less safe ground because she has refused to wave that standard – tea towel rampant on linoleum – which we try to force into her hands.[12]

Brophy thought her name so thoroughly attached to her purported intellectual belligerence that her work never received a fair hearing because of her 'notoriety'. While her 'notorious' reputation has not endured, 'any informed reckoning of twentieth-century literature' that excludes Brophy's writing is, says Steven Moore, 'scandalous'.[13]

Often found nestled alphabetically next to Christine Brooke-Rose in literary encyclopedias and anthologies, such as *The Field Day Anthology of Irish Women's Writing and Traditions* (2002), editors have found it difficult to position her work – is she an Irish writer? A feminist or lesbian writer? Or is she a political activist, biographer or journalist? Interest in Brophy's work, chiefly in *In Transit: An Heroi-Cyclic Novel* (1969), peaked in the 1990s when Mikhail Bakhtin's newly translated

The Dialogic Imagination (1981) exerted considerable influence in literary studies. His concepts of dialogism, polyglossia and heteroglossia appeared to describe perfectly what was regarded as the chief tenets of postmodernist fiction and conveniently corresponded to certain prevalent ideas in feminist theory regarding women's writing and the ways in which it resists the hierarchies of patriarchal discourse with its insistence on logic and rationalism. *In Transit*'s ostensibly postmodernist, or at least poststructuralist, concerns with the slipperiness of signification within language systems made it the focus of scholarly interest in the 1980s; its prescient sexual and gender politics have interested those critics interested in such things. In *The Ethical Component in Experimental British Fiction Since the 1960s* (2007), *In Transit* is considered as an early ethical engagement with gender fluidity.[14] Elsewhere, Jean-Michel Ganteau reads the novel as an example of Sartrean commitment.[15]

To date, there has been only one doctoral thesis (as yet unpublished) focusing wholly on her work, 'Brigid Brophy: Author in the Baroque' (1977). Ten years later, another doctoral thesis, 'The Never-Last Word: Parody, Ideology, and the Open Work' considers Brophy's work, if only rather peripherally, as a point of comparison with Djuna Barnes.[16] More recently, as part of a recent revival of interest in mid-century British literature, a special issue of the journal *Contemporary Women's Writing* was devoted to Brophy, covering her contributions to the Public Lending Right (PLR), animal rights and queer studies. However, as the preface to this issue notes, Brophy remains a neglected writer perhaps due to the fact that it is not easy to categorise her work as either feminist, or theoretical or, indeed, as always perceptibly experimental when compared to her contemporaries, Brooke-Rose, Alan Burns and Ann Quin.

In his introduction to the re-issue of Brooke-Rose's *The Dear Deceit* (2014), Joseph Darlington inaccurately identifies Brophy as a '1950s middlebrow novelist', much like, he claims, Amis and Drabble, who wrote 'Hampstead novels' of middle-class manners.[17] When Brophy attended to the mores of the middle class in *Flesh*, she did so in her own eccentric way, that had nothing in common with the cultivated moralism of the middlebrow novel (indeed, one might add here that Drabble and Amis cannot be wholly written off in such a way). While the settings she chose may have been identifiably middle class, as opposed to the so-called kitchen-sink realism, Brophy brought to her novels a skew-whiff sense of realism modulated by a baroque, often rococo, style often bordering on high-camp.[18] In Susan Sontag's 'Notes on "Camp"' list of what might constitute camp, she includes Aubrey Beardsley's drawings, the novels of Ronald Firbank and Ivy Compton-Burnett and Bellini's operas.[19] Substitute Mozart for Bellini but leave in

Compton-Burnett and one has a workable understanding of Brophy's stylistic and social preoccupations. Along with the work of George Bernard Shaw, she held Firbank's under-recognised short novels in the highest esteem and praised their innovative prose in *Prancing Novelist: A Defence of Fiction in the Form of a Critical Biography in Praise of Ronald Firbank* (1973).[20]

More persuasive than the designation of Brophy as a Hampstead scribbler, is an examination of her work in a 2013 doctoral thesis entitled 'The Avant Postman: James Joyce, the Avant Garde and Postmodernism'. Like Karen Lawrence in *Penelope Voyages: Women and Travel in the British Literary Tradition* (1994), David Vichnar places Brophy in the company of those who have been influenced by Joyce, including B. S. Johnson, Alan Burns, Ann Quin and Christine Brooke-Rose – a group of writers he describes as 'the post-war literary avant-gardes in Great Britain, the USA, and France'.[21] Similarly, Lawrence devotes a chapter to *In Transit* in *Penelope Voyages* (1994), in which she compares Brophy's novel with the 'scandalous' writerly text of Brooke-Rose's *Between*.[22]

An issue of the *Revue of Contemporary Fiction* in 1995 devoted ten pieces to Brophy's work (alongside that of Robert Creeley and Osman Lins) including biographical accounts, short critical essays, and a piece detailing a translator's struggle to render the shifting gender pronouns of *In Transit* into French. In 2020, a collection, *Brigid Brophy: Avant-Garde Writer, Critic, Activist* was dedicated to Brophy's work not only as a writer and critic but also as an important figure in the Animal Rights Movement in Britain. This restoration of her reputation began, to a certain extent, in Avril Horner and Anne Rowe's collection, *Living on Paper: Letters from Iris Murdoch 1934–1995* (2015), in which the importance of Brophy's presence in Murdoch's life as an intimate confidante and intellectual sparring partner is clearly established.[23] Described as a 'polymath' in the style of Raymond Queneau, to whom Murdoch was also attached in intimate epistolary ways, Brophy fell deeply in love with Murdoch and the two women began an often 'stormy but exhilarating liaison' in 1955.[24] Despite her affection for Murdoch, Brophy did not moderate her exacting standards when it came to an assessment of Murdoch's writing. In a letter dated 19 November 1960, Murdoch acknowledges Brophy's 'odd attitude' to her work; 'I confess that I am surprised that you altogether dislike my work'.[25] The two continued to correspond until Brophy's death from MS. Ever the writer, her illness became the subject of her last book, *Baroque 'n' Roll and Other Essays* (1987), written with her characteristic puckish wit.[26] An obituary in the *New York Times* described Brophy as a 'sharp thinker and fierce intellectual who liked a good fight', something reflected in her nonfiction works which 'tended to have provocative, often mischievous points of view'.[27]

Aware that she had been publicly saddled with the 'mantle of pugnacity', Brophy was always chary of unthinkingly adopting new trends in literary 'theory' that claimed to offer radical new readings of writers whose work she knew intimately. One of the more prominent examples of her alleged critical ferocity was her review of Colin MacCabe's *James Joyce and The Revolution of The Word* (1978) in the *London Review of Books*. In his reading of *Ulysses*, MacCabe takes on the defects of the classic realist novel that 'refuses to acknowledge its status as writing'. The realist novel is, he says, essentially duplicitous as it pretends to be 'unwritten', the dim-witted author simplistically using language as a 'window on reality.[28] In her review, Brophy spares MacCabe none of her trademark erudition. Alighting on his central concept of 'an active metamorphosis' one experiences when reading Joyce as opposed to the passivity of unthinkingly gulping down the 'classic realist text', she notes that he uses only George Eliot as a counterpoint to Joyce – a rather inequitable contrast to say the least.

> Certainly, the 'us' for whom reading everyone except Joyce is 'passive consumption' can't include readers of Firbank, who have to perform ecstatic mental leapfrog in order to divine which dialogue issues from which speaker [. . .] Neither can the passive 'us' include anyone who has read Chapter 11 of Volume Two of *Tristram Shandy*: 'The truest respect which you can pay to the reader's understanding, is to halve this matter amicably, and leave him something to imagine, in his turn, as well as yourself'.[29]

Brophy's response might seem somewhat fractious in its demolition of MacCabe's study but it shows her to be a surpassingly well-informed critic with a rare wit and resolute sense of intellectual and aesthetic non-conformism. Her dislike of MacCabe's apparent aversion to realism is illuminating in light of her own writing experiments: 'Fictional narratives are not "transparent" but tinted windows, looking not onto reality but onto invented things (which have a variable relationship to reality)'. She concludes that it is on the 'reader's liking for one nuance of tint rather than another that the writer relies to make the reader choose to read the next novel by the same writer.'[30]

One of the last devotees of the Shavian 'shew' and fond of wordplay of all sorts, Brophy possessed a grammatical virtuosity bordering on pedantry and was not shy of displaying her extensive cultural knowledge, from Mozart to Wimbledon, in her work. As a result, some reviewers and critics characterised her work as overly clever, too tenaciously stylised, and mulishly opinionated; Ian Hamilton purportedly going so far as to tag her with the shamefully misogynist sobriquet of 'Britain's foremost literary shrew'.[31] Even the comments on the dust jacket of one of her own books disapprove of her intelligence: 'Miss Brophy [...] is so clever and so assured that she has no trouble holding the reader's attention' (*New Yorker*). It appears, then, as if Brophy's cleverness was something of a hindrance to her literary success, as Enright points up: 'Brigid Brophy is probably too versatile for her own good, as good goes, and possibly a little too clever, and certainly too much of a writer'.[32] Elsewhere, her work was described as a 'vegetarian *jeux d'esprit*', a description that manages to be somehow simultaneously apposite and impertinent.[33] Some regarded Brophy's wilfully 'cultured' prose as a kind of affectation. Mary (later Lady) Warnock notes her tendency to intellectual insubordination: 'The arguments are often clever. But the air of the schoolboy boldly undermining what he takes to be the schoolmaster's presuppositions detracts from our admiration of their ingenuity'.[34] With some of her novels back in print and with some renewed critical attention, Brophy's work has found a new generation of readers.[35]

'England's lady pundit'

Brophy Antonia Susan Brophy was the only child of John Brophy (1899–1965), a relatively well-known writer in his day, and Charis Weare (1895–1975), a school teacher who had also published a novel written in her twenties. Born in Ealing in 1929, but brought up in Ireland until the age of three with her paternal Irish grandparents, Brophy had a lifelong identification with her sense of Irishness, something evident in *In Transit* with its copious, self-conscious 'Irishisms' and Joycean delight in the pun: 'We speak English as a foreign language, even when we have no other. [...] We Irish had the right word on the tip of our tongue, but the imperialist got at that'.[36] In a piece called 'Am I an Irishwoman?', Brophy describes a sense of outsiderness that was present all of her life: 'I felt a foreigner there [in Ireland]; but I felt a foreigner in England, too. I was brought up to do so'.[37] Perhaps due to this lifelong sense of Irishness, Brophy regarded herself as something of a cultural interloper, once describing herself as an 'urchin graffitist' among the old-boys' networks of the London literati and intelligentsia.[38]

Growing up in a bookish household in which reading and writing were held in the highest esteem, Brophy was an avid reader of long-form prose from the age of five, purportedly reading *Finnegans Wake* at nine. A prodigiously intelligent child, she moved school several times because of the effects of the War before going up to St Hugh's College, Oxford in 1947 on a scholarship to study Classics. However, in her second year, she was sent down for 'unspecified offences,' the precise nature of which remains the object of some speculation but to Brophy remained a source of considerable chagrin for many years:

> I liked Oxford, but it didn't like me [...] Until recently I didn't like to talk about it, but I think it was my sex life. They didn't like my sex life. Nor did they like me arriving drunk in chapel since it was a condition of my scholarship that I had to read in chapel.[39]

This incident not only deprived Brophy of a higher education but would cause her great pain for many years.

Returning to London, Brophy took a series of menial secretarial jobs as was customary for educated young women at the time, one of which was working for a pornographic bookseller, possibly 'somewhere off Tottenham Court Road', like the heroine Susan in *The King of a Rainy Country*.[40] In 1954 she married art historian Michael Levey, author of *The Case of Walter Pater* and several other art history studies, who later would become the director of the National Gallery from 1973 to 1987, and with whom she had a companionable and loving partnership that produced one daughter, Kate, born in 1957, to whom they were devoted, if unorthodox parents. Their marriage was strong and loving but by contemporary standards somewhat unconventional, as testified by Brophy's outspoken views on bisexuality, monogamy and institutional heterosexuality, both *causes célèbres* for the censorious British press. Kate Levey notes that

> For this pair of young freethinkers, wedlock implied none of the traditional bonds or bounds. Where their respective parents had been notably happy in conformist marriages, Michael and Brigid's union was styled on freedom; their conjugal felicity was cemented by their own vision of imaginative and untrammeled love.[41]

Their non-conformist sexual behaviour seemed amenable to both parties in the marriage. She says that when Brophy wrote to Michael Levey stating she was 'at least 50% homosexual', far from being daunted, it 'must have been music to his not entirely heterosexual ears'.[42] What is clear from Kate's account of her parents' marriage is the amount of hard work that Brophy took on to continue being an attentive and dutiful parent, often on her own while Michel was working overseas. While she had been working in temporary jobs, Brophy began to write seriously and published her first fiction in 1953, *The Crown Princess and Other Stories* and *Hackenfeller's Ape*.[43] These were followed by *The King of a Rainy Country* in 1956 before she took what she called a 'sort of emotional gap' in her career until 1962: 'in that intermittent gap I had the child, and this proved to be sufficient occupation for the time being'.⁴⁴

In the 1950s, women's writing in Britain tended to be categorised on one side or the other of a quite clear demarcation between high and middlebrow (that is, more commercially popular) literature. On the one hand, there were the 'serious' women writers such as Elizabeth Bowen, Iris Murdoch, Doris Lessing and Muriel Spark and on the other side of this somewhat inexact divide, Agatha Christie, Barbara Pym, Nancy Mitford, Elizabeth Taylor and Vera Brittain. Save for Spark, whose first novel, *The Comforters,* marked her definitive leave-taking from realism, aesthetic experiment in women's fiction at this time was rare. Middlebrow women's writing exhibited, says Nicola Humble, 'a fascination with domestic space, a concern with courtship and marriage' and the 'minutiae of romantic or familial human relationships'.⁴⁵

For Brophy, the 1960s brought *The Snow Ball* (1964); *Flesh* (1962); *The Finishing Touch* (1963); *Palace without Chairs* (1978); *In Transit* (1969); *The Adventure of God in his Search for the Black Girl and Other Stories* (1973); *The Prince and the Wild Geese* (1983) a children's story, *Pussy Owl* (1976) and a rather unsuccessfully received play, *The Burglar* (1968).⁴⁶ She wrote a substantial number of biographies and full-length critical studies: *Mozart the Dramatist (*1964); two biographical works on Aubrey Beardsley, *Black and White: A Portrait of Aubrey Beardsley* (1968) and *Beardsley and His World* (1976) and one on Ronald Firbank *Prancing Novelist: In Praise of Ronald Firbank*, (1973), a much-neglected writer whose influence on Brophy's own fiction is sometimes discernible, most conspicuously in *The Finishing Touch*.⁴⁷

While neither of her first two works could be considered wholly experimental, *Hackenfeller's Ape* (which won the first novel prize at the Cheltenham Literary Festival) is a curiously eccentric narrative. A satire on animal exploitation, it opens with the drolly named Professor Clement Darrelhyde singing an aria in a 'womanish' falsetto from *The Marriage of Figaro*. Leslie Dock identifies the 'merging, reversing, or reworking of sexual stereotypes' that happen so frequently in Brophy's writing; in *Palace without Chairs*, Fordie, is 'womanish', he wears a shawl and is termed 'dear mother'; the professor in *Hackenfeller's Ape* sings the Countess's song; the narrator of *In Transit* is profoundly confused about their sexual identity and the choral pitches are such that 'males sing soprano, women bass'.⁴⁸ Overturning the species hierarchy between man and ape, *Hackenfeller's Ape* is a fable in which the moral and philosophical questions concerning zookeeping and animal experimentation are scrutinised. As Robert McKay has noted: 'Brophy's fictional simians, Percy and Edwina, are primarily imaginative tropes that serve a philosophical purpose [. . .] for thinking through unresolved questions about human existence'.[49]

Like Brooke-Rose, Brophy was both a writer and a citric and wrote several scholarly, if rather quixotic, literary studies, including one on Freudian psychoanalysis, *Black Ship to Hell* (1962). Her often drolly acerbic literary journalism is collected in the volume *Don't Never Forget: Collected Views and Reviews* (1966) and her non-fiction works include *Religious Education in State Schools* (1967) *The Rights of Animals* (1969); *The Longford Threat to Freedom* (1972) *A Guide to Public Lending Right* (1983) and *Reads: A Collection of Essays* (1989). Ever the controversialist, in 1967 she co-wrote a book with her husband Michael Levey and Charles Osborne called *Fifty Works of English and American Literature That We Could Do Without*, in which she shredded the hallowed literary reputations of, amongst others, *Little Women*, *Wuthering Heights*, *To the Lighthouse* and *Hamlet*. A seditious anti-survey of the English and American canon, *Fifty Works*, deplores Dickens: '*Pickwick Papers* appears to have been written in a series of jerkily spasmodic bouts of inane euphoria'; Mark Twain's writing 'is a vision which can be achieved only by that ruthless dishonesty which is the birthright of every sentimentalist.' A particular joy is Brophy's assessment of Trollope's revived popularity in the postwar years, viewing him as a kind of toothless version of Jane Austen, a writer she revered:

> Trollope is that nice, maundering spinster lady with a poke bonnet and a taste for cottagey gardens whom superficial readers thought they had got hold of when they had in fact got hold of the morally sabre-toothed Jane Austen [. . .] it was not until the 1939–45 war that he became a popular (indeed, a paperback) novelist. Perhaps it was then that the English middle classes discovered that Jane Austen was not what they had supposed and took to Trollope in her place.[50]

On the relationship between her creative writing and her criticism, Brophy once remarked:

> I think that one might guess the masochism in my personality from the fact that I practice criticism as well as creative writing, which would suggest that the critical faculty was very sharpened and was always ready to turn on the creator.[51]

In 1964, the BBC commissioned Brophy to write a radio play, 'The Waste Disposal Unit' (1964) as well as a talk on the sexual hypocrisy surrounding the Profumo Affair, 'The Nation in the Iron Mask' (1963).[52]

Her reputation as a commentator was not surprising for, as Terry Castle notes, Brophy was 'a comet in her day'; as 'stylish and, meteoric and morally à propos as her contemporaries Muriel Spark or Iris Murdoch and in many ways far less fettered than either.' Her 'coruscating essays on fiction', continues Castle, 'visual art, opera, sexuality and camp, pacifism, vegetarianism, the lives of animals [...] were so far ahead of their time, that we are only now beginning to catch up with her'.[53]

The diversity of Brophy's writing, however, posed some difficulties of categorisation and reception. Remarkably varied in both subject and success, her novels were difficult to market as they often had the veneer of realism and of 'women's fiction' and perhaps might have been picked up in a bookshop by readers who enjoyed the work of Barbara Pym or Rosamund Lehmann, even perhaps Doris Lessing. But the intellectual *jeu d'esprit* of her writing did not fit the category of 'domestic romance'.[54] I consider four of Brophy's works here. Firstly, *The King of a Rainy Country*, a condensed narrative of postwar bohemian disaffection and the erotic potential of European travel that exhibits what today might be called a queer sensibility or self-consciousness. With its Bill Brandt cover depicting an indolent androgynous face, *Flesh* is a fablesque tale of Marcus and Nancy, a young, rather non-descript Jewish couple living in not-yet-swinging North London. A year later, she published a 'tart's rococo' of a novel, *The Snow Ball*, that playfully rehearses 'Mozart, sex, and death'.[55] Brophy ended the 1960s with her most renowned work, *In Transit: An Heroi-Cyclic Novel*, a picaresque caper charting the misfortunes of Pat/Patricia O'Rooley who loses her/his sense of gender identity whilst temporarily stranded in an airport.

In 1973, came *The Adventures of God in His Search for the Black Girl: A Novel and Some Fables*, followed by an illustrated children's book *Pussy Owl: Superbeast* in 1976 that was featured on the popular Jackanory TV series and broadcast on the BBC on 22 March 1976. Her last novel, *Palace without Chairs: A Baroque Novel*, appeared in 1978. She also wrote a play: a Shavian comedy of manners, *The Burglar*, was first performed in Brighton then transferred to the Vaudeville Theatre in London on 22 February 1967, where it closed after only ten days. Featuring yet another kind of metamorphosis, or at least a gender transposition with a distinct hint of Alistair Sims's turn as headmistress Millicent Fritton in *St Trinian's*, *The Finishing Touch* (1963, revised in 1987), a 'Firbankian acid-drop' of a novel, (re)imagines art critic-cum-spy, Anthony Blunt, as a lesbian headmistress at a girls' finishing school on the French Riviera.[56]

The Brophyian Experiment

Unlike Quin, Brooke-Rose and Figes, Brophy's experimentalism lies not so much in moving away from the use of third-person omniscient narrator and a largely teleological, if usually pre-digested plot but more in the recasting of these into what she calls her 'baroque method'; a feature common to all her novels and the only aesthetic form for which, she said, her psychology was 'equipped to practise'.[57] This method involves a 'contraposition' and 'inter-penetration' in which the writing delivers, by way of 'contrasting masses' and a 'manipulation of levels' a 'sharply unexpected view – ironic, tragic, or comic':

> It is an architectural method, a manipulation of levels to provided bizarre perspectives [. . .] The form is necessarily highly condensed, because every feature is performing two or three functions; it is technically economical and emotionally intense, inasmuch as surprise is created less by introducing fresh features than by the obliquity and unexpectedness of the views suddenly afforded of those already there.[58]

Brophy's experiments with fiction often consist of introducing unusually positioned slants into pre-existing forms and rearranging familiar parts into a new whole: 'The whole purpose of fiction', she noted, 'is that the writer (and thereby the reader) is transported into some form of life which is absolutely different from his own: and to be transported'.[59] For Brophy, this transportation is produced not through the accumulation of realistic detail and dialogue but by a technique of narrative layering in the 'baroque contraposition' of her novels.[60] Her writing style, she said, serves not merely as 'decoration or as means of communication' but also allows her to pass off some frankness about sexual matters, in particular regarding women's sexual desire.[61] Talking openly of a young woman having four lovers, as Nancy does in *Flesh*, before marriage, was, if not exactly shocking, then certainly rather racy in 1962. This frankness is couched in politely readable forms that seem to conceal, at least on first glance, their lack of moral judgement towards matters sexual which allows many demarcations between gender roles to quietly melt away. The effect of Brophy's prose, at once sharp but rather impersonal, is of an ongoing authorial detachment that distinguishes it from more conventional uses of realism that offer the reader a moral interpretation on the action and the characters. As one critic notes, *Flesh* 'seems to be a novel that pushes realist devices in unusual directions', mixing 'total knowledge of characters with great detachment and neutrality'.[62] Characters in Brophy's fiction appear as if they have been rather self-consciously staged in set pieces and exist on identical narrative equivalence in terms of narrative point of view. Chris Hopkins suggests that in her novels while authorial omniscience is by no means eschewed, it is strictly neutrally applied, leaving the reader with the peculiar feeling that they have encountered 'real' characters and yet not sure at all as to their significance or consequence.[63] With the exception of *In Transit*, which is a different kind of experiment, Brophy's prose often seems to be conforming to realism but in fact, just as she says of her beloved Aubrey Beardsley, the design possesses a 'style that murmurs of perversity', in which 'forms are ambiguous in matter' and always in the 'act of changing from one substance into another.[64]

In May 1969 Brophy and her lifelong friend, Maureen Duffy (herself a noted writer) put together a daringly 'perverse' exhibition, *Heads and Boxes: Items of Prop Art*, at the Mason's Yard Gallery, London. Consisting of 'twenty-five conceptual "heads" crafted from polystyrene wigstands'. The 'heads' were then 'made by attaching or appending various texts and other items, and twenty-nine "boxes," which were small dioramas or three-dimensional collages constructed inside the clear plastic boxes that held the wigstands. As the artists' manifesto puts it, the works are "readymages"'[65]: the visual equivalents 'of poems, lyrics [...] satires, squibs, *marseillaises* or metaphysical extravaganzas'.[66]

Although never part of any literary coterie, Brophy found herself, along with Brooke-Rose, Figes and Quin, included in B. S. Jonson's list of writers that he thought wrote as though it mattered. Brophy always pooh-poohed the term avant-garde, viewing it as symptomatic of a wrongheaded approach to art that seeks to identify and categorise regular and successive waves of change and innovation, with one movement and tendency neatly following its predecessor, all meticulously gathered into one orderly taxonomy organised around the 'before' and the 'after'. In such a schematic, the artists that come 'after' must find a new language, or mode in which to write, a mode that is not only new but one compelled to rail against its immediate antecedents – to wit, Woolf's essay 'Mr. Bennett and Mrs. Brown' (1924). But for Brophy, the novelist need not be always intent upon looking forward for innovation. Looking back, reusing past languages and cadences could be just as innovative: 'To submit yourself to an idiom unfamiliar through disuse is as pioneering an act as to submit yourself to one unfamiliar because it has never been used before'.[67] For Brophy, the aim was aesthetic pleasure; the content imbricated in the form, her approach echoes a kind of Wildean/Firbankian artistic wit that might tell stories with little sense of moral manipulation. In *Prancing Novelist*, Brophy praises Firbank's achievement as a writer who works according to 'the logic of the design rather than the logic of narrative and characterisation', an interesting observation given her criticism of Woolf's vagueness concerning characterisation.[68] For her, Firbank exemplified the ways in which art does not 'progress in the sense that science progresses', along a steady trajectory of new discoveries and developments.[69]

Perhaps somewhat surprisingly, Brophy did not admire Woolf's work. In an excoriating review of *Virginia Woolf* by Dorothy Brewster in *Don't Never Forget*, she notes that as much as she admires Woolf the woman who was indubitably a 'clever and thoughtful literary person', she maintains that her 'experimental fabric was spun to conceal a hole – the absence of characters and incidents, those sheer gifts which are as indispensable to true novelists as tunes to true composers'.[70] She argues that 'great novels are devastatingly particular', whereas 'Virginia Woolf's novels are too devastatingly vague. I lost patience when I discovered (from the luncheon in *Between The Acts*) [. . .] that she thought you need[ed] a corkscrew to open a bottle of champagne'.[71]

The King of a Rainy Country: 'Well, bugger me backwards!' 'Not in those trousers'

Originally published in 1956, *The King of a Rainy Country* was republished in 2012. On the back cover of this reissue, Ali Smith describes the novel's examination of romanticism and disaffection as a 'pitch-perfect novel' that is 'witty, unexpectedly moving and a revelation again of Brophy's originality'. It is, she goes on, 'Entirely of its time, it remains years ahead of itself even now, nearly 60 years later, in its emotional range and its intellectual and formal blend of stoicism and sophistication'.[72] Many of Brophy's novels are concerned with the eccentricities and complications of romantic and sexual relationships and the possibilities of same-sex love which one might have assumed to be uncontroversial in the 'swinging' 1960s. But in fact, this was not at all the case. Brophy's views, in fiction as well as in journalism, on love, marriage and sex displeased many of her readers, earning her the reputation of Britain's leading *provocatrice*. In 1965, she wrote an article called 'The Immorality of Marriage' for *The Sunday Times* in which she systematically picked apart the essentialist logic of 'the natural' division of roles between the sexes that imprisoned women as mothers and housewives: 'Only on the subject of the relation between the sexes do reactionaries start citing "nature" as an ideal'.[73] Men and women, Brophy argued, need no longer adhere to such a primitive logic as the 'one thing which is consistently natural for humans by intelligence and imagination is to improve upon nature'.⁷⁴ She argues that it is indefensible to treat 'half the human population [...] as sub-persons' and insists that women must take advantage of even the smallest glimpses of liberation on offer.⁷⁵ This liberation includes, although she does not say so here, taking pleasure from same-sex desire. *The King of a Rainy Country* playfully and queerly reworks the operatic form, self-consciously using its *clichés* but also exploring their potential for sexual transgression in the cross-dressing *hosenrolle* or *travesti*. Structured as a three-act opera, loosely based on Mozart's *The Marriage of Figaro* with some *As You Like It* thrown in for good measure, the novel tells the story of a young graduate, Susan, who drifts into a job after university temping for a pornographic bookseller, Mr Finkelheim, 'somewhere off Tottenham Court Road'.⁷⁶ She has a relationship with Neale, a diffident young man of 'manageable height' with whom she falls in companionable love at a coffee party (p. 7). While they are exceedingly close temperamentally they do not have sexual relations: 'We were pleased at being coupled as *you two*, but also afraid lest, in the unspokenness of the understanding, neither of us really understood' (p. 9). Language acts as a screen for their feelings:

> Our relationship was verbal: allusive and entangled. Deviating further and further into obliquity we often lost track. 'I don't think I think I know what you mean'. 'We'd better say it openly'. 'Much better. But I'm not going to be the first to say it'. 'Neither am I.' (p. 9)

This tacit agreement sets up a circumlocution around same-sex desire, or, more precisely, non-straight desire that is open to finding its pleasures outside of heterosexuality, playing with the 'constructed silences' of non-straight identity;⁷⁷ silences that are unsurprising given that male homosexuality was still criminalised in 1956.⁷⁸ Neale and Susan are visited by François Dulappe, a young French man, 'facially rather like Michelangelo's David' whom Neale has 'found' in the restaurant where he works at night as a *plongeur* (p. 23). In the events that follow this meeting, including a gently comic scene in the pub, the novel is narrated intermittently in untranslated French for a good six pages, in which we learn that François is 'quair', to which Susan responds 'The English is queer' (p. 27). *King* disturbs the notion that desire can only be located and enjoyed in the conventional locales of the heterosexual marriage, the home and the family and as such, then, might be described as queer writing. Queerness does not, says David Halperin, 'name some natural kind or refer to some determinate object; it acquires its meaning from its oppositional relation to the norm. Queer is by definition whatever is at odds with the normal, the legitimate, the dominant'.⁷⁹ In Brophy's fiction, all characters exist in various states of spoken and unspoken queerness; even the tender feelings that Professor Darellhyde has for Percy in *Hackenfeller's Ape* demonstrate the diversity of intimacies one may experience, even across species. As Lee Edelman has noted 'queerness can never define an identity; it can only ever disturb one',[80] and it permits another way of thinking about erotic relations in the world, about staying open to the multiple possibilities of desire, 'open' says Teresa de Lauretis 'to another discursive horizon, another way of thinking the sexual'.[81] Similarly, Guy Hocquenghem says 'desire emerges in multiple forms' as it is fundamentally perverse; it disrupts categories, disturbs conventions and crosses boundaries, seeing in the most unlikely objects and subjects the potential for eroticism and connection.[82] Queer pleasure, then, is the theme of *King*; the characters are seeking and acting out different kinds of pleasures, just like Nancy and Marcus in *Flesh*. For Susan and Neale, desires are fleeting, fugitive and can switchback on themselves in the most unlikely ways. Both find an ability to take pleasure from becoming – to be in transit rather than in a state of settled arrival: as Neale says to Susan towards the novel's end, 'I kept you travelling hopefully, didn't I? isn't that the kindest things one can can do for anyone?' (*King*, p. 256). As in her later novel, *In Transit* and Brooke-Rose's *Between*, the novel delights in the vagabond possibilities of multilingualism: Neale and Susan happily travel between three languages with ease and Helena says she can 'make love quite eloquently in four' (p. 216).

Working in Mr Finkelheim's dodgy book emporium, Susan happens upon a nude study, *The Lady Revealed*, of an old school friend, Cynthia Bewly, on whom she had a passionate schoolgirl crush. The photo instantaneously prompts crystalline memories of a passionate, understage kiss with Cynthia at their girls' school as a production of *As You Like It* goes on above their heads. The kiss, reminiscent of that between Sally Seton and Clarissa Dalloway, powers the novel's narrative drive; the quest to find Cynthia. Susan's memory of Cynthia was 'like a small photograph in which, if I tried to enlarge it, the detail blurred outwards into nothing' (p. 39). She recalls that a note that Cynthia passes to her in French club is a blank message '- ---- ---'. Susan 'stares down at it, knowing what [she] wanted it to mean' but is too scared to reply to Cynthia who asks her whether she has cracked the code. Susan responds by sending her a coded message in French: '-- -'----' (pp. 62–3). Unable to put their feelings even into letters that might form the basis of words, their passion must be encrypted. This encrypted language surrounded by blanks is a way of exploring the silencing of same-sex attraction at a time when lesbianism in fiction mostly meant misery and an almost certainly tragic *dénouement*.[83] Patricia Juliana Smith has suggested that the novel points up many instances of 'silence and unspeakability' as it slowly reveals Susan's lesbian desire; a process paralleled in the layered book of 'pornography' in Finkelheim's collection.[84] The layers require a concerted effort of seeing otherwise to understand how the surface relates to its 'underside':

> The paper was in fact transparent, but when one looked at the whole thickness of the book it seemed solid [...] As each one went over we could see, from its underside, the small piece of clothing depicted on it, alienated and almost unrecognisable when it appeared alone on the page. The fan gave way to the mask; the skirt vanished, the all over mask was replaced by a black strip [...] the legs became visible. (pp. 37-8)

The careful unwrapping of layers to reveal something unexpected is a quintessential Brophyian technique; in her novels, no one is quite who they seem and can metamorphose at any given point like actors playing multiple roles in a play. This is a world where the plain old surname Bewley is transformed into Beaulieu and where the bookseller Finkelheim, a gentile posing as a Jew, changes his name and accent at will. Neale is most sexually interested in queer male actors but then wants to marry Cynthia. The novel is permeated with a layered design that is filled with female gazes as Susan drinks in the 'planes, spines, and the declivities' of Cynthia's body (p. 41).

The third-person voice describes events with a detached irony, culminating in a reworking of the heterosexual marriage plot. Although Neale marries Cynthia, he enters into a convoluted sexual dance of which Susan tells him, without rancour, that he has 'adopted' her past; that is, he has become a version of Susan's schoolgirl-desiring body (p. 258). In this way, then, he substitutes his uncertainly located desire for that of Susan's thwarted lesbian passion. The potential for sexual fluidity and transformation is everywhere in the novel and abjures any notion of queer shame. Even the tragic ending is lightly handled. The opera diva Helena is found dead in the mountains in suitably operatic tragic style and has sent Susan a box containing Helena's old soiled wedding dress.

The novel might well have been given the subtitle, *The Lady Revealed* to indicate its nimble quest of sexual manners that sees the tentatively bisexual Susan and Neale leave London to track down the former's passionate schoolgirl crush, Cynthia Beaulieu, *neé* Bewley, now a minor film starlet, to Italy where events unfold to allow Cynthia to marry Neale and Susan to fall in love with Helena Buchan. This plot is whimsical and split over its three acts – the middle of which describes Susan and Neale's trip from London to Paris, then from Rome to Venice as coach tour guides to a party of Coke-guzzling, stereotypically crass Americans-in-Europe. A series of obviously flimsy narrative plot devices allows the characters to explore crushes, intrigues, passion and disappointments in a lighthearted and witty manner in 1950s bohemian London with its seedy booksellers and dingy pubs, and then in Paris and Italy.[85] What ensues is a queer caper of mistaken objects of desire, schoolgirl lesbian kisses, capricious film starlets, fading opera divas, who are 'gloriously bisexual' (p. 217) and young men who linger over male nudes but who finally marry the starlet. *King* offers a bracing, sexually optimistic antidote to depictions of sex and sexuality in British literature in the 1950s, which were chiefly focused on the male experience of young men trying to get young women to have sex with them, as in Kinsgsley Amis's *Lucky Jim* (1953). *King* comes just before the social realism of the 'kitchen sink' dramas of Shelagh Delaney's *A Taste of Honey*, first performed in May 1958, and John Braine's *A Room at the Top* (1957), both of which depict far less joyful relations between men and women. The work against which *King* might be most usefully compared in class terms is John Osborne's *Look Back in Anger*, which appeared in the same year. However, *King* has none of the dismal misogyny of Jimmy Porter or the emotional and sexual debasement of Alison, nor the infernal repetition of the domestic space. On the contrary, *King* depicts a joyful, freewheeling eroticism that gestures to new sexual possibilities for young women. In *Promise of a Dream* Sheila Rowbotham recalls how 'little cultural space existed at this time for expressing the sexual freedoms emerging among young women of my generation'.[86]

King oscillates between a baroque, arch realism and self-consciousness; that is, between a self-conscious artfulness and an engagement with the wider social world. But Brophy was opposed to the term experimental, insisting rather that her work followed a baroque design that 'consists of deploying contrasting masses in such a way that each, as well as performing its own function, constitutes a funnel down which one gets a sharply unexpected view – ironic, tragic or comic – of the others'.[87] In this way, Brophy's work is similar to that of Muriel Spark, whose writing is a synthesis of artfully experimental technique and the projection of an external, still-recognisable social world. While this world is often conceived in slightly more artificial form in Brophy's fiction, both writers share an interest in the technique of narrative patterning. As in opera, the sense of individual psychology of characters in the novel is secondary to a set of elaborately orchestrated roles; thus, we get little sense of Susan Neale and Cynthia and Helen as 'real' characters. Brophy once wrote: 'I could no more devote a whole paragraph to describing a person's nature than I could to describing Nature'.[88]

An intricate comedy of sexual manners, *King* is full of highly stylised, often elliptical, disjointed exchanges in which the speakers' words often sail by each other: the novel is a queering of the already camp form of opera and its pantomime-like character.[89] There are no 'thick' social contexts, or familial or personal histories given beyond the self-consciously and often semi-farcical events of the plot that revolve around the chance discovery of a picture of a female nude which leads to an erotic odyssey across Europe. *King*, then, examines the ways in which desire might flow when unfettered from its conventional domestic moorings – an idea given symbolic expression in the image of the shutters in Italian houses and *pensiones*, recalling Robbe-Grillet's *La Jalousie*:

> 'Anyway, what is it about the shutters?'
> 'The slats,' I said.
> 'Yes, it's clever. They give an impression you can see in, though in fact you can't. And isn't that the whole of romance?'(p. 105)

Flesh: 'Nothing is perverse'[90]

> Perhaps what Nancy picked out in him was the potentiality hidden on the reverse side of his personality. If so, she must have been extraordinarily alive herself to such potentialities. (*Flesh*, p. 7)

A year before 'sexual intercourse' began in Larkin's version of Britain, Brophy's third novel about that very subject, *Flesh*, was dedicated to Iris Murdoch. For her part, Murdoch thought it 'a lovely handsome clever book, with excellence on every page'. Writing to Brophy she said: 'You must be the first person who has described sexual intercourse beautifully and well in a book. I like the fine sensuousness of it all'.[91] Some reviewers praised *Flesh* as a witty fable of sexual mores: an 'exceptionally taut and funny novel' that 'never lets her background submerge her characters or override her theme. This is a powerful piece of sophistication'.[92] Others regarded it as a flawed work displaying a 'serious imbalance of structure [. . .] One can only say, in faint praise, that *Flesh* reads like a working notebook for a much longer novel'.[93]

With its sensual Bill Brandt cover from *The Perspective of Nudes* (1962), *Flesh* is related in Brophy's coolly detached narrative style that gives the illusion of straightforward realism but is closer, in fact, to the marvellous logic of a fairy tale or fable. *Flesh* describes the overturning of the power dynamic between male and female sexual desire where the woman is the teacher and authority, the male a malleable disciple. A novel concerned with 'complex gender investments in cultural formations of the ideal body', *Flesh* describes the ways in which a woman may give herself permission to transform a man's virginal body, indeed his whole life, for her own delectation reversing the dynamics of the Pygmalion–Galatea myth.[94] In transposing the male gaze into the female gaze, *Flesh* suggests how centuries of cultural representation have represented women as the erotic object of the male gaze under which women are passively appraised, desired and pursued by men and never the other way around. In Brophy's version of the Pygmalion myth, the woman is the tutor, the sculptor, the elocutionist, and the male the beautiful passive statue or the *ingénue* flowergirl.

A young Jewish couple from North London, Marcus and Nancy meet at a party and marry a few months later. A shy virgin, Marcus is gradually moulded by Nancy into her erotic plaything. Turning him into her biddable sexual *protégé*, Nancy performs a powerful act of sexual creativity upon his male body, rendering it not just a tool of her sexual pleasure but a thing of plasticity that can be shaped at will. She produces in Marcus a strong erotic awakening: 'a new scale of sensuous experience had come within his range – or, rather, possessed him [. . .] like a rainbow cast on his flesh by a window pane'.[95] Brushing aside any notion of female sexual passivity, Nancy is endowed with a capacity to steer her new husband, previously a painfully introverted 'voodoo scarecrow' into new erotic territories. Described at the novel's beginning as being 'like a derelict property suddenly bought up by a speculator' (p. 5) and feminised from the outset, Marcus is an indolent aesthete with an effete interest in art, especially in Rubens, an artist who makes Nancy feel distinctly queasy. A passive figure from the outset, Marcus is 'over-sensitive', his 'acute sensibility' taking its deepest pleasures in 'books, paintings flowers' (pp. 5–6). In a reversal of normative gender roles, Marcus is the 'aesthetic' and Nancy is 'intelligent' (p. 17). Indeed, *Flesh* might be described as the queering of the Pygmalion myth: 'If women are usually seen, for cosmetic reasons, as the more mutable sex, in *Flesh* it is a man who is transformed, both in body and mind, under a woman's skilful hands'.[96]

Like that other uxorious, Jewish womanly-man Leopold Bloom, who enjoys nothing more than a pig's kidney fried in butter, Marcus is a bad Jew, preferring 'pork to other meats' and as a boy was consumed with 'a lust for fried bacon' (p. 9). His principal dilemma at a cocktail party at which he meets Nancy, with her boyishly neat figure and bobbed dark hair like a 'match head', is that being seen eating a sausage might make him 'unmarriageable'. Nancy's first words to him describe her ravenous appetite as she begins to devour those same sausage rolls: 'It seems so silly to be restricted by an old hygienic precaution that may have had some point in the ancient world' (p. 11). Marcus hesitates to respond for fear of sounding 'intellectually aggressive', arguably a feminine fear that has hampered women for centuries as they strove to hide their intelligence behind more marriageable traits like modesty, needlecraft and deference to male authority.

When they first have sex on their honeymoon to Italy, Nancy 'talks to him about what he was to do'. *Flesh* presents women as intensely sexual without any hint of monstrosity accruing to their bodies or lives: 'Nancy did have talent. It was for sexual intercourse' (p. 41). In the 2013 reissue, Richard Kelly notes the subtle ways in which Brophy turns the gender tables, 'without fuss or contrivance, but with great style and acute perception'.[97] Nancy leads Marcus into a new erotic world which is 'limitless, infinitely receding and enticing, because every sensation he experienced there carried on its back endless multiplication of overtones, with the result that the sensation [. . .] was never finished.' A world as 'appropriate and precise as poetry', in Nancy's gift of sexual ecstasy there is 'such a perfect interpenetration of opposites that one could grow as climax out of the other' (p. 44).

In a reversal of the ubiquitous male gaze on the female nude, Nancy appraises Marcus with discerning eyes; he has become a 'disgustingly fat' Rubens figure with 'pendulous breasts' like a women's, but nevertheless she still finds him attractive (p. 122). In *Flesh* then, a man is redesigned, even transformed into a female, by a woman's active desire; her own sexuality is the architect of Marcus's transformation. Brophy, who very queerly loved both men and woman in her lifetime, believed in the 'Freudian recognition of the basic bisexuality of everybody'.[98] Indeed, *Flesh* exhibits many of Eve Sedgwick's definitions of the term queer: 'the open mesh of possibilities, gaps, overlaps, dissonances and resonances, lapses and excesses of meaning when the constituent elements of anyone's gender, of anyone's sexuality aren't made (or *can't* be made) to signify monolithically'.[99] Brophy explains this

> conscious desire to counteract the mythology of literary criticism at the moment, which so often cries that only women can write about women, and only men can write about men. One constantly reads that there are no good parts for women in the theater, because there aren't enough women dramatists. The point is, that Hedda Gabler and Cleopatra were not created by women dramatists. I have a feeling that this is not only a mistaken approach to sex, but also a mistaken mythology of basic mental differences between the sexes, which I don't accept exists.[100]

Marcus is 'plumped up' for Nancy's 'harem' (p. 48); her treatment of Marcus, then, is a reversal of the male–female active–passive binary that has for so long dominated romantic fiction. A 1960s incarnation of Circe, Nancy has a black bob and 'neat', read boyish, figure, and she sets about transforming Marcus into a state of porcine sensuality who indolently indulges his passions for sex, art and food, while being kept by Nancy as a sexual plaything. We might usefully turn here to *Black and White*, and to Brophy's description in Beardsley's work of 'female dandies, female effeminates, even? Or are they male hoydens, male tomboys, boy butches?'[101] Beardsley, she continues, 'translates the male/female mixture into a human/animal mixture', working from mythological fictions of metamorphosis and the 'nostalgic figure of a human/animal mixture'.[102] In what might be called a dandification of realism – its appearance as one thing but underneath something quite different, more arch and ambiguous – Brophy's fiction constantly is also, as noted, fascinated with the transformative perverse potentiality of the human body and, in Freudian terms, the polymorphisity of its desires.

The novel shows a strong female sexual appetite but, despite Marcus's eventual infidelity with the German *au pair*, Ilse, Nancy suffers no torments of jealousy – indeed, she relishes his full erotic transformation. A hint of the fetishist is often at the back of Brophy's writing, like the child lying in bed watching his mother get dressed up for an evening out; her fiction delights in the bejewelling of ordinariness – the moment where the mother becomes the beautiful princess, or Salome in an exotic transmogrification.[103] The atmosphere is constantly open to the queer, the unexpected and the travelling from one state to another. As in *King*, the idea of queerness appears several times in *Flesh*. Polydore, or Polly, is 'queer, insofar as he's anything' (p. 66). Marcus's sister, who is a lesbian, is 'more than a little sweet' on Nancy (p. 50) and Nancy's seduction of Marcus leads them into a fluid space of eroticism unfettered by boundaries and limits.

> Where she led him was a strange world that was not new to him, since he had always known it existed, subterraneanly: a grotto, with whose confines and geographical dispositions he at once made himself quite familiar, [...] every experience conducted him to the next; a world where he pleasurably lost himself in a confusion of the senses not in the least malapropos but as appropriate and precise as poetry – a world where one really did see sounds and hear scents, where doves might well have roared and given suck, where perfectly defined, delightful local tactile sensations dissolved into apperceptions of light or darkness, of colour, of thickness, of temperature. (p. 44)

Given that the year is 1962, this description is striking in its candour. In *Don't Never Forget*, Brophy writes of the ability of women to express sexual desires now enfranchised by contraception: 'they have a taste for sexual intercourse'.[104]

In contrast to Nancy's neat litheness, Marcus broadens and thickens as his sensual nature begins to spread. He goes to work for his Uncle Polydore – Polly – himself an aesthete whose queerness is cultivated through his trade in 'decorative schemas' – sumptuous swags of silk and the lustrous surfaces of eighteenth-century cabinetry. But he would start 'to lust for home' as Nancy begins curing hams in the kitchen (p. 81). As Marcus loves food in the same the way as he loves beautiful furniture, he soon begins to 'settle into a domestic version of a rustic slowness', in which he can enjoy his *'embonpoint'* and develops a camp 'suspicion of a lisp' caught, Nancy thinks, from Polydore (p. 85). His metamorphosis is nearly complete. Marcus begins eating as part of a form of intense uxoriousness; his body softening, filling out, he finds himself lusting for home in ways that effectively effeminise him (p. 80). While Nancy is not wholly pleased with Marcus's transformation into the fleshy, womanly man – 'You're disgustingly fat' (p. 122) – their passion continues, even after his afternoon infidelities with the *au pair*, and they settle into a new definition of marriage.

Reviewing the 1964 English translation of Jean Genet's *Our Lady of the Flowers*, Brophy notes that the language of the novel is composed out of 'the grammatical metamorphosis of "il" into "elle"', a process out of which 'flowers the queer argot'.[105] Crucially, this is a metamorphosis that is 'never fixed' and can reverse itself at any point. Genet's 'personal erotic tastes are transformed into poetry as a 'universal imagery of eroticism', a most 'esoteric sexual perversion that depends upon the reader's imaginative faculty to be aroused to an intangible but all the same completely sensual erection'.[106] *Flesh* shows women as intensely sexual without any suggestion of the femme fatale's *dentata* monstrosity that has so often accrued to women's actively desiring bodies; demonised, says Cixous, 'for being frigid, for being "too hot"; for not being both at once'.[107] Even when Nancy becomes a mother she is not punished for her desire to return to work or for giving up breastfeeding almost immediately: unlike Cixous's women, she is not 'guilty at every turn' – guilty 'for being too motherly and not enough; for having children and for not having any; for nursing and for not nursing'.[108] *Flesh*, then, is a parable of transformative passion that refuses conventional modes of eroticism and permits a woman to be 'hot' in her desires and to possess, with impunity, the power to mould male beauty to her own taste.

The Snowball: Rococo Realism

Another Brophyian novel about sex, and one that contains, moreover, a two-page description of a female orgasm, *The Snow Ball* is a lively reworking of Mozart's *Don Giovanni*, specifically the ambivalence of the 'seduction'. The novel rewrites the sexual politics of the original opera by showing a woman's desire to be the equal of a man's, and also strips away the sexual violence implicit in the original. The novel centres around a fancy-dress New Year's Eve party in an opulent eighteenth-century London residence of Tom Tom and his glamorous wife Tum Tum, who has been married four times and is otherwise known as Anne. She is the longtime friend of another Anne, known as Anna K, who arrives at the party alone, dressed as Donna Anna, 'the only unseducible woman', according to Janet Wolff, 'among Don Giovanni's victims'.[109] The setting is a snowy night; the snow flakes falling like the Joycean snow in 'The Dead', gently suggesting the fragile nature of sexual passion. [110]

After an ecstatic sexual encounter, it is Donna Anna who rejects Don Giovanni at the novel's close, she leaves for home sensuously sated rather than as, in the opera, an object of unsolicited sexual attentions.[111] Described by a contemporary reviewer as 'a sort of prosy musical joke',[112] the novel's rococo style and tone takes the central conceit of an eighteenth-century masquerade ball as this allows for a masked erotic dance between three pairs of romantically entangled characters in a reworking of events in the original operatic plot. There are two women, Anne and Anna K, who have an ex-husband in common; Ruth, the teenage daughter of Jewish couple Rudy and Myra Blumenbaum, who has come dressed as Cherubino with her *amor* Edward. Two minor characters complete the cast – the tiresome Dr Brompius and a man in a Chinese waistcoat who 'looks like a boiled egg', who will later die on the dance floor in the drained lights of the early morning when all the glittering lights of the chandeliers' illumination revert to unglamorous ordinariness – 'mere yellow things' – as reality returns.[113]

Appearance is not fixed to character in opera and as Sam Abel notes, audiences readily suspend their collective disbelief: 'How can aging divas portray young *ingénues*, wooden tenors dashing heroes, and overweight sopranos women dying of consumption, with no protests from the audience?'[114] Opera has the potential for the upsetting of 'proscribed gender role[s]'.[115] An important eighteenth-century form, opera revels in disguise and travesti, as Anna K is informed by Dr Brompius, who urges her to consider the 'whole culture-situation of the period, in which opera is embedded like a jewel in its setting' (*Snow Ball*, p. 71). A fancy-dress party is a masquerade that permits an overturning of everyday rules and for men and women to indulge in some licensed transgression and transvestitism. Masquerade is carnivalesque, allowing all manner of indiscretions, inversions and metamorphoses. As Terry Castle has noted, eighteenth-century masquerades were 'a world of endless, enchanting metamorphosis [...] always with an even more gratifying pattern of transformation: a proliferation of intrigue. Besides thematising mutability through image, the masquerade episode serves as a nodal point for narrative transformation – the privileged site of plot'.[116] Bewigged, bejewelled and transformed into fabulous travesties of their quotidian selves, the partygoers are all disguised. At midnight, Anna K. meets a masked Don who kisses her while she wonders if this mysterious man might share her personal obsessions – 'Mozart, sex and death' – but flees from him only to be reunited a short while later. Donna Anna enters into an erotic game of cat and mouse with this Don up in the minstrel's gallery, both concealed from general view behind the folds of a plush curtain. Their erotic sparring is as intellectual as it is sexual. He tells her: 'I like your beauty spot', so she slowly peels it off before he passionately kisses the place it had occupied between her breasts just after she has told him 'I've been enjoying your terror for some minutes' (p. 120).

Both class outsiders, Don and Donna Anna are 'Cinderellas at this ball' (p. 78) with a mutual interest in Mozart, death and sex. As D. J. Enright observes, 'Anna considers herself too old for adventures and is much concerned with death: a concern not dispelled by Don Giovanni's cheery assurance that sexual intercourse drives out thoughts of death in direct proportion to its frequency'.[117] Finally, they leave the party to consummate this liaison. As in *Flesh*, the act of sexual intercourse is depicted in detail and is focused solely on Anna's orgasm that takes hold with uninhibited sensuality:

> Having only to wait, she – or some part of her, perhaps her hand on his head, perhaps her mouth on his shoulder – convulsively, repetitively and in the end, she felt, abrasively, caressed his body; it was done with the mere idleness of excited yet reluctant impatience [...] as though by digging into his flesh, by pitting him, her fingers or teeth could actually lay hold on the paradox whereby so much thought and strategy in the vertical world went into maneuvering into this horizontal situation where pleasure consisted in something being imposed, in being carried to the point of no return, in an act as unwilled as sneezing, falling asleep or dying. (pp. 139–40)

Again, this joyful depiction of erotic play is a far cry from the joyless bunk-ups in Alan Sillitoe and John Braine that frequently had dreadful consequences for women, or the bitter struggle between Alison and

Jimmy Porter. *The Snow Ball* effervesces with sexual joy and, as in *Flesh*, women's erotic pleasure is depicted as active, unashamed and, above all, freely taken.

The erotic play comes as much from the often unanticipated interaction of wit and intelligence as from the union of physical bodies. This sense of unexpectedness is characteristic of Brophy's baroque technique that positions one scene against another in a series that cuts up the flow of the narrative. Interviewed in the *New York Times*, Brophy described what she defined as baroque in more detail:

> Baroque is the juxtaposition and interpenetration of death themes and life themes – as it were, black marble and white marble. The aim of the design is to bring the reader suddenly round a corner to confront an incongruity – which may be comic or ironic but is always poetic and is always in Bad Taste [. . .] In "The Snow Ball," the surface will still pass for naturalistic [. . .] "In Transit" dispenses with a naturalistic texture and substitutes fire works. But however surrealistically they seem to explode, they are all pinned to the baroque structure, and it should be the form that leaves its impress on the imagination's eyelids when the show is over.[118]

An elegantly plotted set-piece of flamboyancy involving three sets of lovers, *The Snow Ball* describes an opulence teetering on the verge of decadent dissolution into a 'flurry of black beauty spots' (p. 16); among the baroque sumptuousness there lurks a sense of all 'the pure, sweet, all-desirable prettiness of sugar' (p. 19) and an undercurrent of evanescence and decay, and even a touch of malice. Mirroring to some extent Don and Anna, teenagers Ruth and Edward have sex in the back of her father's Bentley, then become embroiled in a petulant post-coital quarrel, which concludes in Ed maliciously throwing a snowball at Anna K's back as she and Don are returning to the party. Anna refuses the shame attached to the signification of this – 'I don't feel aimed at at all' (p. 152) – but Ed is shown to be the poison in the piece as he spitefully writes in the snow on Rudy Blumenbaum's car, 'JEWBOY' (p. 165). As Dock observes, 'most of the descriptions start out as neutral, if not positive [. . .] and gradually, within the passage, the description becomes quite negative'.[119] The décor and settings are always on the verge of a sapping excess:

> From the rooms' shiny surfaces of white, the eye seemed continually slipping off, slipping down, as though your eyelids were being pulled shut and your body being depressed toward floor or bed in a delicious swoon that was half laziness. The whole room tugged with its own gravitation, against the vertical. (p. 27)

Any naturalism in the narrative is unsettled by an unpredictable zooming in on the tiniest of details that linger protractedly on small, mostly decorative, touches such as the flights of sugary cherubs and the bare-buttocked cupids and the description of Anna, a 'newly born cherub in her early forties' (p. 24) applying heavy masquerade make-up before entering Anne's pure white bedroom. This room has been transformed from a maid's room into the 'sheer spirit of rococo' (p. 25) – in 'such an excess of satin purity, so blazoned, as not to be pure at all, but rioting, shameless, like white lilac' (p. 24). The décor is 'anti-natural' in its extravagance – 'brass, silk, Chinoierisie, an ornately scalloped wash basin, more cherubs in parings, all set off with a white Siamese kitten atop the white bed' (p. 27). Brophy and Levey's flat in Brompton Road in Chelsea was testament to this love of anti-naturalist rococo: it was full of 'gilded woodworm-pocked angel, and, among so many objects of desire, the eau-de-nil art deco cocktail cabinet opening onto beveled mirror glass [. . .] Brigid loved pretty, deceptively frivolous things – a sentence by Firbank, a piece of rococo glass'.[120]

The novel's plot is simultaneously (re)interpreted by the diary entries of young Ruth Blumenbaum, the girl Cherubino, whose first ball it is. Her writing, often using abbreviations and encryption, attempts to capture the events of the party in a minute-by-minute account that verges, at times, on a parody of modernist stream of consciousness and also, perhaps, with a Jamesian suggestion of a child's-eye view of adult shenanigans in *What Maisie Knew*. This technique offers a defamiliarised focalisation of the action; the events of the night are pressed like a flower by words in her diary. Ruth's diary gives us the events of the party before the main narrative reveals them:

> Anna K kissed a man in a black mask. Feel there is something awful about all the people in the world. Can't think what they are here for [. . .] they just move around without aim attracted or repelled by each other

but then notes 'None of this expresses what I feel at all' (*Snow Ball*, pp. 47–8). Ruth's diary entries interrupt the action, lending the plot of the novel an air of complete artifice. Ruth's diary emphasizes the sense of queering enigma that pervades the novel – the overheard scraps of conversations and fleeting glimpses of bodies and costumes in this rococo romp.

In Transit: 'Polymorphous as the angels'

Sexual liberation in the 1960s began, John Lucas suggests, with the *Lady Chatterley* Trial in 1959 and ended in 1969 with Brophy's *In*

Transit, which he describes as a 'virtual handbook of transgression'.[121] The sexual transgression of the novel resides primarily in the refusal to accept the conventions of male and female roles in fiction and in language. In Brophy's work, as we have seen, men can sing soprano and women bass, girls can fashion boys into objects of desire and desiring women can take their pleasures and remain unpunished. *In Transit*'s transgression resides not only in the refusal of gender binaries but also in its disregard for the rules of, as Brophy calls, it the 'naturalistic' novel. *In Transit* takes this rule-breaking several steps further. Heterogenous to its very core, the novel, observes Annagret Maack, breaks 'with every convention of the traditional novel'.[122] It is between genres – farce, fairy tale, detective novel, romance and operetta – its textuality a mixture of Joycean badinage, typographic experiments, Steinian punnery and Sternean digressiveness:

> 'To be absolutely frank, what I should most like to resemble is a small but powerful and concentrated bomb. My ambition is to explode and shatter the rules.'
>
> 'Splendider and splendider! You have the true violent spirit of the creative artist. It is by the setting off of bombs inside the existing framework of the arts that new artistic forms come into being.'
>
> 'And yet for all my creative energy I feel impotent,' Och sadly said. 'I can't find anyone who will teach me the rules. So how can I make sure of breaking them?' (p. 193)

In Transit is an intensely jocular text that has some serious points to make about the orthodoxies of language in relation to gender. Not all critics, however, agreed with such an assessment. Some regarded the novel's jokiness and its experimental form as frustrating any consequential content. Representative only of the novel's 'move towards anarchy', *In Transit*'s puns and metafictional conceits thwart any possibility, suggests one critic, of any meaningful engagement with gender politics.[123] Brian McHale disagrees with such an opposition between form and content, suggesting rather that Brophy's anti-novel dissolves 'the unitary real into a number of competing alternative realties governed by different physical laws'.[124] He regards the gendered mutability of the central character Pat/Patricia O'Rooley as part of a longer tradition of 'the inverted and exploded body' that can be 'traced back through such early twentieth-century precursors of postmodernism as Alfred Jarry'.[125] Bodies in one form of transit or other, McHale suggests, have been an important part of literary explorations of the borders and limits of self-hood and language. The inversion and explosion of Pat/Patricia's body involves not only corporeal misplacement but also a surrendering to the semantic vagaries of circumstances. Losing the gender of your main protagonist poses certain fundamental problems for the writer, which are, in the first place, chiefly pronominal ones. However, if we cannot say he or she, it does not follow then, Brophy suggests, that we cannot say 'I':

> I . . . could hardly (could I?) commit myself to a main character at whose every appearance in my narrative I would be obliged to write he/she, his/her, etc.
> For which reason
> I *have*,
>   dear Sir/Madam,
>   to remain
>   Your
>   I
>
> (p. 69)

The novel humorously dissects the logical irrationality of gendered grammar; we are not told the gender of the speaker until section 2, 'Interludibrium', when the interlocutor tells us, 'You'll notice that I [. . .] have trickered you off with mirror effects. For instance, if I were not an I, it could not be I who would be committed to a he/she' (p. 69). We do not learn of a gender for O'Rooley until much later (and even then, it vacillates) but in the meantime it becomes clear that the reader first must challenge the authority of narrative voice. Who is the 'nanny interlocutor' that inhabits the conventional third-person realist narrative? What is this 'shameful hold' that the quest for 'compulsive interlocution' exerts on 'modern literate man'? (p. 14):

> How authors squirm, how they sidle from foot to foot to avoid that compulsion to narration [. . .] They say they are seeking to alienate you. They take aim to fling you an open-ended fiction the book lands legs akimbo, pages open at the splits, less a book than a box of trick tools, its title DO IT YOURSELF KID. (p. 14)

Later we read via the 'I' voice that all narrative elements are mere tricks: 'Am I therefore trying to produce an *effect* of verisimilitude by the non-realistic method of pretending that I cannot now remember remembering what, it is admitted by internal evidence, I did at that time remember quite clearly' (pp. 69–70).

In Brophy's novel, gender follows genre. If the latter is well defined, then perhaps Pat/Patricia's identity will resolve itself into some clearer sign of membership (all puns intended) in his/her corduroy trousers. But s/he soon discovers that this is no thriller, nor detective fiction nor romance. More worryingly for Pat/Patricia, it transpires that in this particular book, 'External war has been declared between content and this form'. The novelist tries but fails to rein in the character and the plot: 'he cramps and clamps his characters in order to cram them inside his narrow story lines' (p. 44), but they will always, suggests Brophy, try to escape from their designated spaces.

After contracting a bad case of 'linguistic leprosy' (p. 11), all meanings become unmoored from things in the world and a beleaguered O'Rooley finds all signification absconding from him/her. There are no useful words, at least initially, to describe his or her gender. All signs of sexual difference have been evacuated from the body, or at least have become invisible, a body that had, until very recently been the site of some essential(ist) truth, a reliable depository of the markers of sexual difference which principally boils down to having or not having possession of the phallus. No longer Evelyn Hillary O'Rooley but Hooligan, he/she becomes a semantic delinquent who 'by night has crept into the hall of sculpture' and 'vandalised the exhibits' by chopping the torsos in two and swapping the Venus de Milo's bottom half for Hermes's top half (p. 72). Signs become increasingly fugitive and O'Rooley begins to struggle to translate even the over-signed, infantilised environment of the airport – that represents 'the true pure feel of the twentieth century' (p. 23) – a space that relies, above all, on the functionality of signs. O'Rooley finds him/herself radically estranged from the surrounding environment, all at once unable to read even the simplest of signs and stuck in the present tense of being perpetually in transit. As in *Between*, the punning reveals a more serious point regarding the construction of identity:

> We are all simply persons slit, split and filleted on a point of logic of our own perceiving. We noticed one day that it is merely arbitrary to suppose any nation or class superior to the rest simply because we happened to be born into it [. . .] Paleface and Back Bottom are interchangeable: what you call the world turned upside down is simply the world to someone who happened to be born on the other side. (p. 27)

Palpating his/her body and clothing for signs of gender is an arduous process for O'Rooley as among the folds, clefts and contours there is no real sign of obvious sexual difference. As all signs become open to translation and interpretation; gender is reduced to a matter of interpretation, requiring a reader/interlocutor to define what is masculine and what is feminine. The clue to gender identity comes only in a bewildering conversation with Betty Bouncer and her husband who finally establishes that O'Rooley is male and was Betty's first date. Betty appears to be 'obviously heterosexual' as she observes the 'heterosexual conventions of speech [. . .] I quite clearly am, must be and can only be A MAN' (p. 111). Consciousness here becomes the search for an interlocutor, a reader of your own signs to help you with the meaning-making activity of narrative. But when Patricia, now reconciled to being female, finds herself on a bizarre gameshow called 'WHAT'S MY KINK?' taking place somewhere in the airport, she strategically 'resolves to be Patrick again' and goes on to win the contest; only as a man, it seems, can one win the game.

Interpolated into the main narrative that oscillates between Pat, Patrick and Patricia is a secondary story of 'L'HISTOIRE DE LA LANGUE D'OC', the title a punning take on *Histoire d'O* (p. 19), described (just like *In Transit* itself) as a 'misprinted mistranslated overestimated sadomastubatory pornofantasy-narrative' (p. 143).[126] In conversation with the professor emeritus, Och, the heroine who speaks only to give her consent to erotic degradation in the original O, becomes a complex, thinking subject who muses on the possibilities of the liberation of the imagination. Hence, there occurs a transposition of the passive, mostly speechless O from the original text into a wily and resourceful interlocutor in this version. While Och is tortured she does not succumb to the silencing and submission of her predecessor O, and is literally and figuratively cheeky: 'By having Oc give "cheek," Brophy parodies the idea that the male is the dominant figure in the scene; here, power resides in the supposedly masochistic "Oc" rather than with "The Master"'.[127]

O'Rooley discovers that, at best, the rules governing gender are often a matter of convention and convenience. One might lose one's member but this has little effect on the essential subjectivity: 'Identity, however, is unloseable [. . .] I have doubted often what I am, but never who' (p. 44). This gestures to *Orlando* (1928), Woolf's 'writer's holiday', in which Orlando learns how to be both: 'Orlando had become a woman [. . .] The change of sex, though it altered their future, did nothing whatever to alter their identity'.[128] While *In Transit* is humorous and 'punny', it also shows how language has the power to shape the social order. As the narrator muses – 'Suppose the structure which, like an organic conveyor belt, has been transporting all my thoughts and experiences all these years is but an arbitrary convention?' (p. 217). A gender fantasia, *In Transit* was ahead of its time in its examination of the relationship of the body to biological sex and to a culturally constructed gendered identity, anticipating some central concepts of third-wave feminism in Judith Butler's *Gender Trouble* (1990).[129] Brophy's anti-novel observes how ideological discourses powerfully shape and regulate the gendering of the corporeal self and policies it pleasures. Pat/Patricia's body becomes 'sexed' by the discursive trappings of convention – language, clothes, and gesture – and above all by the romance narratives of high and low culture that compel the subject to reiterate a series of performances that interpellate the body as male or female. In his review of the novel in *Life*, Robert Phelps recognises Brophy's insistence on the fluidity of identity: the novel suggests that '[a]t his innermost center', a person 'is many things, many appetites, all genders. [...] In his soul, he is as polymorphous as the angels'.[130] This polymorphism is also evident in the disturbance of language in the unconventional form of the (anti-)novel – language is, as Brophy points out, 'one of the hero(in)es immolated throughout these pages' (*In Transit*, p. 214).

A Maverick Feminist

Regarding feminism less as a political undertaking than a sensibility, one which was for her instinctive and therefore in no need of doctrines or manifestos, Brophy was extremely resistant to feminism as an organised political movement. Her recalcitrant attitudes, however, do not invalidate her as an important figure in the history of British women's writing. As Patricia Waugh has noted, not all women writers who experiment with concepts of gender and sexuality in their work have aligned themselves explicitly with contemporary feminism; indeed some of them 'have refused to confine themselves to a narrow feminist agenda and have often taken up positions that are antithetical to those of the dominant feminist politics of their time'.[131] Brophy might best be viewed then, not as an adversary of feminism, but as a dissident or non-conformist feminist thinker. Not easily persuaded by the politics of the Women's Liberation Movement (WLM), Brophy did, however, consider herself to be a 'natural' feminist insofar as she was convinced of the innate equality between women and men, particularly concerning questions of biology in the reproduction and regulation of the nuclear family. Publicly outspoken on the restrictions of monogamous marriage, she argued in 'A Woman's Place' that matrimony was only one of an 'infinitely flexible' number of ways in which human sexual and kinship relations might be arranged.[132] Although Brophy was broadly in agreement with many of feminism's aims, she was sceptical towards feminism as a set of doctrinal tenets; however, such scepticism did not prevent her from writing about what she called the 'sex war'. Brophy, then, was less an anti-feminist than a maverick feminist who, while agreeing with sexual equality, was nevertheless not easily corralled into the involuntary extension of ideology into artistic and intellectual domains.

In typically contrarian style, Brophy seemed to suggest that, on the one hand, she was not committed to any systematic ideological project of feminism and in some of her non-fiction writing her ideas might in fact be regarded as conspicuously, even startlingly, anti-feminist but on the other, her work expresses a manifestly feminist awareness, especially in her journalism. Thus, we get two sides of the famous Brophyian pugnacity: she writes that society ought to ask 'whether it is natural for women to be kept in the kitchen' and that the 'normal and natural thing for human beings to do is [...] to reform society and to circumvent or supplement nature',[133] but also that '[f]eminism may lack allure for individual bookbuyers, but the posse of jackboot feminists can no doubt be counted on to bully institutions'.[134]

Despite Brophy's ambivalence towards feminism, especially in the 1970s and 1980s, it has become unexceptional to read that Brophy was not only an animal rights activist and campaigner for the PLR, but that she was also a devoted feminist. Accompanying the reissues of *Flesh* and *The Finishing Touch*, Richard T. Kelly describes her thus: 'In hindsight Brophy still cuts a singular figure as novelist, critic, feminist, pacifist, campaigner for the rights of authors and of animals and connoisseur of art and opera'.[135] Similarly, in the anthology *Modern British Women Writers*, she is described as a 'vociferous' supporter of feminism.[136] In an obituary in the *Independent* we learn of Brophy's deep 'commitment to causes that were worth fighting for', namely, 'feminism, pacifism, vegetarianism, Public Lending Rights, pornography, and the Vietnam War'.[137] More accurately not suggesting her commitment to feminism, Sebastian Groes describes Brophy as a writer whose sexual politics represented a radical challenge to the 'masculine, humanist "majoritarian" tradition'.[138]

Janet Todd notes that Brophy was, in fact, well known for her 'acerbic anti-feminism'.[139] In addition to the reference to 'jackbooted' feminists', Todd may be referring here to Brophy's critical demolition of *The Handbook of Non-Sexist Writing*, edited by Casey Miller and Kate Swift, in the *London Review of Book* in February 1982, and reprinted as 'He/She/Hesh' in *Baroque 'n' Roll* (1987).[140] At the time Brophy wrote this, feminist debates around the politics of language and representation were at their most intense but this did not discourage her scathing intervention. She disagrees with the feminist assertion at the centre of Miller and Swift's project – one now widely acknowledged – that is, that language has a direct effect on the ways in which we understand the world, and that it has a disproportionately powerful effect on the interpellation of the subjectivity of girls and women: 'Every language reflects the prejudices of the society in which it evolved'.[141] They are clearly engaging here with contemporary feminist debates on culture that began with Simone de Beauvoir's *The Second Sex* and continued with Betty Friedan's *The Feminine Mystique* (1963) and Dale Spender's *Man Made Language* (1980).[142] The argument that everyday language enforces gender stereotypes was, of course, fundamental to the feminist claim that the personal is the political and, further, that the idea of what constitutes the political needed to be extended to encompass, as Kate Millett said, 'powerstructured relationships, the entire arrangement whereby one group of people is governed by another, one group is dominant and the other subordinate'.[143] In this context, then, Brophy's *précis* of Miller and Swift's arguments seems rather perverse:

> These truisms are not enough to establish whether language can and, if so, should be nagged into changing in a programmatic direction [...] Even if you accept the assertion, it does not follow that by changing the language you can change the prejudices.[144]

A rather curious assertion, surely, by a writer whose protagonist Pat/Patricia O'Rooley experiments with gender roles and examines the function of language to influence subjectivity. In her review, however, Brophy unreservedly rejects the notion that language has any discernible effect on the ways in which we understand gender:

> There is not the smallest reason to expect that Britons and residents of the USA will turn non-sexist overnight should Ms Miller and Ms Swift succeed in persuading the 'writers, editors and speakers' [...] to scrap the 'he' in sentences like 'Anyone who converses with *émigré* Hungarians will soon find that he is bewildered by their pronouns' and replace it by 'he or she' or one of the other formulae.[145]

Miller and Swift argue that the 'vocabulary and grammar' of English asserts a world view that upholds a 'white, Anglo-Saxon, patriarchal society' given to 'excluding or belittling women', a claim, Brophy says, that must be taken 'with a pinch of salt'.[146] But in the very next sentence, she adopts a conflicting position on linguistic sexism insofar as it pertains to her own experience. She does not mind at all 'craftsmanship' or 'chairman' as do the authors but was once 'driven to public expostulation' when introduced as an 'authoress'.[147] In a concluding remark that is commensurate with the idea that feminism equals humourlessness (comparable to Sara Ahmed's concept of the 'feminist killjoy') Brophy reprimands the two authors for trying to 'denature' anything in the English language that 'might pass for a joke'.[148] A lifelong advocate of the dexterous pun, Brophy seems here to privilege the right of language to be humorous over any political responsibility, observing that the authors' solutions have the 'depressive effect of sucking the imaginative content out of material that can ill spare it'.[149]

Brophy's resistance to feminism is also evident in her review of Germaine Greer's *The Obstacle Race: The Fortunes of Women Painters and Their Work* (1979). An unequivocally feminist recuperation of female painters in history, Greer's project salvages women painters who have been lost or overlooked in cultural history for reasons of lack of education and training and patriarchal prohibitions on women's labour outside of the domestic sphere. Describing her feminist methodology as a 'singularly squinting vision of our culture', Brophy complains that Greer's one 'shut eye excludes painters who were men, except where they impinge, as teachers, lovers or parents, on painters who were women'.[150] By pointing up the fact that men are missing from this account, Brophy wilfully misses the point that Greer's is a study of the various obstacles that *women* painters have encountered, one of which is patriarchy, not unlike the ways in which Woolf talks of the absence of women writers in the canon in *A Room of One's Own* (1929). To complain that Woolf neglects talking at length about William rather than Judith Shakespeare, parallels Brophy's cavilling critique of Greer's polemical undertaking. In much the same vein, Brophy ventures into feminist baiting territory in an excoriating review of Colin MacCabe's book, *James Joyce and the Revolution of the Word*. Referring to his chapter on *Finnegans Wake* and its 'phallocentric male discourse':

> Can we categorise the text as a feminine discourse despite its articulation by a male pen or must that pen be accounted for? Alas, Mr MacCabe doesn't go on to say what a *female* pen is like and whether it manages to assume a non-phallic shape.[151]

Rather perplexingly however, Brophy's attitudes towards feminism are frequently undermined, even contradicted, in her non-fiction writing. Witness a newspaper article for the *Saturday Evening Post* from 1963, 'Women', in which she discusses the coercive power of the 'confidence trick' of biology that has been perpetrated on women:

> Women are free. At least, they look free. They even feel free. But in reality women in the western, industrialised world today are like the animals in a modern zoo. There are no bars. It appears that cages have been abolished. Yet in practice woman are still kept in their place just as firmly as the animals are kept in their enclosures. The barriers which keep them in now are invisible.[152]

Presciently locating a problematic that would be central to much feminist theory in the next three decades, Brophy here identifies the ways in which nature, invisibly going under the mantle of culture, is used to keep women in invisibly barred cages, and, further, persuades them to acquiesce to the idea that they 'are by nature unfit for life outside the cage', thus maintaining, she says, one of the 'most insidious and ingenious confidence tricks ever perpetrated'.[153] The invisibility of the bars is distressing for a woman, she argues, as she is 'unable to perceive what is holding her back' and thus may accuse her 'whole sex' of 'craven timidity' as they seem to have not 'jumped at the appearance of an offer of freedom'.[154] Women are comforted by reassurances that there is 'nothing shameful in not wanting a career, to be intellectually unadventurous is no sin, that taking care of the home and family may be personally "fulfilling" and socially valuable', all of which is perfectly valid, Brophy says, were it not for the fact that such arguments are 'addressed exclusively to women' and, as such, constitute 'anti-woman prejudice revamped'.[155] Three years later in "Women: The Longest Revolution', Juliet Mitchell writes: 'Like woman herself, the family appears as a natural object, but it is actually a cultural creation [. . .] It is the function of ideology to present these given social types as aspects of Nature itself'.[156] Brophy's views, then, are close to Mitchell's on the ways in which biology has been used as the tool of patriarchal ideology, concluding that society has 'contrived to terrorise women' with the idea 'that certain attitudes and behaviours are "unwomanly" and "unnatural"'.[157] These words also resonate with those of other-prominent feminist thinkers, such as Kate Millet, who argues at length in *Sexual Politics* that patriarchy maintains the most 'tenacious or powerful hold through its successful habit of passing itself off as nature [. . .] When a system of power is thoroughly in command, it has scarcely need to speak itself aloud'.[158]

And yet, Brophy continued to hedge over any identification of herself as a feminist: 'What is a feminist?', she asks Leslie Dock:

> I mean there are many women writers that I admire and I certainly admire any woman who gets on with the job as though she were not a woman. I may have a very slight dislike for, and contempt for, women who make a profession out of being women.[159]

In this interview she mischievously compares feminists to Frenchmen who live in England and

> make a profession out of being Frenchmen [. . .] Perhaps I have the feeling that, if one has no subject matter except feminism, then one is trading on nothing, as though one were to make a career out of proclaiming that grass is green.[160]

Brophy wrote this in the mid-1980s, a time when second-wave feminism was at its height. For Brophy, in this context, to talk of feminists as 'trading on nothing' might sound, to our contemporary sensibilities, distinctly un-feminist; the position becomes more complicated still when she later states in the same interview that she does, in fact, consider herself to be a feminist but one of her own definition. She believed, she said, in women leading by example rather than by any kind of consciousness raising or, worse, didacticism:

> I basically think that the point of Women's Lib is better made by having more Jane Austens and George Eliots, and high-powered civil servants and so on, than by constantly reiterating a truism when you have nothing else to say.[161]

Brophy's rebellious attitudes towards feminism might be compared to Angela Carter's libertarian take on sexual politics in *The Sadeian Woman and the Ideology of Pornography* (1979).[162] Both Brophy and Carter reacted against the Anglo-American feminist aversion to both psychoanalysis and pornography; the latter an important register of broader ideas of social liberty for Brophy.[163] Carter viewed pornography as useful for women insofar as it allowed them to examine femininity as a set of mythologies equally reviled and revered, and to explore 'their own complicity with the fictional representations of themselves as mythic archetypes'.[164] Like Carter, Brophy was in 'the demythologizing business',[165] and her creative work articulates this: 'I feel that mythology is a denial of imagination which I think one has to counter'.[166] Actively desiring subjects, women in Brophy's fiction defy the old myths of female sexuality. In political, intellectual and aesthetic matters, Brigid Brophy was, then, something of a life-long *refusenik*, preferring, just like her much-loved Aubrey Beardsley, to keep 'a foot in either camp – a foot wearing, moreover, a kinky boot'.[167] Brophy's 'kinkiness' was regarded as somehow 'catching' by the conservative British press. In the *Daily Telegraph*'s obituary of Brophy's husband, Sir Michael Levey, there is the implication that Brophy's political views on 'humanism, animal rights, feminism, pornography, homosexual rights, the Vietnam War and religious education in schools (she disapproved of only the last two)' were not only subversive but actually contagiously so – they 'rubbed off on her husband', transmitting themselves sartorially in his adoption of 'loud roll-neck sweaters, black shirts with gingham collars and cuffs, and black velour caps'. He seemed, then, to have 'caught' his wife's perversity when he declared in 1966: '"I'd really rather be dissolute and sexy than respectable"'.[168]

Notes

1. George Stade and Karen Karbiener (eds), *Encyclopedia of British Writers: 1800 to the Present*, 2nd edn, 2 vols (London: Eurospan, 2005–9), pp. 78–9.

2. Terry Castle, sleeve notes, Brigid Brophy, *The King of a Rainy Country* (London: Coelacanth Press, 2012).
3. Brophy, *The Burglar* (London: Cape, 1968), p. 11.
4. S. J. Newman, 'Brigid Brophy', in Jay L. Halio (ed.), *British Novelists Since 1960: Part 1, A–G, Dictionary of Literary Biography*, XIV (Detroit: Gale Research, 1983), pp. 137–8 (p. 138).
5. Brophy, *Burglar*, p. 29.
6. Letter in Christine Brooke-Rose Papers 1893–2005, MS-00532, Harry Ransom Research Center, University of Texas at Austin.
7. Kate Levey, 'Mr. and Mrs. Michael Levey', *Contemporary Women's Writing*, 12: 2 (2018), pp. 142–51 (p. 143).
8. Giles Gordon, 'Obituary: Brigid Brophy', *Independent*, 8 August 1995 <http://www.independent.co.uk/news/people/obituary-brigid-brophy-1595286.html> (accessed 20 April 2019).
9. Christine Brooke-Rose, 'Introduction', in Brophy, *In Transit: An Heroi-Cyclic Novel* (Dalkey Archive Press, 2002), pp. i–vii.
10. Shena Mackay, 'Brigid Brophy: A Short Appreciation', *Contemporary Women's Writing*, 12: 2 (2018), pp. 264–7 (p. 264).
11. Brophy, *Burglar*, p. 10.
12. Irma Kurtz, 'Who's Afraid of Brigid Brophy?', in Brooke-Rose, Correspondence (literary), 2001–2003, Christine Brooke-Rose Papers 1893–2005, MS-00532, Harry Ransom Research Center, University of Texas at Austin (hereafter, HRC), p. 82.
13. Steven Moore, 'Brigid Brophy: An Introduction and Checklist', *Review of Contemporary Fiction*, 15: 3 (1995), pp. 7–11.
14. See Eveline Kilian, 'Discourse Ethics and the Subversion of Gender Norms in Brigid Brophy's *In Transit*', in Susana Onega and Jean-Michel Ganteau (eds), *The Ethical Component in Experimental British Fiction Since the 1960's* (Newcastle: Cambridge Scholars, 2007), pp. 31–49.
15. Jean-Michel Ganteau, 'In Thy Autonomy is Thy Commitment: Brigid Brophy's *In Transit*', in Jean-Michel Ganteau and Christine Reynier (eds), *Autonomy and Commitment in Twentieth-Century British Literature* (Montpellier: Presses Universitaires de la Méditerranée, 2010), pp. 191–202.
16. Leslie Ann Dock, 'Brigid Brophy: Author in the Baroque' (unpublished doctoral thesis, 1977); Sheryl Stevenson, 'The Never-Last Word: Parody, Ideology, and the Open Work' (doctoral thesis, University of Maryland, 1986).
17. Joseph Darlington, 'Introduction', in Christine Brooke-Rose, *The Dear Deceit* (Great Britain and Glentrees, Singapore: Verbivoracious Press, 2014).
18. Brophy, *The Snow Ball* (London: Faber and Faber, 2013); *Flesh* (London: Faber and Faber, 2013).
19. Susan Sontag, 'Notes on "Camp"', *Partisan Review*, 31: 4 (1964), pp. 515–30.
20. Brophy, *Prancing Novelist: A Defence of Fiction in the Form of a Critical Biography in Praise of Ronald Firbank* (London: Macmillan 1973).
21. David Vichnar, 'The Avant-Postman: James Joyce, the Avant-Garde and Postmodernism' (thesis, Université de la Sorbonne Nouvelle, 2013)

22. Karen R. Lawrence (ed.), 'In Transit: From James Joyce to Brigid Brophy', in Karen R. Lawrence (ed.), *Transcultural Joyce* (Cambridge: Cambridge University Press, 1998), pp. 37–45; 'Postmodern "Vessels of Conception": Brooke-Rose and Brigid Brophy', in *Penelope Voyages: Women and Travel in the British Literary Tradition* (Ithaca, NY: Cornell University Press, 1994), pp. 207–36. See also her *Transcultural Joyce* (1998).
23. Iris Murdoch, *Living on Paper: Letters from Iris Murdoch 1934–1995*, ed. Avril Horner and Ann Rowe (London: Chatto & Windus, 2015).
24. Ibid., p. 169.
25. Ibid., p. 215.
26. Brophy, *Baroque-'n'-Roll and Other Essays* (London: Hamish Hamilton, 1987).
27. Sarah Lyall, 'Brigid Brophy is Dead at 66: Novelist, Critic and Crusader', *New York Times*, 9 August 1995, p. 20 <http://www.nytimes.com/1995/08/09/obituaries/brigid-brophy-is-dead-at-66-novelist-critic-and-crusader.html> (accessed 23 April 2019).
28. Colin MacCabe, *James Joyce and the Revolution of the Word* (London: Palgrave, 1979), p. 15.
29. Brophy, 'James Joyce and the Reader's Understanding', *London Review of Books*, 2: 3 (21 February 1980), pp. 8–9 <http://www.lrb.co.uk/v02/n03/brigid-brophy/james-joyce-and-the-readers-understanding> (accessed 20 April 2019).
30. Ibid.
31. Quoting Ian Hamilton, Jennifer Hodgson, 'Afterword', in Brophy, *The King of a Rainy Country* (London: Coelacanth Press, 2012), pp. 269–73 (p. 269).
32. Enright, 'Writer's Fancy', pp. 15–16.
33. Clara Claiborne Park, 'Book World', *Washington Post*, 18 August 1974.
34. Mary Warnock, 'A Hard Time for Satire', *The Listener*, 6 December 1973, pp. 785–6.
35. See David James (ed.), *The Legacies of Modernism: Historicising Postwar and Contemporary Fiction* (Cambridge: Cambridge University Press, 2012); Martin Ryle and Julia Jordan (eds), *B. S. Johnson and Postwar Literature: Possibilities of the Avant-Garde* (London: Palgrave, 2014); Philip Tew, *The Contemporary British Novel* (London: Continuum, 2004); Sebastian Groes, *British Fiction of the Sixties: The Making of the Swinging Decade* (London: Bloomsbury, 2016); Andrzej Gąsiorek, *Post-War British Fiction: Realism and After* (London: Edward Arnold, 1995).
36. Brophy, *In Transit: An Heroi-Cyclic Novel* (London: Macdonald, 1969), p. 35.
37. Brophy, 'Am I an Irishwoman?', in Brophy, *Don't Never Forget: Collected Views and Reviews* (New York: Holt, Rinehart and Winston, 1966), pp. 315–19 (p. 317). Originally published in *New Statesman*, 5 November 1965 <https://www.newstatesman.com/node/165463> (accessed 21 April 2019).
38. Brophy, 'James Joyce'.
39. Kurtz, 'Who's Afraid?', p. 82.

40. Brophy, *King*, p. 11.
41. Levey, 'Mr. and Mrs.', pp. 149–50.
42. Ibid., p. 150.
43. Brophy, *The Crown Princess and Other Stories* (London: Collins, 1953); *Hackenfeller's Ape* (London: Virago, 1991).
44. Brophy, interview with Leslie Dock, *Contemporary Literature*, 17: 2 (1976), pp. 151–70 (p. 155).
45. Nicola Humble, *The Feminine Middlebrow Novel, 1920s to 1950s: Class, Domesticity, and Bohemianism* (Oxford: Oxford University Press, 2001), p. 11.
46. *The Finishing Touch* (London: Secker & Warburg, 1963); *The Adventure of God in His Search for the Black Girl* (London: Macmillan, 1973); *The Pussy Owl* (London: BBC Books, 1976); *Palace without Chairs* (London: Hamilton, 1978); *The Prince and the Wild Geese* (London: Hamilton, 1983).
47. Brophy, *Mozart the Dramatist: A New View of Mozart, His Operas and His Age* (London: Faber, 1964); *Black and White: A Portrait of Aubrey Beardsley* (London: Jonathan Cape, 1968); *Beardsley and His World* (New York: Harmony Books, 1976); 'Foreword', in Elizabeth Smart, *By Grand Central Station I Sat Down and Wept* (London: Panther, 1966); 'Introduction', in Jane Austen, *Pride and Prejudice* (London: Pan Books, 1967).
48. Brophy, interview with Dock, p. 159.
49. On Brophy and speciesism, see Robert McKay, 'Brigid Brophy's Pro-Animal Forms', *Contemporary Women's Writing*, 12: 2 (2018), pp. 152–70 (p. 159).
50. Brophy, Michael Levey and Charles Osbourne, *Fifty Works of English and American Literature That We Could Do Without* (Rapp and Carroll: London, 1967), p. 64.
51. Brophy, interview with Dock, p. 157.
52. Brophy, 'The Nation in the Iron Mask', in *Don't Never Forget*, pp. 50–7, originally a talk for BBC Radio, 1963; 'The Waste-Disposal Unit', in *Best Short Plays of the World Theatre, 1958–67* (New York: Crown, 1968). The Dalkey Archive Press has kept *In Transit* in print and reissued *Prancing Novelist* in 2016. In 2013, in the series Faber Finds, Faber and Faber reissued *Flesh*, *The Finishing Touch*, *The Snow Ball*, *The Adventures of God in His Search for the Black Girl*, *Mozart the Dramatist*, *Black and White* and *Beardsley and His World*.
53. Terry Castle, sleeve notes, Brophy, *King*.
54. Deborah Philips, *Women's Fiction: From 1945 to Today: Writing Romance* (London: Continuum, 2006), p. 1.
55. *The Snow Ball* was produced as a television drama as part of BBC One's Wednesday Play Series, which ran from 1964 to 1970.
56. Michael Caines, Blog, *Times Literary Supplement*, 15 May 2015 <http.timescolumns.typepad.com/stothard/2015/05/rediscovering-brigid-brophy> (accessed 20 April 2019).
57. Brophy, *Burglar*, p. 30.
58. Ibid., p. 29–30.
59. Brophy, interview with Dock, p. 159.

60. Brophy, *Burglar*, p. 29.
61. Ibid., p. 29.
62. Chris Hopkins, 'The Neglect of Brigid Brophy', *Review of Contemporary Fiction*, 15: 3 (1995), pp. 12–17 (pp. 14, 16).
63. Ibid., p. 14.
64. Brophy, *Black and White*, pp. 28, 38.
65. McKay, 'Pro-Animal Forms', p. 160.
66. Brophy and Maureen Duffy, unpublished manifesto and catalogue, in Brigid Brophy Papers, Kate Levey private collection. Cited in McKay, 'Pro-Animal Forms', p. 160.
67. Brophy, *Prancing Novelist*, p. 76.
68. Ibid., p. 67.
69. Ibid., p. 80. See Sam Reese, 'Renaissance Women: Brigid Brophy, Mary McCarthy, and the Public Intellectual', *Contemporary Women's Writing* 12: 2 (2018), pp. 207–21.
70. Brophy, *Don't Never Forget*, p. 183. A review of Dorothy Brewster, *Virginia Woolf's London* (London: George Allen & Unwin, 1959).
71. Ibid., p. 183.
72. Ali Smith, sleeve notes, *King*.
73. Brophy, 'The Immorality of Marriage', in *Don't Never Forget*, pp. 22–7 (p. 26).
74. Ibid., p. 23.
75. Ibid., p. 39.
76. Brophy, *King*, p. 11. Subsequent page references will be given in the text in parentheses.
77. Teresa de Lauretis, 'Queer Theory: Lesbian and Gay Sexualities, an Introduction', *differences: A Journal of Feminist Cultural Studies*, 3: 2 (1991), pp. iii–xviii (p. iv).
78. The Wolfenden Committee Report decriminalised homosexuality between consenting adults, replacing the 1885 Labouchère Amendment. It led to the Sexual Offences Act of 1967.
79. David Halperin, *Saint Foucault: Towards a Gay Hagiography* (Oxford: Oxford University Press, 1995), p. 62.
80. Lee Edelman, *No Future: Queer Theory and the Death Drive* (Durham NC: Duke University Press, 2004), p. 17.
81. Teresa de Lauretis, 'Queer Theory', p. iv. See also Eve Kosofsky Sedgwick, *Epistemology of the Closet* (Berkeley: University of California Press, 1990); Lauren Berlant and Michael Warner, 'Sex in Public', *Critical Inquiry*, 24: 2 (1998), pp. 547–66; Heather Love, *Feeling Backward: Loss and the Politics of Queer History* (Cambridge MA: Harvard University Press, 2007).
82. Guy Hocquenghem, *Homosexual Desire*, trans. Daniella Dangoor (Durham NC: Duke University Press, 1993), pp. 49–50.
83. As, for example, the fate of the lead in the play *The Killing of Sister George*, first shown in 1965 later made into a popular 'lesbian' film. See Kelly Hankin, 'Lesbian Locations: The Production of Lesbian Bar Space in "The Killing of Sister George"', *Cinema Journal*, 41: 1 (2001), pp. 3–27.
84. Patricia Juliana Smith, 'Desperately Seeking Susan(na): Closeted Quests and Mozartean Gender Bending in Brigid Brophy's *The King of a Rainy*

Country', *Review of Contemporary Fiction*, 15: 3 (1995), pp. 23–31 (p. 30).
85. Ali Smith, sleeve notes, Brophy, *King*.
86. Sheila Rowbotham, *Promise of a Dream: Remembering the Sixties* (London: Allen Lane, 2000), p. 116.
87. Brophy, *Burglar*, pp. 29–30.
88. Cited in Hodgson, 'Introduction', in Brophy, *King*, p. xv.
89. Smith, 'Desperately Seeking', p. 23.
90. Brophy, *Flesh*, p. 46.
91. Murdoch, *Living on Paper*, pp. 222–3.
92. Anon., 9 November 1962, *Times Literary Supplement*.
93. Nicholas Monsarrat, 'Review of *Flesh*', *New York Times Book Review*, 2 June 1963.
94. Patricia Waugh, *Harvest of the Sixties: English Literature and Its Background, 1960 to 1990* (Oxford: Oxford University Press, 1995), p. 189.
95. Brophy, *Flesh*, p. 38. Hereafter page numbers are included in the text in parentheses.
96. Richard T. Kelly, 'The exquisite sentences of "Flesh" and "The Finishing Touch" by Brigid Brophy', Faber, 29 August 2013 <https://www.faber.co.uk/blog/out-now-the-exquisite-sentences-of-flesh-and-the-finishing-touch-by-brigid-brophy> (accessed 20 April 2019).
97. Richard T. Kelly, 'Introduction', in Brophy, *Flesh*, p. 1.
98. Brophy, interview with Dock, p. 159.
99. Eve Kosovsky Sedgwick, *Tendencies* (Durham, NC: Duke University Press, 1993), p. 8.
100. Brophy, interview with Dock, p. 159.
101. Brophy, *Black and White*, p. 38.
102. Ibid., p. 42.
103. Ibid., p. 38.
104. Brophy, *Don't Never Forget*, p. 22.
105. Ibid., p. 302.
106. Ibid., p. 303.
107. Hélène Cixous, 'The Laugh of the Medusa', trans. Keith Cohen and Paula Cohen, *Signs*, 1: 4 (1976), pp. 875–93 (p. 880).
108. Ibid., p. 880.
109. Janet Wolff, 'Eddie Cochran, Donna Anna and the Dark Sister', in Janet Wolff, *Resident Alien: Feminist Cultural Criticism* (New Haven, CT: Yale University Press, 1995), pp. 23–40 (pp. 30–1).
110. There is a repeated colour patterning of luxurious black and white in the novel reminiscent of Beardsley's sketches on which Brophy wrote in *Black and White: A Portrait of Aubrey Beardsley*.
111. As mentioned the novel was adapted as a play for the BBC's Wednesday Play series, which included Nell Dunn's *Up the Junction* (1965), Jeremy Sandford's *Cathy Come Home* (1965) and Peter Watkins's *The War Game* (1965).
112. Eve Auchincloss, 'Bad Characters', *New York Times Review of Books*, 24 September 1964.
113. Brophy, *Snow Ball*, p. 171. Subsequent page references are given in the text in parentheses.

114. Sam Abel, *Opera in the Flesh: Sexuality in Operatic Performance* (Boulder, CO: Westview Press, 1996), pp. 11–12.
115. Corinne E. Blackmer and Patricia Juliana Smith (eds), *En Travesti: Women, Gender Subversion, Opera* (New York: Columbia University Press, 1995), p. 6.
116. On masquerade in eighteenth-century literature, see Terry Castle, 'The Carnivalization of Eighteenth-Century English Narrative,' *PMLA*, 99: 5 (1984), pp. 903–16 (p. 907).
117. Enright, 'Writer's Fancy', p. 15.
118. Israel Shenker, 'Brigid Brophy Puns in Response to Questionnaire', *New York Times*, 27 February 1970, p. 28 <https://www.nytimes.com/1970/02/27/archives/brigid-brophy-puns-in-response-to-questionnaire.html> (accessed 10 April 2019).
119. Brophy, interview with Dock, p. 167.
120. Shena Mackay, 'Brigid Brophy: A Short Appreciation', *Contemporary Women's Writing*, 12: 2 (2018), pp. 264–7 (p. 265).
121. John Lucas, 'The Sixties: Realism and Experiment', in Laura Marcus and Peter Nicholls (eds), *The Cambridge History of Twentieth-Century English Literature* (Cambridge: Cambridge: University Press, 2004), pp. 545–62 (p. 545).
122. Annegret Maack, 'Concordia Discors: Brigid Brophy's *In Transit*,' *Review of Contemporary Fiction*, 15.3 (1995), pp. 40–5 (p. 41).
123. Magali Cornier Michael, *Feminism and the Postmodern Impulse: Post-World War II Fiction* (Albany: State University of New York Press, 1996), p. 30.
124. Brian McHale, '"I draw the line as a rule between one solar system and another": The Postmodernism(s) of Christine Brooke-Rose', in Ellen J. Friedman and Richard Martin (eds), *Utterly Other Discourse: The Texts of Christine Brooke-Rose* (Chicago and Normal, IL: Dalkey Archive Press, 1995), pp. 192–213 (p. 197).
125. Brian McHale, *Postmodernist Fiction* (London: Methuen, 1987), p. 173.
126. On the challenges of translating gender pronouns in *In Transit*, see Ina Schabert, 'Translation Trouble: Gender Indeterminacy in English Novels and Their French Versions', *Translation and Literature*, 19: 1 (2010) pp. 72–92.
127. Sonya Andermahr, 'Both/And Aesthetics: Gender, Art, and Language in Brigid Brophy's *In Transit* and Ali Smith's *How to Be Both*', *Contemporary Women's Writing*, 12: 2 (2018), pp. 248–63 (p. 255).
128. Virginia Woolf, *Orlando: A Biography* (New York: Harcourt Brace Jovanovich, 1928), p. 138.
129. Judith Butler, *Gender Trouble* (New York: Routledge, 1990).
130. Robert Phelps, review of *In Transit*, *Life*, 13 February 1970, p. 10.
131. Patricia Waugh, 'The Woman Writer and the Continuities of Feminism', in James F. English (ed.), *A Concise Companion to Contemporary British Fiction* (Oxford: Blackwell, 2006), pp. 188–209 (pp. 192–3).
132. Brophy, 'A Woman's Place', *Enquiry*, BBC Two, 27 January 1965 <http://www.bbc.co.uk/archive/marriage/10510.shtml> (accessed 20 April 2019).
133. Brophy, 'Women', in *Don't Never Forget*, pp. 38–45 (p. 43).
134. Brophy, 'Reviews', *Times Literary Supplement*, 19 July 1985. Cited in

Janet Todd, *Feminist Literary History* (Cambridge: Polity Press, 1988), p. 12.
135. Kelly, 'Exquisite Sentences'.
136. Vicki K. Janik, Del Ivan Janik and Emmanuel S. Nelson (eds), *Modern British Women: An A–Z Guide* (London: Greenwood Press, 2002), p. 47.
137. Christopher Fowler, 'Invisible Ink No 245: Brigid Brophy', *The Independent*, 12 October 2014 <https://www.independent.co.uk/arts-entertainment/books/reviews/invisible-ink-no-245-brigid-brophy-9787629.html> (accessed 20 April 2019).
138. Groes, *British Fiction*, pp. 58, 68.
139. Todd, *Feminist Literary History*, p. 11.
140. Brophy, 'He/She/Hesh', in *Baroque-'n'-Roll*, pp. 61–7.
141. Casey Miller and Kate Swift, *The Handbook of Non-Sexist Writing for Writers, Editors and Speakers* (London: Women's Press, 1981), p. 4.
142. Simone de Beauvoir, *The Second Sex*, trans. H. M. Parshley (London: Vintage, 1997); Betty Friedan, *The Feminine Mystique* (New York: W. W. Norton, 1963); Dale Spender, *Man Made Language* (London: Routledge & Kegan Paul, 1980).
143. Kate Millett, *Sexual Politics* (New York: Columbia University Press, 1970), p. 23.
144. Brophy, 'He/She/Hesh', p. 65.
145. Ibid., pp. 61–7.
146. Miller and Swift, *Handbook*, p. 4; Brophy, 'He/She/Hesh', p. 63.
147. Brophy, 'He/She/Hesh', p. 63.
148. Ibid., p. 64. See also Sara Ahmed, *The Promise of Happiness* (London: Duke University Press, 2010).
149. Brophy, 'He/She/Hesh', p. 62.
150. Brophy, 'The One-Eyed World of Germaine Greer', *London Review of Books*, 1: 3 (22 November 1979), pp. 1–3 (p. 2) <https://www.lrb.co.uk/v01/n03/brigid-brophy/the-one-eyed-world-of-germaine-greer> (accessed 20 April 2019).
151. Colin MacCabe, *James Joyce and the Revolution of the Word* (London: Palgrave, 1979); Brophy, 'James Joyce', pp. 8–9.
152. Brophy, 'Women', in *Don't Never Forget*, p. 38.
153. Ibid., p. 38.
154. Ibid., p. 39.
155. Ibid., pp. 39–40.
156. Juliet Mitchell, 'Women: The Longest Revolution', *New Left Review*, 40 (November–December 1966), pp. 11–37 (p. 11).
157. 'Women', in *Don't Never Forget*, p. 43.
158. Millett, *Sexual Politics*, p. 58.
159. Brophy, interview with Dock, p. 164.
160. Ibid., p. 164.
161. Ibid., p. 164.
162. Angela Carter, *The Sadeian Woman: and the Ideology of Pornography* (London: Virago, 1979).
163. Frank Pakenham, Earl of Longford, *Pornography: The Longford Report* (London: Coronet Press, 1972). In *The Longford Threat to Freedom* (London: National Secular Society, 1972) Brophy responds: 'For most

people pornography does them no large harm and no large good either, they move on to types of books or films that are less repetitive and predictable'.
164. See Sally Keenan, 'Angela Carter's *The Sadeian Woman*: Feminism as Treason', in Joseph Bristow and Trey Lynn Broughton (eds), *The Infernal Desires of Angela Carter: Fiction, Femininity, Feminism* (London: Longman, 1997), pp. 132–48 (p. 138).
165. Angela Carter, 'Notes from the Frontline', in Michelene Wandor (ed.), *On Gender and Writing* (London: Pandora Press, 1983), pp. 66–77 (p. 71).
166. Brophy, interview with Dock, p. 159.
167. Brophy, *Black and White*, p. 32.
168. Anon., 'Sir Michael Levey', *The Telegraph*, 29 December 2008 <http://www.telegraph.co.uk /news/obituaries/4015722/Sir-Michael-Levey.html> (accessed 18 April 2018).

Chapter 4

Christine Brooke-Rose: 'un écrivain dite éxperimentale'

> If one happens to be both a woman and an experimenter, one's work tends to be regarded suspiciously as a doubly different genre, not quite relevant.
> (Christine Brooke-Rose, 'A Writer's Constraints', p. 41)

Writing and/as *dépaysement*

From her early bilingual childhood, Christine Brooke-Rose had an interest in the workings of language, especially in what Ali Smith has called the 'physical mechanics of grammar'.[1] In her first critical work, *A Grammar of Metaphor* (1958) derived in large part from her doctoral thesis she demonstrates the development of this interest showing much of the technical and intellectual dexterity that will prevail in her later writing, both critical and creative.[2] In an interview in 1976, she comments on her lifelong interest in language and metaphor:

> Language is capable of far more subtle ways of metaphoric expression then the stock grammatical ways [. . .] You use the same phrase in a new context and embedded in that new context it acquires a completely different meaning [. . .] what interests me particularly, is the fusion of different discourses.[3]

This interest in the poetic possibilities of language as an almost infinite series of permutations is apparent in all her novels and originates from her early experiences of multilingualism where language is always poised on the boundaries of defamiliarisation as the speaker switches from one system to another, remaining constantly vigilant to the internal rules governing utterance. This vigilance produced in Brooke-Rose a low-level sense of displacement from the comforts of a single native language and culture, and she once remarked how 'unenglish' she had always felt.[4] As Sarah Birch writes, this sense of un-rootedness, what in French is called *dépaysement*, from one linguistic system results in a constant linguistic and cultural locomotion whereby she experienced 'the prismatic effect of viewing one field of knowledge, one language, or one culture through the discursive lens of another'.[5] This sense of outsiderness is unmistakable in much of her personal correspondence. In England, she recalls: 'I used to feel and be made to feel completely out, a mad Francophile [...] I've never wanted to belong to a literary group or a political group'.[6] In Paris, she felt similarly 'out', kept her distance from the Marxist and feminist ferment: 'I didn't join the French literary movements because they were even worse'.[7] She was, as Heather Reyes observes, 'always just outside, an exile both from her own country [...] and from her adopted one, as well as from the theoretical groups with which she has much in common but to which she doesn't quite belong'.[8]

Being labelled as an experimental writer was, for the most part, rather irksome for Brooke-Rose. Generally used imprecisely, the term 'experimental' gestured, she thought, only vaguely to some Joycean idea of wordplay, stream of consciousness or typographic innovation *à la* Apollinaire. She always insisted on a more precise definition of her experimentalism:

> I've had to suffer from this all my career [...] without ever even a brief examination of what I do, so that I get bracketed with, say, Joyce (in praise or blame) simply as experimenter though I'm doing exactly the opposite [...] I want to ask that question: what IS experiment? In what ways do Brigid's experiment differ (from mine – optional) from others, at the time or since. Her main narrative for instance is still in the traditional past tense, unlike the Nouveau Roman or mine.[9]

Her own type of experimentalism was varied and diverse but she still believed in the representative function of language. As her friend, Mike Freeman, wrote to her – 'your formalist non-mimesis is at heart deeply mimetic – i.e. your forms are the most effective way of representing the reality of the world, society, forms of consciousness and culture that we inhabit'.[10] Brooke-Rose was adamant about keeping 'Life', what she called 'the stuff of novels', firmly attached to the art of her writing:

> Life can be made quite, quite dead without craftsmanship, and oh dear, that now taboo three-letter word, art, in other words vison, passion, and a controlling intelligence. Mere life is never enough, any more than mere craft is, because in the end what matters is the quality of the author's mind and personality.

In this review, she is responding to 'Mr Kinsgsley' (Amis) who had declared that a 'writer should not be seen '"doing his stuff"'. Conceding that modernism was a 'healthy and very necessary reaction against mandarin apocalyptese and other dead ends – a reaction which has to be made every generation or so', Amis went on to complain that too many 'imitators' of modernist experimentation 'took that as a licence to write sloppily or flatly'.[11]

A writer who minded little being seen 'doing her stuff', Brooke-Rose's writing was anything but sloppy or flat. A writer, critic and an academic, she spent her life engaged in meticulously exploring the possibilities of language and textuality; she was, as Lorna Sage says, a 'word' and 'writing addict'.[12] Always interested in how language might communicate the fragilities of what she called the 'corpus crisis' of the human condition,[13] her 'discovery of literary theory was important: 'Theory has released an immense hidden strength in me, but it has also made writing more and more difficult, because more and more demanding'.[14] Of all the writers considered in this book, Brooke-Rose provides us with the most systematic account of the rise of 'theory' in the latter half of the twentieth century. She describes how when she came to Paris to teach at Vincennes in 1968, she immediately 'plunged into Lacan's *Écrits*', and then even 'more enthusiastically still into Derrida['s]' *Écriture et la différence* (1967) and *De la Grammatologie* (1967).[15] For Brooke-Rose, theory helped her understand her own writing practices as a novelist: 'the novel's task [. . .] is to stretch our intellectual, spiritual, and imaginative horizons to breaking point'.[16] One of her best critics, Karen Lawrence, takes this further, saying, 'Her novels produce significant experiments in writing and theorizing the novel tradition that fictionally "diagnose" the unreality of twentieth-century life, the conditions that much contemporary theory seeks to analyze and demystify'.[17]

Crucially, Brooke-Rose did not insist on an impassable divide between experimentalism and realism: 'I have nothing against realism [. . .] Even the most experimental, postmodern writer is still basically realistic. They may not be "imitating" reality, in the sense of reproducing a familiar situation, but ultimately they're representing something'.[18] In this respect, then, she agreed with one of Robbe-Grillet's assertions in *For a New Novel: Essays on Fiction* (1965): 'All writers believe they are realists. None ever calls himself abstract, illusionistic, chimerical, fantastic, falsitical'.[19] However, any kind of novelistic technique, including realism, must evolve: 'People can go on writing', she noted,

> the nineteenth-century novel until the year 2000 if they want, but that won't alter the fact it's dead, and that you are simply pouring into old forms a reality that has completely changed. We now have to evolve new forms to suit this new reality.[20]

For Robbe-Grillet, a contemporary writer she admired, this process involved a degree of perspectival and temporal simultaneity, as

Brooke-Rose notes of his writing: 'We are made to see, creator-like, the same objects in different time-scales [. . .] in two or three different process perspectives simultaneously'.[21] Influenced in part by the experiments of Robbe-Grillet, Nathalie Sarraute, OULIPO as well as Samuel Beckett, Brooke-Rose produced a substantial body of work. This chapter considers two novels written in the 1960s, *Out* (1964) and *Between* (1968), alongside a selection of essays and articles in two collections, *Stories, Theories and Things* (1991), in particular, 'Illiterations', 'A Womb of One's Own', and 'Woman as Semiotic Object', and *Invisible Author: Last Essays* (2002). I use her critical writing as primary texts with an awareness that, in many ways, it functions as a critical commentary on her own creative work.

Life, Attempts at

In her experimental anti-autobiography *Remake* (1996), Brooke-Rose informs the reader that she has had a lifelong prejudice against biographical criticism as it panders to the idea of narrative coherence while disregarding the ways in which the 'interference' of the 'absorbing present' frustrates attempts to grasp the past.[22] Noting the influence of poststructuralism on Brooke-Rose's writing, Ellen Friedman argues that this allows her *oeuvre* resistance to the biographers' queries as 'only the text is germane'.[23] While sympathetic to both objections to biographical criticism, it is possible, as was clear in Chapter 2, that one might consider the life of a writer in ways that do not reduce her work to what Pound calls 'laundry-lists',[24] or a forensic search for what Beckett termed the 'offal of experience'.[25] I think it is productive rather than reductive to take into account the events and circumstances of Brooke-Rose's long writing life – her multilingual and peripatetic childhood; her work in the Women's Auxiliary Air Force (WAAF) as an intelligence officer at Bletchley Park; an undergraduate student in philology and medieval literature at Oxford then a PhD in Middle English and Old French; a career as a jobbing literary journalist; a first marriage to a Polish poet; and in 1968 taking up a prestigious academic job in Paris Vincennes then a long retirement in Provence. *Remake* gently parodies this biographical trajectory:

> the baby in Geneva, the little girl in Chiswick, in Brussels, Folkstone, the young girl in Liverpool, in Thornaby-on-Tees, in Bletchley Park, in Occupied Germany, the student in Oxford, in London, the young wife and writer in Chelsea, the traveller in Spain, Austria, Italy, Eastern Europe, Turkey, the less young wife and writer in Hampstead, the middle-aged professor in Paris,

in New York, in Buffalo, Brandeis, Jerusalem, Geneva, Zurich, the old lady in Provence. (p. 13)

In 1923 on the third floor of rue Lévrier in Geneva, Christine Frances E. Brooke-Rose was born to Alfred Northbrook Rose, who was British, and a Swiss-American mother, Evelyne Blanche Brooke, both of whom would end up, in quite different circumstances, entering religious orders, the former as an Anglican monk, the latter as a Benedictine nun. When she was a child Brooke-Rose's family moved between England, Belgium and Switzerland, and as a result she spoke English, French and German with equal fluency. Whereas Kavan deliberately destroyed her own diaries and letters, Brooke-Rose's literary life is accessible though her archives in the Harry Ransom Humanities Research Center, which houses documents, photographs, reviews, MS holographs, lifelong correspondence that move from pen and ink in the 1940s to typewritten correspondence and notes in the 1960s and 1970s to word-processed scripts in the 1980s and finally, to email printouts in the 1990s.[26] In *Remake*, we learn of her early life as a process of *dépaysement* between London and Europe:

> Once upon a time there was a little girl born in French, of an English father, a Swiss mother, herself of an American father and a Swiss mother. The English father lived in London, the Swiss mother in Geneva. That was the first spilt. It didn't work. What does 'it' refer to? The marriage of course. Back to London. Back to Geneva. Back to London. Back to Brussels. Back to back. Forgetting French, forgetting English, learning Flemish, learning German, forgetting Flemish, relearning English etc. (p. 10)

After her parents separated in 1928, Brooke-Rose and her mother went to live with her maternal grandparents in Brussels then returned to London in 1936. At eighteen, Brooke-Rose joined the WAAF and worked for two years in Liverpool. At the outbreak of war, she was recruited to work at Bletchley Park Code and Cipher School as a 'decipherer' of the 'resulting intelligence' called 'CXMSs or Source' that came out of the codes.[27] This was both her first job, and as she pointed out, a kind of higher education where she witnessed the 'real war, seen from an enemy point of view': 'Einsatzbereitschaftbericht, Einsatzmeldung, Einsatzbefehl, from Keitel to Kesselring, from Kesselring to Rommel [. . .] the otherness of the other learned young'.[28]

After the war, Brooke-Rose won a place at Somerville College, Oxford in 1946 and was awarded her BA in 1949. After a brief failed marriage to Rodney Bax who she met at Bletchley, she married the Polish poet Jerzy Peterkiewicz in 1948 and they lived in London where, at UCL, she wrote a PhD, 'The Use of Metaphor in Some Old French and Middle English Lyrics and Romances'. She then worked as a literary reviewer and journalist during which time she began publishing her own writing. A poetry collection, *Gold*, based on an anonymous fourteenth-century English poem 'Pearl', was published in 1955 and was followed by her first novel, *The Languages of Love*, in 1957. Then, by her own admission, came a 'terrible second one', *The Sycamore Tree*.[29]

Brooke-Rose's experiments with narrative began, albeit tentatively, with her 1960 novel *The Dear Deceit*. Based on her father's life – that of a thief, 'a lying mythomaniac, a cheater' (*Remake*, p. 50) – the novel is mostly realist but noteworthy for a reversal of narrative chronology (it is told backwards), a technique unexceptional today, but innovative enough for its time. *The Middlemen: A Satire* followed in 1961, after which she endured two years of very serious illness that returned her, she said, 'to her essential self' but resulted in the removal of a kidney. During her illness and convalescence, she fell out of her habitual reading practices, describing how she 'couldn't read novels, good or bad, about love-affairs, class-distinctions and one-upmanships'.[30] Her attention now turned from fiction to scientific texts, a move unsurprising perhaps for someone who had worked at Bletchley Park. Finding science books full of 'their own curious poetry', they seemed to act as the bridge between her interests in poetics and non-literary discourses. She was especially drawn to the potential of science fiction as a genre: 'One of the main attractions of science fiction is in its structuring paradox in that it both beautifies and neutralizes our fears of science's dehumanization and displays the inexorable "necessity" of science with the "freedom" of fiction'.[31] Some of this narrative freedom is evident in her first experimental novel *Out* that is both the writing out of sickness and the reversal of the hierarchy of sickness and health.

Her early works *The Languages of Love* and *The Middlemen* are both technically competent if undistinguished novels. The latter is a dissection of the vapidity of the advertising industry: 'We are all middlemen, selling to others something we do not own, something we have not made, something we do not intimately understand'.[32] The critical reception of *The Middlemen* was generally positive, one review noting that the novel contained, 'more than one hidden truth'[33] and Anthony Burgess found it 'crammed with wit and intelligence'.[34] Sarah Birch recognises the influence of Muriel Spark's' 'lightness and wit' in these early works that 'share with Spark's work an effort to integrate intellectual pursuits with questions of self-definition'.[35] A four-page letter from Spark (undated but probably from 1960) comments on a draft of *The Middlemen* that Brooke-Rose had sent her. Spark describes the novel, 'as a smashing success' and that she is 'full of admiration' for a book 'packed with latent hysteria'. The novel is 'as obsessive as Robbe-Grillet but not leading into a circular nowhere like his "Jealousy"':

> This is your most serious book in my opinion, for it compels discussion outside the literary consideration of form and style [...] Every book should have a beginning, a middle and an end, and I believe you have done a true English Satire about a society concerned with middles and neglectful of beginnings and ends in their working lives.[36]

Another reviewer was not so kind however, saying it was a 'stylish' novel but finally one about 'shooting deadish ducks'.[37] Later, Brooke-Rose expressed similar 'disappointment' with all her early work, 'easy satires and conventional', but conceded that *The Dear Deceit* was already beginning to 'experiment with the reader's expectations',[38] and was 'written backwards', she later noted with not a little pleasure, 'long before the Amis arrow'.[39]

'"But don't you think, Miss Grampion," said the professor beyond the long, wide table, "that palatal dipthongisation in fourteenth century Kentish may have been optional?"' Thus begins Brooke-Rose's first novel, *The Languages of Love*.[40] With some light 'plotty' action that occurs in a recognisable social context with dialogue that, while arch in its intellectual *badinage,* this novel is nonetheless sufficiently well-ordered to pass as a mostly realist novel and shows some of the gentler irony of Brophy's tale of a bright young postgraduate woman in *The King of a Rainy Country* (1956). Later, described by a reviewer in 1971 as a 'delightful' novel that is 'unconventional in theme', *The Languages of Love* was 'intelligent entertainment' written in a 'tolerably conventional style' in which, unlike her later work, each 'sentence' is 'understandable, with normal grammar rules of grammar and punctuation'.[41] Reading *The Languages of Love* alongside *The Dear Deceit*, both of which Lorna Sage called 'understated anti-novels', the germination of Brooke-Rose's preoccupations with form are perceivable.[42] The impulse behind the second phase of Brooke-Rose's writing after 1964 is evident from a letter in which she admits her intense dislike of Iris Murdoch's writing style (not unlike, as we have seen, Brophy's own feelings):

> She's an example of everything I've struggled against, i.e. keeping very archaic narrative forms but getting praise for 'original' content (which soon ceases to be original if it doesn't affect the form, eg [sic] novels about, say, football, or the working class, or ex-colonials, etc, etc). Of course the content was not of that kind, it was rather of a metaphysic magical kind, but the same applies, professionally: it didn't interest me if she went on writing sentences like 'she thought, her heart sinking a little' and such. I've written about this so-called narrator's vice (in fact perpetual author-comment).[43]

As is evident from this letter, even in her personal correspondence, Brooke-Rose was an exacting critic who possessed an uncommonly wide-ranging understanding of literary criticism that included a comprehensive historical knowledge of literature from medieval French to contemporary writing and literary theory. From her teaching post at Vincennes, Brooke-Rose could see that just over the English Channel there was an ignorance of the emergence of 'theory' in France – she called this the 'international "university" gap [. . .] few wanting to know what was going on or had gone on elsewhere'.[44] In a lengthy review, 'The Nouveau Roman', she elaborates on this:

> we do not, in Britain, go in much for 'movements', 'school', and 'philosophies'. We do not have an existentialist novel or a phenomenological novel or a structuralist novel, or even, really, a Marxist novel. Our tradition is an empirical one of trial and error. What we do have is a handful of talented individuals who each do something different, without theories almost.[45]

As noted, Brooke-Rose wanted her novels to push the reader to 'breaking point',[46] and what fascinated her was 'the desire nay the absolute need to transgress all the forms of the carefully built model'.[47] This transgression, though, countenanced no allegiance to one school or movement, thus she resolutely refused to be part of any group, even narratology, with whom she had some sympathy but finally, could not cope with 'narrative and its complexities'.[48] Her broad critical palate is noted in a review of *Stories, Theories and Things*, where David Seed says 'one of Brooke-Rose's most engaging characteristics as a critic was her ability to avoid many of the pitfalls of continental theorists such as dogmatic generalization and a tendency towards abstraction'.[49] She is able to discern how narrative and rhetorical devices work, and shows in her own writing how to put into practice her dictum, 'to transgress intelligently one must know the rule'.[50]

Brooke-Rose did not join the feminists in Paris and, as we shall see presently, her attitude to feminism as a literary-theoretical movement was, initially at least, one of thoroughgoing scepticism. She objected in particular to Anglo-American feminism's apparent return to character analysis and plot summary that exemplified an approach to literature that acted 'as if nothing had happened from the pre-Twenties on except perhaps the Freudian and Marxist schools, with a bit of Nietzsche or Benjamin or what have you thrown in'. One reviewer of Brooke-Rose's *Stories, Theories and Things* notes her obvious scepticism towards feminism, observing that she was:

> clearly at odds with many of the ideas to have emerged from the feminist literary criticism, including the belief in a specific and separate 'female' way of writing. She is baffled by the celebration of 'flux and chaos and primitive

perceptions'. And she asks why feminist critics have been so eager to define a female aesthetic when the category of the 'aesthetic' itself has such ambiguous resonances, many of them expressive of male hostility to the 'feminine'.[51]

Rather than focusing on one sex or other, we should aim for, Brooke-Rose says, echoing Brophy's own views, a 'pleasantly neutered position' and 'a delightful bisexualism'.[52] However, belonging to one sex had an immediately deleterious effect on her life after her PhD when she was not put forward for any academic jobs like the 'boys' who were her contemporaries as her supervisor 'assumed that I was doing it for fun before producing a family'.[53] Likewise, in *The Languages of Love*, Julia Grampion, after passing her viva, a rare enough event in 1957, is asked, 'What do you want with a PhD anyway?': 'You're not the academic type. You should be writing detective stories'. She replies, 'Whatever career women take up, they have so much more against them than men. They're bound to look like battle-axes by the time they get there'.[54] The idea of female intelligence is understood here as something ugly, deformed; a petrifying force set in opposition to sexuality and one to be avoided at all costs by 'attractive' women. To be a clever woman, as we have seen in the case of Brophy, was not much of an asset in the 1960s.

Finding no luck, then, in an academic career, Brooke-Rose continued to write novels, critical works and reviews, living a busy if rather unconventional life for a married woman with Jerzy in a tiny flat in North London. Her second stage as a writer began with *Out* in 1964, followed by *Such* in 1966 and *Between* in 1968 a year that marked another significant turning point in Brooke-Rose's life when she was asked by Hélène Cixous to take up an academic position as Professeur en Anglo-Américain à l'Université Paris VIII (often erroneously cited as the Sorbonne).[55] Jonathan Coe writes that 'it's tempting to see Brooke-Rose's decision to accept a teaching post in Paris at the end of the Sixties as a wholesale rejection of Britain's reactionary literary culture'.[56] But it is just as likely that the failure to secure an academic position as well as the breakdown of her marriage to Jerzy left Brooke-Rose free to take up Cixous's offer and leave for France where she would live for the rest of her life. Thus, she began and ended her life as a European and has often been referred to as an 'European intellectual'.[57]

Literary Influence:
'well on the way to becoming a 'lady novelist'[58]

Reading Samuel Beckett's second novel *Watt* (1953) was a turning point in Brooke-Rose's artistic practice. In a review of the English translation of *The Unnamable* in 1958 also, she expressed her exhilaration at reading Beckett's prose that allowed her to see the potential of working with decomposition and decreation in novelistic form. Thus, in 'Samuel Beckett and the Anti-Novel' she advocates a 'good airing' out of the postwar British novel that might turn it 'inside out' and leave behind 'straight' writing' whose 'main concern is to tell a story about persons recognizable as human beings in recognizable situation'. 'It seems necessary' she says, 'to the development of the novel or the play that every now and then antinovels or anti-plays should be written'.[59] She explains how Beckett's 'simple and unfigurative', even 'colloquial' language might, confound those, she says 'who are so anti-experiment' (p. 39). Beckett, she observes,

> uses this carefully mundane language to describe incredible things in ordinary context or, more usually, ordinary things in an incredible context. This puts what he writes about slightly out of focus, as if observed, not so much by a foreign visitor as by someone outside the human race, outside the world and time. (p. 40)

The 'slow motion' dwelling of Beckett's eye on detail and patterns that emerge and accumulate from these details are detectible in her first 'experimental' novel, *Such* (1964) that has echoes of his 'weird almost mathematical style' in *Watt* (p. 41). The disturbance of the hierarchy of significance is also important for her:

> Beckett writes of something utterly pointless and unimportant as if it were important, using the language we use of big ideas and great passions [. . .] By reducing all our big hopes and small activities to the same nothing, he creates something out of the nothing which is behind them all. (p. 43)

She deeply admired Beckett's work for its ability to work with 'an almost mathematical precision" and his 'scientific attitude to language' and for its 'humorous play with all the possible permutations of the simplest situation, as if each had its own philosophical existence'. She valued his approach that revealed 'the mock "scientific" but also in some way truly scientific attitude behind the poetry' that 'seemed to [her] to be the only way of dealing with both inner and outer reality in this age of the uncertainty principle in physics' (p. 11). Not for her then, the separation between literature and science of the 'two cultures' model proposed by C. P. Snow, who declared in 1959 that the 'intellectual life of the whole of western society is increasingly split into two polar groups'.[60] Adam Guy suggests that *Out* demonstrates the main tenets of Heisenberg's uncertainty principle in *Physics and Philosophy: The Revolution in Modern Science* (1958): 'the element of the Copenhagen Interpretation that registers most pervasively in Brooke-Rose's work is the idea of unavoidable distortion necessitated by acts of observation, along with the profound epistemological implications that ensue'.[61] In a 1957 review for the *Times Literary Supplement*, Brooke-Rose demonstrates this interest in the relationship between science and art: 'The development of phenomena, modern physics shows, is correlative to the development of consciousness, yet in spite of this the behaviour of the "unrepresented" is invariably assumed [. . .] to have remained unchanged'.[62]

Between 1956 and 1968, Brooke-Rose was a prolific critic, reviewer, and freelance literary journalist. An exacting commentator, she believed that 'A critic's job is to direct the reader, with a new outlook, back to the works in question', and she wrote on a wide range of literary and cultural topics for several leading newspapers and journals.[63] Many of these pieces reveal the evolution of her thinking on narrative form. In a review of Frank O'Connor's *The Mirror in the Roadway* she observes that although O'Connor's 'ideas on realism are extremely vague and shifting', she nonetheless 'sympathizes, since realism is a vague and shifting concept'.[64] Her article, 'Anatomy of Originophobia' alludes to the 'new provincialism in literary criticism' that has a 'healthy no-nonsense attitude to so many established cults' and risks proving 'fatal' as it suggests a 'firm belief that the English-speaking world is the only one that counts'; even American literature, on this view, is considered as 'foreign' literature.[65] In 1961, she wrote an astutely prescient article called 'The Vanishing Author' for *The Observer* accompanied by a photograph of Nathalie Sarraute, Alain Robbe-Grillet and Marguerite Duras on a visit to London the same year. All three of these writers, she noted, write anti-novels that take 'the novel form very seriously', in which the 'author is constantly mocking and destroying his chosen form'.[66] She goes on to say that these *nouveau romanciers*, while all different in the particulars of their work, eliminate 'Old techniques' in order to reveal the presence of the author to the reader; 'In effect', she continues, 'they place the characters and action at a point equidistant between author and reader, like a game being watched'.[67] Later, in *Invisible Author*, she will recall this piece and the ways that it anticipates, 'though of course more naively', Roland Barthes's, 'The Death of the Author', by seven years and Foucault's comparable proclamation in *L'Archéologie du savoir* (1969).[68]

Reading, then subsequently translating, Robbe-Grillet's novel *Dans le Labyrinthe* in 1959 was also a transformative moment for Brooke-Rose.[69] She had previously expressed her admiration for Sarraute's 'critical ideas' in *The Age of Suspicion* (1963 [1956]) which, in her view, challenged some longstanding conventions in the realist novel, in particular, the idea of the 'le petit fait vrai'.[70] In this study, Sarraute also dispels the idea that character is of any central importance: no longer able to read characters off the objects and context as in realist fiction, her main character, she says, has 'lost everything; his ancestors, his carefully built house [...] his body, his face [...] his personality and, frequently, even his name'.[71]

Brooke-Rose was fascinated by Sarraute's thoughts on the distinction between realism and formalism:

> Sarraute in a way goes back to Hegel, but without the decorative implication, by insisting that the true realists are those that look so hard at a changing reality that they have to invent new forms to capture it, whereas the formalists are epigones who come afterwards, take over these once unfamiliar but now ready-made forms and poring them into perfectly familiar reality that anyone can see.[72]

Brooke-Rose admired Sarraute's careful attention to writing in a precise style that is commensurate with the subject matter. In a review of *Childhood* (translated by Barbara Wright), she notes how Sarraute uses language 'to catch, in the present tense, through contradictory voices and with an incredibly subtle notation' both the transience of the surface of memory but also what exists underneath the threshold of consciousness – what Sarraute called the 'subconversation' of her writing. Finally, however, she concluded that Sarraute's novels seemed to her never to 'pass from the realm of abstract feelings to what I call the how'.[73] She thought that focusing only on a novel's content ran the risk of 'taking form for granted as a mere window on reality', but equally regarded any exclusive 'attachment to form that excludes all else' as 'totally withering'.[74]

This necessary interlacing of form and content is highlighted in her review of Robert Pinget's *The Inquisitor* (*L'Inquisitoire*, 1962) and Michel Butor's *Degrees* (1961 [*Degrés*, 1960]), in which she writes of her excitement about the ability of the *nouveau roman* to imbue things and people with a 'new intensity and in so doing they appear not less but more "real"'. These new novelists, she argues, are 'making us relearn to live each moment so that, as on holiday – it is sufficient for people and things merely to be, without reference to something happening'.[75] Thus, a stripping away of the determining causality of plot and a repudiation of an exaggeratedly rich symbolic significance of the material world is not, in her view, antithetical to realism. 'I am so often called antirealist', she says but regarded herself on the contrary as 'a sort of naive mimetist, going back to essentials as if to strengthen them or to honour them'. She was adamant that she was 'not antirealist, if by realism one means representation, and I do not think a writer can be antirepresentational: language is representational'.[76] Brooke-Rose cautions us to be aware of the differences between realism and the merely realistic: 'Whenever I slide into a realistic scene, say a love scene or something like that, something happens later to destroy it, to show that these are just words on a page'.[77]

Experiments in Realism

Thus, after reading Beckett and the *nouveau romanciers*, Brooke-Rose's writing altered dramatically. Recognising the possibility of an aesthetic 'in-betweenness' in novelistic narrative, she believed that the two modes of narrative, realism and its putative opposite, can be present at different times in the same writer – 'There is', she says, 'room for both'.[78] For her, experimental writers and what she calls 'consolidating writers' are both concerned with testing how far language can get purchase on experience in the world. Unlike B. S. Johnson, whose loathing for realism was well known and publicly expressed, Brooke-Rose did not deride realism; in fact, she professed her admiration for many realist writers; what troubled her was not realism itself but what she regarded as the encouragement of a simplistic, 'very diluted' act of identification with characters.[79] This was, she thought, a problem with the rather stagnant reading cultures in postwar Britain rather than with literary form itself, which is always open to the possibility of turning itself inside out if the conditions are encouraging. For her, realism *per se* was not the enemy. Rather, she viewed it as a term that was frequently mishandled and used, often erroneously, to suggest the aesthetic antithesis to experimentalism, reminding us in 'Illiterations', that the *nouveau roman* was originally called 'nouveau réalisme'.[80] In *For a New Novel: Essays on Fiction* (1965), Robbe-Grillet argued that the novel 'has fallen into a state of stagnation' so much so that is it is very difficult to imagine that as an art-form it could survive for long without some 'radical change': 'The minds best disposed to the idea of a necessary transformation, those most willing to countenance and even to welcome the values of experiment remain, nonetheless, the heirs of a tradition'.[81] For Brooke-Rose, the writing of Beckett and the theories of the *nouveau roman* as well as her lifelong interest in Ezra Pound's poetry, in particular his technique of repeating phrases that allows a recontextualisation of language, all influenced the techniques employed in *Out*. But she warns us not to take these influences too far. In 'Invisible Author, she notes how lazy 'label-clichés' have 'unanalytically' fixed her work as examples of 'the *nouveau roman* in English', despite the fact that this is only actually true of *Out*, after which she tries out 'different things in each novel'.[82] She accepts that she admired Robbe-Grillet's ideas of a 'speakerless present [. . . an] impersonal, speakerless (narratorless) narrative', and his method of 'reliving incidents and collocations of data with omissions, shifts, or added detail', but emphasises that her own work is not a copy.[83] She notes that, unlike Sarraute and Robbe-Grillet, she always seeks out humour and wit in her writing whereas the *nouveau roman* 'takes itself very seriously'.[84] Reading Beckett and the *nouveau romanciers* inspired her to move away from the constraints of Free Indirect Discourse and the third-person omniscient narrator used in her early novels to the use of a narratorless present tense, which had been developing in her mind for some considerable time.[85]

Inevitably there have been claims that Brooke-Rose was influenced by postmodernism but Lorna Sage, for one, refuses to be mired in this rather predictable debate. Viewing Brooke-Rose's writing as one that involved 'a kind of double-take about realism', Sage notes how she was 'charmed by the notion of the novel as the site of verbal play, by polyglossia, by split "selves"' and also by the possibility of puns as they all 'promised a kind of liberation from origins, from "place", in the form of gender, class, nation. Brooke-Rose longs for [. . .] what Barthes called textual *atopia*, placelessness'.[86] It is this liberation, then, that constitutes Brooke-Rose's vagabond writing; her atopian delight in wandering within and around language, seeking out its edges and curves and its roads less taken. This leaving behind of home was often literal for her writing practice; to write she needed to leave behind any domestic routines and 'be completely cut off'.[87]

Brooke-Rose's development of thinking about language can be traced back to *A Grammar of Metaphor* (1958), when she was still working on what kind of a writer she wanted to be and how to 'see everything differently' in a language system that always returns to notions of the real.[88] In her efforts, Brooke-Rose considers the possibility of a 'double take on realism' in which she considers a 'sliding scale of' writers positioned on a continuum of their relation to reality. 'At one end', she says, 'there are those 'who reflect little on the conventions of their craft and take them over happily as a sort of readymade net to catch a not too slippery fish called reality'. Others, 'painstakingly examine and remake every knot in that net, only to find a harpoon or a beowulfian wrestling-match under water would have been better [. . .] and then that the monster was imagery anyway'.[89] These extremes of approaches can conclude in oblivion for both the work and the writer. The 'naïve' writer of popular fiction 'takes over the conventions of a literary craft when they have already become a cliché', is momentarily commercially successful, even mildly critically lauded, but this soon fades and the book sinks into obscurity. The experimental writer fares little better. Her craft may have been harder to accomplish; skilfully wrought out of the wrestling of imaginary monsters and countless sleepless nights spent challenging the conventions, it is finally dismissed as 'over-technically conscious' and, like the less accomplished writer of 'literary fiction', is also 'relegated to pulp'.[90] But Brooke-Rose is too generous a writer, too perspicacious a critic, to believe that things can be so simply understood. She knows that even the most technically unreflective writer might well have just as carefully considered the technical aspects of her writing as much as the *bona fide* experimenter who may, in fact, have very little to say. In short, she understands, and sympathizes with the various techniques of what a writer may or may not do with her work to achieve certain effects. As Sage astutely observes, 'It is the middle-distance focus and the rounded character that she wants to avoid, not the raw material of others and otherness'.[91]

As both a writer and a critic, Brooke-Rose was keenly aware of the 'fundamental inseparability of elements that critics and teachers have to separate' and that any creative work must necessarily hold often quite incongruent, even jarring, elements together in a 'precarious suspension of disbelief'.[92] Relatively rare for her time (and even now) Brooke-Rose was as comfortable writing about literary theory as she was writing experimental novels and in her long teaching career teaching she moved effortlessly, if not always lucratively or critically successfully, between the two. However, once retired from teaching she was reluctant to accept invitations to speak about her critical work, preferring to be considered as a writer rather than as an academic. Returning to Somerville College in 1993, she gave a lecture in which she broached the 'vexed question' of the experimental novel: 'What does it mean? Is it a genre? Just as "women's novels" seem often to be treated as a separate genre (out of fear? timidity? scorn? ignorance?)'.[93] An 'unidentifiable category', the experimental novel, Brooke-Rose says is 'a ragbag of anything so far uncategorized or unfamiliar or undefinable, undefinable because its constraints are either unperceived or different in each case'.[94]

Theory Wars

Aware of what Sage calls the 'fashionable desiderata' of Derrida, Barthes, Foucault, Kristeva and Cixous, Brooke-Rose was always wary of the tendency to conflate theory with criticism; interested in the former, mostly language-based theories of subjectivity and constructions of reality in language, she remained single-mindedly committed to the latter.[95] With characteristic perspicacity, she explains this to a student:

> the whole point of the theoretical (or rhetorical) revolution in the sixties and seventies was to do things criticism didn't and couldn't do, and not to do things it could (e.g. evaluate). Many Cultural Studies people, and Feminists in particular, think they're doing Theory when in fact they plunge straight through the texts to its cultural themes, not seeing the text, and much criticism today has become plot or theme summary or even ideological rewrite.[96]

Here, she is attentive to the complex relationship between writing and criticism, citing Shelley, Coleridge, Sidney and Wordsworth as examples of writer/critics of a particular type: 'behind their practice lies their philosophy, their contradictions, their sea changes, their readings and misreadings'. She insists that it is those 'writers with minds that touch ours' that transmit ideas and not 'rhetoricians, who merely observe, categorize, and directly or indirectly, prescribe, post-factum'.[97] In *A Rhetoric of the Unreal*, she develops these ideas on t/Theory: it is not, she says, 'empirical reality but a literary artefact' and is 'rarely as scientific as it purports to be' in its pose of supposedly objective detachment. Used improperly, or rather unskilfully, to prove what the critic is seeking, theory becomes 'a rigid system' deprived of the 'contrary richness' of literature, the best of which can dodge its dogmatic rigidity. If a critic forces the 'theory' onto this richness, she will find in the poem, or story or novel, only 'what fits theory' and this participates in what Brooke-Rose calls the 'worst kind of subjective criticism'.[98] Little wonder then, that in 'Illicitations' she declares that she is more interested in shifting 'fictional conventions' than making fiction bend to the theory.[99]

Often at odds with the radical politics that accompanied the new theoretical mode that she encountered everywhere on her arrival at Paris Vincennes, initially called Le Centre Universitaire Expérimental de Vincennes,[100] Brooke-Rose recalls in *Remake* that 'Every pedagogic problem [was] politicized in a blind fanaticism of Gauchistes and Communists, everyone having to speak'.[101] Much to her personal annoyance, politics produced frequent disruptions of her teaching at Vincennes, a role she took immensely seriously, and she often regarded student protests as bothersome interruptions to her working day.[102] Such irritation notwithstanding, she was happy to teach and read theory as it helped corroborate some of her thinking:

> I must have been feeling for both contemporary and later deconstructions of the notion of identity as a male humanist concept, a deconstruction already incoherently incipient in Virginia Woolf [...] On authorial

identity, I remember writing an article called 'The Death of the Author' for *the Observer* in 1961, some seven years before Barthes' essay of the same name (1968/1977), though of course more naively, but also less finalisingly dogmatic, and eight years before Foucault's demonstration that the concept "author" is a construct out of specific operations.[103]

In a letter to Glyn White,[104] she describes in detail her 'technique of absolutely objective narrative narration' used in *Thru* and repeated in variations of constraint elsewhere.[105] She was also interested in what she called the 'personal atmosphere' of the writing that evokes, in a variety of ways, 'an atmosphere of time, place and character – including the author's own [...] I won't call it style because that's a dirty word now, but it includes style'. This 'atmosphere', she argued, can only be produced by 'the exact word for the exact detail (whether one detail or twenty-five is immaterial) personally and uniquely observed, and placed in a context made unique and personal by observation and imagination, in short by hard thinking'.[106]

I consider now two novels, *Out* and *Between*,[107] as illustrative of one stage of her experimental work in which she begins using 'a narratorless past tense' that provides a method of 'miming a consciousness' that is 'both reflective and unreflective'.[108] As stated, I will read Brooke-Rose as both a writer and a critic as she never insisted on a clear distinction between these two activities, calling herself 'one of the few novelists who is also a long practicing critic'.[109]

OUT: 'all the new-waving should not be left to the French'[110]

On the contexts of writing *Out*, Brooke-Rose recalled a trip to France with Jerzy where she suddenly fell seriously ill: 'I was rushed to the clinic and operated on – I lost one of my kidneys – and had a very bad time recuperating. But as I lay on the bed I started writing *Out*'.[111] *Out* is a novel about the state of being 'out'. Those who were out are now in and vice versa; a movement necessitating a fundamental shift in the hierarchy of signification system, namely, the complete reversal of 'the irrationality of racism', then called the 'colour bar'.[112] In a 'pronounless, present tense' the novel recounts a near-future society that is run according to the quasi-meaningless slogan 'diagnosis prognosticates aetiology', in which the 'colourless', that is the white people, are now the displaced, diseased and unemployed; whereas the coloured people are now 'in' and rule this new world. Published in 1964 and the winner of the Society of Author's Travelling Prize, *Out* takes malady as its central metaphor, not only of the physical body but also of meaning and language that have been upended by an unspecified catastrophe. Written, says Brooke-Rose, in 'very short bursts', the novel's depiction of exhaustion and redundancy 'exactly reproduced the state of illness' that she was in: 'I started writing a sentence and fell back on the pillow exhausted'. The technique of the novel was almost instinctively experimental in that she was not 'consciously trying anything' but 'groping' towards a new way of writing.[113]

The events in the novel occur sometime after a geological and ontological catastrophic event, described only as the 'displacement', that has resulted in an over-warmed society of ultra-surveillance that has reconfigured geographic space across the world into Afro-Eurasia, Sino America and Chinese Europe. In a fundamentally discriminatory feudal society of privilege versus exploitation and discrimination based upon the external nuances of skin colour, the Asseti tribe now are the rulers of this new world while the Colourless live in Settlements away from the rulers in the Big House; an obvious reversal of the plantation–slave dynamic. The temporality of the post-settlement is blighted and the citizens of this new world are compelled to live in a confusingly perpetual present – 'It's because of there being no past, and no future, ma'am, it's so difficult, living in the present' (p. 124) the white man tells Mrs Mgulu, one the few named characters, the owner of the 'big house', who prides herself on her liberalism towards the lower white race. Now at the bottom of the social pile, white men's privilege has been utterly displaced; they are now sickly and weak and thus condemned to permanent redundancy, compelled to visit the 'Labour Exchange' for their daily 'dole-pills'. Increasingly scrutinised by the surveillance technologies of this new society, the consciousness of the 'colourless' atrophies. They subsist only on a Beckettian gruel that is described repeatedly in all its globular repugnance and are dying out, due to their lack of immunity to the post-catastrophe environmental contamination.

Out is concerned with many types of 'outness', including obsolescence, redundancy, sickness and, in a larger narrative sense, the very existence of white Western society. Performing as a sign of all kinds of 'outness', the sickly white protagonist is, in all senses, redundant; he cannot find employment not only because of the colour of his skin but also because only white people have been afflicted with the 'sickness'. With little ontological purchase on this post-displacement world and operating with a ruined subjectivity and diseased body, the elderly protagonist asks his wife, Lily: 'Who am I? Who was I?' (p. 170), knowing that 'Knowledge certain or indubitable' is unobtainable (p. 60). In terms of narrative reliability, he can be counted on for very little, as readers can only access what Brian McHale describes as his 'obsessive, damaged consciousness'.[114] Locked out of the discursive systems governing this new society which seems to consist of shifted geopolitical areas such as the Orwellian 'Chinese Europe' and 'Afro Eurasia', he experiences the world as intermittent unreality in which dialogue and communication are always uncertain – 'This dialogue does not necessarily occur' (p. 48) – or, another, equally negative possibility, is that 'the conversation has wholly occurred and is wholly sane but is beyond the grasp of sick white reasoning' (p. 109). Described by B. S. Johnson as a 'deeply intellectual' novel, *Out*, he says, attempts to provide 'something very close to the multiplicity and simultaneity of natural experience'.[115] More than this though, *Out* depicts the evacuation of humanity from the protagonist and as such it is, as notes Brooke-Rose, more influenced by Beckett's 'despair of the human situation' and demonstrates the 'stripping off of man', denuding him of all 'his *accoutrements*'.[116]

A melancholic, often mournful, tone articulates the end of a stage of humanity; one that involves a loss of identity, ontological orientation and the idea of foundation: 'It is impossible ever to see the beginning of anything because at the beginning the thing is not recognisable as anything distinct and by the time it has become something distinct the beginning is lost' (p. 196). With beginnings and origins lost the novel is, then, a 'dialogic elegy on the loss of the self – or of a subjectivity that is undergoing such a radical, socially imposed and experimental rewrite that the man's consciousness is dying in the process'.[117] This loss of origin and of grand narratives, including the ability to construct a cogent narrative out of stable linguistic utterances, is replaced by diagnostic technology in a process of cognitive and affective dispossession. The protagonist is told by his inquisitors at the Labour Exchange that he 'can't even think' (p. 20). As art has been expelled from this new society, the need to think in complex, interpretive ways is no longer required – becoming yet another form of redundancy in the novel. All that is needed now is a recording of phenomenon that can be reduced to easily readable data: 'The sequence has occurred' (p. 48).

Technology is central to the evacuation of human essence as it allows the exposure and disclosure of the fundamental elements of human consciousness – memory, thought and imagination – qualities that make humans different from each other, unpredictable and potentially subversive. Seeing all though a mechanical lens, the machines strip humans of their essential humanity and one might plausibly argue that what is imagined in the novel is a kind of post-human society. The displacement that has occurred has reoriented society, and has transposed ontology as well as geography, resulting in a 'displacement from cause to effect', one of several phrases that are constantly repeated, mantra-like, throughout the novel. To investigate these new effects in this displaced social and economic order, technology is used to scrutinise individual subjects and to turn what was previously inside out. For example, the 'psychoscope' is a piece of technology that allows the practitioner to see inside the patient 'right down to his extracted absolute of [his] unconscious patterns', as well as to scrutinise all the 'up-and-down tendencies' that make up every human's conscious and unconscious life. The machines produce biograms that expose consciousness to the operator and render memory and deep subjectivity to so much output of data. The logic of this new global order is bureaucratic, scientific and, above all, ruled by the mechanical. All efforts are taken to secure a diagnosis of the malady of the human condition – the telescope, microscope, teinoscope, broncoscope, periscope psychchope and the oscillograph all see past the body into the mind, punctuated by an Orwellian-like slogan, 'diagnosis prognosticates aetiology', a 'rule universal in all fields' that has become an 'article of faith' (p. 139).

Of *Out*, Brooke-Rose noted

> My protagonist is a sick old man who cannot get a job and cannot remember his previous status [. . .] This exactly reproduced the state of illness that I was in, so in that sense of retention it was still a very mimetic novel.[118]

The whole text is an excursion through his uncertain apprehension of the external world, presented in repetitive, elliptical and speculative forms. Events are rendered as baseless hypotheses subject to the general condition of sickness. Things may happen, may have happened, have yet to happen or will not happen at all. It matters little; 'Knowledge certain or indubitable is unobtainable' (p. 60). And yet the machines continue their work on diagnosing humanity:

> Your profile is coming up very clearly indeed on the oscillograph, and the profile provokes its own continuation, did you know that, the profile moulds you as it oscillates? Diagnosis provokes its own cause did you know that? To put it more succinctly, diagnosis prognosticates aetiology. (pp. 138–9)

All memory has been emptied out of the protagonist. He cannot recall what his profession was in the past, before the displacement; reflecting on this loss, as Little says 'achronologically',[119] he speculates, was he a humanist, gardener, a welder, an electrician, or a fortune teller? – 'there's no future in that, not nowadays' (p. 62). He may well have been a psychopath, as he tells the hospital doctor, who dutifully writes this down as if it were a *bona fide* career (p. 197). Later, however, another doctor who gives him his psychoscope can see that he is not being serious; 'We have a sense of humour, yes?' (p. 132). Humour, like art, which has been banished from the new world order, is suspect and irregular and as such must be eradicated as it has the potential to subvert the mechanical order of things by making language lively and communicative. Humour requires an audience to verify the effect of its comedy; it also needs a dexterity of hearing that is alive to the offbeat nuances of language. In this new post-crisis world there is no room for such jocularity or for any sense of nuanced communion with another. Frequently the protagonist is uncertain not only of his own identity and sense of subjectivity, but also of what he is hearing and experiencing; who are these speakers, what are these discourses that circulate endlessly, repeatedly and sterilely around him? They are variously 'scientific laws', 'articles of faith' and 'universal rules' that become increasingly forensic with increasingly little empathy or ethical content. Despite the fact that he is probed by the psychoscope to the depths of his consciousness and innermost thoughts, the protagonist is, somewhat paradoxically, never sure that anyone can actually hear him when he speaks; if one can't be heard, if one's language is inaudible then the subject slowly and gradually disappears.

In terms of its use of reverse racism, *Out* may be read as an inversion, or a reworking, of the colonial gaze in Robbe-Grillet's *La Jalousie*, which focuses on white characters in a colonial setting.[120] But one cannot disregard the contexts of the Apartheid which use an absurd racialised logic to legitimise the subjugation of one group by another. In South Africa, the 1953 Bantu Act and the Pass Laws resulted in the system of Apartheid setting up interdictions, prohibitions and thus institutionalised racial discrimination that insured whites remained separate from blacks. On 21 March 1960, sixty-nine black demonstrators were massacred by police as they protested against laws that required all 'Blacks' to carry a pass book, a version of which is included in *Out*. The Sharpeville Massacre was widely covered in the British press and could not have failed to be in Brooke-Rose's consciousness as she wrote parts of *Out* from her convalescent bed.[121] Indeed, in an interview in 1991, Brooke-Rose confirmed that the context for writing *Out* was unquestionably political and social: 'it's about the colour bar. Can you have anything more social than that?'[122] Apartheid's irrational logic, what she described as 'a world without explanation',[123] underpins the novel's sense of unreality and strangeness resulting from the displacement of those categorised in law as non-white that imposes on this population not only poverty, sickness and unemployment but also a lasting sense of a psychotic logic of which Frantz Fanon had spoken with powerful conviction in *Les Damnés de la terre* in 1961, a work that Brooke-Rose would most likely have known and even have read in its original French.

A perversity of logic underpins all racism: 'We have no prejudice that's an article of faith. But there is an irrational fear of the Colourless that lingers on, it's understandable, in some cases, even justifiable, with the malady still about, well, it makes them unreliable' (p. 51). As a French speaker, Brooke-Rose may also have been aware of another important anti-colonial work, Albert Memmi's *Portrait du colonisé, précédé par Portrait du colonisateur* (1957), with a preface by Jean-Paul Sartre, in which he condemns the violent absurdity of colonialism and its denial of rationality:

> There are neither good nor bad colonists: there are colonialists. Among these, some reject their objective reality. Borne along by the colonialist apparatus, they do every day in reality what they condemn in fantasy, for all their actions contribute to the maintenance of oppression.[124]

Repetition, Repetition, Repetition and Reception

'It is impossible to know', notes Natalie Ferris, writing of *Out*, 'whether events or images are singular or generative, successive or progressive. The memories of past occurrences, the dim recognition of a dialogue before him, or the visions of an inhospitable future form his present'.[125] The repetition of events with only tiny alterations and the absence of any past tense produces a narrative that effectively evacuates all sense of history from the society and obstructs any notion of a future. This is suggestive of the ruined time of slavery and, later of colonialism, that strips agency and personhood from each subject, evoking some of Memmi's ideas. The repetition with only tiny alterations is also part of the rejection of temporality in the novel. With no past tense, the entire narrative unfolds in a continuous present tense that effectively evacuates all sense of history from the society and obstructs any notion of a future: 'It's because of there being no past, and no future, ma'am, it's so difficult, living in the present' (p. 124).

In the *Illustrated London News*, the reviewer regarded *Out* as a 'meticulous reconstruction' of a diseased mind but complains of the novel's 'nightmare technique: not recommended for beginners'.[126] To narrate new realties, imagined or otherwise, to rid the novel of its naïve 'pretending' was, as Karen Lawrence notes, part of Brooke-Rose's quest to find 'survival strategies for the genre of the novel'.[127] This entailed experimentation with new forms of telling that might create a different kind of story, even if it is, in some cases, the 'absent story' that demands a new kind of engagement with the idea of story.[128] Correspondingly, Lorna Sage suggests that Brooke-Rose's writing might seem superficially 'distant and characterless' but that, in fact, her work necessitates a different kind of reading: 'experimental fiction, being in some sense more like poetry, actually needs to be read aloud to live in reader's heads – a special and pleasing irony, when you consider that it's a throwback to orality [...] and diametrically opposed to deconstructionist notion that it's the written word that liberates multiple plays of meaning'.[129] To read the 'voice' in *Out*, then, is to involve oneself in its experimental techniques that initially appear formidable in their semantic repetition and estrangement of any sense of plot or narrative progression.

One of these techniques is a forensic sense of vison, hence, *Out*, begins with a microscopic description, one repeated throughout the text, of two flies lingering on a trousered knee:

> — *Would you rather have your gruel now or when I come back from Mrs. Mgulu?*
>
> The question is inevitable, but will not necessarily occur in that precise form.
> — Two flies are making love on my knee.
> — Flies don't make love. They have sexual intercourse.
> — On the contrary.
> — You mean they make love but don't have sexual intercourse?
> — I mean it's human beings who have sexual intercourse but don't make love.
> — Very witty. But you are talking to yourself. This dialogue will not necessarily occur. (p. 12)

The absence of story is emphasised by the repetitive and increasingly anaesthetised nature of language in the novel. Experience and events become 'collocations of data with omissions, shifts, or added detail, as if through the expanding and contracting lens of memory and imagination; but instantaneously, merging with direct experience'.[130] Much, then, is demanded of the reader; a fact recognised by Brooke-Rose who actively sought to make readers more aware of her writerly techniques. Norman Shrapnel's review in the *Guardian* acknowledges the effort required in such a *scriptible* text: 'She puts words and paragraphs to productive hard labour, busily controls pace and stance, trains and tracks her camera eye, and launches whole vocabularies of medical science-fiction on her new wave straightforwardly?'[131] This view is repeated by another reviewer in *The Tablet*, who describes *Out* as a 'strange and immensely intelligent novel' offering an 'analogue of the human condition [...] an over rationalised world'.

> Hypnotic catalogues of medical terms, several lines printed upside down, frequent repetitions, an uneasy ambivalence which now seems to be recounting a fact and now a fantasy; these are some of the devices that will perhaps

exasperate a reader who begins by questioning the very purpose of a novel that so resolutely expels all the usual concessions to comfort. But none of them is without justification, for Ms BR is evidently working out a wholly new way of exploring the forgotten places of human hope. Whether she is right to work it out on not-so-captive readers is another matter.[132]

Thus, readers are asked to read *Out* actively as it stages the disappearance of narrative or at least in its eschewal of the past tense and its 'narrator-less narrative' rehearses the refusal of deep temporality or psychology. In a sense the novel goes nowhere; it has no tension or plot or dénouement or reliably stable point of view and, while not devoid of humanity and pathos, it resists all acts of naïve 'identification' between text and reader, never permitting what could have been a gripping dystopian novel to fully emerge. *Out* combines, says Lawrence, 'Robbe-Grillet's myopic, cold descriptive sentence with Beckett's agnostic list of possibilities played out in the narrative'.[133] One review of the novel notes: 'The future world of *Out*' is a 'detailed quasi-scientific observation of phenomena [. . .] But it is hard to feel that this procedure helps the novel's arguments, despite the intelligence with which Miss BR handles it'.[134] Some critics commented on the Beckettian tones of the novel. For example, in *The Scotsman*, Boswell notes this influence in the ways in which 'certain phrases recur throughout the book, spiralling upwards and out, often with a shift of emphasis on the way'. The reviewer also notes that while Brooke-Rose is not 'a cosy writer' she is 'considered pretty well the leading exponent of the anti-novel in this country', but he maintains that while *Out* is experimental insofar as it 'dispenses with a straightforward plot', it is not an anti-novel.[135] Elsewhere, a reviewer states, 'I don't mean to imply that Miss Br's sharp talent is imitative. No doubt it is merely the exigencies of the anti-art service into which she has pressed it (temporarily, one hopes) that conjures up the ghost of Malone'.[136]

On the whole, *Out* received mixed reviews. Writing in *The Spectator*, Kay Dick notes that the novel allowed Brooke-Rose to 'free herself from social and personal trivia' of her previous works which were 'witty and satirical views of contemporary, mostly metropolitan' society. *Out* shows 'remarkable courage', but it is not 'an easy book and demands intense concentration because it makes no concessions. This does not imply incomprehensibility. On the contrary, it strikes vivid images in terms recognisable to all of us'.[137] W. J. Nesbitt concluded that *Out* was a 'bold but difficult experiment' employing 'impenetrability, distortion, and repetition', resulting in a novel that is 'unsatisfying' but 'technically [. . .] interesting'.[138] A reviewer in the *New Statesman* takes Brooke-Rose to task for its perceptibly 'French' influences, comparing it to Raymond

Williams's novel, *Second Generation*, 'Mr W neglects fantasy and form; Miss BR neglects just about everything else' and has

> trotted out the whole Left Bank box of *trucs* – meaningless confusions, solipsistic riddles, obsessive galaxies of 'objective' scientific terms. Vague incantations like 'diagnosis merely prognosticates aetiology' are passed around like fake currency; imitations of epistemology peep out from each repetitive paragraph.

Out belongs, the review continues, to a

> genre which one can't exactly stigmatise as well-established, but which is none the less fashionable – in a sense – for that. Although it is difficult to work up much indignation for a package which isn't yet rich enough to be glossy, there is some voguish ballast in the cargoes of enthusiasm that come, from Paris, via John Calder, for the anti-novel. A minority is no more guaranteed right than guaranteed wrong, and avant garde literature is this country is too sickly a growth to be guaranteed anything – even alive.[139]

Elsewhere, a review in the *Evening Standard* review described *Out* as possessing 'Vibrant echoes of Huxley and Orwell, portentous display of medical terms, and occasional rich undergraduate purple – but a worthwhile try'.[140] The most insightful review, however, was Myrna Blumberg's, 'Out's out – it's in to be anti' in the *Guardian*. In an interview in her Hampstead flat, Brooke Rose tells Blumberg that she regards *Out* as 'an extension of the anti-novel'; a novelistic experiment largely critically overlooked in Britain. She complains of being treated in British literary culture as a 'promising newcomer': 'I know what I'm doing now.' Acknowledging that her early novels took a 'conventional god's eye view' she says that while this broadly realist narrative technique 'suits some purposes, such as the portrait and of a society on a fairly broad canvas' it cannot deal as well with the expansive sense of outsiderness that is central to *Out*, and which necessitated a different narrative style in order to speak about what she, as author, could not imagine, namely, 'what it's like to be a negro'. The ambition of *Out, then,* is to find a narrative form appropriate for the presentation of an unfamiliar point of view, a mostly silenced one. For once, she viewed the results favourably: 'for the first time in my life I'm a hundred percent satisfied with a book. I've achieved what I set out to do'.[141]

Between: ~~To Be~~

By the time she moved to Paris, Brooke-Rose had already written *Out, Such,* and *Between,* with *Thru* coming later in 1975. Each of these works moved further 'one way or another,' says Frank Kermode (a long-term admirer of her work), from the 'comfortable tacit agreement between author and reader as to the relation of fiction to reality'.[142] All four novels renegotiate this relationship between language and reality, and between reader and writer, unmistakably anticipating Barthes's ideas of the *lisible* and the *scriptible* in S/Z (1970) and *The Pleasure of the Text* (1973). The lipogrammatic constraint avoiding the verb 'to be' in *Between* is, of course, echoed a year later in Georges Perec's *La Disparition* (1969) written without the letter 'e'.[143] Brooke-Rose's knowledge of poststructuralism and the OULIPO-style constraints she sometimes imposed on her writing have been emphasised in the critical reception of her writing, helping to categorise her as a wilfully difficult writer, one whose 'whose work could take artful pains to dispense with seemingly indispensable linguistic foundation stones'.[144]

Between (1968) represents the evolution of Brooke-Rose's experiment with narrative form described in *Stories, Theories and Things* thusly: '*Between* deals with (?), explores (?), represents (?), plays around with (?), makes variations on (?), expresses (?), communicates (?), is about (?), generates (?), has great fun with (?) the theme of/complex experience/ story/of bilingualism'.[145] The narrative is situated in the organising consciousness of an unnamed female narrator who slips in and out of languages, countries and memories. Moving between fourteen languages and set in the liminal spaces of planes, hotels and the peripatetic world of international conferences, *Between* completely omits the verb 'to be' – one of the many constraints Brooke-Rose would set herself in her writing. Reformulating some of her earlier thinking in *Invisible Author* and *Stories, Theories and Things*, she considered this constraint as not only technical, but also one challenging the reader's assumptions about the function of identity in literature. *Between* uses, she says, a 'non-narrating narrative voice' thus 'there is no separate narrative voice from that of the character [. . .] the distinction between hetero-and homodiegetic is collapsed, as in most Beckett'.[146] Working as a simultaneous translator, the nameless narrator travels from one country to another, digressively weaving her meditations on language and translation between two non-linear, framing 'stories'. The first of these describes the course of a marriage annulment, the second, follows an exchange of love letters written in Medieval French.[147] In a broadly affirmative review in the *Daily Telegraph*, Robert Baldick concludes that the novel is 'engaging' but with its multilingualism, 'some knowledge of French, with a smattering of German, is necessary for full enjoyment': 'The result is a painfully vivid impression of the tedium of life travelling the world and translating other people's clichés: fortunately – and this is a tribute to Miss Brooke Rose's art – very little of the tedium brushes off on the reader'.[148]

I have chosen, as indicated, to focus on *Between* rather than *Such* as it addresses questions of gender in Brooke-Rose's experimental writing and as such is more germane to the ongoing concerns of this book. The novel probes the marked feminine of Romance languages: those 'long lost code of zones lying forgotten under layers of thickening sensibilities reveal how women must always learn to translate themselves into the logic of the universal masculine 'he'.' In its 'groping inside language and forms', *Between* examines how women find themselves negotiating language in the world in different ways to men (p. 468), but crucially does not endorse Helene Cixous's concept of *écriture féminine* in its examination of gender and language.[149]

As previously noted, Kinsgsley Amis thought the failure of experimentalism in Britain was because 'its intake of human stuff was so low'; in other words, he regarded that innovation in form was always at the expense of consequential content.[150] But Brooke-Rose was no mere dabbler in the recondite. She was a 'firm believer in fiction that has content, information' – for her 'it was important to get everything right',[151] and that 'people are, and will always be, the stuff of the novel'.[152] In *Between*, 'human stuff' occurs both at the personal and historical level, and this takes place around various acts of translation made by the unnamed bi-lingual translator, who has lived between two languages and cultures both during and after the war and now makes her living 'passing on other people's ideas'.[153] The role of the female translator is significant as it indicates how women position themselves in the linguistic world and also the need for a kind of neutral re-writing. As Sarah Birch notes, 'While she awaits her birth in her own voice, she can only speak though the voices of others, but this "speaking though" also constitutes her struggle to get out'.[154] It might also be said that the personal story is a translation of the wider European postwar histories in which the protagonist is involved; chequered pasts that require rewriting of wartime sins, cleaning out the dark areas in an act of linguistic whitewashing. To qualify as translators, she and her German lover Siegfried must obtain a 'Persil-Schein certificate denazifying us whiter than white' (p. 473). Words she has heard during the war, such as 'Schweinnhunde! Kommunisten! Sozialdemokraten! Homosexuelle Juden!' must be now forgotten, cleansed from her memory: 'You will understand these things later my child, but remember now, your uncle did only his duty as a Party member' (p. 526).

The events of *Between* unfold in layers of memories, repetitions, flashbacks and a continual movement around European cities and across different languages. While the temporal and spatial coordinates are always shifting on a micro-level, the historical context for the novel is recognisably that of postwar Europe. Travelling from one country to another, the narrator interlaces her meditations on language and translation between two fragmentary framing 'stories'; one that describes the course of a marriage annulment, the other, following an exchange of love letters between the narrator and an older French man, Bertrand, written in Medieval French. Passive, neutral and largely invisible – the woman functions as an impartial, almost imperceptible, channel connecting two parties whose motives are often not clear, suggesting that seeing one's life from a series of fluctuating perspectives is another act of translation.

Between opens between 'the enormous wings' of a jet plane, the body floats between 'doing and not doing', between countries and lovers; between 'two social orders', and, above all, between language and body (p. 395). The narrator, an unnamed woman who works as a simultaneous translator, is in perpetual transit between European cites – Prague, Rome, Paris, Athens – attending conferences trying to find equivalences for words across cultures, peoples and places. She works listening, translating, interpreting, reformatting, all the while relaying the words of others. Her role requires her to be invisible; a transparent, neutral in-between channel connecting several parties. The narrative cuts back and forth from the interior of the plane to a conference translation booth to various hotel rooms where a chambermaid might come in and wish the occupant 'buenos dias, Morgen or kalimera' (p. 396), to thoughts of the end of her marriage, sightseeing trips in a variety of European countries, a dialogue in love letters between the translator and the balding, paunchy Siegfried and a house ('que voulez-vous dire "un cottage?"') in Wiltshire. All of this occurs across multiple languages and cultures, suggesting that seeing one's life from fluctuating perspectives and grammatical fissures is another act of translation that, as Karen Lawrence suggests, is 'a technique for exploring fixings and releasings of positionality'.[155] Language might fix us into a culture but switching languages can emancipate us from the limitations of monoculturalism.

The Enemy Point of View

As is the case with *Out* and *Such*, *Between* refuses plot in the conventional sense of beginning, end and narrative linearity but nonetheless contains a recognisable 'story'. Circuitously, we learn that the 'I' is a bi-lingual woman, born in France before the Second World War to a

French mother and a German father. Her father leaves when she is very young and she is sent by her mother to study in Germany and to live with her father's relatives but then war breaks out and she finds herself trapped in Germany, caught between two cultures and languages that are now understood not as geographical neighbours but in terms of allies and enemies. She is never to see her mother again. After the war is over, 'I' finds herself in the French Zone in the newly partitioned Berlin. Now married to an English airman, she must account to the authorities for her wartime 'between–ness'. Carefully explaining her linguistic dexterity to the monolingual Americans who are suspicious of her wartime translation work from French to German: 'What did you do. You will excuse these questions Fraulein but in view of your nationality we must make sure of your undivided loyalty total ignorance dissidence change of heart' (p. 489).

She is now considered a politically suspect citizen, as she has been constantly moving (in transit) between the language of both ally and enemy. What is it that has she actually heard? Her interrogators view 'other' languages (that is, not English) as simple mechanisms able to be unlocked in the act of translation and to deliver direct equivalences, an approach which ignores the idea that perfect translation is impossible and that there might exist at the heart of every language a certain level of untranslatability. *Between* suggests that we need to understand untranslatability, not as an obstruction to communication, but as an always-dynamic condition of active difference that compels the listener as well as the translator to be active to the question 'what difference does it make?', a repeated refrain in the novel. As Lawrence Venuti notes, translation is 'constantly engaged in signalling those differences to constituencies and institutions in the receiving situations, and constantly inventive in finding the linguistic and culture means to make as productive difference in that situation'.[156] So, even when we think we know the most reliable translation for a particular word we must remain vigilant of the slippage between a translated word and what it might mean in different places and contexts. The margin for error is considerable: 'If you read a word in your own language, it can come out like a pun: "lecheria," in Spanish, for example, which means milk shop, but of course, she [the translator] reads it as "lechery." And that kind of disorientation is very personal to me'.[157]

The idea of home, the rural house in Wiltshire, is constantly translated, becoming increasingly unreal as she attempts to explain the word 'cottage' in different languages: 'que voulez-vous dire, un cottage?' is a repeated refrain. Can it truly be the case, she wonders, that the word cottage has no equivalent outside of English? Is it a 'piccolo chalet', or a 'box a refuge a still small centre within the village within the wooded countryside within the alien land' (p. 418). The otherness of other languages (not English) 'block the text', suggests Brooke-Rose, 'rather like the ideograms in Pound', arresting our attention around ideas of semantic, linguistic and affective equivalence.[158]

Translation is an activity that is at once intellectual and physical. Siegfried, the narrator's lover, who is also a translator, uses his brain, eyes, hands, ears and voice in the act of translation:

> He lip-reads the speaker on the dais through the small glass booth and in the next split second hears the expected English syllables of problems we should consider today for the sake of mutual understanding the advancement of learning the true state of things that pour into the earphones through the distant brain way up and out into the mouthpiece in simultaneous German. (p. 407)

'On one level,' the translator notes, 'one hardly ever listens. On another one has to understand immediately you see because the thing understood slips away, together with the need to understand' (p. 429). The novel suggests that mishearing, mistranslation and misinterpretation are often at the heart of human relations and problems, both at the intimate level of love and in the discourses of enmity and diplomacy. What do we really mean when we speak? We do not always say what we mean. And vice versa. But we must remind ourselves that behind the rules of *langue*, the syntax and the grammar, exists the 'Misch-Masch of tender fornication' that is the unruliness of the *parole* where words 'fraternized silently beneath the syntax, finding each other funny and delicious' (p. 447).

Read more historically, the act of translation is crucial at this moment where peace in postwar Europe depends on so many fragile lies and truths behind the Persilshein: 'we must surely acknowledge that these vital lies have more energy than so many of the fragile truths that surround us in this supposedly rationalistic age so dominated by masculine upward myths' (p. 505). Relatively new after the War, by the 1960s simultaneous translation was used routinely in international conferences and congresses set up in the processes of the reparation and modernisation of Europe post-1945.[159] The translator works for the Agricultural Aid Commission, a Conference of Irrigation Engineers, and Congresses of Semiologists and Demographers. In the 'bombed out hallowed structures' of postwar Europe, accurate communication and a consensual version of 'truth' are urgent matters. Language, the novel suggests, possesses a powerful ability to collaborate in the construction of truth – 'Structures of power, even when they appear to depend on physical force, in fact depend on the assistance and cooperation of innumerable individuals for the administration of physical force' (p. 509). The act of translation and interpretation always requires a bridging of (at least) two human worlds – that of the speaker and the audience, with the translator a silent meditating presence in between. *Between* examines the differences between two (or more) things, often languages, and how these might be traversed, made less different, more equivalent, but without the semantic violence of erasure or exclusion: 'We live in an age of transition between one social order and another and we must effectuate that transition or die' (p. 462).

But the translator finds it hard to translate her own being into the world. In a text that rejects the verb 'to be', she has difficulty knowing who she is and cannot say 'I am . . .': 'she doesn't know who she is, she is always translating from one language to another and never quite knows to which language she belongs'.[160] Thus, existence becomes activity rather than being and suggests that we can live without saying definitively 'I am' this or that; if you cannot say what something is, then you must describe it by its function, what it does in the world. Accordingly, the whole consciousness of the novel, what McHale calls its 'interior discourse', is ascribed to the voice of the 'I' but only in terms of doing rather than being.[161] This concept is rehearsed in the repeated appearance of a bedside bottle of mineral water. It is always water and mineral and in a bottle but designated by a shifting series of names on the labels in multiple languages: 'Vichy water', *'eau de Vichy,' Vichywatten,' 'l'eau qui petille'*, and 'Spa Monopole' (p. 475). Thus, she describes things in the world but always avoids saying 'it is' or they are'. Likewise, describing a door without saying this 'is a door', we read, 'Ausgang. Exit. Push, Tirez. Drücken.' We know this refers to a door, but we learn of this object in the world through its doing rather than being. The door only comes into meaning, that is, into being though a shared familiarity with its action not through its sign in the world.

A reviewer in the *TLS* notes: 'Miss B-R sets aside the familiar opposition between the word-spinner and the full human being [. . .] while the comedy is very much there, it is firmly controlled by a self-derisive and vulnerable consciousness'.[162] Brooke-Rose often uses humour to get to what she calls, the 'swift live thing' at the heart of writing.[163] 'One thing I have against the French school is, on the whole – I don't want to mention any names – but on the whole there is very little humour'.[164] In her dexterous multilingual wordplay and the liberal use of punning, humour is fundamental to Brooke-Rose's work and the pun is the cornerstone of this humour: 'The pun is free, anarchic, a powerful instrument to explode the civilization of the sign and all its stable, reassuring definitions'. Puns 'open up' she says, 'a different dialectic with the reader' (*Thru*, p. 607). Not unlike the solver of cryptic crossword puzzles, punning shows off the speaker's facility with language, both native and second and third, forcing the listener/reader to engage with something other than language as information. A kind of queering of everyday language also seen in *In Transit*, the polysemous nature of punning arrests language as metaphor; and this, in turn, has an effect on narrative momentum. Punning is a kind of perverted meaning, compelling words to be read as encrypted code rather than as flow, thus slowing down the reading process. Arresting the logical flow of language, punning is a refusal to go anywhere in terms of dialogue and narrative progression. *Between* is frequently humorous and 'punny', but it also reveals the susceptibility of language to ideological manipulation, pointing up its ability to whitewash itself with its own sly manoeuvres. Brooke-Rose is, notes one review, working very obviously with Structuralist theories but she manages to lighten these by putting 'the abstract etymological theorizing of Levi-Strauss and the Structuralists into tangibly crumpled light-weight suits' that allows the theory to 'have a sense of humour'.[165]

The 'Problem' of French Feminism

When she started to write *Between*, Brooke-Rose wanted the novel to be unmarked by gender and effectively to have 'no sex'.[166] But she was seriously blocked with writing until she gave the central consciousness a female identity after which she began to feel more sure of herself: 'It's one of the few novels I felt certain about. It was the best of all so far, and I knew it was a very original idea, so there we are'.[167] While it is feasible to read many parts of *Between* through the lens of feminist theory, as is the case with Brophy it is no straightforward undertaking to call Brooke-Rose a feminist. As Lorna Sage notes, Brooke-Rose deliberately kept a 'lifetime's discreet silence' on being a woman writer until she published 'Illiterations' in 1991.[168] Replying to a doctoral student's letter in which she asks her an 'overvast' question on her relationship to feminism, Brooke-Rose's response is enlightening:

> There are lots of Feminisms. Some of the best are Deconstructionists, the next best, or useful, are the recuperators or re-readers of feminine texts (good relationship but not always good critics), the worst are very naïve indeed, still with 'essentialism' (essential femininity, ethnicity etc.) Obviously I'm in much in all three (Pm, Pst, F) but each has become a ragbag term. I'm closer to French feminism.[169]

This last claim is rather confusing as Brooke-Rose regarded, as we shall see, French feminism as the most serious exponent of an immutable female essence although it might be said that her work pre-empted Cixous's advocating of 'sweeping away syntax' in 'The Laugh of the Medusa', just not in the cause of any biological essentialism.[170]

A latecomer to feminism, Brooke-Rose's highly developed 'analytic capacity' encouraged her to sit back and observe the development of French feminism post-1968 and of the various factions and competing definitions within that vexed term. 'Christine did not', Cixous explained in an interview, 'come for women'.[171] It is certainly the case that the establishment of Cixous's Centre d'Etudes Féminines in 1974 was of limited interest to Brooke-Rose. It soon became clear to both Cixous and Brooke-Rose that she did not consider herself primarily a woman writer and it was increasingly evident that they each had quite 'different investments' in Vincennes and so drifted apart in the following years. Speaking in an interview in 1991, Brooke-Rose confesses,

> I was and still am impatient with some types of feminism, but it's true that I have been very much concerned, especially in the eighties, with women's place in language, as opposed to the experimental male writer [. . .] but it is all part of my experimenting with different discourses, juxtaposing them and clashing them, rather than a specifically feminist concern.[172]

In the same interview, she rebuffs the idea that bilingualism and polyglottism is associated with a 'specifically female predicament' (p. 153). Writing of how she was blocked when she first started writing *Between*, she decided to

> make her a woman not so much because of bilingualism, but because of this idea that a translator merely transmits other people's ideas, and this is sort of a cliché about women, it's a view that a masculine world has and has had for many many centuries about women. (p. 154)

The interviewer pushes her on the question of feminism: 'you seem to oppose the idea of women's writing', *écriture féminine*', to which Brooke-Rose responds:

> the radical feminists are very much against the androgynous-great-mind stance which was Virginia Woolf's. I am rather for it. Clearly any great mind or indeed any human being has a great deal of feminine and masculine in him, and all male writers have always had a lot of feminine in them.

Women, she continues, have tended to accept 'the male point of view' for generations and centuries' and thus 'have always read as men [. . .]

and it's time that men also learn to read as women' (p. 157). However, as noted in Chapter 1, she had 'always been suspicious of all movements and labels which create blind obsessions. A writer, man or woman, is essentially alone, and will be "good" or "bad" independently of sex or origin'.[173]

The central question for Brooke-Rose was the constitution of the 'specificity' of women's sexual difference.[174] Unconvinced by the Kristevan idea of feminine subjectivity as essentially 'exploded, plural, fluid', definitively outside of linearity and rationalism,[175] she notes that many of the techniques that are claimed as feminine fluidity, nonlinearity and openness have all been used by men, a fact now 'explained away as femininity erupting first in male writing'.[176] In 'A Womb of One's Own', she further develops some of these ideas suggesting, rather controversially, that some of the problems of women's invisibility as experimental writers are made 'worse by some of the feminists themselves' (p. 223) as they insist upon the idea that a women's identity is predicated upon 'a primitive flux and chaos of the pre-symbolic', of the semiotic and the amniotic; 'Are flux and chaos in fact what feminists should defend? And, as corollary, are they entitled to defend it?' (p. 230). In short, she asks, is the womb, and by extension its reproductive functions, what provide the basis for an understanding of femininity? In this way, then, she takes to task both Kristeva and Cixous in her objection to their privileging of the biologically-based irrationalism of the pre-Oedipal and the pre-symbolic as a 'gross over-simplification, which flourishes only at the cost of much sliding and a good deal of loose thinking. Perhaps that is the point? Loose thinking as feminine specificity' (p. 231). The antithesis of a loose thinker, Brooke-Rose was insistent that 'art is above all about ordering' (p. 234). Thus, she concluded that feminists 'shouldn't actually want this, this is going back to the primitive and flux and flowing and all that'.[177]

> Flux and chaos, for all their undoubted vitality and necessity as a means of achieving tolerance, integration, wholeness, are nevertheless at the moment more in danger of threatening all that we hold dear in civilisation today. Moreover, control and logic (etc.) as well as 'symbolic' rather than purely 'semiotic' expression can hardly be said to be absent from the best and most incisive feminist criticism.[178]

If she eschewed the flux of 'womb music' Brooke-Rose did, however, see the possibilities in deconstruction's collapsing of binary logic: 'Inverting the polarities, (writing/voice, nonbeing/being, etc.)', she says, 'produces dizziness and fear (and resistance). But could the ultimate effect not be reequilibration, which should produce (and has produced) flights of creativity'.[179]

If Brooke-Rose explicitly shunned the label 'woman writer' she readily acknowledged that 'male outsiders enter the canon more easily than women do'[180] and that women have had particularly acute difficulties in being recognised as serious writers: 'It take centuries, generations of artists being allowed and expected to practise their art and to show themselves practising it, rather than just looking pretty at a spinet as an asset on the marriage market' (p. 253). She also argued that the refusal of women's creativity was a result of 'men's unconscious' that perpetuates the 'deep phallocratic fear of women' that has led to the 'total occultation of women from the writing process' with the exception of 'disguised autobiography' that is allowed to women as it is not regarded as 'not creative' (p. 258). By way of illustration, in *Stories, Theories and Things*, she recounts an anecdote in 'Woman as a Semiotic Object' in which she remembers her despair at trying to make Umberto Eco understand the gendered nature of some linguistic constructions. Despairing of Eco's inability to see how gender is so deeply embedded into language, she wondered if even semioticians, usually alive to all shades of linguistic nuance, were 'unconsciously nostalgic for nice, deep, ancient, phallocentric, elementary structures of significance' (p. 249). Finally, women writers, she argues also face problems of comparison and imitation as well as a fundamental difficulty in belonging as men 'belong to groups', whether the canon or society, whereas traditionally 'women belong to men' (p. 262).

Brooke-Rose did not see sexual difference as any more important than any other kinds of human difference, including race and nationality and was wary of any theory that unyieldingly sought to make gender politics its central concern – something she readily acknowledges in one of her testy epistolary exchanges with her estranged sister, Doriel Rose, when she describes herself as 'dreadfully intolerant of dogmatism without the knowledge and analytic capacity I have worked so hard for but NOT of genuine, natural ignorance e.g. students'.[181]

She concludes in 'Illiterations' that a kind of bisexualism of both writing and reading is the best way forward to counter one of the main problems in the question of women's writing, namely 'men's reluctance or inability' to identify with women characters as women do with male ones'.[182]

> Whatever is the case, it would surely be a good thing if more men learned to read as women [...] so that the bisexual effort, which they have metaphori-

cally appropriated at the creative end, should not remain so wholly on the women's side at the receiver's end. Both should read as both, just as both should write as both. And one of the ways in which this delightful bisexualism should occur is in a more open intelligent attitude to experiment of all kinds by women. (p. 264)

Chapter, End of

Christine Brooke-Rose was a consummate writer. In an essay from 1977, she writes what might be considered as a manifesto for her own work, describing it as:

> Playing at what you can do, working at what you can't do. Trying to join the two, trying to heal the infinitive splits one of which is the split between poetry and narrative, which once upon a space time were one and the same thing.[183]

Of her life she said, 'I had huge fun, and am happy that I devoted my life to writing'.[184] After her retirement she refused any invitations to speak in a purely scholarly capacity, preferring (once again) to be considered as a writer rather than a critic. Her fears of falling into complete oblivion, what she continually referred to in her letters as her failure to 'pierce through', have been recently invalidated as a new generation of readers are rediscovering her wit and rigorous critical intellect in her surpassingly thought-provoking *oeuvre* of experimental writing.

Notes

1. Ali Smith, 'The Armchair, the World', *Times Literary Supplement*, 24 March 2006, p. 21.
2. Brooke-Rose, *A Grammar of Metaphor* (London: Secker & Warburg, 1958).
3. Brooke-Rose, interview with David Hayman and Keith Cohen, *Contemporary Literature*, 17: 1 (1976), pp. 1–23 (p. 3).
4. Brooke-Rose, *Remake* (Manchester: Carcanet, 1996), p. 149.
5. Sarah Birch, *Christine Brooke-Rose and Contemporary Fiction* (Oxford: Clarendon Press, 1994), p. 3.
6. Brooke-Rose, 'A Conversation with Christine Brooke-Rose', interview with Maria del Sapio Garbero, in G. N. Forester and M. J. Nicholls (eds), *Verbivoracious Festschrift Volume 1: Christine Brooke-Rose* (Great Britain and Glentrees, Singapore: Verbivoracious Press, 2014), pp. 144–65 (p. 144).
7. Brooke-Rose, 'Christine Brooke-Rose: The Texterminator', interview with Tom Boncza-Tomaszewski, *Independent on Sunday*, 27 March 2005, p. 128 <https://www.independent.co.uk/arts-entertainment/books/features/

christine-brooke-rose-the-texterminator-8427.html> (accessed 13 May 2020).
8. Heather Reyes, 'The British and Their "Fixions," The French and Their Factions', in Ellen G. Friedman and Richard Martin (eds), *Utterly Other Discourse: The Texts of Christine Brooke-Rose* (Chicago and Normal, IL: Dalkey Archive Press, 1995), pp. 52–63 (p. 58).
9. Brooke-Rose, Correspondence (literary), 2001–2003, uncatalogued material, Christine Brooke-Rose Papers 1893–2005, MS-00532, Harry Ransom Research Center, University of Texas at Austin. Hereafter, HRC.
10. Mike Freeman, letter to Christine Brooke-Rose, 24 September 2004, Christine Brooke-Rose Papers 1893–2005, MS-00532, HRC.
11. Brooke-Rose, *The Observer*, 7 January 1962. R12574, Series II: A, Reviews by Christine Brooke-Rose, 1955–1984, Christine Brooke-Rose Papers 1893–2005, MS-00532, HRC.
12. Lorna Sage, 'Review of Amalgamemnon', *The Observer*, 18 November 1984, p. 29. R12574, Series II: B, 15.17, Christine Brooke-Rose Papers 1893–2005, MS-00532, HRC.
13. Christine Brooke-Rose, 'Thru', in *The Christine Brooke-Rose Omnibus: Four Novels – Out, Such, Between, Thru* (Manchester: Carcanet, 1986), pp. 577–742 (p. 736).
14. Brooke-Rose, *Stories, Theories and Things* (Cambridge: Cambridge University Press, 1991), p. 13. Hereafter, Brooke-Rose, *Stories*.
15. Brooke-Rose, 'Remaking', in Christine Brooke-Rose, *Invisible Author: Last Essays* (Columbus: Ohio State University Press, 2002), pp. 53–62. Originally a lecture, British Council Conference, September 1996; published in *PNR*, 113, 23: 3 (1997) <https://www.pnreview.co.uk (accessed 20 April 2019).
16. Brooke-Rose, *Stories*, p. 189.
17. Karen R. Lawrence, *Techniques for Living: Fiction and Theory in the Work of Christine Brooke-Rose* (Columbus: Ohio State University Press, 2010), p. 5.
18. Brooke-Rose, 'A Conversation with Christine Brooke-Rose', interview with Ellen G. Friedman and Miriam Fuchs, in Friedman and Martin (eds), *Utterly Other*, pp. 29–37 (p. 37).
19. Alain Robbe-Grillet, *For a New Novel: Essays on Fiction* (New York: Grove Press, 1965), p. 157.
20. Brooke-Rose, 'Women in Their Own Write: A Novel Theory', interview with John Hall, *The Guardian*, 16 November 1970, p. 9.
21. Brooke-Rose, 'The Baroque Imagination of Robbe-Grillet', *Modern Fiction Studies*, 11: 4 (1965), pp. 405–23 (p. 420).
22. Brooke-Rose, *Remake*, p. 6. Subsequent running page references to individual texts will be given in the text in parentheses.
23. Ellen G. Friedman, 'The Resisting Author: An Introduction', in Friedman and Martin (eds), *Utterly Other*, pp. 9–18 (p. 9).
24. Ezra Pound, letter to Harriet Monroe, 29 December 1927, in *The Selected Letters of Ezra Pound, 1907–1941*, ed. D. D. Paige (New York: New Directions, 1970), pp. 215–16 (p. 215). See also Eveline Kilian, '"My publisher urged me to write an autobiography": Christine Brooke-Rose's Experiment with Life Writing', in Lucia Boldrini and Julia Novak (eds),

Experiments in Life-Writing: Intersections of Auto/Biography and Fiction (London: Palgrave Macmillan, 2017), pp. 79–102 (p. 80).
25. Samuel Beckett, 'Dante ... Bruno. Vico ... Joyce', in Samuel Beckett, *Disjecta: Miscellaneous Writings and a Dramatic Fragment*, ed. Ruby Cohn (New York: Grove Press, 1984), pp. 19–34 (p. 19).
26. Also preserved in this archive are reviews of her essays, academic books, novels and collections of criticism along with letters responding in detail to the doctoral theses.
27. These are Brooke-Rose's corrections to the information on her life at Bletchley Park annotatated on the draft of *Utterly Other Discourse*. Ever attentive to factual inaccuracies, she corrected the author's description of 'a unit of British intelligence called "Ultra"': 'no, the intelligence was called Ultra higher up or in the field'. She also adds that she did not only 'help decipher' but actually 'deciphered' the 'resulting intelligence'. G10692, Series III: 28.8–10 Christine Brooke-Rose Papers 1893–2005, MS-00532, HRC.
28. Brooke-Rose, 'Remake', in Friedman and Martin (eds), *Utterly Other*, pp. 19–28 (p. 22). Also in *Remake*, p. 5. In HRC archives of personal correspondence, there is a letter dated 4 Janauary 1946, Group Captain E. M. Jones RAF describes Brooke-Rose's WAAF service in hut AA7 between 19 May 1941 and 1 January 1946. She was 'one of a large number of young women who were carefully selected for ability and reliability [. . .] Even in this company she proved herself one of the best, and in consequence she was promoted to a job which called for ability, initiative, and a capacity to accept responsibility, far above the average.'
29. Brooke-Rose, 'The Texterminator', interview with Tom Boncza-Tomaszewski. Brooke-Rose thought *The Sycamore Tree* 'really bad' and when Muriel Spark suggested that the Hogarth Press reprint her early novels, she wrote to Christine Carswell on 2 October 1985 saying that 'I wouldn't want it reprinted'. R12574, Series III: A, 16.10–11, Christine Brooke-Rose Papers 1893–2005, MS-00532, HRC.
30. Friedman and Martin, 'Introduction', in *Utterly Other*, pp. 9–17 (p. 11).
31. Brooke-Rose, *A Rhetoric of the Unreal: Studies in Narrative and Structure, Especially of the Fantastic* (Cambridge: Cambridge University Press, 1981), p. 74.
32. Brooke-Rose, *The Middlemen: A Satire* (London: Secker & Warburg, 1961), p. 2.
33. 'Good for a Laugh', *Manchester Evening News*, 22 August 1961, R12574, Series II: B, 15.9, Christine Brooke-Rose Papers 1893–2005, MS-00532, HRC.
34. Anthony Burgess, *Yorkshire Post*, 7 September 1961.
35. Sarah Birch, *Brooke-Rose*, p. 24.
36. Muriel Spark, letter to Brooke-Rose, R12574, Series II: B, 15.9, Christine Brooke-Rose Papers 1893–2005, MS-00532, HRC.
37. Simon Michael Bessie, letter to Brooke-Rose, 5 June 1961, R12574, Series II: B, 15.9, Christine Brooke-Rose Papers 1893–2005, MS-00532, HRC.
38. Brooke-Rose, interview with David Seed, *Textual Practice*, 7: 2 (1993), pp. 247–57 (p. 250).

39. Notes for interview with Tom Boncza-Tomaszewski, from uncatalogued papers, 1893–2005, MS-00532, HRC.
40. Brooke-Rose, *The Languages of Love* (London: Secker and Warburg, 1957), p. 5.
41. 'Eccentric, Obscure but not Negligible', *The Auckland Star*, Saturday 27 March 1971, R12574, Series II: B, 15.5, Christine Brooke-Rose Papers 1893–2005, MS-00532, HRC.
42. Lorna Sage, *Moments of Truth: Twelve Twentieth-Century Women Writers* (London: Fourth Estate, 2001), p. 202.
43. From uncatalogued papers, 1893–2005, MS-00532, HRC.
44. Uncorrected MS of 'Parallels and Paradoxes: The Story of a Literary Friendship', for Frank Kermode's *Festschrift*, p.8, from uncatalogued papers, 1893–2005, MS-00532, HRC.
45. Brooke-Rose, 'The Nouveau Roman', *Times Literary Supplement*, 7 August 1969, pp. 881–2 (p. 882).
46. Brooke-Rose, *Stories*, p. 189.
47. Brooke-Rose, 'Self-Confrontation and the Writer', *New Literary History*, 9: 1 (1977), pp. 129–36 (p. 135).
48. Brooke-Rose, *Stories*, p. 27.
49. Brooke-Rose, interview with David Seed, *Textual Practice*, 7: 2 (1993), pp. 66–74. Online version pp. 247–57.
50. Brooke-Rose, *Stories*, p. 26.
51. Laura Marcus, Susan Wiseman, Judith Still and Mary Jane Drummond, 'Reviews: Mapping the Modern', *Women: A Cultural Review*, 2:2 (1991), pp. 179–200.
52. Brooke-Rose, *Stories*, p. 264.
53. Brooke-Rose, 'Parallels and Paradoxes', in Anthony Holden and Ursula Owen (eds), *There are Kermodians: A Liber Amicorum for Frank Kermode* (London: Everyman, 1999), p. 4.
54. Brooke-Rose, *Languages*, p. 8.
55. For example, in *Times Literary Supplement*, 12 August 1994.
56. Jonathan Coe, 'The Experimental Woman', *The Observer*, 7 April 1996, p. 15.
57. In 1987 she was the subject of a BBC literary documentary, *Bookmark*, that played up her Frenchness by filming her strolling along the banks of the Seine and swishing across the Vincennes campus in a cloak, her cut-glass vowels somewhat at odds, perhaps, with teaching at this most radical of campuses. 'Yorkshire Ripper, Melvyn Bragg, Christine Brooke-Rose', *Bookmark*, BBC video, 7 May 1987, at G10692, Separated material, 1893–2005, MS-00532, HRC.
58. Colin Wilson, *The Sunday Telegraph*, 27 August 1961.
59. Brooke-Rose, 'Samuel Beckett and the Anti-Novel', *The London Magazine*, 5: 12 (December 1958), pp. 346 (p. 38). Subsequent references are given in the text in parentheses.
60. C. P. Snow, *The Two Cultures* (Cambridge: Cambridge University Press, 1993), p. 3.
61. Adam Guy, '"That's a scientific fact": Christine Brooke-Rose's Experimental Turn', *The Modern Language Review*, 111: 4 (2016), pp. 936–55 (p. 943).

62. Brooke-Rose, 'Mental Participation', *Times Literary Supplement*, 6 September 1957, p. 537.
63. On Queneau, see Christine Brooke-Rose, 'Viewpoint', *Times Literary Supplement*, 1 June 1973; on Simone Weil, *Times Literary Supplement*, 16 November 1956; on jazz, 'Ye Olde New Orleans', *Time and Tide*, 23 August 1958; on Al Alvarez, *Times Literary Supplement*, 3 March 1961. Other notable reviews cover Ivy Compton Burnett, Iris Murdoch, Alistair McClean, Robert Pinget, Frank Kermode, and Indian travel writing. R12574, Series II: A, various, and G10692, Series III: 26, 1893–2005, MS-00532, HRC.
64. Brooke-Rose, '*The Mirror in the Roadway*: Review', *Time and Tide*, 20 July 1957.
65. Brooke-Rose, 'Anatomy of Originophobia', *Times Literary Supplement*, 19 May 1961, p. 308.
66. Brooke-Rose, 'The Vanishing Author', 12 February 1961, R12574, Series II: A, 14–15, 1893–2005, MS-00532, HRC. She also cites Karol Irzykowski's *Paluba* (Warsaw: Wiedza, 1948 [1903]); Joaquim Maria Machado de Assis, *Memórias Póstumas de Brás Cubas*, serialised in *Revista Brasileira*, 1880; Andre Gide's *Les Faux-monnayeurs* (Paris: Gallimard, 1925); Thornton Wilder's *The Skin of Our Teeth* (New York: Harper & Brothers, 1942); Antoine Furetière, *Le Roman Bourgeois* (1666); and E. T. A. Hoffman's *Lebensansichten des Katers Murr* (1819–21) as examples of anti-novels.
67. Corrected MS for the *Guardian* 1984. R12574, Series I: B, 14.9, Christine Brooke-Rose Papers 1893–2005, MS-00532, HRC.
68. Brooke-Rose, 'Remaking', in Brooke-Rose, *Invisible Author*, p. 58.
69. Like her contemporaries Barbara Wright and Barbara Bray, Brooke Rose was a skilled translator from French to English, winning the prestigious Arts Council Translation Prize in 1969 for her translation of *Dans le Labyrinthe*. See G. N. Forester, '*In the Labyrinth*, translated by Brooke-Rose: A Review', in Forester and Nicholls (eds), *Verbivoracious*, pp. 86–92 (p. 91).
70. Brooke-Rose, 'Subscript', interview with Lorna Sage, in Brooke-Rose, *Invisible Author*, pp. 169–80 (p. 172).
71. Nathalie Sarraute, *The Age of Suspicion: Essays on The Novel*, trans. Maria Jolas (New York: George Braziller, 1963), p. 213.
72. Brooke-Rose, 'A Writer's Constraints', in Brooke-Rose, *Invisible Author*, (pp. 40–1).
73. Brooke-Rose, 'Invisible Author' (p. 12).
74. Ibid., p. 15.
75. Brooke-Rose, 'Review of Robert Pinget's *The Inquisitory* and *Degrees* by Michel Butor', *The Sunday Times*. In HRC undated galley proofs TXRC98-A40. It is likely that it was published in 1966 after the English translation of *L'Inquisitoire* (1962). R12574, Series II: A, 'Reviews by Christine Brooke-Rose, 1955–1984, 1893–2005, MS-00532, HRC.
76. Brooke-Rose, 'A Writer's Constraints', pp. 41, 47.
77. Brooke-Rose, interview with Hayman and Cohen, p. 4.
78. Ibid. (p. 92).
79. Brooke-Rose, 'A Conversation', interview with del Sapio Garbero, p. 156.

80. Brooke-Rose, 'Illiterations', in Friedman and Fuchs, also in Brooke-Rose, *Stories*, and in Forester and Nicholls (eds), *Verbivoracious*, pp. 41–59. She also provides a useful synopsis of some of these techniques in Brooke-Rose, 'The Baroque', pp. 405–23.
81. Robbe-Grillet, *New Novel*, p. 17.
82. Brooke-Rose, 'Invisible Author', p. 17.
83. Brooke-Rose, 'The Author is Dead Long Live the Author', in Brooke-Rose, *Invisible Author*, pp. 130–55 (p. 153).
84. Brooke-Rose, *Rhetoric*, p. 330. In Heather Reyes's doctoral work, she examines the influence of Italo Calvino and Umberto Eco, drawing in particular on Eco's 'Form as Social Commitment' in *Open Work*. 'Form must not be a vehicle of thought; it must be a way of thinking', and must break up the ossification of stereotypes: 'our feelings and emotions have been frozen into stereotypical expressions that have nothing to do with our reality'. Umberto Eco, *The Open Work*, trans. Anna Cancogni (London: Hutchinson Radius, 1989), pp. 141–2. This, argues Reyes, can be traced back to *A Grammar of Metaphor*. See her 'Delectable Metarealism/Ethical Experiments: Re-reading Christine Brooke-Rose' (unpublished doctoral thesis, Birkbeck, University of London, 1998).
85. Ibid.
86. Lorna Sage, 'A Place for Displacement', *Times Literary Supplement*, 12 August 1994, p. 21.
87. Boswell, 'Writer Out on a Limb: Boswell Meets Christine Brooke-Rose', *The Scotsman*, 17 April 1965, 1893–2005, MS-00532, HRC.
88. Brooke-Rose, *Stories*, p. 12.
89. Ibid., p. 12.
90. Ibid., p. 12.
91. Sage, *Moments of Truth*, p. 190.
92. Brooke-Rose, *Stories*, p. ix.
93. Brooke-Rose, 'A Writer's Constraints', in Brooke-Rose, *Invisible Author*, p. 41.
94. Ibid., p. 41.
95. Sage, *Moments of Truth*, p. 198.
96. Letter to Helga Hansen, 3 February 1997, G11681, Series II: Correspondence, 1996–1999, 1893–2005, MS-00532, HRC.
97. Brooke-Rose, *Stories*, p. 12.
98. Brooke-Rose, *Rhetoric*, p. 15.
99. Brooke-Rose, 'Illicitations', *Review of Contemporary Fiction*, 9: 3 (1989), pp. 101–9 (p. 102).
100. On the history of Paris VIII, see Paul Cohen, 'Happy Birthday Vincennes!: The University of Paris-8 Turns Forty', *History Workshop Journal*, 69 (2010), pp. 206–24.
101. Brooke-Rose, *Remake*, p. 166.
102. Interview with Ian Hamilton, 'Yorkshire Ripper, Melvyn Bragg, Christine Brooke-Rose', *Bookmark*, BBC, 7 May 1987, at G10692, HRC.
103. Brooke-Rose, 'Remaking', in Brooke-Rose, *Invisible Author*, p. 58. She erroneously remembers the article here as 'The Death of the Author'.
104. Brooke-Rose, letter to Glyn White, 4 February 1998, G11681, Series II, 1893–2005, MS-00532, HRC.

105. See 'The Nouveau Roman', a review of John Sturrock's *The French New Novel: Claude Simon, Michel Butor, Alain Robbe-Grillet*, *Times Literary Supplement*, 7 August 1969. HRC, Series II: 15.1.
106. Brooke-Rose, 'Mood of the Month', XI p. 50, R12574, Series II: 15.1, 1893–2005, MS-00532, HRC.
107. The following abbreviations are used: *LL*, *The Languages of Love*; *ST*, *The Sycamore Tree*; *DD*, *The Dear Deceit*; *MM*, *The Middlemen: A Satire*; *LLEO*, *Life, Life, End Of*; *IA*, *Invisible Author*; *STT*, *Stories, Theories and Things*.
108. Uncorrected MS of Invisible Author, p. 17, 1893–2005, MS-00532, HRC.
109. Brooke-Rose, 'Invisible Author', in *Invisible Author* (p. 2).
110. Ian Hamilton, 'A Network of Urban Tensions', *The Telegraph*, 19 November 1964.
111. Brooke-Rose, 'The Texterminator', interview with Tom Boncza-Tomaszewski.
112. Brooke-Rose, 'Invisible Author', in *Invisible Author*, p. 17.
113. Brooke-Rose, 'Conversation' with Friedman and Fuchs, pp. 31–2.
114. Brian McHale, '"I draw the line as a rule between one solar system and another": The Postmodernism(s) of Christine Brooke-Rose', in Friedman and Martin (eds), *Utterly Other*, pp. 192–213 (p. 193).
115. B. S. Johnson, 'View/Reviews: 'Telling Stories is Telling Lies . . .', *Vogue*, 1 October 1966, p. 18.
116. Brooke-Rose, 'Women in Their Own Write', p. 9.
117. Judy Little, *The Experimental Self: Dialogic Subjectivity in Woolf, Pym, and Brooke-Rose* (Carbondale: Southern Illinois University Press, 1996), p. 135.
118. Brooke-Rose, 'Conversation' with Friedman and Fuchs, p. 31.
119. Little, *Experimental Self*, p. 7.
120. Morton P. Levitt reads the novel as a parody and an 'inversion' of *La Jalousie*, in Levitt, 'Christine Brooke-Rose', in Jay L. Halio (ed.), *British Novelists Since 1960: Part 1, A–G*, Dictionary of Literary Biography, XIV (Detroit: Gale Research, 1983), pp. 124–9. See also Reyes 'Delectable Metarealism'. The MS of *Out* at the Harry Ransom Center contains Brooke-Rose's annotations which provide a fascinating metacritical paratext to Reye's readings. R12574, Series I: A, 4–5, 1893–2005, MS-00532, HRC.
121. In 1964, the year *Out* was published, Nelson Mandela was sentenced to life imprisonment for his membership of the ANC.
122. Brooke-Rose, 'A Conversation', interview with del Sapio Garbero, p. 150.
123. Brooke-Rose, 'Invisible Author', in *Invisible Author*, p. 16.
124. Jean-Paul Sartre, 'Preface', in Albert Memmi, *The Colonizer and Colonized* (New York: Orion Press, 1965), pp. xv–xxvi (p. xv).
125. Natalie Ferris, '"I think I preferred it abstract": Christine Brooke-Rose and Visuality in the New Novel', *Textual Practice*, 32: 2 (2018), pp. 225–44 (p. 236).
126. *Illustrated London News*, 5 December 1964. All subsequent contemporary reviews of *Out* cited are located in R12574, Series II: B, 15.10, 1893–2005, MS-00532, HRC.
127. Lawrence, *Techniques*, p. 90.

128. Brooke-Rose, 'Illiterations', pp. 52–3.
129. Sage, 'Place for Displacement', p. 21.
130. Brooke-Rose, 'The Baroque', p. 418.
131. Norman Shrapnel, 'Between Prophecy and Fantasy', *The Guardian*, 13 November 1964.
132. *The Tablet*, 21 November 1964.
133. Lawrence, *Techniques*, p. 29.
134. 'New Novel', *The Listener*, 19 November 1964.
135. Boswell, 'Writer Out on a Limb', *The Scotsman*, 1965.
136. 'The New and the New Novel', *Times Literary Supplement*, 30 September 1965, p. 847.
137. Kay Dick, 'The Magic Mountain', *The Spectator*, 1964, p. 614.
138. W. J. Nesbitt, 'Faulkner and Nabokov Again', *The Northern Echo*, 20 November 1964.
139. 'Novelties', *New Statesman*, 13 November 1964.
140. *Evening Standard*, 10 November 1964.
141. Christine Brooke-Rose, interview with Myrna Blumberg, 'Out's Out – It's in to be Anti', *The Guardian*, Saturday 7 November 1964, p. 9.
142. Frank Kermode, 'Flinch, Wince, Jerk, Shirk', *London Review of Books*, 28: 7, 6 April 2006, p. 17.
143. Warren F. Motte Jr (ed.), *Oulipo: A Primer of Potential Literature* (Lincoln, NE: University of Nebraska Press, 1986).
144. Margalit Fox, 'Christine Brooke-Rose, Inventive Writer, Dies at 89', *New York Times*, 10 April 2012 <https://www.nytimes.com/2012/04/10/books/christine-brooke-rose-experimental-writer-dies-at-89.html> (accessed 20 April 2019).
145. Brooke-Rose, *Stories*, p. 6.
146. Ibid., p. 7.
147. A year later, Brigid Brophy published her post-Joycean anti-novel, *In Transit*, a similarly 'difficult' experimental text.
148. Robert Baldick, 'Clash at the Embassy', *Daily Telegraph*, 31 October 1968.
149. The HRC archive contains notes and letters passed between the two at this time.
150. David Lodge, *The Novelist at The Crossroads and other Essays on Fiction and Criticism* (London: Routledge and Kegan Paul, 1971), p. 18–19.
151. Kermode, 'Flinch, Wince', p. 17.
152. Brooke-Rose, *Remake*, cited in Ellen G. Friedman, 'The Resisting Author', in Friedman and Martin (eds), *Utterly Other*, pp. 9–18 (p. 12).
153. Brooke-Rose, *Between*, in *Brooke-Rose Omnibus*, pp. 391–576 (p. 426).
154. Sarah Birch, *Brooke-Rose*, p.81.
155. Karen R. Lawrence, '"Floating on a pinpoint": Travel and Place in Brooke-Rose's *Between*', in Friedman and Martin (eds), *Utterly Other*, pp. 76–96 (p. 86).
156. Lawrence Venuti, 'Translation, Empiricism, Ethics', *Profession*, 10 (2010), pp. 72–81 (p. 80).
157. Brooke-Rose, 'Conversation', with Friedman and Fuchs in *Utterly*, p. 32.
158. Ibid., p. 32.

159. Simultaneous translation was used extensively for the first time at the 1947 Nuremberg Trials.
160. Brooke-Rose, 'Conversation', with Friedman and Fuchs in *Utterly*, p. 32.
161. McHale, 'I Draw the Line', p. 198.
162. 'Loded Language', *Times Literary Supplement*, 31 October 1968, R12574, Series II: B, 15.12, 1893–2005, MS-00532, HRC.
163. Christine Brook-Rose, *A ZBC of Ezra Pound* (London: Faber, 1971), p. 13.
164. Brooke-Rose, interview with Hayman and Cohen, p. 60.
165. John Whitley, 'Girl in a Glass Booth', *The Sunday Times*, 3 November 1968, p. 62.
166. Brooke-Rose, *Stories*, p. 6.
167. Brooke-Rose, interview with Lawrence, in Lawrence, *Techniques*, p. 205.
168. Sage, *Moments of Truth*, p. 178.
169. See Brooke-Rose's correspondence with Canepari-Labib in her PhD thesis 'Word-Worlds: The Refusal of Realism and the Critique of Identity in the Fiction of Christine Brooke-Rose', 1998, G11681, Series II: Correspondence, 1996–1999, HRC.
170. Hélène Cixous, 'The Laugh of the Medusa', trans. Keith Cohen and Paula Cohen, *Signs*, 1: 4 (1976), pp. 875–93 (p. 886).
171. Hélène Cixous, interview in Natalie Ferris, 'Manna in Mid-Wilderness', in G. N. Forester and M. J. Nicholls (eds), *Verbivoracious Festschrift Volume 1: Christine Brooke-Rose* (Great Britain and Glentrees, Singapore: Verbivoracious Press, 2014), pp. 281–8 (p. 284).
172. Brooke-Rose, 'A Conversation', interview with del Sapio Garbero, p. 153.
173. Brooke-Rose, *Stories*, pp. 225–6.
174. Ibid., p. 227.
175. Julia Kristeva, 'Women's Time', trans. Alice Jardine and Harry Blake, *Signs*, 7:1 (1981), pp. 13–35 (p. 19).
176. Brooke-Rose, *Stories*, p. 229.
177. Brooke-Rose, 'A Conversation', interview with del Sapio Garbero, p. 157.
178. Brooke-Rose, *Stories*, p. 233.
179. Brooke-Rose, 'The Dissolution of Character in the Novel', in Thomas C. Heller, Morton Sosna and David E. Wellbery (eds), *Reconstructing Individualism: Autonomy, Individuality, and the Self in Western Thought* (Stanford, CA: Stanford University Press), pp. 184–96 (p. 195).
180. Brooke-Rose, *Stories*, p. 251.
181. Brooke-Rose, Letters, 25 October 1994, G10692, Series II: B, 28.2, 1893–2005, MS-00532, HRC.
182. Brooke-Rose, *Stories*, p. 264.
183. Brooke-Rose, 'Self-Confrontation and the Writer', *New Literary History*, 9: 1 (1977), pp. 129–36 (p. 136).
184. Brooke-Rose, letter to Richard Martin, 24 June 2003, G11681, Series II: 34, 1893–2005, MS-00532, HRC.

Chapter 5

Eva Figes:
'there must be freedom to experiment'

Eva Figes's experimental writing has suffered from particularly long-standing critical neglect. Even in Friedman and Fuchs's seminal *Breaking the Sequence,* she does not, unlike Quin and Brooke-Rose, merit an individual study despite claims early in the book that Figes, along with Kathy Acker, Gertrude Stein, Brooke-Rose, Dorothy Richardson and Woolf have all produced an alternative narrative territory in which 'the feminine, marginalized in traditional fiction and patriarchal culture, can be expressed'.[1] Like most of the writers examined in this book, Figes's work tends to refuse any alignment with a particular concept of the 'feminine'. Although some of her writing explores women's social and cultural roles, it is also concerned more broadly with questions of memory, history and the difficulties in articulating alienated subjectivities which results in, what Robert Nye describes as, a 'poetry of the inarticulate'.[2] Figes's bilingual German-Jewish identity is, I suggest, an important part of this faltering poetics in her writing practice as it allows her to consider the ways in which language constructs the subject as an outsider or marginal. Figes regarded herself first as a German, then as a Jew in wartime Britain and so could, as Brooke-Rose says of her own writing, explore the world from the 'enemy viewpoint' which she extends to incorporate the kinds of marginalisation suffered by women.

'Rule one: never speak German'[3]

Born Eva Unger on 15 April 1932 into a family of upper-middle-class assimilated German Jews, Figes came from a family of four: her father, Peter Edward Unger (1904–73) and mother, Irma Alice, *née* Cohen (1905–91), and a brother, Ernst. In November 1938, after a business trip to Berlin, her father was arrested during the events of Kristallnacht and temporarily imprisoned in Dachau, the first of the Nazi concentration camps situated on the outskirts of Munich. On his release in 1939, after the family bribed his way out of the camp, the family prepared to flee from Germany, initially finding only Bangkok willing to take them in as Jewish refugees.[4] Eventually, though, they were permitted to enter Britain where they settled into a life which, while not one of hardship, was noticeably less affluent than the the one left behind in Berlin. Soon after their arrival in England, Eva's maternal grandparents, who had not been able to join them on their flight, were imprisoned and subsequently died in Trawniki, a concentration camp south of Lublin in Poland. The young Eva was not aware of this until later and recalls no explicit allusion to the Holocaust in her childhood until she was thirteen, when her mother sent her to the local cinema with nine pence where she 'sat alone in the dark and watched the newsreel of Belsen'.[5]

The family originally settled in north-west London where the children were sent to the local primary school but in 1941, to escape the Blitz, they temporarily moved out of London and Eva and her brother were sent to boarding school at Cirencester, Gloucester. During the war, Figes's father was in the British Army and took part in the Normandy landings and then worked processing foreign refugees in a special army unit. After leaving her North London primary school, Figes attended Kinsgbury Grammar School until 1950, the recipient of a State Scholarship. She went on to read English at Queen Mary, University of London from where she graduated with honours in 1953. In 1955, she married John Figes, a fellow graduate in history. They had two children, Catherine-Jane and Orlando, but the marriage lasted only seven years and they divorced in 1962.

For Figes, the physical effects of the Second World War resounded long into the 1960s and 1970s, and the emotional and psychological repercussions much longer as described in three autobiographical works that described her early life and the ways in which she became aware of herself as an outsider – a German-speaking Jew in wartime England. In *Little Eden: A Child at War* (1978) she describes how, as a child, she realised that as a German speaker in England her 'foreignness' was charged with a particular significance that, although tolerated at school, could turn treacherous at any moment. She quickly adapted to these new linguistic conditions and learnt that to be accepted in England she should 'never speak German' as it had 'become the tongue of lunatics and maniacs'.[6] Her mother forbade the children from speaking any German during wartime, a prohibition that inevitably led to a feeling of double-consciousness in the young Figes who felt a keen awareness of loss around the silenced language. There was no sense of Jewishness inculcated in the children at home so, on being called a Jew by another child at school for the first time, Eva was bewildered by the 'unnamed tensions that attached themselves to this state of being' (p. 129). She was deeply disturbed by the idea that others could identify her with a label 'planted' upon her 'so bewilderingly', and that 'other people [could] know things about me that I did not myself' (p. 73). This sudden awareness of her Jewishness made Figes increasingly sensitive to silence: 'things unsaid, hinted at, a dark horror at the heart of the family which could not be spoken about but brooded over the dining table, turned small disputes about everyday trifles into momentous schisms' (p. 129). Figes describes the anxiety that this silence provoked and how once it began to be articulated she was transformed into a conduit for guilt, 'I found myself like a lightening [sic] conductor, suddenly charged with what for me became a guilt of horrendous proportions' (p. 129). A powerful presence in her early life, this silence seemed to be at odds with the external life she led which was secular and, to all intents and purposes, 'English'.

Outside of *Patriarchal Attitudes*, most critical work on Figes (of which there is very little) has focused on the articulation of the trauma of the post-Holocaust generation, defined by Marianne Hirsch as the 'postmemory' generation', in whom the damage of the Holocaust was transmitted intergenerationally by memories and stories.[7] Oblivious of her Jewishness until this playground interpellation, Figes would later situate her sense of outsiderness in the broader historical context of her familial history that was distinctly European, expressed here in a 1978 article, 'The Long Passage to Little England' in *The Observer*:

> England does not share the European experience. German troops never marched down Whitehall; men were not rounded up and shot or sent to labour camps; there were no gas chambers on the outskirts of Surbiton or Tunbridge Wells; no partisans, no collaborators and no bitter aftermath of retribution. This enabled a lot of English people to see life after 1945 as a continuation of life before the war.[8]

The sense of being an interloper into what she calls Englishness (never Britishness) is manifested in a prevalent sense of foreignness in much of Figes's fiction. Her protagonists, both male and female, are often agonisingly aware of the discrepancy between their consciousness of self and the external world, exacerbated by the tensions between being at home and being adrift in the world. As one critic notes, Figes's writing abounds with the 'multifarious narrating I s' which oscillate between 'home and away', the 'here of loneliness and ghostly sites' and the 'there then' of 'nostalgic pasts'.[9] Deep memory, often repressed and buried, functions as a Bergsonian version of a second self in many of Figes's novels and necessitates a different level of articulation that often runs concurrently with the external self in the exterior world or, as is sometimes the case, overwhelms this exterior self.[10]

Like Brooke-Rose, after graduating Figes worked for fifteen years in publishing and journalism and was a regular contributor to *The Guardian*, especially to what was then called 'The Women's Page'. She wrote articles and editorials for several newspapers and magazines including *The Observer*, *The Guardian* and *Vogue*, and also worked as an editor for major publishing houses including Longmans, Weidenfeld and Nicolson, and Blackie. In 1973, she taught for two terms at University College London on a Cecil Day-Lewis fellowship.

Figes produced a wide and varied compilation of written works: thirteen novels, three (semi-)autobiographical works, four critical works, various short stories, radio and television plays, children's books, about a dozen translations of French and German novels, and numerous critical pieces published in journals and magazines. Like Brooke-Rose, Figes was a writer and critic, and is best remembered for *Patriarchal Attitudes: Women in Society* (1970) which remains, along with Germaine Greer's *The Female Eunuch*, published the same year, a central work in the history of British feminism.[11] She wrote another book on women, *Sex and Subterfuge: Women Writers to 1850* (1982) and edited *Women's Letters in Wartime, 1450–1945* (1993), as well as an earlier critical study, *Tragedy and Social Evolution* (1976).[12] From 1987, she became the co-editor of Macmillan Women's Writers series, a role which gave her a good oversight of the landscape of second-wave feminism and the varieties of women's writing. Also like Brooke-Rose, Figes was a talented translator – translating two novels from German to English for Calder and Boyars – Renate Rasp's *A Family Failure* (1970) and *The Deathbringer* by Manfred von Conta (1971).[13]

While she began writing novels in the 1960s, Figes did not become a full-time writer until 1967. Her first novel, *Equinox*, was published in 1966, followed by *Winter Journey* in 1967 for which she won the Guardian Prize for Fiction. *Konek Landing* in 1969, was followed by *B* (1972), *Days* (1974) and *Nelly's Version* (1977). The next decade saw Figes continue to experiment with novelistic form in *Waking* (1981), *Light* (1983), *The Seven Ages: A Novel* (1986), *Ghosts* (1988), *The Tree of Knowledge* (1990), *The Tenancy* (1993), and *The Knot* (1996). In addition, she wrote two children's novels, *The Banger* (1968) and *Scribble Sam* (1971) and two short stories: 'Obbligato, Bedsitter' (1975) and 'On the Edge,' (1983). Her last works saw her returning to her German Jewish past in *Tales of Innocence and Experience* (2003) and

Journey to Nowhere (2008), an account of postwar Zionism.[14] She also wrote an art historical study *Light: with Monet at Giverny (2007)*.

Given the timeframe of my study, I am limited to the examination of only three of Figes's experimental novels in this chapter, all of which were published in the 1960s, but it is important to note that Figes continued to experiment with temporality and disarticulation in her subsequent novels, in particular, *B*, *Days* and *Nelly's Version*. The first novel examined here is *Equinox*. Published in 1966, four years before *Patriarchal Attitudes*, it anticipates many of its arguments regarding women's exclusion from the public domain and their difficulties in finding a meaningful life outside of the home and marriage as well as their struggles to continue writing in the face of cultural and ideological obstacles. A discernibly feminist novel, *Equinox* is narrated in fragmented passages that oscillate between the interior and exterior world, expressing the dissatisfaction of a young, well-educated married woman who is compelled, after she loses a baby, to resume the role of homemaker and to relinquish all her ambitions of becoming a poet. While *Winter Journey* moves away from a feminist theme, it articulates another sense of outsiderness in the form of old age and its attendant physical and psychological alienation. Narrated from the temporally fragmented point of view of an elderly man, Janus Stobbs, the narrative fluctuates temporally between past and present as he descends into the chill landscapes of dotage and obsolescence. The final novel examined in this chapter is *Konek Landing*, a work that Figes once confessed was her favourite. Described on its cover as a 'novel of a man treading the path of Steppenwolf and Siddhartha', it recounts the wandering statelessness of Stefan Konek, a survivor from the Jewish ghetto on the run from persecution in a landscape that resembles the devastated landscape of postwar Europe. In the same way that I considered Brooke-Rose's critical writing on gender as important for her creative writing, I look at *Patriarchal Attitudes* in relation to Figes's position on feminism which, although robustly unequivocal in this work, did not lead to any formal participation in the feminist movement in Britain in the 1970s and 1980s. I turn first to Figes's place in postwar Britain's experimental writing 'scene' and her involvement with the loose-ish association of writers in the Writers Reading Group headed by B. S. Johnson.

Down with 'shabby chicanery': The Writers Reading Group

While Figes would pursue her own artistic and intellectual path, as much as in fiction as in her non-fiction writing, she was part of a loosely defined collection of British experimenters consisting of herself, Ann Quin, Alan Burns and B. S. Johnson, which became informally known as the Writers Reading Group.[15] In his biography of B. S Johnson, *Like a Fiery Elephant* (2004), Jonathan Coe describes Johnson as the trailblazer of the group, a veritable 'one-man literary avant-garde of the 1960s' but recognises that that there were 'other avant-garde writers around at the time (Alan Burns, Eva Figes, Ann Quin, Christine Brooke-Rose spring immediately to mind)'.[16] However, these writers did not enjoy anywhere near the level of fame of Johnson simply because, Coe suggests, 'they were not as good at putting their names about'.[17] In a review of Coe's biography, Figes noted that despite the social and class differences within the unofficial group, they all shared an interest in the future of the British novel: 'Johnson and I were contemporaries, and although very different in terms of background [...] we shared a common vision about where the novel should be going, or rather, where it should cease to go.[18]

Despite their differences, and the infrequency of their meetings, Figes recalled that they 'were all huggermugger',[19] and that she felt saddened when the group came to an end in double-tragedy with the deaths of Johnson and Quin: 'shortly after these two deaths, Alan Burns, closer to both of them than I had ever been, chose to dig himself into an American university, and stayed there. Their loss still makes me feel solitary, and bereft'.[20] In a later interview in 2010, Figes reiterates her sense of loneliness as the only 'survivor' of the Group:

> We all rather stuck together as a sort of group. We were all very young, and in a way I felt very lonely afterwards because I felt I'm the only one who has survived [...]. They've all either given up or they've killed themselves, and they've got very little to show for it.[21]

Dedicated to finding new forms that might challenge the popularity of social realism in the postwar British novel, each of the writers in the group possessed, Figes notes, 'very different talents and preoccupations' but all 'shared a common credo, a common approach to writing' that was concerned with 'breaking up conventional narrative, with "making it new" in our different ways'.[22] She notes their communal discontent, with what Johnson called the 'shabby chicanery' of conventional realism where the reader is so drawn in by the artificial linearity of the plot that he 'believes', says Johnson, he 'is doing anything but reading a novel'.[23] Figes echoes his views: 'All of us were bored to death with mainstream "realist" fiction at a time when, in England, it seemed the only acceptable sort. We all used fragmentation as a starting point, and then took off in different directions'.[24] For his part, Alan Burns thought that the novel had become 'stuck fast in its 19th century rut': Once a fresh, even ground-breaking way, of narrating the world, realism now, he argued, 'gives off that stink of staleness and old age'. With his characteristic coruscating wit, he *précised* his abhorrence of commercial realism in an essay entitled 'The Disintegrating Novel':

> The boredom the boredom the boredom the boredom the boredom.
> An intensely dramatic account of a love affair between a French politician and a beautiful empty desperately insecure model.
> The boredom the boredom the boredom the continuous unmitigated incapacitating tedium.
> A school teacher dying of an incurable disease spends her last months in a dilapidated cabin on the sea coast where she makes a curious friendship with a wandering Indian. Who publishes who criticises who publicises who sells who buys who reads this predigested pap?[25]

While aesthetic change in music and the visual arts was 'now accepted', even, in some cases, becoming part of the 'establishment' in the 1960s noted Johnson, literature, and especially the novel, was frozen in a time lag and continued to rely heavily on a nineteenth-century mode of storytelling: 'the neo-Dickensian novel not only receives great praise, review space and sales but also acts as a qualification to elevate its authors to chairs at universities'.[26] John Barths's notion of the 'used-upness of certain forms or exhaustion of certain possibilities'[27] was unquestionably in the zeitgeist and clearly Johnson's ideas on the exhaustion of realism seem influenced by Barths when he said of realism: 'no matter how good the writers are who now attempt it, it cannot be made to work for our time, and the writing of it is anachronistic, invalid'.[28]

The group gave a reading entitled 'Writers Reading' at the Institute of Contemporary Arts in London on 27 November 1969, an event attended by lesser-known writers – Paul Ableman, Sarah Broadhurst, Carol Burns, Barry Cole, Rayner Heppenstall and Stefan Themerson.[29] The clearly stated aim of the group was the creation of a 'new audience' for 'prose writers concerned with new forms, styles, and language', but discussion over the ways this might be achieved were not were not always harmonious.[30] As noted in the minutes of the group's second meeting, the points discussed 'took some length of time in very rowdy conditions without any basic decisions arising. All are pending further debate'.[31] Writing about this event in 1978, Figes said that the group had attempted to 'change the face of fiction', but later noted with some regret that '[w]e have failed to change the English literary scene, or it has failed us'. Despite this putative failure the group showed a plucky determination even in the face of anticipated adversity: '[w]e are prepared to be writers facing a barrage of questions, friendly, interested or downright hostile'.³² A promotional pamphlet produced by the group suggested that they encouraged both agreement and rowdy dissent; they wanted 'to start a dialogue through audience participation and/ or protest'.³³ Keenly aware of the entrenched attitudes and the cultural and intellectual domination of what Figes called the 'literary establishment', she and other members of the group also acknowledged that the conservative reading habits of the British public were 'not a mythical Aunt Sally'. Bemoaning such tame literary appetites, she says, 'in England nobody really expects writers to have the intellectual calibre of, say, a philosopher or a mathematician' and 'the review columns and the bestseller lists confirm the cosily middlebrow' [...] people expect novelists and playwrights to entertain, not tax their thinking overmuch'.³⁴

At their first meeting, the group comprising of Burns, Figes, Johnson and Quin, 'resolved to invite: Jim Ballard, William Burroughs, Maureen Duffy, Michael Frayn, Alan Sillitoe'. Duffy, who was a close friend of Brigid Brophy and worked with her on the PLR campaigns, recalls this time as one of exhilarating change and full of new possibilities for writers: 'we were absolutely trying to do something different as a group'. Part of the excitement was the new class make-up of both the PLR campaigners and the members of the Group, many of whom were the first in their families to go to university. PLR was, in part then, a response to this changed class base of many new writers who could not rely on stipends, annuities, and private incomes. Although Johnson was certainly sympathetic to the aims of PLR, he was, recalls Figes, anti-everything – 'always aggressive, even belligerent':

> I remember him throwing paper darts into an audience to campaign for Public Lending Right. I remember sitting next to him at a very rowdy and enjoyable Annual General Meeting of the Society of Authors where he called for the instant resignation of the entire Committee of Management because of their handling of the PLR issue.³⁵

For her part, Figes saw PLR as essential support for writers such as herself, a single mother bringing up two children and only able to write in 'short periods', often 'not more than an hour a day' when her children were at school.³⁶ In 1972, she wrote 'Public Larceny Right' for the *New Humanist* and urged the editor to widely distribute the piece to the Publisher's Association, Society of Authors and the Bookseller's Association 'and see what happens'.³⁷

In addition to PLR, the formation of the Arts Council in 1946 was a vital source of funding for many writers in the 1960s. As recalled by John Calder in his memoirs, the new Labour government actively encouraged arts and culture: 'Jennie Lee became Arts Minister, and suddenly there was money for the arts in greater abundance than ever before, and this included literature [...]. Money was made available to help writers trying to get known who had sufficient talent'.[38] An important step in the relationship between the state and arts, the formation of the Arts Council aimed to directly support writers and artists.[39] For experimental writers, the problem of money was even more pressing as their work had limited popular and commercial appeal. Acutely aware of the need to earn money as the sole provider for her two children, Figes was extremely grateful for the Arts Council's help and acknowledged that it supported emerging writers who wanted to try something different and difficult with the form of the novel: 'there must be freedom to experiment, to make mistakes, to fail, to shock – or there can be no new beginnings'.[40]

Figes was a different kind of experimenter to Johnson, who had very specific, even, one might say, rather unbending ideas about what experiment meant in terms of the novel, and believed that form was considerably more important than the content: 'What happens is nothing like as important as how it is written, as the medium of the words and form through which it is made to happen to the reader'.[41] This formally purist position, however commendable in aesthetic terms, ran the risk of rendering his writing unapproachably prescriptive:

> I want my ideas to be expressed so precisely that the very minimum of room for interpretation is left. Indeed, I would go further and say that to the extent that a reader can impose his own imagination on my words, then that piece of writing is a failure. I want him to see my (vision), not something conjured out of his own imagination. How is he supposed to grow unless he will admit others' ideas?[42]

Adopting a didactic, even cantankerous, position *vis à vis* the reader, Johnson's 'vision' nonetheless constituted a 'belligerent critique of the conservatism of modern British writing and an impassioned apologia for his own methods'.[43] Frank Kermode however, was critical of Johnson's experiments and considered his book of pages in a box as merely tinkering with the material aspects of the book; a method that did not always produce any progression in narrative form *per se*:

> Johnson's plan to revolutionise the novel came down to the use of 'devices' intended to disrupt ordinary forms of attention by involving the physical book itself, the material base of writing, in unusual ways, as if to take revenge on it for a long history of tyranny [...] Johnson was very serious about these innovations, but they kidnap the notion of experiment or estrangement by making it appear that the violation of narrative order in the interests of what

he thought of as truth must be blatant. In fact these tricks simply prompt one to ask what the point of this sort of innovation really is.[44]

Kermode's views are comparable to those of Brooke-Rose on Johnson's experimental techniques. In an interview, she noted that while Johnson 'did a great deal to defend experimental writing', he was not, finally, an experimental writer: 'His stories belong to the then fashionable drab socio-realism'.[45] Here, she identifies the tensions that exist between the sometimes rather conventional kernel of Johnson's writing and the external 'violation of the narrative order' that formed a significant part of his experimentalism. In 1985, looking back at the activities of the Writers Reading Group, Figes recalls how Johnson frequently took his mission of 'truth-telling too literally' but that he was, in fact,

> being consistent in his own way to a belief that Ann, Alan and I all shared with him: the belief that the seamless 'realist' novel is not only not realistic, but a downright lie. Of course all fiction is a form of lying, but the realist novel is a dangerous lie because people have come to believe it.[46]

Different Grids

Figes's own position on what constituted experimentalism was noticeably less dogmatic than Johnson's. She acknowledged that her work could vary substantially both in theme and technique from one text to another depending on her intellectual interests at the time and that she preferred not to 'impede' herself by following one style or technique in every novel. In an illuminating interview with Manuel Almagro and Carolina Sánchez-Palencia in 2000, Figes talks about her own work in terms of its experimentation, emphasising that formal innovation should never occur at the expense of intellectual content:

> I think a writer has to have something to say and one thing leads to another. Occasionally, I've written a book which seems very unlike me because I get interested in a subject and that requires a certain technique to do it.

She recognises that many writers do 'unconventional things' with prose form but often lack, in her view, much in the way of cogent ideas. In the same interview, she notes that she does not carry out the same approach to experiment time after time but accepts that 'sometimes you have to have several attempts until you find the right form'.[47] The right form can be closely aligned to the ethical content of the individual work. Referring to Günter Grass, who was both a close friend and political ally and from the 'same generation that witnessed what happened in Europe', Figes comments that many writers enjoy a position in society that enables them to 'say certain things' and therefore have certain moral obligations: 'to express the defence of certain rights and values' and that they are 'lacking in responsibility if they don't'.[48] She reiterates this position in an essay, 'Accustomed as I Am to Public Speaking' (1973), maintaining firmly that a writer 'must have the same political commitment as any other citizen, "must" because there is no room for sitters-on-the-fence. If you are not for you are against, and inaction and apathy become guilt by default'.[49] On this view, then, the content of an experimental novel is not secondary to the innovative prose style but fundamental to its aesthetic and ethical project.

Writing in 1968, Figes comments on the disparity between different kinds of prose writing that are given the label experimental: 'at no time in the past have books as different, say, as *Malone Dies* and *Anglo-Saxon Attitudes* been awarded the same generic label and criticised as though they had anything in common'.[50] Often circumspect about pronouncing herself an experimentalist, Figes believed that 'a good writer is not "experimental"', that is, she does not (or, by implication, should not) set out to be so but rather that 'there are experimental stages, certainly, but you do not commit yourself to print until you know you have got where you wanted to get'.[51] Figes talks of her search for a 'different grid' for writing, one that might represent 'new models of reality' only attainable 'by a painful process of trial and error'.[52] Placing the idea of experimentalism and the question of realism into a longer time-scale, she concludes that writers simply offer some comments on the 'nature of reality' and if these are successful they 'become internalised by one or more generation and become accepted as reality itself'.[53] Her own writing, she says, is informed by her desire to show that, on the whole, life is 'not conscious,' and that the realist novels of the past portrayed a 'false reality'; finally, she writes of her desire to 'make a direct emotional impact [and] break through the rational prose structures'.[54]

By her own acknowledgment, Figes had three specific influences on her work – each a specific source of joy as well as despair in terms of the development of her own craft. She was a lifelong reader of Kafka to whom, in her early twenties, she says that she responded with passionate intensity: 'It was like having the top of my head completely blown off' and revealed to her that in literature 'anything was possible'.[55] She was also a close reader of Virginia Woolf. After reading Woolf's diaries, she came to believe that she shared an affinity with her approach to writing – she 'was very much like me' – but rather disconsolately supposed that 'she's done it all, there's nothing new under the sun really'.[56] It was only after Figes had produced her own substantial body of work that she felt sufficiently confident to return to Woolf's work and found that, like Woolf in *A Room of One's Own*, she regarded the novel as a still relatively open form for which 'all the rules had not been laid down' and was, therefore, particularly suited to continuing remoulding and revision.[57]

Figes also greatly esteemed Beckett's writing, which seemed to her to reflect her 'own very dark view of the world'; conceding that she was writing in the wake of Beckett, she declared that he 'had gone as far as anyone could go' in one particular direction. Describing herself as 'a much more local writer' than Beckett whose real interest, she thinks, is in writing about men, Figes says: 'when he writes about women, like Winnie in *Happy Days*, he makes her an idiot. And women know about black holes as much as men do'.[58]

An intriguing insight into Figes's writing techniques is to be found in her 1968 essay, 'Interior Landscape'. Stressing the importance of form, she notes: 'you cannot formulate new ideas in an old form [. . .] the interests of any novel must be inextricably bound up with the way in which that novel is written, its structure and language'. But she emphasises that she does not consider herself 'part of a vanguard', rather 'that others are fighting a rearguard action [. . .] based on a conception of the novel which is rooted in the nineteenth century'. Thus, writers of highly conventional realist novels merely blindly replicate the

> superficial techniques of a bygone era without understanding the original motivation which produces those techniques, presumably on the assumption that if it worked in the past it will work now – 'What's good enough for George Eliot is good enough for me' is the argument.

Admitting that she finds it 'difficult to establish any sense of communion with other people who write in such a way', she also is aware of being dismissed 'as avant-garde, though I cannot see anything avant about it: after all Kafka was born in 1883 and could easily have been my grandfather, likewise Joyce and Proust'.[59]

> Just as people now accept Turner sunsets and will buy them in a debased form people recognise in *Dr Zhivago* a kind of construction which they have been taught to associate with great novels of the past. What they fail to recognise is that when these techniques evolved they were to some extent new and were evolved in order to communicate new ideas, the personal *Weltansshauung* of the writer.[60]

Identifying the evolution of contemporary fiction as one that moves away from realism, Figes argues that the boundaries between prose and poetry have once again been 'broken down' as prose writers become increasingly concerned with the poetic – 'Death', 'personal sensibility', the 'fuller exploitation and exploration of language – images as metaphor, ambiguity, subtle rhythms'. This is ignored by those she calls the 'traditionalists' who go on 'formulating theories about what the novel "should be", as though Adam Bede were comparable to Clarissa Harlow, as though there were some kind of outer yardstick of reality'.

> By and large the interest of the serious novelist has moved away from the social scene, from the action and interaction between individual and society [. . .] to the world of the single individual, the private and interior landscape which we assume to some extent we hold in common [. . .] this new assumption does not imply a flight from reality, as the traditionalists would suggest. The theories of Freud have as much bearing on our lives as those of J. M. Keynes.[61]

The last of the group to survive, Figes continued to write into older age and became, like Brooke-Rose, habituated to being 'increasingly neglected', particularly, as by 2000, the term postmodernism had usurped that of experimentalism.[62] With its ready-made grids of irony, transgression and Derridean-inflected linguistic play, postmodernism was a *bona fide* international literary movement that had its own advocates and detractors with whom she felt little connection.

Patriarchal Attitudes: Re-angling Women's History

Like Brophy and Brooke-Rose, Eva Figes wrote about the ways in which women have been 'largely man-made', an insight introduced in the opening pages of Simone de Beauvoir's *The Second Sex* which was translated into English in 1953, but only began to find receptive political ground in the 1960s. Published in 1970, *Patriarchal Attitudes*, represents an important milestone in the development of British feminism.[63] Figes would comment later that: 'I think I became a literary critic mainly because of my feminism because I began to realise that women writers were either neglected or misunderstood'.[64] *Patriarchal Attitudes* appeared, Figes said, at exactly the moment that 'echoes of the American women's movement were beginning to reach Britain', and formed part of a political environment in which 'women worked together with such a sense of communion and unity of purpose'.[65] In an introduction to the 1978 edition, she wrote of the overwhelming response to the book in the form of a 'massive postbag' reflecting the growth of feminism in Britain: 'Women's workshops sprang up all over the country; almost every college had its feminist group, and women's associations of long standing and of all kinds suddenly joined in the growing chorus demanding women's rights'.[66]

Somewhat deprecatingly describing her own *oeuvre*, Figes said, 'I have written only one rational polemic, whilst I am the author of six highly irrational and emotional novels'.[67] Already moderately well known in Britain as a novelist, after the publication in 1970 of this 'polemic' *Patriarchal Attitudes*, Figes enjoyed substantial national and international success, earning her a reputation as an important feminist critic. Published just a month before *The Female Eunuch*, *Patriarchal Attitudes* joined other influential feminist works published the same year in Britain and the United States: Kate Millet's *Sexual Politics*, Robin Morgan's *Sisterhood is Powerful: An Anthology of Writings from the Women's Liberation Movement* and Shulamith Firestone's *The Dialectic of Sex: The Case for Feminist Revolution*.[68] Using a figurative device that encapsulates the representational mechanics of women's oppression, *Patriarchal Attitudes* begins with the image of a seductive mirror in front of which women dance in a 'hypnotic trance' believing that this image is truly 'herself'; at once, her only reality and sole destiny.[69] Locked into this reflection, women cannot draw any knowledge from elsewhere as the mirror authorises her only reality: '[...] because she thought that image was herself, it became just that' (p. 15). It is crucial to note, Figes says, that the mirror is 'distorted' as it was 'created by men' not by both men and women 'for joint aims' (p. 17). The mirror forms part of a 'whole hall of mirrors' which is 'male-created' and immovable (p. 18). This 'hall' is composed of centuries of male lawmakers, philosophers, artists and scientists, all of whom have created and regulated women's 'whole code of morality' (p. 19). However, male domination and the policing of womanhood is only part of the problem. Self-absorbed collusion in their own oppression is a crucial consideration too, as a 'great majority' of women remain entranced by the image in the mirror and 'subside meekly or gracefully' into the roles. However, there are some 'really determined' women for whom that role is 'inadequate, and satisfactory or simply unavailable' assigned to them (p. 19). She quotes from George Eliot's 1856 essay on women's writing, 'Silly Novels by Lady Novelists', in order to show how writing, in particular the novel, might be a liberating space for women: 'No educational restrictions can shut women out of the materials of fiction, and there is no species of art which is so free from rigid requirements. Like crystalline masses, it may take any form, and yet be beautiful' (p. 19). 'History', Figes asserted, 'has to be re-angled' to account for women's invisibility, something considered later in *The Tree of Knowledge*, in which she examines Biblical representations of women.[70]

Somewhat structurally resembling *The Second Sex*, *Patriarchal Attitudes* is an analysis of the cultural, religious and biological origins of women's oppression. Women are taught to be, Figes says, 'an uneasy combination of what [a man] wishes her to be and what he fears her to be, and it is to this mirror image that women have had to comply', non-compliance runs the risk of social denunciation 'since the standard of womanhood is set by men for men and not by women, no relaxation of standards is allowable, choose either an absolute woman, or nothing at all, totally rejected' (p. 17). Like Brophy's views in 'The Immorality of Marriage', Figes challenges the primacy of the natural in terms of gender:

> what is a 'natural' man or woman? One is forced to answer that there is no such thing, unless one concludes that, since man is a social animal, his 'natural' condition is to be artificially conditioned, with variations in time and place. For centuries, the word 'nature' has been used to bolster prejudices or to express, not reality, but a state of affairs that the user would wish to see. (p. 13)

Crucially, Figes recognises that it is possible for women to have, as Patricia Waugh says, a 'rational, coherent, effective' agency in the world and at the same time, be subject to the fragility and paradoxes of human subjectivity which, for women, often involves living intellectually compromised lives because of the demands of domesticity, marriage and childrearing.[71] Pursuing these thoughts, *Patriarchal Attitudes* examines, amongst others, comments on women by Rousseau, Shakespeare and, of course, Freud. But it is to the noted sexologist, Havelock Ellis, to whom Figes initially turns, arguing that in *Man and Woman: A Study of Human Secondary Sexual Characters* (1894), he presents an important argument

> We have to recognise that our present knowledge of men and women cannot tell us what they might be or what they ought to be, but what they actually are, under the conditions of civilisation. By showing us that under varying conditions men and women are, within certain limits, indefinitely modifiable, a precise knowledge of the actual facts of the life of men and women forbids us to dogmatize rigidly concerning the respective spheres of men and women.[72]

These 'conditions of civilisation', what we now understand as cultural and ideological factors, are then, the subject of *Patriarchal Attitudes*. Included in the first chapter, 'A Man's World', are several proclamations on women's natural role of homemaker and helpmeet in society by a range of male commentators including Sir John Newson who in 1964 wrote an article in *The Observer* on his views concerning the training of girls to become homemakers, to become, as Figes puts it, to become 'a man's satellite' (p. 32). The destiny of girls, Newson argues, 'is to develop into housewives and mothers, all activities confined to that of the private and the domestic sphere in which they can exert limited moral control over the family, primarily in their role as wives and mothers' (p. 30). Women exist in this capacity by 'sustaining or inspiring the male [. . .] what infuriates a rather esoteric group of women is that they want to exert power both through men and also in their own right, and that is almost impossible'.[73]

Women in the 1960s

As noted earlier, a series of liberal reforms began in 1965 with the abolition of the death penalty, the partial decriminalisation of homosexuality and the legalisation of abortion in 1967, the end of theatrical censorship in 1968 and the reformation of British divorce laws in 1969. These socially progressive legislations formed the political background to a decade that would go on to assume semi-mythological status as one of widespread social and sexual permissiveness and a movement away from the more conservative postwar sensibility of the 1950s. This narrative of the 1960s, systematically reiterated, as the 'swinging' decade is one that dies hard in the popular imagination but many critical studies of the period suggest that how one experienced the decade depended on class, age, ethnicity and gender.[74] As Brian Harrison notes,

> Most people who lived through the 1960s did not feel that they were collectively experiencing an outlook special to a decade [. . .] But once the decade could be viewed complete, the phrase 'the sixties' became identified with throwing off old inhibitions, conventions, and restraints.[75]

He suggests that the decade might be characterised by several manifestations of revolt and dissent, particularly by youths, all of which originate from a reaction against 'wartime austerity and puritanism'.[76]

In the midst of, and in contrast to, the so-called permissive society was the entrenchment of the ideal of home-owning and domesticity. As observed by cultural historians, the period from the middle of the 1950s into the 1960s was one in which domesticity and home life for women was promoted as the ideal goal in life.[77] The concept of homemaking was established as the foundation of family life for all classes. After the end of rationing the home functioned as an indicator of modernisation and the majority of women across all social classes, many of whom had worked during wartime, found their destinies bound up with the domestic space of the home.[78] For middle-class women, domesticity changed considerably as they were now expected to carry out all the housework previously carried out by domestic help, doing 'chores which their mothers would have employed other women to perform'.[79]

Throughout the 1960s women were being educated to university level in increasing numbers, but their fundamental goal in life, educated or not, was that of being a wife, mother and homemaker; marriage was typically the end of the middle-class young woman's intellectual activity, with few women continuing to work after marrying, and even fewer after having children.[80] An article by Lois Mitchison (daughter of Naomi) in *The Guardian*, 'The Price of Educating Women' questions the value of a university education for girls who were not going to enter the workface.[81] Going to university, she says, is merely a 'frill for a girl who is likely to marry in her early twenties', and while educated women may be a more sociable companion and a 'better housekeeper', how can society justify spending state money on women who will do little more than read a 'book on child welfare' or follow a recipe?'[82] But there are even more 'obviously disastrous consequences of a university education for women' that results in feelings of discontent and guilt 'about their work in the home'.[83] She goes on to place the blame for this dissatisfaction with domesticity on the education institutions themselves: 'some schools and colleges lay the foundations of later guilt by assuming that careers and celibacy are the highest aims for women, or even the normal aims'.[84] Such attitudes towards women's education and paid labour forcefully conditioned women to accept their domestic destinies.[85]

Yet Another (Surprisingly) Reluctant Feminist?

Perhaps somewhat unexpectedly for a writer who became best known for her feminist criticism, Figes exhibited a residual kernel of ambivalence towards feminism as a movement and resisted being described as a 'woman writer'. Writing in a popular magazine, *London Look*, in 1967 Figes says 'I was very worried that I was going to be labelled as a woman writer and I didn't want that kind of image. I think in many cases that there is truth in that criticism of women'.[86] Of *Konek Landing* she said: 'I am trying to perceive as a human being not as a woman. I prize detachment. People who aren't detached are inclined to write the same book over and over again. Writing, for me, should be a progression, a kind of endless exploration'.[87]

Despite her advocacy for feminism, not only in *Patriarchal Attitudes* and *Sex and Subterfuge,* but also in her journalism and other writing,

Figes was extremely reluctant to describe herself, or be described, as a feminist:

> I don't like to be labelled that way (as 'a feminist') because it seems to me that the things I'm writing about are things that affect all human beings, whichever gender they are [...] every citizen has a duty to stand up for certain rights and certain values, but a writer not only has a duty as a human being but has the opportunity to express it either in journalism, or in novels, or in essays, or whatever. I think it lacking in responsibility if they don't do it.[88]

Furthermore, she rejected the idea of her novels as feminist, suggesting that, as a writer, she is palpably less interested in the wider politics of the feminist movement than with an examination of 'women's emotions. Women don't stop feeling vulnerable because of feminism'.[89] Interviewing Figes for the *Guardian* in 1993, Jan Moir remarks on her ambivalence towards feminism to which Figes responds by saying that while she was broadly sympathetic towards its aims she always refused, just like Brophy and Brooke-Rose, to become 'an actual devotee' of the 'burgeoning Women's Liberation Movement'.[90] These pronouncements may appear to sit rather awkwardly against her journalism and her work in *Patriarchal Attitudes* and also with her commentary on feminism for several popular publications that show to what extent *Patriarchal Attitudes* had reached into popular culture beyond the more obviously radical publications such as *Spare Rib*. However, while Figes remained agnostic about what she called the 'vexed question of secondary sexual difference' with regard to women's attitudes and aptitudes, she was nonetheless very clear that if women are 'required to choose between marriage and a career' it amounts 'to repression on a monstrous scale' (p. 9, 12). Her first novel, then, addresses the domestic thwarting of women's desires and ambitions. Before proceeding to my reading of this novel, it is worth quoting at length from a less well-known piece of Figes's work, 'The Largest Minority', in which she writes of the changing attitudes to motherhood in the postwar decades:

> The generation of educated women who grew up at the end of the Second World War were restrained from militancy, not only because they formed a much smaller minority, but because at the time it was fashionable to emphasise the importance of continuous personal contact between a mother and her young children [...] So the ranks of angry young women are swelled by the middle-aged, now redundant mothers who have come to feel that too large a personal sacrifice was demanded of them for those short years of active motherhood, and that they have been cheated of any hope of realising other ambitions in their middle age.[91]

Equinox: The Stillborn Poetess

Equinox (1966) depicts the stalemate that marriage and domestic life often represented for educated women. The novel examines the institution of marriage as a state of 'interlocking neurosis' (*Equinox*, p. 86) and the restrictive roles available for women outside of both matrimony and domesticity.[92] In ways that anticipate many of the ideas in *Patriarchal Attitudes*, *Equinox* recounts fragments of the life of a middle class, educated woman, a poet, who finds her intellect wasting away in the role of the 'bourgeois little housewife' (p. 6). Not long after its publication, Figes confessed in an interview that she was 'thoroughly ashamed' of the novel as it was a 'thinly disguised' quasi-autobiographical work which, although 'distinguished perhaps by poetic language', was not 'challenging in any other way'.[93] It is striking that Figes's objection is to the novel's autobiographical content that attenuates, she believes, its artistic achievement. Commenting on this further she said: 'the husband was not my husband really, though he had certain characteristics of my husband; he was me. I split myself into several bits: the husband was German-Jewish like me, and the woman herself was another aspect of me'.[94] In some ways, this is a clear-sighted self-criticism that acknowledges the strong presence of her life in her art, but dismisses, or neglects, the novel's more submerged themes of speechlessness and memory. Composed of fragmented, episodic prose, the narrative weaves in and out of the not-always fully identified consciousness of each protagonist in snippets of free-floating dialogue that is both spoken and unspoken: 'I must get away soon. I must. Once I was called Reading and said I must get away soon and Martin said don't think about them anymore, marry me. The trap is endless, sprung from generation to generation' (p. 129).

It is implied that Liz Winter had once consulted her doctor with a minor malady (accompanied by her husband Martin), and was given the advice, 'Tell your wife she ought to have a baby [. . .] it gives them something to do' (p. 16). We learn gradually that Liz has been pregnant but lost the baby six months into the pregnancy; a traumatic experience communicated in disjointed fragments throughout the book, sometimes accompanied by lines of poetry, or annotated by dispersed fragments lamenting the inadequacy of her language to find expression not just of this trauma but of the supposed innate naturalness with which women should approach the processes of conception and pregnancy:

> I'd find myself quite speechless, quite unable to communicate in any way, quite unable to understand how it all happened or how I got here at all.

What's this bond supposed to be, anyway, how does it all keep going, this idea of maternal feeling and so on. People don't learn anything just because they conceive, they don't just suddenly understand how to feel just because they give birth. Why should they? (p. 159)[95]

Liz rejects the *diktats* of the naturalness of a women's maternalism that restrict her to the small, private spaces of domesticity that define and regulate her whole life. She longs to leave behind the confines of her home in all its unchanging silence and lassitude: 'I want to stop thinking about where to get a plumber when it thaws [...] what to do in the evenings and the weekends and the long empty spaces between hours when nothing has to be done. I want to run, fast' (p. 75).

The novel opens with the image of air travel; watching planes landing at the airport where she is picking up her husband who has been on one of his frequent trips aboard, Liz thinks 'things can happen here, movement and magic, and soft air and sun can pick you up in an embrace and take you wherever you want to be. Just name a place' (p. 7). But for her, stasis and stagnation is everywhere. The lack of ability to travel, literally or figuratively, is one of the main themes of Figes's debut novel. Liz feels trapped in the monotony of marriage and being a housewife and worries that she 'is not equipped for anything' and thus needs another kind of language to articulate herself into the world: 'I can use words I know, but you have to use words for something, you can't spin them around in a vacuum to make pretty patters. And I'm in a vacuum, I don't have a life'. Her husband dismisses this kind of thinking as 'brooding' and discourages any self-reflection on her part. For him, 'marriage is a side-issue' whereas Liz is wholly defined by its boundaries (p. 11).

She attempts to return to writing poetry after her baby dies but is confronted with her own loss of sensation that further silences her:

The grey gulf of non-being is in me The dull despair

The grey gulf of non-being is yawning

Yawning with the boredom of no pain, no feeling

The grey gulf or getting nowhere The pain of not feeling any

Nothing

Write it down. Fool. (p. 26)

Trying to find writerly inspiration, she reads William Blake but still finds that she cannot access her own voice with which to express her thoughts; 'brainy Liz' becomes the 'stillborn poetess' (p. 120) who is struck dumb by grief and boredom: 'I can't say anything. Afraid of committing myself even to paper. I make myself try, failing all real urge, but the reluctant, dumb thought gets lost half-way to expression' (p. 27). This sense of inarticulacy is strong: 'You should write it down, it says something [. . .] But how often do you even want to say something, have even a single original image?' (p. 75). The nullity she feels gradually comes to the forefront in the narrative as dialogue recedes into the background: 'Throw words and hope they will ring on pavement, or explode like a hand grenade or at least a small toy firework. Meaning grows out of the word itself, unfolds like a seed and sprouts in all directions, bearing strange-tasting fruit.' (p. 76). Set against these faltering attempts at poetic articulation, she sees her 'reluctant, dumb thought' get lost 'half-way to expression' (p. 27).) In between long passages of intense, almost lyrical, interiority there are snippets of excruciatingly hackneyed prose in the style of the popular Mills and Boon romances that are self-consciously inserted into the prose. The descriptions of trite romance counteract the actuality of marriage: 'As he put his arms around her a warm wave of desire swept over her. She closed her eyes. This was what she had been waiting for all her life' (p. 22). Shifting between interior and exterior narratives that emphasise an increasingly wide gulf between her thoughts, her intellect and the way she is expected to be in the external world, Liz finds herself wondering 'just what happened to all that potential juvenile brilliance' (p. 141).

Negotiating the troughs of post-partum depression, Liz meets an almost complete absence of emotional understanding from her philandering husband, Martin, a scientist, who is always urging her to adopt a more scientific approach to life and death: '[T]ry a different way of looking at things, objective rather than introspective'. She should try, he suggests, to 'skim along' life like he does, and to regard the baby's death as an ordinary technical failure of the 'transfer of oxygen from the mother's blood' (p. 16). Bored one day at home, she takes to reading some of the scientific textbooks at Martin's suggestion and encounters purely technical renditions of certain scenarios of life and death and, in particular, reproduction and birth. The emotional aspects of her loss are subdued by the objectification of the process of reproduction that is reduced to a 'procreative machine': 'In the chromosomes, proteins are involved both in a structural role and as enzymes, synthesizing nucleic acid during replication of the generic material' (p. 27). However, she uses the science books to help her with the 'insane' act of writing (p. 76). By finding words for the sucking detachment that invades her life, Liz is helped by the disinterestedness of the scientific texts she reads: 'Every million years or so an elemental atom is created out of nothing [. . .] I am nothing, cold, clear and empty. I'm a stranger to my own life, none of it means anything to me' (p. 95). The effect of these scientific expositions is a drawing back of Liz's thoughts into a kind of elemental interaction with the universe.

Comprised mostly of interior monologue interspersed with more free-floating prose fragments, the novel's 'story' of Liz's unfulfilled life was treated rather dismissively by a reviewer in *The Guardian* as the familiar 'theme of female frustration in the NW3 belt' but concedes that the novel 'lifts this to new heights of dignity and appeal. The ego bound heroine finds no escape from the daily round of brooding, never a moment to put her thoughts up'. But the review praises the novel for its 'austerely passionate style' that 'finally elicits 'total sympathy' for the plight of the protagonist'.[96]

With few people to whom she can talk, Liz's only real intimacy is with herself, her own thoughts and her writing and thus she resorts to silence for prolonged periods. She enters into a rather desultory affair with John, the dissatisfied husband of Frances, another trapped housewife, a harried mother of three children who feels that she is 'curled up in a shell' with a 'pebble blocking her exit' (p. 134). The affair is dismally predictable and perfunctory, lacking in any substantial intimacy. Abbreviating the mundane melodrama of the extramarital affair, Figes telescopes the emotionally charged conversations generic to all adulterous lovers and a commonplace in domestic fiction:

I can't leave her There are the children
She can't stand on her own feet
I'm in a mess, I've always been in a mess But I love you
Whatever that means [. . .]
Yesterday I was thirty

I'm not sure about love. (p. 134)

Liz longs to leave behind the domestic landscape of 'unchanging silence and lassitude'. She feels trapped in the unchanging stasis of domesticity: 'I want to be one of the passengers, travelling hopefully, leaving stale thoughts behind with last year's shoes [. . .] flit, leave no roots . . .' (p. 74). In *Patriarchal Attitudes,* Figes identified the economic and political foundations of sexual inequality, specifically women's role as home makers and non-participants in the public sphere. Capitalism, she argued, has kept women economically dependent on men as it insisted upon 'the sex-role division of woman at home, man at work' a state that is upheld by the institution of marriage in which Liz finds herself trapped.[97]

Attempting to escape this domesticity, then, Liz finds an editorial job in publishing but on returning to the public sphere she very quickly grasps the extent to which the world outside of the domestic domain is shaped around men. She finds herself thrust physically into the male space of work: 'Men everywhere, walking the streets, crowding the tubes and buses, coming into the office and out at the station . . .' She cannot pass unnoticed in this male public space; as she moves around, she is followed by the collective male gaze with its 'cruel predator eagle eyes' (p. 73). And yet, just as Figes notes in *Patriarchal Attitudes*, Liz finds herself desiring definition by this male gaze:

> I'm any woman. My body will grow old and I want to keep it young [. . .] I want to be loved, cherished, protected. I also want to be worshipped from not too far away. I want to stand on my own feet with someone holding both hands [. . .] I want you to think me beautiful even though I know that's not true. I also want the taxi driver to think me beautiful. (p. 136)

Slowly though, work becomes a self-actualising practice for her and allows her to project outwards into the world of connection and sociability and away from the sequestered confines of home and its petty concerns with household maintenance and food; a 'Strange life alone alive in the dark: completely separate and apart' (p. 14). As Anne Oakley observed in her groundbreaking study of women's housework: 'Women's domesticity is a circle of learnt deprivation and induced subjugation: a circle decisively centered on family life'.[98] The deprivation in *Equinox* is both emotional and intellectual: 'Something is happening to me: you can count the moments when something is happening to me' (p. 13). Returning to work allows a partial alleviation of this deficiency of event; she muses 'what's so special about work? Something to do, action, I am in command, pay packet, projects aired, decision already taken' (p. 134). She doubts her intellectual abilities in her job: 'being a woman can make anyone stupid [. . .] I'd be a first-class editor if I wasn't a woman' (p. 13). Work allow hers, in the most literal sense, a way of moving outside of the domestic space to involve oneself in a shared project. For men, this project is taken for granted as they are taught to project outwards onto the world: 'I am any man [. . .] I want to tell other people what to do, and why they ought to do things . . .' (p. 136), but such authority requires a woman/wife to recognise and facilitate its legitimacy:

> I want someone to come home to. Someone who understands everything and who will leave me alone to get on with my own work when I need peace and quiet. But who appreciates my work, can make positive comments [. . .] also I want to stay in command. A Greek goddess who cooks well. (pp. 136-7)

Liz's constant feelings of inarticulacy are mirrored in the repressed memories of her husband, Martin, a scientist whose approach to life is cautious, buttoned-up and rational. A German-Jewish child, he was sent to England on the *Kindertransport* and Liz often imagines him as part of an 'endless stream of thin and ragged people' (p. 32), but he is mute about his Jewish past; he 'never talked about his past to anyone, and most people had no idea' and he tells Liz that he 'put it away' (p. 156). As readers, we learn only circuitously that his parents were murdered by the Nazis:

> She thought about Martin in the first days she knew him, his veiled hostility to a civilisation which had liquidated his parents scientifically, the way cattle are disposed of, his love and hate for the English way of life which had allowed him to grow up in security but condemned his parents to death. (p. 72)

Martin's childhood memories are transferred into Liz's unsettled mind and she begins to dream of him as a 'a small boy with cropped hair and protruding ribs' (p. 32), and of Holocaust images of 'rotting bodies' and ominous trains. While Martin is mostly silent about his Jewishness, he understands that he feels survivor-guilt and says at one point: 'What kind of Jew am I, anyway? Look at these hands, they're alive and strong [. . .] And they have no right to be alive at all' (p. 32). This second story of Martin's experience as a German-Jewish refugee haunts *Equinox* but is left uncharted: it is not until *Konek Landing* in 1969 that Figes begins to more fully examine the ways in which this refugee history is intimately bound into her own experience of Jewishness in postwar Britain.

The reception of *Equinox* was largely favourable, with most reviewers affording as much attention to Figes's writing style as to its feminist themes. In *The Observer,* one review notes, 'Miss Figes handles the interior monologue convention with genuine tact', and that her 'methods needs no justification since she makes it seem the obvious way to handle the material'.[99] *The Evening Standard* called *Equinox* a '[p]erceptive novel' – 'Courageous, honest and ultimately depressing'.[100] In *The Sunday Telegraph*, Francis King wrote that the main character in *Equinox* is a 'neurotic and, highly intelligent and self-willed women' and that Figes writes of her frustrations with 'a beautiful exactitude and sensitivity to the nuances of words' despite the fact there is some unsuccessful material in the novel that is 'too voluble and too intense to carry total conviction'. He complains that men are depicted as if they were 'members of an alien species', and of 'some restless time switches' but that despite these limitations, *Equinox* is a novel 'to be recommended warmly'.[101] Less laudatory is Richard Mayne's review in the *New Statesman* who views it as a novel of an 'eternally glum heroine' and suggests that Figes should have avoided 'the appearance of self-pity' in order to pay more attention to the theme that treats 'the growing acceptance of human limitations'.[102] In the *Daily Telegraph,* the novel is described as a 'promising first novel' but the reviewer undercuts this praise by patronisingly reducing the narrative to a case of undiagnosed but 'severe post-natal depression' which presents as 'moody introspection'.[103] A review in the *Times Literary Supplement*'s commends the novel as one of 'scrupulous honesty', noting that Figes is 'another good woman novelist' but 'perhaps one day she will just be a good novelist'.[104] Another reviewer calls *Equinox* a 'scrupulously intelligent if typically contradictory addition to the New Feminism; half SOS, half warning shot', the novel is a 'general lament for all women' as well as a 'pained insight into the imbalance between the European and the English consciousness', using a narrative technique in which 'interior monologue finally banishes dialogue from the book'.[105] Kenneth Allsop admits that he is less than fond of any experiments in fiction and typically, he says, he 'flinches from unpunctuated prose', but finds the novel 'remarkably fine' and '[M]icroscopically introspective'. He also recognises its experimental techniques that splinter the potential ordinariness of the narrative's themes: 'Miss Figes has orchestrated her book in a beautiful manner. Sometimes it is written in the first person sometimes the third; paragraphs of delicate prose alternate with flat journalist quotes and snippets of banal dialogue'.[106] These experiments with interiority continue in *Winter Journey*.

Winter Journey: Ice Creeping

Its title inspired by Schubert's *Winterreise*, *Winter Journey*, was Figes's second novel but one she regarded as her first, as her dislike of *Equinox* was so strong that she would eventually discount it from her *oeuvre*. Taking Schubert's image of a melancholy winter landscape as a model for the gradually frozen immobility of old age, she shapes the narrative of the elderly Janus Stobbs who wanders around a dreary war-pocked urban setting alone with his unruly agitating memories, 'lonely and rejected by society'.[107] She later noted that this novel was 'the first time that I was really in control of what I was doing', and that it represented a 'big advance' in her artistic practice as a novelist.[108] Initially rejected by Secker, as they wanted, said Figes, another 'acceptable middle-brow novel' in the mould of *Equinox* and thought a novel about a war veteran battling the disturbing vagaries of his scattered memories and the difficulties of poverty and old age of limited commercial appeal. With the influence of Anthony Burgess, the novel was finally published by Faber to largely positive reviews, many of which noted its apparent debt to Beckett.

Awarded the Guardian Fiction Prize in 1967, *Winter Journey* is a slim volume structured into five sections designating parts of a single bleak winter's day, Early Morning, Mid-Morning, Noon, Afternoon and Night, in the life of Stobbs, a widowed war veteran who lives alone with his memories in a run-down flat in London whose cracked walls and dilapidated interiors are at one with his ailing body and mind as it decomposes: 'the sun dying, ice creeping. And then night. Sounds in the dark are objectless, my lost children, birds. Black slack sack back'.[109] Almost completely deaf, Janus experiences voice as pure interiority so that the narrative mostly functions from the inside out; that is, the external of world of Janus's past and the present is filtered through his singular subjectivity 'to create', notes Robert Nye, 'the moment from inside, vividly, patiently, admitting every ounce of its current ambiguity, so that his sentences read like heart beats'. In choosing this technique, Figes 'goes beyond gesture to fix the most fugitive moments of existence' in her prose and this produces the impression of 'a richness of life going on, being lived from one word to another'.[110] In a review of the novel, Barbara Bray, Beckett's translator, calls the novel a 'quiet little book' that 'salutes the purity of Samuel Beckett's prose but doesn't make any foolish attempt to imitate the inimitable'. Noting its imperfections such as the superfluous 'pushmi-pullyu device' of the title and some other 'small over-deliberateness' in its composition, Bray concludes that *Winter Journey* nonetheless is a 'bitingly sharp and convincing' piece of writing that 'gives a remarkably direct and concentrated illumination of a life' and of the 'physical present' of its protagonist.[111]

The impulse to write about a central protagonist whose faculties are in decline and whose life is now composed primarily of memory rather than experience, derived, in part, from Figes's reading of Faulkner: '*The Sound and the Fury* impressed me as having explored new areas of human perception, which hadn't been done before. I chose to work with an old person, because everyone who survives becomes old'.[112] Memories become a series of voices that keep Janus awake at night in a constant fragmented whisper of memories and past traumas that meander between the personal, his wife Nora and his children, Ted and Nana, and older memories of 'the abdication, coronation, D-Day, VE-Day' and more random snippets from the news and his life: the 'girl who got murdered in the signal box', of botched abortions 'bloodstained knitting needles' and 'Sally Simpson coming to work eight months gone' (p. 24). The disorder of Janus's thoughts follow no pattern; they are associative and have their own sense of generation and contribute to the disruption of linear temporality in the novel – a technique that Figes so admired in *The Sound and the Fury* (1929). Like Quentin, Janus is obsessed with the ticking of a clock beside his bed that marks out the emptiness and narrowing of time and is the 'mausoleum of all hopes'. Explaining that she set out to write about a person who was alienated and marginalised not by identity, as in *Konek Landing*, but by the human condition of ageing, Figes said 'I wanted to write a book about being old, the defective human being, to write through someone whose faculties weren't a hundred percent'.[113]

Janus is inhabited, often haunted, by voices, many of which are distressing and even accusatory, that revisit him in the shrinking spaces of the present. They also construct for him an alternate reality of a polar mission – Scott's journey to the Antarctic is a symbolic framing structure in which he imagines himself slowly moving towards a state of frozenness, and finally death. Like the natural world that is interposed into the novel, Janus's consciousness is subject to sudden brief flourishing and then inexorable decay: 'everything running into everything else and distinct, wildly illogical logic' (p. 97). A continuation and intensification of the movement towards interiorisation of voice and the eschewal of signposted dialogue that marks much of realist writing, the novel's depiction of ageing and infirmity is permeated with the atmosphere of decay, stasis and a gradual freezing over of all life: 'No thaw [. . .] the sun dying, ice creeping [. . .] Skin stays slack, nothing renews' (p. 10). Janus lives in the fading traces of the past with the knowledge that his death has already begun.

Beginning in mumbling inarticulacy – 'Numm bll num mun ssoo sss tck' – the novel opens in a semi-lucid dream state in which Janus believes he is back in his old house. He wakes only to find he is in the cold dark of his dingy, cold flat at 4 o'clock in the morning and he is back alone, a 'leftover' in the newly modernising postwar wasteland of 'towers and motorways and old crusts of concrete' (p. 12). Living on the very edge of society, he is infirm and in his old age almost wholly invisible to those around him, and frequently wonders to himself 'Where is the care?'. We learn only obliquely that Janus is an elderly veteran who was involved in an unspecified armed battle during the war, again never named as the Second World War, but some local details are suggestive of his past: 'Stalingrad, that was a cold place' (p. 24). One reviewer notes the pathos of Janus's faltering consciousness: 'we feel the stammer of that old heart [. . .] as if we had inherited [. . .] the pain of all his experience, and the pulse of will that keeps him going'.[114]

Janus is not a kindly old man who has learnt life's lessons and is now reconciled to a benevolently insightful old age; living has given him little insight or compassion and his descent into old age is not stoically noble or redemptive but rather petty and crotchety, his days full of small victories against his doughty landlady, Mrs Griffin. He has 'unearthed no peace in the accumulation of experience' and 'his thoughts are stupid' and often ungenerous. He casts a critical eye over his daughter, Nan, and her coarse unkindness to her son, Dan, whose youthful exuberance and energy is a hindrance to her household routine of drudgery and complaint. Nora's voice and presence haunts Janus throughout the day but it is not always fondly remembered:

> she was always at war, fighting what she didn't have and couldn't get [. . .] What was she on about? What did she expect? Should have given her the flat of my hand like my mother would say, then she'd have felt something all right. (p. 25)

Relations between men and women are strained and restricted by strictly regimented gendered activities in the home that sours any peaceable companionship.

Janus's infirmity and virtual deafness inevitably drew comparisons with Beckett. Consequently, as Nye notes 'all the odds and sods of Janus's pointless existence are drawn together in a jerky, rambling style that is [. . .] reminiscent of Beckett in that it makes a kind of poetry of the inarticulate'.[115] Such inarticulacy, Nye claims, makes Figes, 'a real realist' whose writing offers 'much that seems threatening to one's necessarily limited experience of "real"'. Figes's novel, he suggests, touchingly elicits 'the empathy for impotence of extreme age found in some of Beckett's finest writing'.[116] But this is not Beckett. Beyond the obvious similarity of the corporeal and mental dilapidation of old age, *Winter Journey*'s prose is attached to a more concrete, less ontologically abstract, sense of the speaker's world and subjectivity. The social and historical contexts of Janus's life are more easily discernible from the fragmented elements of the interior discourse. In short, we can more readily piece together an external existence in *Winter Journey* than we might do in *The Unnamable* or *Endgame*, in particular by the material marks of the war scattered throughout text – the 'Velveteen cloth on the Anderson shelter'; 'Remember walls have ears, Coughs and sneezes spread diseases. Make do and mend' (pp. 13–14). Janus is filled with his memories of the violence of the war:

> Morris lost two fingers on his left hand at the Battle of the Somme (one of them) [. . .] A great glass tower for a finger or two and a pile of smoking bricks. Not only fingers. Wet sheets flapping in alleys between high walls of sooty brock and a clatter of small hard boots down the iron stairs. Alf, nip down to the corner and alf a pahnd of tuppeny rice. And the girls chanted a pennuth of chips ter grease yer lips and aht yer goes. Pigtails flapping and skirts cut down to size but still far too long, the colours toned down with too much wash and wear. Tom Morris saved Alf's life, though the boy lost one

eye and his mother. Got kids of his own now, moving out shortly to a new house in Stevenage. (pp. 47–8)

The novel presents a strong sense of the postwar dilapidation of London. All around Janus is the construction of new tower blocks: 'a great black shadow now, eating space. It takes my window light, my sky' (p. 26). The space around has been laid to waste and has not been improved by half-heated modernisation:

> Waste blowing across waste ground, too many cars. The old city is crowded out, crumbling, walls overlapping, no room for anyone or anything, cracks appear and don't get mended [. . .] now empty houses cave in on themselves and 'turn to dust'. (pp. 46–7)

The past is literally collapsing – the 'old city is crowded out, crumbling, walls overlapping' (p. 46). The rickety housing in which he lives is doomed, but, paradoxically, the new tower blocks seem sterile in comparison to the 'bombsite blossoms, flourishes, birds nest in niches' (p. 28).

Like Scott of the Antarctic, Janus is in danger if he stops moving and succumbs to the cold. A repeated refrain is 'keep moving':

> You've got to keep moving, that's the main thing make an effort. Pull yourself up by the elbows, bootstrings, anything. Keep muscles working, circulation going, bowels open regularly, all your faculties in working order. [. . .] It's not easy sometimes but then pan in sink water to soak is never easy light off and you have to decide whether it's worth it or not want not want not not not not I always say where the window shut where the river turns. (pp. 31–32)

While much of the novel is interior monologue, there are passages that mimic the back and forth momentum of linear conversation and the drawing out of details that forms the mainstay of conventionally realist fiction, which, in their information-rich sentences, move the plot forward. But in Figes's novel, no significance is to be gleaned from these exchanges:

> 'Morning, Tom,'
> 'Morning, Janus.'
> 'Cold wind,'
> 'Reckon it'll snow.'
> 'A nip.'
> 'A nip.'
> 'Still, not bad for January.' 'Can't complain.'
> [. . .]

> End of conversation. (pp. 48–9)

This reveals little beyond a perfunctory phatic exchange and the prose moves directly back to the stumbling minutiae of the third-person narration: 'Clouds moved silently, vaporized water awaiting another condensation. Morris scratched his tough grey stubble [...] Tick tock. Morris's windbags wheezed in their calcified casing and one jacket button snapped of its last thread' (pp. 49–50).

In an interview, Figes explains the ways in which silence, stumbling and failure work in *Winter Journey*. While these might contribute to confusion and frustration on the part of a reader who expects a more immediately comprehensible narrative pattern and plot, it is a process that requires some sustained effort to process the discontinuities of language used in such a way. Janus realises that 'reason comes to a stop, isn't a straight line, is so far, then it ties itself in knots, no one could disentangle them again' (p. 15). '[S]omehow', says Figes, 'you have to have an ear' for the knots and tangles of discontinuity and to accept that the process of living (and the proximity of death) does little to provide coherence.[117] Her techniques drew a mixed reception.

In a press release from Figes's publishers, Jay Bail describes it as a 'potently avant-garde novel' full of 'loose flowing poetry, meaningless conversation' which heightens the 'already high-pitched situation'.[118] Some reviewers cared little for this technique: the *Library Journal* of January 1968 called it a 'tough sledding' of a novel, and that while it 'may tempt those readers who prefer to feast on stream-of-consciousness or experimental works instead of more conventional fare', this soon becomes a 'confusing game for the reader and often leaves him stumbling over the pebbles of poetic prose scattered along a somewhat arid plot'. Initially sympathetic to Figes's techniques in the novel, the reviewer concludes that the reader's patience is sorely tried and that he/she 'wearies of the whole thing by the end'.[119] A review in the *Glasgow Herald* is discernibly negative in its assessment of Figes's technique, suggesting that the novel '[O]scillates between mucoid brutality and Eng.Lit. poesy' that makes 'for difficult engagement with the reader'.[120]

Konek Landing: Trauma and Memory

Figes's third novel, and the first to deal explicitly with the traumatic events of the war on a personal level and, more broadly, of 'the extermination of the Jews',[121] *Konek Landing* represents a significant evolution of her writing – she would later regard it as a novel possessing 'a breadth of vision, that no other book of mine will ever have'.[122] Originally planning to 'write the narrative straight', Figes soon found that she

> couldn't stand it written that way, it was so boring, and I suddenly saw a very complex narrative. I really pushed language to its limits, rewrote the same paragraph 6 times, became very conscious of syllables and vowels. I became obsessed with vowels.[123]

The language in *Konek Landing* is testimony to this aesthetic ambition:

> the wind blowing warm in the sun through the woman's dark hair high drying grass scratching her long skirts dark bushy brows gathered in a frown as she squinted through the sun at a blue summer sea from the top of the headland; paused now to pull at a grass stalk, put it in her mouth, picked a large ox-eye daisy, flung the stalk tough and bitten dry now no more juice away and pulled angrily at another, unthinking. (p. 131)

Citing *Konek Landing* as her most artistically successful and favourite book, Figes was disappointed then, when it was 'unhappily treated by everyone else':

> I put more into it than into any other book. I felt most about it. Though it was a dead end in some ways, which is why I went onto other areas [. . .] on the whole people found it difficult and tended to think it was pretentious [. . .] I thought the book wasn't actually difficult to read, everyone tried to read it too fast, I'd adopted a style such that 500 pages became 200 pages with the same content. People should have taken notice of all those commas and read the pages slowly.[124]

Commas aside, *Konek Landing* received a variable critical reception. Jonathan Raban described it as a 'cross between Kafka and Beckett' that is a 'dun-coloured, piece of "serious", semi-experimental fiction' comprising 'endless series of interior monologues, fragmentary encounters and gloomy nightmares', that quickly become 'monotonous and often incomprehensible'. The novel's 'difficult surface', Raban continues, 'seems unjustified by any fundamental complexity of connection,' concluding that even 'the language seems to have died of undernourishment in this European wasteland'.[125] Elsewhere, William Trevor is more appreciative of Figes's experiments with language in which 'streams of consciousness murmur at one another'.[126] What Figes has created in the novel, he says, is a 'reality that one wants quite urgently to be involved with. As with some of Joyce, and most of Beckett, the effort required is part of the involvement'. The 'dense, difficult style perfectly matched the predicament of Konek that in the end no other style would have as effectively conveyed the rudiments of this man's life'.[127]

Declaring that she had got the idea of the *Konek Landing* from 'a very bad television series about a stateless seaman', Figes noted that she felt 'an enormous excitement' about the novel and would later consider it an important event in her life,[128] not only as a writer but also as an adult whose childhood exile and life-long sense of displacement had, for the first time, found some artistic expression: 'I wrote out my hang-ups about Germany and the European story in that book' (p.36). This 'story' transfigures Europe (never mentioned by name) from a place of Enlightenment and civilisation to one of peril and persecution that resulted in great waves of exile during and after the war but also one full of gaping absences and a death-haunted present. The novel allowed Figes to think for the first time about her past and the ways in which her childhood was traumatised by the physical and psychological upheaval of sudden departure and the subsequent deracination that produced within her a permanent condition of otherness: 'I didn't realise how dramatic the whole thing had been until my early 20s when I was psychoanalysed [. . .] I became aware of my sense of guilt [. . .] I may need to come to terms with the whole business of human cruelty' (p. 37). She later said that she 'never thought about [her] German-Jewish past again in the way [she] did before' she wrote *Konek Landing*: 'It was a problem I had to solve in a purely personal way, facing up to human cruelty [. . .] my parents' attitude was one of unmitigated bitterness toward the country they had come from' (p. 37)

The story of Stefan Konek, 'a survivor of the ghetto and an orphan', is drawn not only from Figes's own history of exile but also from that of her family's maid, Edith, who they had to leave behind when they fled from Berlin to England (p. 37) In a later non-fiction work, *Journey to Nowhere*, Figes describes conversations that she had with Edith, who had found her way back to the family after the war. When the family left Edith was forced into what was called a *Judenhaus*. After the Law on Tenancies with Jews was passed in Germany on 30 April 1939, Jews were stripped of all their possessions and property and forced to live in houses that were always overfull and allowed little privacy. Edith tells Figes: 'It was awful. I can't begin to tell you. Overcrowded everybody crammed together' (p. 78). Edith is the only living witness of this horrific past and she is confined in its traumatic repetition: 'it became clear to me that Edith did not live in the real world. She was stuck in the past' (p. 106). She is only able to identify herself with those who 'find themselves having to confront ghosts from the past, lost ones who will not rest in peace, who have no resting place where we can place our offering' (p. 139).[129] Edith is, for Figes, 'just one of the many, countless faces without names who had been part of a vanished world from which I had escaped. From which Edith, too, had' (pp. 100–1). Figes does not however, turn this Holocaust narrative into a crude story of loss and redemption. Rather as, Brian Cheyette has observed, she creates 'more generalised images of displacement and loss [...] characterised by a refusal to turn past trauma into simple stories'.[130] This process of generalisation is central to *Konek Landing* as the narrative of Konek's life of dispossession and displacement achieves an archetypical potency that refuses any resort to mawkish solace.

Dispossessed, parentless and pursued, Stefan Konek is one of those 'countless faces', although his story, unlike Edith's, takes place in unspecified places and his perpetuators are never identified.[131] Significantly, the words 'Jew' and 'Nazi' are never mentioned, rather we learn metonymically of the latter in their 'tunics' and the former are referred to by the nuns in the orphanage as 'boys of your race' (*Konek*, p. 25), one of the 'inbred races' (p. 15). This absence of specific identity renders the narrative more archetypal and the natural imagery that suffuses the beginning and the end of the novel suggests the cyclical nature of human history and the ubiquity of cruelty and violence. Konek's story of 'landing' becomes literalised – a sloughing-off of civilisation and returning to nature: at the novel's close he becomes a 'willing sacrifice' to a tribe of primitive peoples (p. 158). An orphan survivor of the ghetto, Konek is handed over to a series of people and institutions to be protected and is compelled to assume various identities over the course of his short vagabond life.

Structured into three major sections, 'Inland', 'Shores' and 'The Island', the narrative moves in fluvial associative waves at times using streams of consciousness, interior monologue and, at others, a more conventional, third-person narrative. The novel is, says Kenneth Graham, 'intense and clever, sparing with articles, pronouns, connectives', the narrative moves, not by plot, but rather by a 'deep visionary murmur, hard delphic spasms' that are 'very painful'. He also notes Figes's use of primitive archetypes: 'waves, pools, seeds, cupboard/womb, bonfire'.[132] The novel begins with an evocation of the natural, primitive world in which the human does not feature for some considerable time:

> It began where the tide ran, the water rocking, air and water and air; there, you might say, the cradle of life. Weigh of water ran and sank and ran, advanced and retreated, left small circles, air enclosed in liquid, which glistened in the bright hot sun. (p. 9)

Out of this deep geological time, emerges a 'four-legged creature' from the sea who struggles up onto two legs. Living in the trees with gnawing hunger, the figure hides in a 'pile of mouldering timbers', terrified of the rats but but even more of the 'dangerous predator that lurks outside the door on two legs' (p. 13). This is Stefan Konek, as yet unidentified; he has become primitive man in the natural world, reduced to an inconsequential living figure distinguishable as human only by his progressive method of perambulation. He lands on earth, or rather crawls out of the sea onto land, after being shipwrecked: 'a four-legged creature pulled himself upright on two legs, tottered but balanced finally, and swung himself into the safety of the trees' (p. 11). This human figure has been left alone 'to find his way back with two pin-points of light' (p. 12). Gradually, the narrative reveals that this moment comes long after a childhood spent being hidden away in cupboards and attics for hours at a time; unable to speak, or move, the family live compacted on top of each other, 'six not counting him' taking turns 'to shit in the buckets' (p. 17).

> [Legs beginning to prickle, back aching, feet dead how did I pass the time wriggling toes pee-ed into my pants once sniffing dipped fingers into the warm trickle licked at it how did I ever get through the first I was a caveman she suggested that so I wouldn't make a sound because the lion was prowling about outside in the forest waiting to get his jaws into me gobble me all up so I sat there very quiet for what must have been hours holding my breath listening men's voices once I heard them then I was really frightened. (p. 14)

In his terror, Konek is all the while desperate for his mother to come and finds himself surviving on the memories of stories she invented for him to mitigate his fear. Konek's recollections of that time are a stream of memories in which the division of punctuation is dropped in favour of unimpeded flow:

> they were shouting so I thought if they take her away who is going to let me out no one started to cry then called out mummy softly at first then louder when I was sure they had gone. (p. 14)

This technique, familiar from modernism, was noted by some critics in the novel's reception: 'Syntax, time sequence, and any conventional connection between events have been abandoned in favour of a quasi-poetic language, whose effects are achieved by startling juxtapositions of images and occasional sharply observed scenes'.[133] Another review notes its Beckettian influences, both 'emotionally' and 'stylistically':

> If it's somewhat inflexible in tone and mood, mainly capable of communicating a sort of tormented sensitivity, one must also admit that Miss Figes's narrative is dense and concentrated, often verbally apt and delicately expressed. But that is not enough to make it a satisfactory novel.[134]

The lack of 'satisfaction' expressed here is repeated in many reviews which comment on a loss of clarity in the novel that is the result of a lack of any cogent linking narrative that might have helped piece together these poetic fragments. However, Susana Onega suggests that while the novel resists the expression of 'the traumatic events in linguistic terms', that is, in a linear narrative, it employs 'sustained use of archetypal symbols and the imposition of an all-encompassing mythical pattern that facilitates the transmission of trauma sensorially and empathically instead of logically'.[135]

The novel is divided between Konek's time as deserter from the navy somewhere in postwar Europe, and his disjointed memories of a childhood spent hiding away from unidentified persecutors in cupboards and attics first with his parents and then by himself. After he loses his family, Konek makes his way as an orphaned child, around him a city devastated by war:

> Chaos, piles of brick and crumbled mortar, rubble which spilled onto pavement, no street signs, wanderers passing on foot, wrapped round in rags or barefoot, staggering under bundles or pushing household clutter on small handcarts, bicycle handlebars, also dragged small weary children or babies who whined find. Soiled uniforms, pants and no tunic, or only a tunic, all parties stripped off, but warmer than civilian clothes. (p. 31)

Waking up in 'a strange bed' one morning, his parents nowhere to be seen, Konek is taken in by Aunt Edith, who tells him

> of course mother or father will come back, but just for now you are going to have a nice holiday with auntie, and just for a game you are going to have a new name. You are now Pavel Zuck. (p. 22)

He is then taken to be put in care of the nuns at a convent where life is harsh and punishment frequent. He meets Jan with whom he escapes from the convent only to be captured and then sent to a home for boys where he learns to read and write. Jan and Konek go on the run again and end up among two strangers, Nelly, who mistakes him for her lost son '[m]any years ago now' (p. 57), who is also called Stefan, and her daughter, Lili. The household is oppressive with '[n]et curtains across the windows, stuffy, radiators full on' (p. 58) and a butterfly collection: 'each creature the rusted pin stuck through its dry back, one wing dropped off':

> Afraid to breathe fearing that the expelled air the breath coming out of him would send the dusty grubs to their final disintegration him held with lungs caught holding the foul air pinned there the pin itself crusted with rust: pain

through nerve ends, recognition, a collection of trivia uglier than old leaves ... (p. 60)

This section is followed by a blank in the narration covering several years during which the only thing that is clear is that Konek is in prison, paying for an accidental murder committed by Jan, his orphanage friend. After several failed attempts to find a job and establish an affective relationship with Hannah Brest, the half-sister of Jan's wife, Konek becomes a seaman on board the *Christina*. A version of the medieval Ship of Fools, the *Christina* is full of crippled and demented war survivors and convicts like Stefan. But he soon finds himself shipwrecked on an island by the novel's end and is sacrificed by its native population. The passivity of Stefan is striking; he can do nothing to escape his fate and now waits for his life to end. Figes offers no redemption or consolation in *Konek Landing*, suggesting that Stefan's destiny is inescapable from the moment we learn of his fugitive status at the beginning of the novel.

In a review of the novel, 'Back to Berlin', Linda Talbot says that *Konek Landing* is 'thick with the deprivations defined in poignant detail', and that Figes's poetic language gives 'the impression of the lived-in moment'. Less positive is a review somewhat belittlingly entitled 'A Rabbi's Family Saga', which describes the novel's technique as impenetrable: 'one stream of consciousness is pretty well as unreadable as the next one'.[136] A review in the *Sunday Telegraph* observes that Figes is more talented than 'her overdone themes of a woman in domestic despair' had suggested in *Equinox* and that *Konek Landing* gives 'fuller rein to her gifts'. Praising the novel's 'shimmering prose', the reviewer concludes that it is a 'startlingly beautiful' if 'difficult' book, 'but one which repays the effort' of careful reading.[137] Not all reviewers, as noted, appreciated Figes's prose style. In *The Scotsman*, Derek Stanford accepts that her method makes for an 'unusual degree of relation', but 'somewhat batters the reader's mind with its long assault of phenomena. It must be taken slowly to avoid the impression of garbled confusion'.[138]

Indeed, the novel, and all Figes's works examined here, require slow and careful reading to fully apprehend the complex layers of memory and suppressed emotion that resonate through the prose. Her writing as noted earlier, points to an essential inarticulacy or hesitation that gestures to another way of speaking trauma. In *The Imagination on Trial*, Figes noted that John Berger felt that *Konek Landing* made 'a physical impact' on him as a reader; the result, Figes believed, of her quest to push 'language to its limits' in all of her writing.[139]

Notes

1. Ellen G. Friedman and Miriam Fuchs (eds), *Breaking the Sequence: Women's Experimental Fiction* (Princeton, NJ: Princeton University Press, 1989), p. 4. Figes is briefly compared to other 'contemporary experimentalists' Toni Morrison and Marilynne Robinson, as their writing tends 'towards lyricism and poetic language' (p. 32).
2. Robert Nye, 'A Dull Head Among Windy Spaces', *The Guardian*, 7 April 1967, p. 7, Reviews of *Winter Journey*, press cuttings, 1967–1968, MS 89050/7/5, 1966–1971, Figes Archive, BL, London.
3. Figes, *Little Eden: A Child at War* (London: Faber and Faber, 1978), p. 19.
4. Figes, 'The Long Passage to Little England', *The Observer*, 11 June 1978, p. 14. Hereafter, 'Little England'.
5. Figes, *The Observer*, 1969. Cited in Eva Tucker, 'Eva Figes Obituary', *The Guardian*, 7 September 2012 <https://www.theguardian.com/books/2012/sep/07/eva-figes> (accessed 12 April 2018).
6. Figes, *Eden*, pp. 19, 22. Hereafter, running page numbers from primary texts will be given in the text in parentheses.
7. Marianne Hirsch, 'The Generation of Postmemory', *Poetics Today*, 29: 1 (2008), pp. 103–28; Marianne Hirsch, *The Generation of Postmemory: Writing and Visual Culture After the Holocaust* (New York: Columbia University Press, 2012). Figes's work is included in several anthologies of Jewish writing. See Bryan Cheyette (ed.), *Contemporary Jewish Writing in Britain and Ireland: An Anthology* (Lincoln, NE: University of Nebraska Press, 1998); Susana Onega and Jean-Michel Ganteau (eds), *Ethics and Trauma in Contemporary British Fiction* (Amsterdam and New York: Rodopi, 2011); Cheryl Verdon, 'Forgotten Words: Trauma, Memory and Herstory in Eva Figes's Fiction', in Nadia Valman (ed.), *Jewish Women Writers in Britain* (Detroit: Wayne State University Press, 2014), pp. 116–34; Beate Neumeier, 'Reading Matters: "Marginal" British Jewish Writers', in David Brauner and Axel Stähler (eds), *The Edinburgh Companion to Modern Jewish Fiction* (Edinburgh: Edinburgh University Press, 2015), pp. 279–88.
8. Figes, 'Little England', p. 14.
9. Marilena Parlati, '"Treble exposure": Fissured Memory in Eva Figes' Fiction', in Helen Thomas (ed.), *Malady and Mortality: Illness, Disease and Death in Literary and Visual Culture* (Cambridge: Cambridge Scholars, 2016), pp. 129–43 (p. 133).
10. Henri Bergson, *Time and Free Will: An Essay on the Immediate Data of Consciousness*, trans. F. L. Pogson (London: George Allen & Unwin, 1910), p. 126.
11. Figes, *Patriarchal Attitudes: Women in Society* (London: Faber, 1970); Germaine Greer, *The Female Eunuch* (London: MacGibbon and Kee, 1970).
12. Figes, *Sex and Subterfuge: Women Writers to 1850* (London: Macmillan, 1982); *Tragedy and Social Evolution* (London: Calder, 1976); Eva Figes

(ed.), *Women's Letters in Wartime, 1450–1945* (London: Pandora, 1993).
13. Renate Rasp, *A Family Failure: A Novel*, trans. Figes (London: Calder & Boyars, 1970); Manfred von Conta, *The Deathbringer: A Novel*, trans. Figes (London: Calder & Boyars, 1971). Other translations by Figes include Martin Walser, *The Gadarene Club* (London: Longmans, 1960); Elisabeth Borcher, *The Old Car* (London: Blackie, 1967); Bernard Grzimek, *He and I and the Elephants* (London: Thames & Hudson, 1967); George Sand, *Little Fadette* (London: Blackie, 1967); and *The Musicians of Bremen: Retold by Eva Figes* (London: Blackie, 1967).
14. *Equinox* (London: Secker & Warburg, 1966); *Winter Journey* (London: Faber and Faber, 1967); *Konek Landing* (London: Faber and Faber, 1969); *B* (London: Faber and Faber, 1972); *Days* (London: Faber and Faber, 1974); *Nelly's Version* (London: Secker & Warburg, 1977); *Waking* (London: Hamish Hamilton, 1981); *Light* (London: Hamish Hamilton, 1983); *The Seven Ages: A Novel* (London: Hamish Hamilton 1986); *Ghosts* (London: Hamish Hamilton, 1988); *Tree of Knowledge* (London: Sinclair-Stevenson, 1990); *The Tenancy* (London: Sinclair-Stevenson, 1993); *The Knot* (London: Sinclair-Stevenson, 1996). In addition, she wrote two children's novels, *The Banger* (London: André Deutsch, 1968); *Scribble Sam* (London: André Deutsch, 1971). She also wrote two short stories: 'Obbligato, Bedsitter', in Samuel Beckett et al., *Signature Anthology, 20* (London, Calder & Boyars, 1975), pp. 33–47; 'On the Edge', in Julian Evans (ed.), *London Tales* (London: Hamish Hamilton, 1983), pp. 51–9. Her last works saw her returning to her German-Jewish past, in *Tales of Innocence and Experience: An Exploration* (Leicester: W. F. Howes, 2003); an account of postwar Zionism, *Journey to Nowhere: One Woman Looks for the Promised Land* (London: Granta, 2008).
15. Eva Figes, 'B. S. Johnson', *Review of Contemporary Fiction*, 5: 2 (1985), pp. 70–1 (p. 70).
16. Jonathan Coe, *Like a Fiery Elephant: The Story of B. S. Johnson* (London: Picador, 2004).
17. Ibid., p. 3. 'John Calder wanted to organise a group of these writers into an avant-garde school of writing like the *nouveau romanciers* in France or the *Gruppe 47* in Germany'.
18. Figes, 'Everything Gets Worse', *The Guardian*, 5 June 2004 <https://www.theguardian.com/books/2004/jun/05/biography.jonathancoe> (accessed 18 April 2018).
19. Figes, 'The State of Fiction: A Symposium', *New Review*, 5:1 (1978), pp. 38–9.
20. Figes, 'B. S. Johnson', p. 70.
21. Figes, interview with Sarah O'Reilly, May 2010–June 2011, *Authors' Lives*, C1276/38, Sound & Moving Image Catalogue, British Library, London. Hereafter, BL.
22. Figes, 'B. S. Johnson', p. 70.
23. B. S. Johnson, 'Introduction', in B. S. Johnson, *Travelling People* (London: Constable, 1963), p. 21.
24. Figes, 'B. S. Johnson', pp. 70–1.

25. Alan Burns, 'The Disintegrating Novel', *Books and Bookmen*, 15 (September 1970), pp. 6–7, 53. Cited in in James Vinson (ed.), *Contemporary Novelists* (New York: St Martin's Press, 1976), p. 212.
26. B. S. Johnson, 'Introduction to *Aren't You Rather Young to be Writing Your Memoirs?*', in B. S. Johnson, *Well Done God! Selected Prose and Drama of B. S. Johnson*, ed. Jonathan Coe, Philip Tew and Julia Jordan (London: Picador, 2013), pp. 11–31 (p. 15).
27. John Barth, 'The Literature of Exhaustion', in Malcolm Bradbury (ed.), *The Novel Today: Contemporary Writers on Modern Fiction* (London: Fontana, 1977), pp. 70–83 (p. 71).
28. Johnson, *Aren't You*, p. 14.
29. B. S. Johnson, W: correspondence, 1960–1969, MS 89001/5/1/39, B. S. Johnson Archive (1933–2004), British Library. The minutes of this initial meeting record that the group agreed to invite 'Jim Ballard, William Burroughs, Maureen Duffy, Michael Frayn, Alan Sillitoe' to join the group.
30. Ibid.
31. Ibid.
32. Eva Figes Archive, BL, London, Johnson correspondence, 1960–1969.
33. B. S. Johnson, B: correspondence, 1965–1973, MS 89001/5/1/3, B. S. Johnson Archive (1933–2004), BL, London.
34. Draft MS, 'The Interior Landscape', 1968, Articles and reviews by Figes, Figes Archive, BL, London.
35. Figes, 'B. S. Johnson', p. 71.
36. Figes, interview with Alan Burns, in Alan Burns and Charles Sugnet (eds), *The Imagination on Trial: British and American Writers Discuss Their Working Methods* (London: Allison & Busby, 1981), pp. 31–9 (p. 39).
37. Figes, 'Public Larceny Right', *New Humanist*, 1972.
38. John Calder, *Pursuit: The Uncensored Memoirs of John Calder* (London: Calder, 2001), p. 275.
39. See Charles Osborne, interview with Peter Firchow, in Burns and Sugnet (eds), *The Imagination*. For further discussion on the relationship between writers and the Arts Council, see Peter Firchow (ed.), *The Writer's Place: Interviews on the Literary Situation in Contemporary Britain* (Minneapolis: University of Minnesota Press, 1974).
40. Jennie Lee, 'Theatre and the State', *Hutchinson's Theatre Annual*, 1970–1. Figes admitted that she 'couldn't go on writing novels and bring up a family without an Arts Council subsidy', in Eva Figes, 'Writers in protest over PLR', *The Guardian*, 24 April 1975, p. 5.
41. Johnson, *Aren't You*, p. 12.
42. Ibid., p. 28.
43. Coe, *Fiery Elephant*, p. 13.
44. Frank Kermode, 'Retripotent', *London Review of Books*, 26: 15, 5 August 2004, pp. 11–13.
45. Brooke-Rose, 'Christine Brooke-Rose: The Texterminator', interview with Tom Boncza-Tomaszewski, *Independent on Sunday*, 27 March 2005, p. 128 <https://www.independent.co.uk/arts-entertainment/books/features/christine-brooke-rose-the-texterminator-8427.html> (accessed 13 May 2020).

46. Figes, 'B. S. Johnson', p. 71.
47. Figes, interview with Manuel Almagro and Carolina Sánchez-Palencia, *Atlantis*, 22: 1 (2000), pp. 177–86 (p. 178).
48. Ibid., p. 182.
49. Figes, 'Accustomed as I Am to Public Speaking', *New Humanist,* February 1973.
50. Figes, 'The Interior Landscape', *The Running Man*, 1: 1 (May–June 1968).
51. Ibid.
52. Figes, 'Note', in Giles Gordon (ed.), *Beyond the Words: Eleven Writers in Search of a New Fiction* (London: Hutchinson, 1975), pp. 113–14 (p. 114).
53. Ibid., p. 114.
54. Figes, interview with Burns, in Burns and Suget (eds), *Imagination*, pp. 33, 35.
55. Figes, interview with Almagro and Sánchez-Palencia, p. 184.
56. Ibid., p. 185.
57. Figes, *Patriarchal Attitudes*, p. 19.
58. Figes, interview with Almagro and Sánchez-Palencia, p. 185.
59. Figes, 'Interior Landscape', p. 58. Figes Archive, BL, London.
60. Ibid., p. 58.
61. Ibid., p. 58.
62. Figes, interview with Almagro and Sánchez-Palencia, p. 180.
63. For usefully detailed accounts, see Sheila Rowbotham's *The Past is Before Us: Feminism in Action Since the 1960s* (London: Pandora, 1989) and Anna Coote and Beatrice Campbell's *Sweet Freedom: The Struggle for Women's Liberation* (London: Picador, 1982). Both works examine the sexual aggression endured by women on the left from their male counterparts.
64. Ibid., p. 180.
65. Figes, 'Why the Euphoria Had to Stop', *The Guardian*, 16 May 1978, p. 9.
66. Figes, *Patriarchal Attitudes*, p. 8.
67. Figes, Letter, *Times Literary Supplement*, 1 November 1976, p. 1426. Figes Archive, BL, London.
68. Kate Millet, *Sexual Politics* (New York: Columbia University Press, 1970); Robin Morgan, *Sisterhood is Powerful: An Anthology of Writings from the Women's Liberation Movement* (New York: Random House, 1970); and Shulamith Firestone's *The Dialectic of Sex: The Case for Feminist Revolution* (New York: William Morrow & Company, 1970).
69. Hereafter, *PA* with page references given in the text in parentheses.
70. Figes, interview with Almagro and Sánchez-Palencia, p. 184.
71. Patricia Waugh, *Feminist Fictions: Revisiting the Postmodern* (London: Routledge, 1989), p. 6.
72. Havelock Ellis, *Man and Woman: A Study of Human Secondary Sexual Characters* (London: Walter Scott, 1894), p. 442.
73. Figes, *The Observer*, 11 October 1964. Articles and reviews by Eva Figes, Figes Archive, BL, London.
74. See Sheila Rowbotham, *Promise of a Dream: Remembering the Sixties* (London: Allen Lane, 2000); and Elizabeth Wilson, *Only Halfway to*

Paradise: Women in Postwar Britain, 1945–1968 (London: Tavistock Publications, 1980).
75. Brian Harrison, *Seeking a Role: The United Kingdom 1951–1970* (Oxford: Oxford University Press, 2011), pp. 473, 479.
76. Ibid.
77. Graham Crow, 'The Post-war Development of the Modern Domestic Ideal', in Graham Allan and Graham Crow (eds), *Home and Family: Creating the Domestic Sphere* (Basingstoke: Macmillan, 1989), pp. 14–32 (p. 20). By 1957, 2.5 million flats and houses had been built, a large proportion of which was social housing. See John Burnett, *A Social History of Housing 1815–1985*, 2nd edn (London: Methuen, 1986), pp. 249, 286.
78. See Claire Langhamer, 'The Meanings of Home in Postwar Britain', *Journal of Contemporary History*, 40: 2 (2005), pp. 341–62; Niamh Baker, *Happily Ever After?: Women's Fiction in Postwar Britain, 1945–1960* (New York: St Martin's Press, 1989), pp. 68–73, 161–4; Pearl Jephcott, 'Women, Wife and Worker', Education Commission Report (London: London School of Economics, 1960); Pearl Jephcott, Nancy Seear and John H. Smith, *Married Women Working* (London: Allen & Unwin, 1962); Viola Klein, *Britain's Married Women Workers* (London: Routledge & Kegan Paul, 1965); Simon Yudkin and Anthea Holme, *Working Mothers and their Children: A Study for the Council for Children's Welfare* (London: Joseph, 1963).
79. Langhamer, *Meanings of Home*, p. 346.
80. This overall picture is more complicated, however, as the number of women in employment actually increased. See Stephen Brooke, 'Gender and Working Class Identity in Britain in the 1950s', *Journal of Social History*, 34: 4 (2001), pp. 773–95.
81. Lois Mitchison, 'From the Archive, 8 January 1960: The Price of Educating Women', *The Guardian,* 8 January 2015 <https://www.theguardian.com/education/2015/jan/08/women-careers-higher-education-archive-1960> (accessed 14 May 2020).
82. Ibid.
83. Ibid.
84. Ibid. Here, Mitchison revisits a piece from an article called 'Future Shock' in which she notes how much had changed for women in the intervening twenty-seven years. She no longer thinks that 'the answer is stop educating women' who want to marry and have children as 'Feminism' and 'legislation' have 'made a difference to all our views'. See Lois Mitchison, 'Future Shock', *The Guardian*, 30 June 1987 <https://static.guim.co.uk/sys-images/Guardian/Pix/pictures/2015/1/6/1420548422496/Lois-Mitchison-30-June-19-001.jpg> (accessed 8 May 2020).
85. See Sarah Aiston, 'A Good Job for a Girl? The Career Biographies of Women Graduates of the University of Liverpool Post-1945,' *Twentieth Century British History*, 15: 4 (2004), pp. 361–87.
86. Figes, *London Look/Life* 1967, Articles and reviews by Figes, Figes Archive, BL, London.
87. Carole D'Albia, *London Life/Look*, 1967, p. 45, Reviews for Winter Journey, Figes Archive, BL, London.
88. Figes, interview with Almagro and Sánchez-Palencia, pp. 180–2.

89. Figes, interview with Laurel Graeber/ James McConkey, in James McConkey, 'Get Thee Behind Us, Freud'/ 'New Beginnings in Middle Age', *New York Times*, 25 September 1988, p. 9 <https://www.nytimes.com/1988/09/25/books/get-thee-behind-us-freud.html> (accessed 1 April 2019).
90. Figes, interview with Jan Moir, 'The Feminist That Time Forgot', *The Guardian*, 27 October 1993, p. 8.
91. Figes, 'The Largest Minority', in William Benton (ed.), *Britannica Book of the Year* (London: Encyclopaedia Britannica, 1971), p. 670 <https://archive.org/stream/in.ernet.dli.2015.147390/2015.147390.Britannica-Book-Of-The-Year-1971> (accessed 21 June 2019).
92. Hereafter, all page references will be given in the text in parentheses.
93. Figes, interview with Burns, in Burns and Sugnet (eds), *Imagination*, p. 34.
94. Ibid., p. 34.
95. This is reminiscent of Rachel Cusk's denunciation of the naturalness of maternal feelings in her *Outline* trilogy.
96. Norman Shrapnel, *The Guardian*, 28 January 1966, reviews for *Equinox*, press cuttings, 1966, MS 89050/7/4, Figes Archive, BL, London. Subsequent references to contemporary reviews of *Equinox* are also from this archival source.
97. Figes, *Patriarchal Attitudes*, p. 71.
98. Ann Oakley, *Housewife* (London: Allen Lane, 1974), p. 233.
99. Stephen Wall, *The Observer*, 1967.
100. *The Evening Standard*, 25 January 1966.
101. Francis King, *The Sunday Telegraph*, 1966.
102. Richard Mayne, *New Statesman*, 4 February 1966, p. 169.
103. *Daily Telegraph*, 27 January 1966, p. 21.
104. *Times Literary Supplement*, 17 February 1966.
105. *The Sunday Times*, 23 January 1966.
106. Kenneth Allsop, *The Spectator*, 28 January 1966.
107. Figes, interview with Burns, in Burns and Sugnet (eds), *Imagination*, p. 34.
108. Ibid.
109. Figes, *Winter Journey*, p. 10. Hereafter *Winter*, and pages references are given in the text in parentheses.
110. Robert Nye, 'Dull Head', p. 7.
111. Barbara Bray, undated press review. This and subsequent references to contemporary reviews of *Winter Journey* are from press cuttings, 1967–1968, MS 89050/7/5, Figes Archive, BL, London.
112. Figes, interview with Burns, in Burns and Sugnet (eds), *Imagination*, p 35.
113. Ibid., p. 34.
114. Bill Webb, 1967, p. 3.
115. Nye, 'Dull Head', p. 7.
116. Ibid.
117. Figes, interview with Almagro and Sánchez-Palencia, p. 184.
118. Jay Bail; no further details on the press clipping.
119. *Library Journal*, 3 January 1968.
120. Elizabeth Mayor, 'Different Witnesses', *Glasgow Herald*, undated.
121. Figes, interview with Burns, in Burns and Sugnet (eds), *Imagination*, p. 37.
122. Ibid.

123. Ibid., p. 36.
124. Ibid., p. 36.
125. Jonathan Raban, 'Family Scrapbook', *New Statesman*, 5 September 1969, p. 315, Reviews for *Konek Landing*, press cuttings, 1969-1970, MS 89050/7/6, Figes Archive, BL, London. Subsequent references to contemporary reviews of *Konek Landing* are also from MS 89050/7/6, Figes Archive, BL, London.
126. William Trevor, 'Family Ferocities', *The Guardian*, n.d.
127. Ibid.
128. Figes, interview with Burns, in Burns and Sugnet (eds), *Imagination*, p. 36. Hereafter, page numbers are given in the text in parentheses.
129. In *Journey*, Edith tells of how after the war many Germans were kind to her but others only pretended to be so that could obtain what was called a *Persilschein*; a play on words used by Brooke-Rose in *Between*, it came to mean de-nazification rather than its original military meaning certifying a clean bill of health.
130. Cheyette, *Contemporary Jewish Writing*, p. xlvii.
131. Subsequently referred to as *Konek* with page references given in the text in parentheses.
132. Kenneth Graham, 'Wastelandmarks', *The Listener*, 4 September 1969, p. 319.
133. Ferber, 'Disembodied', *Times Literary Supplement*, 18 September 1969.
134. Benedict Nightingale, 1969.
135. Susana Onega, 'Affective Knowledge, Self-Awareness and the Function of Myth in the Representation and Transmission of Trauma: The Case of Eva Figes' *Konek Landing*', *Journal of Literary Theory*, 6: 1 (2012), pp. 83–102 (p. 83).
136. Fred Urquhart, *Oxford Mail*, 4 September 1969, 890507/6, Figes Archive, BL, London.
137. Janice Elliot, *The Sunday Telegraph*, 7 September 1969.
138. Derek Stanford, *The Scotsman*, 27 September 1969.
139. Figes, interview with Burns, in Burns and Sugnet (eds), *Imagination*, p. 108.

Chapter 6

Ann Quin: Forms Forming Themselves

Introduction

Like Brigid Brophy, Ann Quin began writing from an early age. Soon developing a sense of language as a way of accommodating uneasy and fugitive thoughts, the young Quin became fascinated by the ways in which narrative could transform reality: 'I lived in a dream world and created dreams out of everyday situations until nothing ever seemed what it appeared to be'.[1] The transmogrification of everyday life into another more intense version, not quite its opposite, rather a strange, oneiric reverberation of the original, is a characteristic feature of her work which takes the familiar space of the domestic and the heterosexual couple into which she interposes 'foreign' or interloping elements that disturb the environment. Quin noted that her writing always required something inherently disquieting in its midst, an element of aberrant disorientation that will dislocate and set adrift the settled and the stable: this was, she said, a 'point that opens for the magic usage of things' and allows for the penetration of, what she calls, the 'real' into writing.[2] The idea of a 'magic' interruption into the quotidian in her work estranges the commonplace and the ordinary, transforming it into something more exaggeratedly theatrical and transient. Alan Burns, to whom she was very close, describes her writing as inhabited 'by shadow images, areas of association, which slip further and further away from the text. She has this talent for throwing off ripples of association, and that's very fine, it's her best quality, her subconscious quality'.[3]

Already an avid reader of Virginia Woolf from her childhood, sometime in 1965 Quin came across Woolf's diaries – an important moment in her aesthetic practice. Woolf's writing, she noted, 'came across beautifully, a lot of her dealing with form reminds me of my own concerns'. She also admired the poetry of William Carlos Williams: '[he]

has such a movement in his writing, such a vivid sense of light and shade tinged with humour'.[4] From the influences of these writers who 'deal' with form, Quin constantly sought ways of writing fiction that did not conform to the template of the contemporary realist novel that seemed to her to be aesthetically very dull and unadventurous. Her experiments with the limits of interior monologue in *Berg*, intercalated textualities in *Three*, the highly experimental dual narration technique in *Passages*, cut ups and pop-art collage in *Tripticks* (1972) resolutely cast off the 'he said', 'she said' mode.[5]

It is futile to speculate what kind of career Quin might have gone on to have but her reputation as an experimental writer is only now beginning to enjoy some belated recognition in various studies offering a reappraisal of mid-century British writing. There has, as Ian Patterson notes, been something of a revival in Quin's work: 'After scarcely even maintaining a cult reputation among writers in the years since her death, she's reappeared like a revenant who'd been lurking in dark corners, and now everybody's writing about her'.[6] Disregarding the hyperbole in the latter half of this statement, it is certainly the case that work on Quin has had a modest flourishing.[7] Patterson concludes that Quin's writing can be best read in an 'internationalist milieu' outside of what he derides as 'English narrowness and its "safe comfortable rituals, the monotony that keeps the fantasies moving" [. . .] You can feel that hatred of monotony throughout her work, a restlessness, an unsatisfied feeling, both in the characters and in the work itself'.[8] *Berg*, *Three* and *Passages* depict characters who are all uncomfortable within the confines of traditional domesticity; indeed, as Phillip Stevick observes, in all four of Quin's novel 'the characters are never at home'.[9] Her work is marked by a pervasive atmosphere of transience and vagabondage in which the idea of home and domesticity is vexing and often cloyingly limiting – Berg's mother, Edith, still exhorts him to wear woollen underwear when the weather turns chilly; the homey dinners in *Three* often turn to drama and disappointment. *Passages* and her last novel *Tripticks* move even further away from any settled notion of domesticity, taking place 'on the road' in Greece and America.

A Vagabond Writer

Born in Brighton on 17 March 1936 to a Glaswegian mother, Anne Ward (*neé* Reid), and an Irish father, Nicholas Montague Quin, Ann Quin was brought up in Ovingdean, a village on the outskirts of Brighton, at the time a working- to lower-middle-class area. An only child, in circumstances that are not wholly clear, Quin had an older half-brother, with whom she 'fell desperately in love' following their first meeting when she was fourteen. The Quin household was by no means affluent but there is no mention in her correspondence or biographical writing of significant financial hardship during her childhood. She has often been labelled a working-class writer but while this remains a rather speculative assertion concerning her upbringing, it has more validity as a claim about her writing life. More than any of the other writers considered here, Quin experienced draining financial difficulties for much of her writing career alleviated only temporarily by two fellowships and an Arts Council Grant. To sustain her life as a writer Quin had to work extremely hard, often travelling from Brighton to London and back every day and sometimes writing all evening after a full day's office work as a typist. Later, living in London in dingy, ill-heated bedsits, she would write every night after work, often to the point of exhaustion.

Her parents' marriage ended when her father, 'a failed opera singer',[10] conceivably more vaudeville than Wagner, left her mother soon after Quin was born, although it is clear from her correspondence that she met her father again at least once.[11] Although the family were not religious, Quin was sent to a Catholic School, the Convent of the Blessed Sacrament, presumably for the discipline of the nuns and as she says in the short biographical piece, 'Leaving School', 'to be brought up "a lady". To say gate and not gaite'.[12] In terms of elocution at least, her education was a success as she left school with a pronounced RP accent that belied her class background.[13] By her own admission she 'sleepwalked' through school and left at seventeen with only one GCE in English language (she failed English Literature), all dreams of study in the Sixth Form by windows that 'overlooked the boys' college', now dashed.[14] While her Catholic education transformed her accent, it did not result in either academic excellence or ladylike acquiescence, rather its 'realistic culture' bequeathed her, she said, a 'death wish and a sense of sin. Also a great lust to find out, experience what evil really was' (p. 16). Despite an inauspicious academic start in literary terms, Quin was passionate about reading and, in an effort to avoid her nightly school homework, she worked her way diligently through Greek and Elizabethan drama, Chekhov, Lawrence, Hardy, and Dostoevsky's *Crime and Punishment* but, as noted, it was Woolf who made a lasting impression upon her and, in particular, *The Waves* (1931) which revealed to her 'the possibilities of writing' (p. 16)

As well as literature Quin also loved the theatre and spent many weekends 'queueing up for a seat in the Gods at the Theatre Royal to witness a fantasy world that relieved my many desires, frustrations' (p. 17).

In 1953, after leaving school, she began work as an assistant stage manager for a repertory company, the closest she could get to being on stage herself. She harboured hopes of becoming an actor, but instead gathered props, cleaned the stage, sewed, made tea and laughed at 'camp jokes [she] didn't understand' (p. 18). Despite these lowly tasks, Quin remained enamoured of the theatrical life. However, following a minor slip-up she was dismissed from her ASM job and returned 'to the world of books'. She continued to write poetry that was 'mainly religious and surrealistic' (p. 19); one poem, 'The Lost Seagull' about a gull 'with a damned soul' won her a prize of a ten-shilling book token.

Still fascinated by the theatre, Quin attempted to become an actress and secured an audition at the Royal Academy of Dramatic Art. Once there, however, she was immobilised with stage fright: she 'began, froze, asked to start again, but was struck dumb, and rushed out, silently screaming down Gower Street'. Abandoning any theatrical ambitions, she resolved instead: 'I would be a writer. A poet' (p. 19). This interest in the dramatic arts can be traced in her writing as she often uses heightened theatricality as a means of twisting and exaggerating what might otherwise have been rather mundane domestic plots, such as *Three* (1966), into self-consciously over-agitated drama often overlaid with a quasi-mythical structure. A father quest story like *Berg* (1964) becomes a tawdrily comic murder with more than a discernible sense of vaudeville and blackly humorous slapstick. *Passages* (1969) takes the form of a Greek drama in places, becoming a countercultural rewriting of the Antigone myth; *Three* has a central conceit of a play that the three central characters are rather desultorily rehearsing.[15] Giving up on thespian life, Quin decided that learning typing skills would be her 'bread and butter', and so signed up for a secretarial course and worked on and off as a typist between 1955 and 1961.[16] She found a job in London at a newspaper office in Fleet Street but remained living at home with her mother, which made for long days commuting between London and Brighton. Struck down with appendicitis that rendered her bedridden for some time, Quin was reluctant to return to work, so prolonged her convalescence while studying painting part-time and falling in love with an art student referred to only as 'Heathcliff' in 'Leaving School' (p. 20). During these years, Quin wrote, by her own admission, some 'beautiful love letters', as well as journals and poetry, but dared not yet call herself a writer.

Deciding not to return to London, Quin found a new job at a solicitor's office in Brighton, a position she found exceptionally tedious, sustained only through her two years there by 'the world of love' that she enjoyed outside of work. In time, Quin and 'Heathcliff' separated and, heartbroken, she 'tackled London again' (p. 20) After finding work as secretary for the foreign rights manager at Hutchinson and Company publishers, she remained there for two-and-a-half years between 1956 and 1958, during which time she became a manuscript reader for new authors. Still seriously short of money, Quin rented a room in Soho where she lived 'on potatoes' and 'saved on gas by going to bed' with her typewriter perched on her knees (p. 20). Such unpropitious conditions notwithstanding, between 1955 and 1961 she worked on two novels, 'A Slice of Moon' and 'Oscar', both of which she would destroy after failing to find a publisher for them.

Later, Quin worked in another solicitor's office in London and at night allowed men to 'wine and dine' her but felt guilty when she 'refused to invite them up for coffee afterwards', thus reneging on the unspoken rules of the sexual contract that women had to endure (p. 21). Escaping a muggy London summer, she went to Cornwall, bearing another 'half-finished novel', to work in a hotel for the holiday season, at the end of which she moved back to Brighton and she suffered her first episode of serious mental health crisis. This is described in 'Leaving School' as a time when 'she dug holes' in the garden, 'lay in them weeping' and woke up 'screaming, convinced my tears were rivers of blood, that my insides were being eaten away by an earwig that had crawled into my ear' (p. 22). Once recovered, Quin returned to London where she worked on her second novel, *Three*, in 'an attic kind of place' with a 'partition next to [her] bed' that 'shook at night from the maneuverings' of her neighbouring lodger (p. 23). On 9 October 1959, she found a job as a secretary at the Royal College of Art Painting School in Wimbledon and moved into a small flat in south-west London, where she wrote every night after work for three years, working on *Berg*.[17] As is evident then, paid work was central to Quin's life, or, stated differently, the burden of finding money to enable her writing and finally to be taken seriously as a novelist was a perpetual struggle for her, only temporarily improved by two fellowships and an Arts Council Grant. In a letter to John Calder, she complained that a serous lack of money was a constant impediment for her writing: 'What I don't want to do is to begin worrying about some bloody office job when I'm in the middle of or towards the completion of a book'.[18] The gendered nature of Quin's impecunious situation was noted by Alan Burns, who, after her death, wrote:

> I, as any writer, will feel always a hostility to any society so little responsive to the situation of its artists. If they are women, that response will be even more meager and self-secure. What Ann Quin wanted, was time free to work – sans the least sentimentality or enlargement, either by her or anyone else.[19]

Quin's peripatetic life was, at times, painful and unsettling for her but she was acutely aware that she enjoyed many aspects of her vagabondage:

> In a way I feel like a leaf blown down, drifting, there seems nothing to catch on to, and any moment I will be swept up and lie rotting in the gutter – why this eternal wanting to escape from one thing or one place to another, I never seem happy to settle down anywhere for long.[20]

Changes of Fortune

Quin's luck changed when John Calder, the renowned publisher of Beckett, Duras and Robbe-Grillet among others, accepted the MS of *Berg* in 1963 and it was published the following year. Its publication allowed Quin to think of herself as a writer for the first time and she regarded the novel as a kind of apprentice-work – a working-out of future directions:

> it's been a good exercise, something anyway I had to write, not so much 'to get out of my system', but more as a sort of map I had to plan out, find several routes, and arrive at a point, an area, so to speak, that would open on to other areas, other routes.[21]

The critical acclaim that *Berg* received almost immediately established Quin as an important new writer and she was consequently awarded two major fellowships, the Harkness and the D. H. Lawrence, allowing her to travel to America between 1965 and 1967 where she lived for some time, in Placitas near Albuquerque, New Mexico and at the Lawrence Ranch in San Cristobal.[22] She travelled extensively in the US, visiting Iowa, Maine and New York City. She also began a relationship with the (married) poet Robert Creeley and experimented with all the recreational drugs and transgressive pleasures on offer on the US countercultural scene, including LSD, peyote, avant-garde poetry and daily erotic flagellation at the hands of Creeley. Relieved, albeit only momentarily, of pecuniary pressures, Quin was finally able to concentrate on her writing and her reading.

Returning to Britain with Creeley for a short while in 1965, they both attended the International Poetry Incarnation at the Royal Albert Hall on 11 June, the participants in which read like a roll-call of the international avant-garde poetry scene in the mid-1960s and included Allen Ginsberg, Kurt Schwitters, Lawrence Ferlinghetti, Gregory Corso, Harry Fainlight, Alexander Trocchi and Andrei Voznesensky.[23]

Quin published her second novel, *Three*, in 1966 about a triangular relationship between a married couple and a young woman, S. The book is dedicated to Bob and Bobbie, almost certainly a reference to Robert Creeley and his wife Bobbie. The relationship with Creeley was over by 1966, after which she formed a relationship with another poet, Robert Sward, but they split up two years later in 1968. The fellowship money gone, Quin once again 'desperately need[ed] some money' and so returned to Britain where, aware that Alan Burns had recently received a substantial Arts Council grant, she set her sights on obtaining something similar which was a lifeline for struggling writers.[24] Her third novel, *Passages*, based on her experiences travelling in the Mediterranean, was published by Calder and Boyars in 1969 but at this point she was suffering from what she called 'terrible depressions' and was feeling 'almost suicidal at times', a state that she attributed 'partly to lack of money'. On hearing that she had been awarded £1,000 from the Arts Council, Quin said she 'felt pretty high for the day, but that aint stopped the depressions!'[25]

In the period when she was waiting for the outcome of this Arts Council application, Quin become involved in the Writers Reading Group's inaugural event in 1969 where she performed her 'reading' in total silence. Alan Burns recalls how

> she came onto stage and she just sat and looked at people, she wouldn't say a goddam word! She just stared, she either implied or she actually stated that we sort of 'think-communicate', we can communicate more in silence than with someone actually putting words across.[26]

Like Figes, Quin was part of the loose association that was the Writers Reading Group. As noted in Chapter 5 the group's mission was to unite these writers by 'a profound interest in prose as a form of expression and not simply as a medium for story-telling'.[27] However, apart from her silent reading, Quin had little to do with the group subsequently. Nevertheless, after her death, just a few months before B. S. Johnson's suicide, Giles Gordon wrote to Calder and Boyars for information on Quin so that he might dedicate the book *Beyond the Words: Eleven Writers in Search of a New Fiction* to both her and Johnson.[28]

A short time before her death, Quin was approached by a director who was interested in adapting *Berg* and making it 'queer'.[29] With a script penned by the photographer for the quintessential Swinging London film, *Blow-Up* (1966), the adaptation was 'better than [Quin] thought possible, and with the addition of a '"pot psychedelic" scene brought into it: on the beach! Mother dies by putting head in gas oven. Son stabs father at the end'.[30] Also, and rather surprisingly perhaps, around this time Quin becomes involved with the writer Henry Williamson, an anti-Semite Fascist supporter, forty years her senior and best known for his novel *Tarka the Otter* (1927).³¹ Such an eccentric choice of partner might be understood in the context of a father-complex but Williamson's right-wing politics remains something of a conundrum in terms of Quin's life.

In 1969, Quin's £1,000 grant was used for what turned out to be an ill-fated trip across Scandinavia. Calder notes that the Arts Council ignored his suggestion to dole out the grant in smaller portions as he thought her Harkness-funded American trip so full of drugs and alcohol that it did not produce any significant creative work. Immediately cashing her cheque into 'liquid currency', Quin boarded a plane to Dublin then, via London and Amsterdam, ended up in Sweden, where her mental health deteriorated very rapidly.³² The trip ended badly – she was found 'near a canal in Stockholm' 'nearly frozen, weeping, unable to speak' and was hospitalised in Sweden for five weeks before returning to England where she spent some time at the Atkinson Morley's Hospital in Wimbledon, a neuro-rehabilitation institution renowned for its pioneering approach to neuroscience.³³ Writing from the Baillie Ward in the hospital, she related this episode to Creeley in March 1970:

> I ended up in Sweden after a crazy flight from London via Dublin, Copenhagen, Oslo [. . .] I got caught up in some occult underground movement, and then also a political movement which involved the Russians and the Chinese following me; of course none of the psychiatrists believe what I tell them, they all think I'm suffering from persecution mania and that half the threatening signs I saw were just in mind.³⁴

In 1971, Quin had a serious recurrence of mental health issues. She was sectioned under the 1959 Mental Health Act and taken to Springfield Hospital, Tooting after she was caught 'stealing a Vicar's blanket'. She wrote to Creeley of the challenges in trying to find lucidity, what she called 'Getting the threads together inside my head', and that 'achieving good, or least stable, mental health was always a difficult adventure & one that I continually confront head on then a retreat then back again'.³⁵ In a short piece, 'The Unmapped Country', Quin writes of the experience of psychiatric hospitalisation and treatment: 'She saw the hospital; staff in their hygienic armour of white approach a struggling body. The raising of a needle, the filling of it, hands holding the body down, eyes unable to see when the needle would sink into the flesh'.³⁶ Without question, Quin suffered from severe mental health problems and experienced periodic crises but the assertion that her writing, its technique and content, was simply and wholly a manifestation of what Philip Stevick terms 'her own troubled mind' dismisses the experimental daring and richness of her *oeuvre*. As we saw with Kavan, a woman writer who suffers from poor mental health often has her work wholly pathologised and reduced to the manifestation of a diseased psyche.[37]

By 1972 Quin had published four novels, and had travelled extensively in Europe and the Americas and now was determined to complete, and further, her education. To this end, she enrolled in Hillcroft Community College (not Richmond College) and lived with her mother at weekends. It appears that her tutors there did not give her any special treatment – 'they seem not to have appreciated her importance as a novelist'.[38] Although her marks were not distinguished, she did sufficiently well to win a place on the newly established Creative Writing Programme at the University of East Anglia.[39] The idea of the routine of academic life seemed to her to offer another way of approaching being both a writer and a reader. In an article for the *Guardian* in 1973, she described the financial hardships she continued to undergo:

> Before I came to Hillcroft I had to supplement my income as a writer by part-time secretarial work: not only was I bored, but I also felt extremely insular, and the idea of having a whole year of systematic study, to attend lectures, participate in seminars and tutorials and discuss what I was reading with other people seemed to me ideal.[40]

The course at UEA started in October of 1973 but by September Quin was dead. Seen by some fishermen at twilight on the beach by Brighton pier taking off her clothes, Quin walked into the sea and drowned. Her body was not found for a week as it had been carried by the strong Channel tides down the coast to Shoreham-by-Sea. Quin was thirty-seven years old.

A 'Singular and Single' Woman

As we have seen, over the course of her short life Quin travelled extensively and as soon as she got some money she left Britain. Her first advance from Calder for *Berg* gave her the chance to go to Greece and Turkey. It was an arduous journey, during which she encountered riots in Istanbul and had to make her way back via Brindisi and Milan before finally arriving back at Folkestone. Quin expressed a strong desire to be peripatetic and nomadic, refused to conform to the traditional female roles of being a wife and homemaker, believing that conventional domesticity would impede her creativity:

> I like being on my own. I find a certain peace and stillness which is necessary for writing and to live with someone would cut in on this always [. . .] I've often thought that what I really need is a wife.[41]

Interviewed by Nell Dunn in *Talking to Women* (1965), Quin talks of this desire for independence, pointing out that for women this is too often compromised by marriage and motherhood that obliges them to relinquish any outside life and become submerged by domesticity. She talks of the pressures on girls and women to think about their future only in terms of marriage and maternity – 'people want to see you married off' (p. 187). Women have been 'so bogged down until recently', she continues, and are only now starting to be 'freed out of the kitchen sink' and are only just beginning to realise 'the possibilities that they have' (p. 193). The kitchen sink, a symbol for contemporary domesticity since *Look Back in Anger*, stands metonymically for all domestic encumberants or 'paraphernalia':

> part of the married state [...] is having a place, and leading a life which involves the paraphernalia of existence such as cooking utensils [...] What seems to me to be so remarkably difficult about life is to be able to live or have one's relationships in a sort of fluid space without it picking up a whole lot of paraphernalia as one goes along. (p. 204)

She describes herself as 'a singular girl, singular and single' who must find for herself 'day-to-day rhythms' outside of marriage and family (p. 208). Quin believed that, in general, 'women have much more to cope with' than men, and that being economically dependent on a man binds them into a domestic contract that allows them little personal freedom and almost no possibility of writing – 'I feel that is very difficult for women to cope with family and create' (p. 187). The repetition and confinement of married domesticity is the antithesis of the 'fluid space' in which one can remain free and open to possibilities, both positive and negative.

> Ann I think women are very different in many ways. Men are always trying to assert themselves, a certain vanity, and women are not so conscious of trying to assert themselves, they're much more adaptable – they like playing a role that a man will throw upon them, they have many roles, there's a lot of the chameleon in women.
> Nell Which do you like being with the best?
> Ann Both (p.193)

This desire to be both male and female, comparable in some ways to Brooke-Rose's 'delightful bisexuality' and Brophy's 'polymorphous as the angels', is discernible in *Three* in S.'s diaries: 'Dual roles/ realised./ Yes yes/ yes/ be a boy./ If you like./ Anything./ Be/ Just be' (p. 114). Quin was aware that being a woman writer was often rather limiting, saying that 'I find difficulty in being a writer and a woman where lots of men are very unsure of me'. Wary of a talented woman, men, she said, 'are liable to put me down and treat me from a physical angle which gets me very frustrated and I then try to assert myself and hate myself at the same time for having to do this and hate the man' (pp. 193–4).

As we saw in Chapter 5, even though the 1960s saw significant improvements for women's autonomy and equality, these legislative changes trickled down into the intimate spaces of sexual behaviour only very slowly. In a posthumously published short story, 'B. B.'s Second Manifesto', Quin captures perfectly the unexamined misogyny and sexual narcissism of 1960s male hipsters:

> Wish I hadn't had so many women, it's like a machine in the end. This chick I lived with, just a convenience, screwed her every night, again in the morning, get up at eleven and know she had cooked some breakfast. Jesus it gets so boring. She was a nymphomaniac, that was her trouble. I want it to mean something, not just sex. All these chicks dote on one, that's why I've given them up.[42]

It must be emphasised, however, that Quin was not in any overt sense a feminist writer and there is no evidence that she identified or even sympathised with the aims of the feminist movement either in Britain or America. The representation of women in her novels is ambivalent to say the least; at times there is even a pronounced undercurrent of misogyny in her work – the 'bitch goddess' sexuality of Judith Goldstein in *Berg* and Berg's smothering mother; in *Three*, Ruth is a neurotically idle and frigid wife who has had extensive plastic surgery to keep her looks; and the obsessively insecure female character in *Passages* is in a perpetual state of chaos. Moreover, ambiguous sexual violence, and even rape, is never far from the triangulated erotic structures that she creates in her novels. That said, Quin was acutely aware of the inequities between male and female writers in the 1960s and understood that it was certainly more difficult to be taken seriously as a woman writer, recalling dispiriting meetings with publishers who seemed to be more interested in her looks than her manuscript. Elsewhere, she noted the disadvantages of being a female writer. Male writers

> can quite happily go on with their creating yet have a wife, mistress, children etc. without it upsetting him too much, besides doesn't he get all the attention and comforts from the woman, ah it was a sad day when the seed entered the wrong ovum and I was conceived a girl, sure now I would have made a wonderful man besides people take more notice of a male writer no matter what blarney he gushes forth, Oh woman is halfway in mid-stream and can never quite reach the bank but has one leg in the estuary and misses the boat out to sea although I think a lot of men do but at least they are given the opportunity of drowning in the ocean and not in a mere river?[43]

As much as Quin wanted the 'ocean' as the medium for her work rather than a backwater, she very often found herself the only woman at literary, especially poetry, events, recalling in a letter to Robert Sward how she went to meet the poet John Logan, 'in a motel room, about fifteen poets, wd. be poets turned up, I the only ah female! We did some reading; I read bits out of new work very badly, was v. nervous, read much too quickly'.[44]

Listening in the audience to Creeley reading poetry at the 1965 Berkeley Poetry Conference, Quin found his poems that alluded to her intensely discomfiting: it was 'difficult to accept [Creeley] reading poems, that seemed to me so very personal, in public [. . .] I needed a glance of reassurance, a word of recognition, I did not, could not find it'.[45] After the Berkeley reading, Quin thought she had been 'rejected'.[46] Her comments here reveal a distinctly feminist sensibility about the male stifling of female voices and of the restrictions of being cast as a kind of muse: 'I found myself so often speechless [. . .] seeing myself as some awkward dumb female clinging to female irrationality, and then by some twist feeling so bloody vulnerable'.[47] This version of her as both faltering and unreasonable was devastating for Quin and certainly must have had some impact on her extreme anxiety about public readings.[48] It is possible (though, of course, by no means certain) that her attitudes towards feminism might have developed more fully had she lived to see the political and social progress made by feminism from the 1970s onwards.

Quin's sense of her writing as a vulnerable 'kind of involuntary commitment', came at some considerable cost, both psychological and physical. On receiving the first proofs of *Berg* she was bodily and psychologically overwhelmed:

> The proofs [of *Berg*] finally arrived, I couldn't open them, and spent the whole day vomiting from anxiety and depression. Eventually the galleys lay all over my room. The dream had been realized, but reading what I had written seemed someone else's dream.[49]

This splicing together of textual and bodily disorder gives us an insight into how Quin approached her writing; often painfully throwing herself into the task of creativity which was for her, part instinct and part craft. Creeley said of her writing: 'she was fascinated by ways in which the "seriality" of prose, the mode of its continuities, might be altered, and these later books are tests of that possibility in part'. He was certain that if she had lived Quin might have been able to resolve 'entirely the division between her conscious experiment and that intrinsic gift of initial story-telling, which was hers in every possible sense'.[50] One critic pointed out: 'To all the correspondences, parallels, echoes [Quin] would at times attach a significance that appeared almost superstitious. Her books, the characters and events in her books, or so she seemed half to believe, were anticipatory of her own experience'.[51] The suggestion here that Quin's writing sometimes prefigures her own life is an interesting take on the relationship of a writer's life to her art, returning us, in different ways, to the earlier discussion of Kavan's writing but still suggestive of an overly reflective rather than refractive relationship between the two. It is likely that Quin wrote into her novels some versions of her own unrealised fantasies and Oedipal struggles and then, later, her experiences with drug-taking, bisexuality and *ménages à trois*, but as important is the poetic form which these assume in her writing.

Berg: 'Oedipus with athlete's foot'[52]

'Doesn't every narrative', Roland Barthes asks in *The Pleasure of the Text*, 'lead back to Oedipus?'[53] Quin's first published novel, *Berg*, is nothing if not an Oedipal tale. By the time she began writing the novel, we know that she had some knowledge of Freud as she notes in a letter to Carol Burns she had read 'no. 7 volume 1, on anxietyneurosis, obsessions and phobias etc'.[54] Elsewhere, Quin noted *Berg* had its roots in her own relationship with her absent father:

> I came across (oh yes, of course, in the Oresteian Trilogy – thank you v. much, a delightful surprise!) the fact that Oedipus means sore feet. Do you remember at the end of *Berg* the father is going to take up chiropody? One could say Jung's collective unconscious at work here I suppose. But the truth of the matter was – my own father, when I last saw him, said he was going to be a chiropodist.[55]

Narrated in broken glimpses, oneiric fragments and outbursts framed by a temporality shuttling between past and present, *Berg* relates a murderous, paranoid Oedipal quest involving voyeurism, mistaken identity, taxidermy and cross-dressing, all of which culminates in the stabbing of a ventriloquist's dummy that the protagonist mistakes for his own father. With its blackly comedic set-pieces, the novel combines the pantomime or theatrical bedroom farce with the darker energies of Greek drama and faux *fin-de-siècle* decadence. Hence, when the novel was reissued in 2001 by Dalkey Archive, Giles Gordon noted that it 'had absorbed the theatrical influences of John Osborne'.[56]

For the most part, the reception of *Berg* was positive but, rather inevitably, Quin's techniques were compared with those of the *nouveau roman* and in particular to those of Nathalie Sarraute, a famous 'Calder writer'. A review in the *TLS* determines that Quin had 'undoubtedly been influenced by such French novelists as Sarraute and by the *nouvelle vague* movement in the cinema', but acknowledged that *Berg* was 'something of a breakthrough in the sense that, for the first time, these techniques have been used to produce a novel that is both wholly English in atmosphere and quite unpretentious'.[57] Stevick, however, maintains that Quin had not, in fact, read any of these French novels:

> What some of the early reviewers guessed was that *Berg* bore a relationship to Nathalie Sarraute and some of the modes of the new French novel. What they could not have known is that Quin had not read the French novelists whom she was seen to resemble.[58]

According to Stevick, Quin was not interested in 'rendering mind' either in the style of the *nouveau romanciers* or by what he calls the 'early modernist' influence; rather she 'began to invent ways of representing the inner life by drawing on her own troubled mind, by introspection and a set of conventions largely of her own devising'.[59] While it is commendable that Stevick attempts to rescue Quin from some of the lazier comparisons to the French novel, it is wholly less so that he attributes her aesthetic practice to her psychological issues which are seen to disallow her from any intellectual attentiveness to the cultural contexts around her. He is also mistaken about Quin's knowledge of Sarraute's work.

While it is not entirely verifiable precisely how much of Sarraute Quin had read, we know for certain by the early 1960s she had read *Portrait of a Man Unknown* (first translated into English in 1958) as she notes in a letter to Carol Burns, 'without being too profane it reminded me a little of my own work'.[60] A reading list Quin sent to her friend Larry Goodell (one she called her 'Quinology') contained three works by Sarraute – *Portrait of a Man Unknown*, *Tropisms* and *The Age of Suspicion* suggesting that Quin was indeed well-acquainted with her writing.[61] Furthermore, we know from Rayner Heppenstall's *The Master Eccentric* that Quin attended a reading by Sarraute at Better Books organised by John Calder in 1964,[62] at which it is highly likely that Sarraute talked about her participation in the aesthetic agenda of the *nouveau romancier* that she defined as a writer who 'is wary of the abrupt, spectacular types of action that model the character with a few resounding whacks; he is also wary of plot, which winds itself around the character like wrappings, giving it, along with an appearance of cohesiveness and life, mummy-like stiffness'.[63]

In several reviews in the French press, *Berg* is regarded as being unmistakably influenced by the *nouveau roman* – 'Ann Quin a lu Alain

Robbe-Grillet'.[64] Giles Gordon, however, places Quin's work in a slightly wider tradition that ranges from Beckett, Burroughs, Creeley, Duras, and Claude Mauriac to Henry Miller, Pinget, and Robbe-Grillet.[65] Noting that Quin's work could not wholly escape some of the influences of such strikingly unconventional writing, Marion Boyars notes that she possessed a very individual style and if any influences are to be found in her later work, it seems more appropriate to name people like Robert Creeley and John Cage.[66]

Despite its innovative prose style that meanders between various foci of interiority and a text 'undifferentiated by punctuation or mise-en-page', finally *Berg* has little in common with the hygienic, pared-down compactness of the *nouveau roman* and the cool detachment of Robbe-Grillet's *La Jalousie*.[67] Its depiction of sexual shenanigans in an insalubrious boarding house has a distinctly postwar, slightly seedy, British quality that, at times, is reminiscent of the domestic violence and cross-dressing disguises in the *commedia dell'arte*-inspired Punch and Judy show. The atmosphere of *Berg*, like Judith Goldstein's fashion sense and décor, is more than a little bawdy. Reviewers discerned influences on the novel other than the *nouveau roman*. In the *New Statesman*, John Fuller criticised the action of the novel as 'a farrago' that represented the 'quintessence of Calderism': 'The headlong prose, the ending-at-the-beginning, the whole arch apparatus of the over-serious, derives, one supposes, from Beckett *et al*. The insubstantiality and wordy portentousness are the writer's own'.[68] For her own part, Quin affirmed her admiration of Beckett and affirmed that her influences were drawn from a European rather than British intellectual tradition: 'I would say if I have been influenced by anyone it would be a mixture of Sartre, Beckett and Ingmar Bergman'.[69] In fact, the novel's title might well be a play on the latter's name.

The narrative circles around a central revenge plot that is always threatening to get out of hand, and, at times, even to disintegrate completely; maintaining a firm grasp on events is arduous not just for the reader but also for the characters. Mingling inner thought with external event with no distinction or separation between the two, the only conventional narrative occurs in the letters that Berg writes home to his mother Edith, the spurned wife who has no idea that her son is scheming to kill his father in the unnamed, out-of-season seaside town. The plot follows a clearly defined, if thoroughly perverse, logic; it is a distorted Oedipal whodunnit that delights in mistaken identities to the extent that the murder that occurs is a *faux* homicide of Berg's father's ventriloquist dummy who happens to be dressed in his suit.

Despite the kernel of realistic detail in *Berg* in the form of its physical settings, Quin had no interest in writing *Berg* as a conventionally realist novel and expressed a deep and abiding antipathy towards writers who leant on what she regarded as worn-out literary modes: 'Then there's W.B.O & Co., (Wesker, Braine, Osborne) and they frankly stink with their dumb 19th century prose. Ugh'.[70] Writing from America she mocks the staidness of British literary culture: 'And as for Miss Murderdock who is considered the leading woman novelist over there. Well fuck'.[71] Paddy Kitchen, a close friend of Quin's, wrote that Quin 'was not one of those authors who self-consciously strove to be an innovator, rather she had to seek a different form for each theme which occupied her mind'.[72]

Berg takes its central narrative trajectory from the blackly comic (and botched) patricide in which events take place as if they were on a stage in the process of 'threading experience through imaginative material, acting out fictitious parts'. The action in the boarding house occurs against a soundtrack drifting over from the Palais de Dance: 'Berg lay back; the waves of jazz, or a slow waltz crowded in upon the necropolis of cells'.[73] The novel's opening epigraph functions both as an overture – something akin to the 'Sirens' section of *Ulysses* – and as a parodic *résumé* of a realist plot: 'A man called Berg, who changed his name to Greb, came to a seaside town intending to kill his father'. The novel is indeed about Alistair Charles Humphrey Berg, born 3 March 1931, a nauseating anti-hero with 'curled webbed toes'. Mistreated as a 'changeling' in his childhood, 'cissy Berg' is now a peripatetic patricidal 'hair restorer' who sells, out of a shabby suitcase, a tonic that promises to make men's hair regrow and to 'Defeat Delilah's Damage', the first of many allusions to *femmes fatales* with their alluring *dentata* sexuality achieved by layers of lacquer and artifice – Judith's lashings of mascara, 'dyed hair', 'well-powdered face and [. . .] unnaturally tinkling voice' (p. 13). A resuscitator of dead bodily functions, Berg sees himself as the avenging hero in a perverse morality play – a 'Pirandello hero in search of a scene that might project him from the shadow screen on to which he felt he had allowed himself to be thrown' (p. 48). Berg has dedicated his life to the murder of his errant father, the various abortive attempts at which form the structuring action of the novel.

With his case of wigs and tonics, Berg takes lodgings in a down-at-heel seaside guest house; a large house divided into bedsits using makeshift partitions, an arrangement typical of postwar Britain in which nearly half the population lived. This congregation of multiple occupants living cheek-by-jowl in what had previously been a single-family dwelling made for cramped living quarters where privacy was in short supply. Such close-quartered living, though, is perfect for Berg's murderous plans as he has managed to rent a room adjoining that of his fugitive father, Nathaniel Berg and his lover, Judith Ann Goldstein. Only a wooden partition separates the two and Berg spends a great deal of his time with his ears pressed to this room divider trying to 'find out how they lived' or furtively peering through their keyhole (p. 2). This partition functions in both literal and metaphorical ways – its division of two distinct spaces is linked throughout the novel by several references to cracks, seams and fissures that separate one space, state or mood from another and in particular the internal from the external. The partition or divider also forms a part of the process of estrangement in the novel wherein the known and the familiar is made uncommon or foreign; transmuted into something that seems recognisable but is in fact deeply other – demonstrated most markedly by the ventriloquist's dummy that is mistaken for the Oedipal body. The lifeless but lifelike dummy body is echoed in other lifeless objects in the novel – taxidermy, a dead budgie (Berty) and a dead cat (Seby), fur, and arrangements of waxed fruit and dried flowers – all of which might suggest the essentially desiccated aspect of realist detail. This mummification of the material environment is reminiscent of Woolf's 'Modern Fiction' (1921) that criticises fiction that insists upon 'an air of probability embalming the whole so impeccable that if all his figures were to come to life they would find themselves dressed down to the last button of their coats in the fashion of the hour'.[74] Far from providing 'probability' to the narrative, however, Quin's use of detail renders the signifiers of the material world strange and extraordinary – the meanings of objects have been perverted and made deviant. Again, this is different to the ways in which language is stripped back in the *nouveau roman* in which nameless characters slide in and out of hygienic sexual intrigue with studied nonchalance. *Berg* is full of artificially overstuffed prose and a sticky kind of slapstick that swings riotously between first- and third-person viewpoints infused by the stink of vomit, underarm sweat and the cheapest of perfumes. Witness Berg sitting in Judith's room:

> He sat once more on the velvet-covered couch, with its lumps of cat fur still clinging round the sides. A waiting room can hardly compare, a corner of a room her smile, the blue orange fangs of the gas fire, the flickering of the television [. . .] I've got cramp in my right knee, oh dear, no it's all right stay where you are Mr. Greb, it often gets me, bad circulation that's all. (p. 41)

The scene clings to the very edges of realism – the cat fur, the gasfire, the rumpled sofa, but forces these details into an incongruous estrangement with the result that the internal and external are indissoluble in the blending of inner voice and outer objective detail. Some critics strongly objected to what they saw in the novel as rehashed modernism. Criticising the novel for its 'oppressively heavyhanded' simulation of modernist writing, one reviewer in the *New York Times* remarks that *Berg*'s 'artily sordid imagery' would have been considered avant-garde in 1922: 'Interior monologues dissolving into dreams, heavily underscored Oedipal churnings – all attest to the existence of Joyce, Freud and Eliot', all of whom 'are wholesome influences'; however, 'what should be a subtle montage of emotional states is all too literally spelled out'.[75] Elsewhere, another reviewer describes Berg's 'run-on sentences' as imitatively *'rechaufée* and *derriere garde'*; modernism after the main act.[76] What is missed here, I think, is the essentially burlesque nature of *Berg*. Its deliberately extravagant and overstated excesses hold together the Oedipal slapstick and the darkly farcical murderous imbroglio in which Berg attempts to kill his drink-sodden, lecherous father who, at one point, attempts to seduce his own son who is dressed in Berg's father's mistress's clothing while he is dressed in Judith's clothes. More vaudeville than tragedy, the novel gestures to its own absurd extravagances at various junctures:

> Such an absurd, fantastic idea: To take his father's corpse back home to Edith – the trophy of his triumphant love for her! In a Greek play they'd have thought nothing of it, considered it to have been a duty, the final act of what the gods expected from their chosen hero. (p. 106)

Am-Dram Abjection

The three main characters, Berg, Judith and Nathaniel (Nathy) Berg are like performers in a perverse vaudeville play or, as Giles Gordon points out in the novel's introduction, like characters in a Jacobean drama with its predisposition to sexual perversity, revenge and disguise which render human bodies uncanny. The grisly slapstick that alternates with the relentless inner monologue of *Berg* has been described as a 'mixture of the surreal, the whimsical and the macabre', influenced in places by the English music-hall tradition; its 'overdetermined atmosphere of seedy blowsiness is vaguely reminiscent of Archie Rice in Tony Richardson's film of *The Entertainer* as well as early Graham Greene'.[77] The sense of an external world in *Berg* is diluted but not wholly absent – it takes place in a largely recognisable British seaside town that has railway stations, parks and music halls, but all is rendered out of focus as if seen through a smeared screen, or a 'window blurred by out of season spray' (p. 1). Any sense of realism is unsettled by the self-consciously overwrought allusions that come thick and fast in the novel: Essau, Judith and Delilah; *fin-de-siècle* Decadence, Egyptian symbolism and Greek drama, Oedipus, Jocasta and Eumenides. The strong sense of perversity and exaggeration in *Berg* borders on the cartoon-like Grand Guignol and, as noted, Punch and Judy.[78] However, at times, there are more disturbing undertones to Alistair Berg's life story, with suggestions that he was sexually abused as a child by an uncle – and then becomes a cruel child who kills a cat, smashes birds' eggs and peeps through keyholes at his parents. As an adult, he is still peeping and now struggling with his sexual responses to women that are infected by his childhood Oedipal eroticism – he once brought back home a 'giggling piece of fluff' but he was 'incapable, apologetic, a dry fig held by sticky hands' (p. 4). His childhood punishments at the hands of his mother are highly eroticised:

> The white arms with veins, dimples and wrinkles at the elbow; you static over her knees, she rhythmically moving, the pleasure in her eyes, the pleasure that was yours. The sheer delight of not giving in to a single cry, and afterwards running out, blinking back the tears, whistling, splashing yourself with water. Later her sighs, her soft kisses covering the bruises, the wiping away of blood that took longer, far longer than the cause. (p. 121)

Propelled by his unconscious incestuous love for his abandoned mother, Berg must kill his father to avenge her: 'I must recall the precise feelings that have nurtured the present circumstances, when nothing at all from outside interfered, not even thoughts of time past, present, or time future, when doubts of my own reality have dwindled away' (p. 22). The action in the novel evolves like dramatic events on a stage, albeit with an absence of linearity: 'How separate from it all he felt, how unique too, no longer the understudy, but the central character as it were, in a play of his own making?' (p. 77). As suggested above, the novel creaks with the badly made props of amateur dramatic theatrical sets; the objects and setting look real but on closer scrutiny are replicas merely imitating the real thing. Judith's room is stuffed with dead and preserved objects, flowers, taxidermy, fur and waxed fruit, all of which are emphasised by the not-quite-alive ventriloquist's dummy that hovers on the borders between life and death, waiting for external animation. This suggestion is reproduced in the novel's closure when the landlady of the boarding house tells Berg: 'Funny thing is my new tenant now, the one who's moving into the room you used to have, reminds me a little of Mr Berg [senior]' (p. 166). His father, far from being dead, is alive, well and living next door. He is, in Berg's eyes, literally back from the dead in what might be read as the resurrection of the patriarch.

The transformation of the familiar and the everyday into the alien and the strange (even the distinctly un-cunning plan of changing his name from Berg to the ludicrous Greb is an example) is a continual movement in *Berg* and might be productively read through the Kristevan notion of abjection. The body is always in the process of being abjected in the novel, beginning early on when a semi-stream of consciousness communicates Berg's sexual formation:

> Longing to be castrated; shaving pubic hairs. Like playing with a doll, rising out of the bath, a pink jujube, a lighthouse, outside the rocks rose in body, later forming into maggots that invade the long nights, crawled out of sealed shells and tumbled between the creases in the sheets [. . .] Later Uncle Billy, home on leave, drink, drenched with sweat and tobacco smells, drawing you over his knee; kissing taboo, you just confirmed, it's dirty, not the thing to do, leads to other things. (p. 4)

Like some of Kavan's writing, *Berg* is situated in close proximity to the condition in which the boundaries between life and death/deadness, as well as kinship boundaries, are easily broached: life and reality become like 'stage effects' (p. 86), faces become 'puppet-like' (p. 69), artificial flowers mingle with real ones, and Judith's heavy mascara becomes 'spider legs' (p. 43). As Kristeva says, abjection revolves around 'the border of my condition as a human being'.[79] This border is represented in *Berg* by the partition that separates Berg's room from that of Judith's and his father's; it is the demarcation between two essential states in the novel and is constantly being poked and prodded at by Berg – he wants to see through the division but is nauseated, repelled, by what he sees when he puts his eyes to the hole in the partition. For Loraine Morley, the abject in *Berg* is most noticeable in 'the nebulous hinterland between patriarchal subjectivity and sexual identity, on the one hand, and the abject state of maternal engulfment on the other; the impossible choice between a violent, violating language [. . .] and silence'.[80]

Some reviewers were less tolerant of the queasy sense of abjection pervading the novel:

> If [*Berg*] were as repellent as Miss Quin tries so hard to make it, it might be something to worry about, or at least to notice. But the deliberation with which she makes every wall, every ceiling, every flagstone cracked, and, wherever possible, puts insects into the cracks, the care with which she describes Berg (alias Greb) taking the skin off the top of his cup of cocoa and draping it over the corpse of a moth on the saucer, the inevitability of the bird's death, or the cat's death [. . .] must give the game away even to the most easily offended reader. It isn't simply *ad nauseam*, but beyond that into pure tedium.[81]

Recognising but not naming here the Kristevan image of the abject *par excellence* – the skin that forms on the surface of hot milk – the reviewer believes the efforts to repel are overdone. But *Berg*'s overdone-ness, its self-consciously hyperbolic sense of abjection, is the point. The novel deliberately stages a queasily disproportionate excess that suggests the melodrama that characterises the Oedipal plot is a dead, and deadening, narrative form that has too-long shaped the logic of novelistic narrative and is now only artistically permissible as a farce along the lines of Alfred Jarry's *Ubu Roi* (1896). The Oedipal plot has become so hackneyed and vaudeville, said Louis Aragon in 1923, that should 'any author use it, he would be hissed off the stage'.[82] For Berg, the novel is a 'play of his own making' (p. 77), a play that so predictably turns around the mother's statement to her son: 'There you see that's your father who left us both, you'll have to do a lot to overcome him Aly before I die' (p. 46). Quin anticipates the hissing and the booing and so amplifies *Berg*'s vaudeville aspects in order to demonstrate the ludicrous hold that the Oedipal plot has on narrative form.

The tripartite entanglement of *Berg* in which exchanges and substitutions occur between three characters holed up in an eccentric, perverted even, version of domesticity, is revisited in Quin's next novel, *Three*, in which a couple, Ruth and Leonard, remember their now-dead house guest, given only the designation S., through her audio diaries and notebooks that she has left behind and with which each becomes obsessed. While clearly not a literal Oedipal narrative in the style of *Berg*, the triangulated desire of *Three* gestures to the difficult position of the third person in relation to a twosome.

Three: 'Recipes for the Unexpected Guest'

Pursued by a compulsion to jeopardise such a bourgeois stronghold.[83]

Published in 1966 two years after *Berg*, *Three* is the second of Quin's four novels, one that she described as her 'ménage book', a 'collage' made up 'of other peoples' letters [. . .] receipts, bills, etc'. In a letter to Carol Burns, she suggested that her research for the novel sourced material from her experience of being the third wheel in the relationships of three other couples: 'that's where you, Alan, Frank, Paddy, Myra and James come in'.[84] She notes her preference for friendship with couples: 'I have often found myself at my best, a kind of security when with two other people, most of my friends are couples, & I suppose automatically play the role of the child'.[85] She was particularly close to Alan and Carol Burns who looked after her when she was unwell. In a letter to Marian Boyars, Quin wrote: 'I have another three weeks to convalesce, and am going to stay with the Burns as from next Saturday, and hope to be in full circulation in London by June 5th'.[86]

Unlike the slapstick grotesqueries of the *ménage à trois* in *Berg*, the mood of *Three* shows more in common with the *nouveau roman*'s enigmatic surfaces. The novel begins with a terse report of a death that both foreshadows and shapes an investigation into another mysterious death: 'A man fell to his death from a sixth-floor window of Peskett House, an office-block in Sellway square today. He was a messenger employed by a soap manufacturing firm' (*Three*, p. 1). Gradually we learn that the novel is an attempt to piece together the story of S., a wholly absent character who exists only in texts made up from audio recordings, diaries and the texts, both aural and written, that she has left behind. S. has died, possibly by her own hands, or has possibly been murdered; it is never wholly clear how she met her death: 'I mean we can't really be sure could so easily have been an accident the note just a melodramatic touch' (p. 1).

Exhibiting influences not only of the *nouveau roman* but also of Black Mountain poetry and contemporary cinema, *Three* is a technically accomplished piece of writing in its use of three distinct narrative modes used to narrate the 'story' of S. In his review of the novel, B. S. Johnson notes the composite narrative structure in which 'spaces approximate hesitations in speech', and are set alongside the more obviously 'straightforward' descriptions in the form of diary entries.[87] There is yet another voice in *Three*; the unnamed third-person narrator who watches over Ruth and Leonard and whose point of view is interwoven with their speech in a series of dispersed and disjointed exchanges. These different layers of narrative produce the novel's inscrutability and undecidability that turn around the triadic structure. Ruth and Leonard are a middle-class couple whose lives are briefly but tragically interrupted one summer by the visit of a young woman, named only as S., to their seaside home. S. has come to convalesce after what they believed was an illness but what actually turns out to have been an abortion. The idea of the guest, the interloper and intruder into the established domestic sphere, is an intriguing one as it permits, even facilitates, a disruption of the symmetrical twosome of the couple. As in Ali Smith's *The Accidental* (2005), the arrival of an outsider offers the possibility of examining and defamiliarising the *status quo* of the existing relationship into which this third party enters and sabotages. A guest is, by definition, a transitory, vagabond figure who resides momentarily in the abode of others and is an observer of their habitual life: 'Habits. Their habits fallen into easily. Perversely' (*Three*, p. 56). This life is replayed for Ruth and Leonard through S.'s observation in her diaries and recordings and makes for disquieting reading and listening, finally making Ruth feel 'like an intruder in her own life' (p. 124). The essential unknowability of a guest in one's home, especially a temporary one, is revealed in highly disconcerting ways when Ruth and Leonard have access to S.'s notebooks, audio diaries and lists that reveal both her past and her fantasies and renders their own relationship wholly strange through her own interloper's gaze: as Ruth notes, 'Funny how she observed us, quite honestly I would never have recognized ourselves from her descriptions'. There is a clear sense from her diaries that S., the trespasser, has been manipulating both Ruth and Leonard: 'Mantis-like I hang over many desultory designs, toy with subterfuges' (p. 56). These designs and subterfuges produce a sexual triangulation similar to that of Robbe-Grillet's *La Jalousie* and the putting into question of the third-person narrative omniscience has definite continuities with his objections to the 'omniscient, omnipresent' narrator who can appear 'everywhere at once, simultaneously seeing the outside and the inside of things [. . .] knowing the present, the past, and the future of every enterprise.'[88]

The idea that a third-person narrator possesses any ability to provide a privileged insight into human behaviour is challenged in *Three*. Despite the various layers of narrative points of view in the multitextuality, the reader is little the wiser by the novel's end as to the actual existence of the events. Narrative points of view move between the first and third person but each fails to elucidate the other and produces ever more complicating uncertainty – indeed, the more detail included in these sections the less 'real' anything becomes. S.'s lists may appear representational but in fact are, as Brian Evenson notes, part of the novel's use of mimesis 'that has undergone a subtle disorientation' and as a result 'decelerates the reading process', as the narrative demands 'that one constantly step back and reread, re-envision what one has begun to think. This inflects a certain tentativeness on the narrative process, further destabilizing the reading experience'.[89] This disorientation is evident in S.'s lists of objects in the couple's house that seem to mock the accoutrements of middle-class domesticity that is defined by the accumulation of appropriate signifiers of bourgeois taste:

Sofa. Flora-impregnated.
Chippendale chairs. Unchipped. Upholstered in blue.
They call turquoise.
Persian rugs. Second skins. For them.
Warm napkins
Silverware pawns. Salt-cellar dominates.
Rooms soundproofed.
Paintings
not hung
too small. Not small enough. But still-lifes she used to do.
Burglar-proofed.

China plates
on the wall. Glass doors. Concealed lighting. White curtains
transparent. (pp. 20–1)

The solidity of these objects is only superficial, however, and behind them is the 'paraphernalia' of constant affective and physical maintenance requiring

specialists
psychiatrists
analysts
masseurs
osteopaths
palmists
clairvoyants. (p. 26)

Later, Ruth in her own diary entry, towards the end of the novel, writes that 'everything here has substance gives security. A home we have built up together' (p. 124). Keeping the boundaries of the house and its bourgeois objects safe is a full-time job for Ruth and Leonard as their home is constantly beleaguered by trespassers who vandalise and destroy:

Throwing
fireworks
into the swimming pool. Stampeded
round the statues [...]
In the dark. They screamed. Tore flowers out. She buried
her face in cushions. Crying. Hands covered her ears. Then they
left. When the storm passed. A trail of torn flowers left.
Plants. Broken bronze pieces.
Littered paths. (p. 103)

The broken lines here are clearly more formally reminiscent of poetry and work to defamiliarise what might be otherwise banal descriptive details in the narrative.

Superficially, Leonard and Ruth's marriage is functional but not, at base, an especially happy one: 'The toleration politeness that brings a basic relationship a certain smoothness in day to day living. But never laughter' (p. 124). There are intimations that the child Ruth wants has not been possible – the '[N]usery done in eggshell blue. Empty' (p. 21), and she 'plans to be put on an adoption society's priority list' (p. 25). The atmosphere in the house is one of joyless lethargy punctuated by outbursts of sexual frustration and, finally, horrific sexual violence as Leonard rapes Ruth: 'Her hand came out, fists against him, in space, areas of darkness around him. He caught hold of her arms, and pulled her down under him' (p. 128). Their relationship is narrated in passages of incoherent dialogue that show communication between them consisting of tense half-understandings. Deploying run-on sentences with no speech marks, these sections give no indication of the speaker:[90]

> Do you think she was in love with you [. . .] Good heavens what makes you say that Ruth? Well it's conceivable after all you're attractive lots of young girls look at you I've noticed and don't pretend you hadn't realised that. I wasn't denying it. How long did you in fact know her Leon before – well before I met her? Can't remember exactly came to work for me let's see must be a year or so. Did you know she had an abort – abortion? When? Before she came here in fact that's what she said and not the illness we were led to believe. Oh. Is that all you can say Leon? What is there to say I know you don't agree with that sort of thing but she was a practical girl in many ways. [. . .]. More tea love? (p. 78)

S.'s life and death is a mystery at the beginning of the novel, one that is only intensified by the textual material she leaves behind. The enigma that surrounds her, however, is never solved despite the expectations that her tapes and diaries might be revelatory; indeed, the ending of the novel raises more questions than it resolves and as such strongly resists any kind of hermeneutic revelation or closure. After S.'s disappearance/ suicide/murder, Ruth and Leonard each become obsessed by recovering her voice through reading her diaries and listening to a series of tape recordings left behind. Both become furtive in their separate pursuit of S.'s words and the eroticised desire to penetrate the conundrum of what she left behind becomes an obsession for them, but each is reluctant to admit this to the other. When Ruth asks Leonard if he has read any of S.'s diaries, he strenuously denies such a suggestion saying, 'Good God no practically impossible her writing so illegible takes an age to wade through a page' (p. 51). Such unreadability might function as a metaphor for the novel itself as it composes its textures from empty surface and depth, forms itself from blanks and enigmas and provocative snippets all leading, finally, to unilluminating dead-ends. What Ruth and Leonard glean from S.'s diaries and recording does not illuminate, but rather casts a posthumously unreliable gaze on themselves that makes for deeply uncomfortable reading. It becomes evident that S. has been intruding upon their private life in ways that echo the trespassers' violation of Grey House: 'Today I came across L's diary [. . .] Nothing very much apart from some little black crosses, which seem to be some kind of code' (p. 65). This code is never revealed to the reader and remains one of many enigmatic puzzles leading only to non-resolution.

We learn of S.'s life in a series of texts that are the transcripts of the audio recordings but which, as noted, typographically have the appearance of line broken poetry that, when read across the whole novel, might be regarded as a form of experimental autobiography for Quin that shares some similarities with Brooke-Rose's anti-autobiography *Remake*:

> Kneeling
> on hot tennis courts. Tarmac clinging. Hymns chanted.
> Hell Mary full of grapes. Our Father who farts in Heaven.
> Authority of those allowed to wear veils. Black in Retreat. Smuts
> on smug foreheads. In honour of Ash Wednesday. The one who
> had epileptic fits. Wanted to be Bernadette in end of term play.
> Prayers delivered for a moment's release. From Irregular Verbs.
> The Angelus. The lavatory. Refuge for comics. Pornography. (p. 36)

Noting the experimental composition of the novel, Sylvia Bruce observes that 'when viewed from the appropriate distance' the novel 'resolves itself into a model of tautness and precision (sculptural, yet also cinematic)'.[91] This resonates with Quin's comments on what may have been an important visual influence on the novel, Alain Resnais's *L'année dernière à Marienbad* (1961). With a screenplay by Robbe-Grillet, the film's enigmatic mood of detachment depicts the erotic tensions between a threesome and is full of static scenes that are like photographic snapshots rather than moving pictures. Quin refers to the film in some correspondence – 'a photo holds the image, is static, and therefore imprints itself more firmly by not having sideeffects, or the infringement of past and future, isn't this was [sic] Last Year at Marienbad tried to bring off?'.[92]

At one period, the working title for *Three* was *The Chameleon*, a perhaps unsurprising title for a novel that demonstrates an interest in performance; all three characters are 'shadow players', 'indifferent to each other's interpretations on revolving stages' (*Three*, p. 124). They perform roles in the novel that often seem to be part of a charade. As Evenson notes, S.'s 'diaries are less about preserving facts than about asserting, even performing, a self, and providing a world to go with it'.[93] S. devises a 'plan' for 'their amusement' that involves masks and gestures and they are each given designations of A, B and C.

> Suggestion A walks past B and C. A might turn. Stop. Shrug. Walk on. B and C watch. Perhaps follow A. Or separate. Pos-sibly disappear together. Variations endless.
> Grimaces behind expressionless faces.
>
> (p. 21)

The three of them perform these mime plays in the 'sunken theatre' of the swimming pool in which the statues, 'disembodied pieces of bronze stone', made by Leonard form a vital part of what Ruth calls his 'frankly grotesque [. . .] little charades' (pp. 6–7):

> She certainly had talent for those mime plays for instance. Oh those I must say I never had much time for them. You joined in readily enough Ruth. What could I do remain passive outsider to all your games then? (p. 6)

As in *Berg*, *Three* exhibits some interest in *travesti* or cross-dressing, epitomised by the dancing 'girls' in the nightclub that Ruth and Leonard visit, who turn out to be 'dancing boys' playing their parts with relish and authenticity. Later, compelled by a compulsion to 'jeopardise' the 'bourgeois stronghold' of Ruth and Leonard, S. slips into the couple's bedroom and dresses up in Ruth's clothes:

> Walk into their room. Lie on her bed. His. Confront the mirror. R's latest lipstick, dress, hats at all angles. Her wardrobe on one side full of toys. Huge teddy bear with an eye missing. Pity she doesn't keep a diary. Letters immediately destroyed – an animal covering its tracks. (p. 61)

S. is far from what she initially seems; an innocuous young woman in need of temporary care. Simultaneously a malevolent interloper and needy child, she is desperate for recognition and inclusion and dresses up as Ruth in an effort to usurp the wifely role of Ruth with whom she also wants an intense intimacy: 'Except I wonder if it is not a certain role she plays with me, when we are on our own' (p. 142). Ruth plays her own role in her physical transformation. She has had plastic surgery; her new face is a mask version of her former self, photographic images of which she burns as she cannot bear to look at her face before its alteration.

S.'s death is reported in a brief newspaper report: 'The unclothed body of an unidentified young woman, with stab wounds in back and abdomen, was found yesterday by a lake near Sugarloaf Mountain. A bloodstained angler's knife and hammer were also found' (p. 131). Thus, the novel ends as it began, with a reported anonymous death. In each case, there is a reduction of a human life to terse reportage, which is, nonetheless, affecting in its concision; perhaps all the more so when we imagine the same journalistic terseness with which Quin's own death must have been reported.

Three received mixed reviews in several important newspapers and magazines. Comparing it to early Woolf, *The Spectator*'s review called it a 'skillful book that needs reading more than once'.[94] However, the reviewer goes on to qualify this, saying that 'readers may feel the same confusion as did the early readers of Virginia Woolf who had to contend with her swivelling viewpoint'. The same review also notes Quin's 'sensibility', which, he says, 'fills every character to the brim so that they don't exist in their own right' and have no 'appreciable difference in tone of voice or cast of mind'. The review concludes disparagingly, suggesting that the novel does not achieve sufficient emotional detachment: 'perhaps it's women' who write in such a way; unable to create characters that are removed from their own feelings, they end up creating 'mountains out of molehills'.[95] Another critic notes Quin's 'feeling for words' but bemoans the lack of indicative punctuation that frustrates the reader's comprehension as she 'even refuses to provide' them with 'such guidance as punctuation can give, and he may have an exasperated sense that she could have spared him a good deal of bewilderment if she had not been so scornful of commas, semicolons, and quotation marks'.[96] The reviewer concedes, however, that despite this dearth of narrative lucidity, 'the characters become surprisingly clear as the novel develops', and that the novel is 'not without drama'.[97] In the *New York Times*, Daniel Stern notes the 'vivid, supple prose' of *Three*, declaring that the novel is 'what used to be called "experimental"'; this as a text in which the 'center of consciousness shifts so swiftly as to be confusing; there are long sections of a diary written in a kind of blank verse; the three main characters are referred to as L, R and S for much of the book'. He too notes that there are 'no quotation marks' and criticises the ways in which Quin's 'almost arbitrary experimentalism' rests upon the 'sterile "tradition of the new" (as Harold Rosenberg calls it)' that, while laudable, does not, unlike Beckett, Jorge Luis Borges, Nabokov, develop 'out of an inner need'.[98]

> Section by section, the book fragments itself down to the fragmentary end. One is left with shards of consciousness, of domestic and sexual lives and rag-ends of fantasies. This is itself no criticism. It is rather that the quarrels of L and R are, underneath the elegant language, quite banal. The sexual difficulties smack of conventional mismating. And the fantasies – even when enacted – seem to have little to do with the people themselves. Here is, I think, the reason why I was left unmoved: finally, it is the human beings who engage one or who do not. Miss Quin has relied on her extraordinary gift for language to salvage people who, I am afraid, are beyond salvation.[99]

Stern concludes by saying that while 'Quin gives signs of owning her own voice' she is somewhat paradoxically, 'shackled by speaking in an old-fashioned tongue'. This observation is, I think, unfounded. Quin's voice in *Three* is anything but old-fashioned but is still, in some places, noticeably in thrall to an experimental zeitgeist in which she is yet to find her own creative expression.

Passages: 'the whole thing frankly Ann, spells Experimental in caps'[100]

Shortly after the publication of *Passages,* John Calder and Marion Boyars wrote a letter in support of Quin's Arts Council Grant:

> Ann Quin is, in our opinion, one of the most gifted and talented young English writers. In the last five years, she has developed from a promising straight novelist into a new direction of prose writing, exemplified in her new novel, PASSAGES, which is totally original and despite its complexity, extremely successful artistically. She exercises a complete economy and control of style, and, at the same time, takes the reader on a journey of the imagination, exploring many levels of consciousness.[101]

Described by one reviewer as 'just the thing for the French',[102] *Passages* takes the idea of journey and travel as its central thematic and aesthetic mode and represents, according to critic Lorraine Morley, 'a bold statement of [Quin's] writing's increasing liberation from textual and sexual conventions'.[103] Dulan Barber suggests that 'the metaphor of the journey is made over into the very substance and form of the book itself' and that the novel's energy 'derives from its extraordinary alliance of classicism and chaos'.[104] A review in the *Times Literary Supplement* describes the novel as a 'juxtaposition of precisely caught experiences' that works together with 'the confused overall shape of the story' to 'suggest exactly the reactions of the traveller whose senses acquire a new responsiveness to detail'. Written when Quin was still living in America, the novel takes as its geographical basis a trip she took to mainland Greece and the islands in 1964.[105] Finding herself caught up in the political unrest in Turkey, Quin sent a postcard from Corfu to John Calder rather dramatically proclaiming, 'S.O.S. £.s.d. needed – desperate. Istanbul riots'.[106]

Like *Berg, Passages* is a quest narrative of sorts. The female character travels to Greece in search of her lost brother who may be dead or alive: 'Not that I've dismissed the possibility my brother is dead. We have discussed what is possible, what is not. They say there's every chance. No chance at all' (*Passages*, p. 5).[107] The quest has little solidity and no defined centre – a vagueness mirrored in the only other character's journal entries belonging to an unnamed male which suggests his past life has somehow failed both professionally and privately: 'He writes a book, that turns out a great success. He travels, lectures, and goes to academic parties, flirts entertainingly with Professional wives/daughters. He marries again. He could be called "the successful man"; yet still he faces the mirror and says: Where did it all go wrong?' (p. 49) The man and woman are being trailed, or perhaps not, by an unidentified persecutor and are thus frequently in a state of transition; endlessly in passage to the next hotel room and set of strange encounters.

Quin's most experimental text to date (before *Tripticks*, her final work), *Passages* was, she wrote in a letter to Calder, her favourite book 'if only because I don't yet fully understand all the levels in the work!'[108] Composed of two major strands of narrative the novel moves back and forth between these two sections with events and impressions becoming increasingly chaotic and incoherent; the novel describes its own texture as one composed of 'pattern[s] formed, collected. Dislocated from moment to moment' (*Passages*, p. 26). The female section is impressionistic, fluvial but also emotionally detached from any connection with its surroundings, moving erratically between first- and third-person narration and between descriptions of the present – 'The hotel that seemed some other place, in another city. Where she was alone. Where she walked spaces between furniture' (p. 70), and the past – 'another person, Another life. A time in her childhood. On a swing in large gardens [...] had it ever happened?' (p. 75). The man's passages are written in the form of a journal annotated with several subheadings such as 'Notebook of a Depressive', 'Dream' and 'On the Train', the marginalia filled with comments on the main passages as well as with references to mythology, especially to the Sirens, Medusa, the Bacchae, Aphrodite, the Sphinx, Dionysius and Minotaurs. This left-hand marginalia forms yet another version to the events and, in many places, is an elucidation of the woman's behaviour in her sections of the novel:

	Femme fatale
	Teasing
	Flirtatious
Often she gets	Quick
Pretty high then	Witty
She forgets which	Mysterious smiles
role she had	Wears false eye lashes and hair piece
started with,	Appears to know all the secrets/perversions
and a delightful	of love/love making, and will by the way she
mixture of them	gestures, smiles, promises all, then laughing
all appears,	suddenly withdraw and dance with someone
leaving the man	else.
confused or even	(p. 44)
more infatuated	

Several specific references in the margins to mythology are taken (without attribution) from Jane Harrison's *Prolegomena to the Study of Greek Religion* (1903), fitting for a novel that revisits and deconstructs

Greek drama. Quin had been rereading Harrison alongside other books on Pueblo mythology:

> Strangely enough I had been reading Jane Harrison's book on Greek Religion, and had been thinking how very similar the rituals, the ceremonies/respect/ fear for the 'underworld' was to the Indians sense of it all; anyway the book [on Pueblo religion] draws comparisons with the Greek legends, so it all seems to tie up with some of my own conclusions.[109]

The experiments in *Passages* are different to those in the previous two novels and present a new challenge to the reader in terms of how to approach the words on the page; in the annotated sections it is almost impossible to read the two sections simultaneously – one has to choose an order of reading which influences the way in which the narrative might be understood. As Evenson notes, *Passages* contains 'more stylistic variation' and a 'more aggressive exploration of the technical possibilities of prose' than in her previous work.[110] In *Berg* and *Three*, third-person external narration plays a significant role. In *Passages*, however, the use of the third person seems to be a series of masked disguises or personae assumed by the various narrating first-person voices, which destabilise any sense of the third-person narration's reliability. There are, to be sure, multiple references to masks in the novel and at times the action consists of a series of roles being rehearsed and performed in various venues.

The two narrative viewpoints belong to an unnamed man, a Jew, who 'talks Hebrew' in his sleep, and a woman 'in her middle thirties', a chameleon-type figure who, 'playing at Antigone' has come to an unnamed Mediterranean country, most likely Greece (named only as 'this country') to find her brother who may or may not already be dead. A military coup appears to have taken place – the 'political situation here is intolerable' (p. 35) – they are often asked for their papers and all movement becomes perilous.[111] Copious amounts of sex, bondage, wine, and hallucinatory narcotics – 'oblong coloured pills' (p. 58) – all contribute to an atmosphere of Dionysian excess that unspools across a narrative that moves between the alternating narratives in which the roles between the anonymous man and woman are always being reversed 'from day to day', structured by the fluctuating role-playing of a 'master–slave situation' (p. 90), brimful of '[c]ounterpoints, contradictions, improvisation in roles [they] assume' (p. 61). There is no discernible dialogue or verbal exchange in the novel; what discourse is there is fragmentary and crafted into disjointed, cut-up dream sequences inserted into the prose.

At one point, the man puts into two columns the attributes of them both. The woman is defined as 'folly/ eccentricity/ obsessive', whereas his character is given as 'Carefulness/ observance/ mindfulness/ watchfulness' (p. 31). However, these characteristics are not fixed throughout the book and it is very often the case that the roles/definitions are tangled between these two columns, producing a sense that these are not two voices at all, but in fact just one that seems to travel between male and female; 'who is it today that inhabits me?' (p. 111). Thus, the idea of passages as both a verb and a noun takes on another meaning regarding identity which is in a constant state of passage on the way to something else: 'Something to be said for remaining in a place far off, without name, without identity' (p. 97). For both the man and woman, identity is a form of improvised reaction to their immediate environment and feelings and this is articulated in the vagabond writing of *Passages*:

> Forms forming
> themselves.
> Defining the
> centre of things.
> No counterpoints.
> No intersections/
> linears.
> Improvisation. (p. 31)

This intermingling of the two gendered viewpoints is so condensed that it might imaginably be considered as one composite voice that is indeterminately gendered, or bi-sexed, that moves between male and female, reminiscent of Brophy's Patrick, Patricia, Pat, BARBARA, Bunny, Slim, Evelyn Hilary O'Rooley in *In Transit*. *Passages* is a novel that is, suggests Nonia Williams, 'always in transit across and through different passages of text'.[112] The two portions of the male and female writing are connected only in the most contingent way; they give different versions of similar events but with no sense of certainty that either are correct or true; the two characters are '[m]ore and more unable to observe, determine the truth of things, share an experience' (*Passages*, p. 29). The female section is often significantly more in flux 'pattern[s] formed, collected. Dislocated from moment to moment' (p. 26), while the male section is outwardly more logical, offering cooler observations of character and situation. But neither section remains fixed in these positions and this changeability is mirrored in many places in the novel where one event, situation or thought dissolves into another.

> We walked down to the beach, and sat against drift wood. I watched his cigarette light up a part of his swollen face. Track of light the moon made on the sea. Three hundred yards the beginning of that where she could lift both feet up and walk on water. Grains in wood his fingers traced, she entered. Land

many oceans spilled into. The way landscapes entered a room. Rooms she went through, corridors. Doors she opened onto carpets that grew towards trees, branches through walls, windows. Soft green light she touched, and was touched by. The scuttling of a crab or some other sea creature passed between them, over the wood. Movement under sand. Shifting of sand in front, behind. Flying fish between waves, those that fell out of the sea, fell back. These she listened to. And the sound of insects. (p. 69)

Almost imperceptibly, the 'he' metamorphoses into 'she'. Such narrative mutability of the gendered subject allows for a different kind of perceiving subjectivity that is always in passage and not moored to one perspective or another. In this way, then, as Lorraine Morley observes, 'a complex sexual subject emerges [. . .] of different discourses; the male (masculine) journal, the female (feminine) stream-of-body-consciousness, a self-reflexive "I," and a mythic imaginary'.[113] The state of being itinerant is reiterated throughout the novel. We read of the man's desire 'to disappear – to go on a journey suddenly, without telling anyone, leaving no address' (p. 97). For the two sections, the male and female passages, the idea is to 'arrive finally at a unit with contradictory attributes never moulded or fused together, but clearly differentiated' (p. 111). Hence, all states of being and temporality are permeable; there is only the most fragile of borders between sleeping and waking, day and night and past and present, the mythological marginalia providing a backdrop of primitive temporality.

If *Three* was her *ménage a trois* work then *Passages* is, by Quin's own account, her 'pornographic' book.[114] There are several sexually graphic scenes in the novel depicting sado-masochistic sex, especially involving the use of a whip, one of which Quin described as 'gt. orgy scene', that is a continuation of the master–slave dynamic.[115]

> the three
>   lay there, their legs, arms linked in the formation of a dance. Under the chandelier they moved slowly. He in the middle hardly moved, watching the two women circle. Their backs arched, breasts thrust high, forward. The leather strap he passed through suspenders. Black slithered across white, between the less black. His head raised, then bent. Arms spread out from the white sleeves. He balanced a whip in each hand. The girl strapped to the chair. Her head swayed over the back, hair hung down. Legs apart, fruit placed between. [...} Sound of whip meeting flesh, into a rhythm, slow at first. (p. 25)

The erotic scenes are highly mannered set-pieces, possessing a curiously static quality like *tableaux vivant* that strips all participants of any specific identity as they become players in scenes composed for a nameless gaze. Sex is detached from any affective attachment and is mostly anonymous:

> No sense of who touched her,
> who she was stripped by, who woke her as soon as she tried to sleep.
> Who beat her with sticks, whips on the soles of her feet. (p. 71)

Cruelty towards others, in particular the transgression of the incest taboo was flirted with in *Berg*, albeit in significantly less explicit ways. Here, taboos are openly transgressed:

Drawing of a third Siren's eye by two strokes only, without the pupil: the sightless eye, eye in death/ sleep/blindness.	Sometimes she talks in her sleep. Names I don't know. Some secret language. She says I talk Hebrew in my sleep, yet I only know a few words in that language. There are moments when she looks at me startled, not really seeing me, perhaps thinking I am someone else. The walls shift in patterns, colour, shapes behind her head, and I think I am somewhere else. At home perhaps, when the murmurs are Mother's, made from her bed, the light shining from the kitchen, stopping in a blade of light at the foot
Image of myself as Bar-Lgura, the Semetic [sic] demon sitting on the roof and leaping down on them all.	of the bed. How I hated Mother then. Day after day (and nights, long nights) of pain. Windows closed, curtains pulled, thin-walled box rooms. Death, the smell of it, of sickness permeated everything. Nurses, doctors came and went, she thought were the family. I made her hot drinks and thought of pissing in them. I wanted to screw my sister in front of her and Father. (p. 37)

As a woman writer at that time, Quin was unusual in her graphic accounts of sexual activity likely influenced by the prevalent 1960s countercultural fascination for transgressive Dionysian energies as they permitted an exploration of Eros, a refusal of order and repression of the primitive drives. Using the Greek myths of Orpheus and Narcissus, Herbert Marcuse's *Eros and Civilisation* (1955) praised the childlike naïveté of what became known as the Age of Aquarius for its quixotic interest in the Dionysian refusal of the *principium individuationis* in favour of communality, erotic freedom and play.[116] This play is highly ritualised in the novel and Quin seems to be aware of a wider contemporary interest in the Theatre of Cruelty, part of a countercultural Nietzscheanism that 'emerges' in the 1960s, says Peter Sedgwick, 'as an expression of the feeling of ecstasy that accompanies the sense of loss of the individual self'.[117] Sexual encounters are fuelled by all manner of intoxicating substances that produce hallucinogenic states only ever half-remembered in the morning. No stranger to hallucinogenic drugs, Quin very contentedly experimented with narcotics during her time in America. In an interview in the *Guardian,* Quin talks of her experience with drugs including Peyote and LSD:

> If I'd stayed in England and not taken drugs, it would have taken me ten to 15 years to reach the particular stage that I reached then. Peyote verified and made concrete things I'd thought about, and made fantasies more real. It made an outer reality, and outer landscape seem equivalent to an inner landscape. It seemed to make all things possible. I just found that when I did write, it all seemed to tie up.[118]

Thus, as we saw with Kavan's heroin use, LSD or peyote did not produce Quin's writing; rather, it intensified what was already there – that is, a pronounced appetite for intense physical and psychological experience. A short passage from the novel speaks to this:

> He   Are you happy or unhappy?
> She   That's not a very important question
> He   You live with such frenzied intensity
> She   Because there's nothing else to do – I
>   would be eaten up with reality. (p. 85)

The novel becomes rather incoherent in places when the experimentation tips over into such arcane ambiguity that it lacks any sense of readerly presence. One critic suggested that the 'fusion between what is experienced, dreamt of and thought, reveals an 'alien territory that is mostly 'well suggested' but otherwise the novel is 'irritatingly opaque and elliptical'.[119] By its conclusion, *Passages* resembles a piece of private writing; confessional, inward-looking and almost unfathomably encoded. Quin recognised the novel's peculiarity, calling it a 'strange strange piece of writing, perhaps even I don't know what it all adds up to.' As with the arrival of the proofs of *Berg*, the process of writing *Passages* took its toll on Quin:

> Actually exhausted myself in finishing the book, so much so that I had a kindabreakdown, when I lost my speech [. . .] all caused, I guess, thru not so much 'overworking' but lower strata happenings: mainly that the book is about a woman in search of her brother; the pressure to finish the book by November was a kind of subconscious desire to meet the anniversary thing of my half brother's death – the loss of speech too I guess was a kind of projection of myself with Ian's death – the virus that hit his lungs.[120]

The intensity of Quin's writing also seemed to drain her readers and many reviewers regarded *Passages* 'as difficult and alienating.'[121]

An immensely talented novelist, Ann Quin was, said Robert Nye, 'admirably alive to the elusiveness of what happens between people, to what is lost in conversation, and to the possibilities of the English language for suggesting these little communicative lacunae'. The best of her writing, he said, 'hoarded words as if they were pebbles washed smooth by huge seas of experience'.[122] A tragedy, then, that this hoarding ended so soon.

Notes

1. Ann Quin, *The Unmapped Country: Stories and Fragments*, ed. Jennifer Hodgson (Sheffield, London and New Haven, CT: And Other Stories, 2018), p. 17.
2. Ann Quin, letter to Robert Sward, 18 July 1968, MSS110, Series 1: boxes 1–16, folders 1–197: 321.3.5, Robert Sward Papers, Washington Universities Library (WUL). All references to Sward Papers are from this source.
3. Alan Burns, 'Blending Words with Pictures', *Books and Bookmen*, 17: 10 (July 1972).
4. Quin, letter to Robert Creeley, MSS031, Series 1: Correspondence, box 11, folder 78.3–6, Robert Creeley Papers, 1944–1978, Department of Special Collections, WUL. See also Robert Creeley MSS 194-61, Indiana University, Bloomington and Creeley Papers, 1950–2011 M0662, Series 1: Correspondence, 126.11–12 (23 December 1964–2 October 1965 and 22 October 1965–20 September 1990), Department of Special Collections and University Archives, Stanford, CA.
5. Quin, *Tripticks* (Chicago and Normal, IL: Dalkey Archive Press, 2002).
6. Ian Patterson, 'Her Body or the Sea', *London Review of Books*, 40: 12 (21 June 2018), pp. 29–31 (p. 29) <https://www.lrb.co.uk/v40/n12/ian-patterson/her-body-or-the-sea> (accessed 21 May 2019).
7. A conference in Manchester on women's experimental writing had papers devoted to Quin's work. See also recent PhD theses on her writing: Chris Clarke's 'Tracing the Ethical Dimension of Postwar British Experimental Fiction' (University of Southampton, 2015) and Nonia Williams's 'Designing Its Own Shadow: Reading Ann Quin' (University of East Anglia, 2013). A special issue of *Women: A Cultural Review* in 2020 is dedicated to Quin. See also Nonia Williams, '"Infuriating" Experiments?', in Kaye Mitchell and Nonia Williams (eds), *British Avant-Garde Fiction of the 1960s* (Edinburgh: Edinburgh University Press, 2019), pp. 193–214. The reissue of *The Unmapped Country: Stories and Fragments*, ed. Jennifer Hodgson (London: And Other Stories, 2018) has been central to the revival of interest in her work.
8. Patterson, 'Her Body or the Sea'.
9. Philip Stevick, 'Voices in the Head: Style and Consciousness in the Fiction of Ann Quin', in Ellen G. Friedman and Miriam Fuchs (eds), *Breaking the Sequence: Women's Experimental Fiction* (Princeton, NJ: Princeton University Press, 1989), pp. 231–9 (p. 234).
10. Robert Buckeye, *Re: Quin* (London: Dalkey Archive Press, 2013), p. 9.
11. Quin writes: 'What shook me at first was that he was "an old man", in

fact seemed and looked so much older than Mother; I was pretty shaky when meeting him "under the clock" at Victoria station!' Quin, letter to Robert Sward, 2 July 1967, MSS110, Series 1, Correspondence: boxes 1–16, folders 1–197: 321.2.19, Sward Papers, WUL.
12. Quin, 'Leaving School', p. 15.
13. Quin, 'Reads from *Three*', *Extensions of Poetry* <https://duende.bandcamp.com/album/ ann-quin-reads-from-three> (accessed 1 May 2019).
14. Quin, 'Leaving School', p. 17. Running references in the text in parentheses.
15. Quin, *Three* (Chicago and Normal, IL: Dalkey Archive Press, 2001); *Berg* (Chicago and Normal, IL: Dalkey Archive Press, 2001); *Passages* (Chicago and Normal, IL: Dalkey Archive Press, 2003).
16. Quin, 'Leaving School', p. 18.
17. Her time at the RCA coincided with the emergence of British pop art that would include David Hockney, R. B. Kitaj and Peter Blake, whose cut-up, collage technique for the cover of The Beatles' album *Sgt. Pepper's Lonely Hearts Club Band* became iconic.
18. Quin, letter to John Calder, 20 November 1964, LMC 2196, Series II, box 52: 2–5, Calder and Boyars MSS, 1939–1980, Lilly Library, Indiana University, Bloomington, Indiana. All references to the Calder and Boyars archive are from this source.
19. Robert Creeley, 'Ann Quin: A Personal Note', unpublished manuscript, Carol Burns Papers, courtesy of Nonia Williams.
20. Quin, letter to Paddy Kitchen, quoted in Paddy Kitchen, 'Catherine Wheel: Recollections of Ann Quin', *London Magazine*, 1 June 1979, pp. 50–7 (p. 53).
21. Quin, letter to Carol Burns, August 1962, Carol Burns Papers. I had no direct access to these so I am quoting from Nonia Williams's private collection. I thank her for permission to do so.
22. In April 1964, before she went to America, Quin stayed at a Carmelite Community in Aylesford Priory in Kent. See Brocard Sewell, *Like Black Swans: Some People and Themes* (Padstow: Tabb House, 1982), p. 184.
23. The event was filmed by Peter Whitehead and released as a short documentary, *Wholly Communion*, available on DVD from the BFI.
24. 28/5/69, MSS031, 11.78.3–6, Creeley Papers.
25. Quin, letter to Larry Goodell, 25 September 1969.
26. Alan Burns, p. 405, cited in Julia Jordan, 'The Quin Thing', *Times Literary Supplement*, 19 January 2018 <https://www.the-tls.co.uk/articles/the-quin-thing> (accessed 12 May 2019).
27. Alan Burns and B. S. Johnson, *Writers Reading* (London: J. & P .Weldon Ltd, 1969), p. 1.
28. In a letter to Boyars, Gordon wrote: 'First, can you tell me the year of Ann Quin's birth. This is for the book's dedication, to her and Bryan Johnson. Second, can you send me up to 250 words of biographical information, listing in particular her publications. Again, I'm afraid this is urgent. Thanks'. 15 March 1974, LMC 2196, Series I: Correspondence, box 52: 4, Calder and Boyars MSS.
29. MSS110, Series 1: boxes 1–16, folders 1–197: 321.2.17, Sward Papers, WUL.

30. MSS110, Series 1: boxes 1–16, folders 1–197: 321.2.24, Sward Papers, WUL. The adaptation did not come to fruition at this time but was made into a film in 1989 called *Killing Dad*. John Calder, *Pursuit: The Uncensored Memoirs of John Calder* (London: Calder, 2001), pp. 272–3.
31. Henry Williamson, *Tarka the Otter: His Joyful Water-Life and Death in the Country of the Two Rivers* (London: Chiswick Press, 1927). Letters from Williamson to Carol Burns suggest that he and Quin were involved a couple of years earlier, between 1963–4, when Quin was going to the Burns's Swain's Lane cottage in Dorset. I am greatly indebted to Nonia Williams for this information and for permission to quote this material.
32. John Calder, *Pursuit: The Uncensored Memoirs of John Calder* (London: Calder, 2001), pp. 272–3.
33. On finding out that Quin was a writer, the Senior Registrar at Atkinson Morley Hospital, Dr Toms, wrote to Marion Boyars asking for a copy of her work: 'Thank you very much for sending me Ann Quin's edition of "Passages". I would be grateful if you could let me have the promised copies of "Berg" and "Three" as soon as possible because comparison between the books is important in order to follow the course of Miss Quin's thinking.' 11 March 1970, LMC 2196, Series I, box 52: 4, Calder and Boyars MSS: See also a letter to Boyars from Dr Harnjd, 23 January 1970, LMC 2196, Series I, box 52: 4, Calder and Boyars MSS.
34. Creeley Papers, 2/3/70.
35. Quin, letter to Robert Creeley, 9 December 1971, MSS031, Series 1: box 11, folder 78: 4, Creeley Papers, WUL.
36. Quin, *The Unmapped Country*, p. 159.
37. Stevick, 'Voices', p. 232.
38. Francis Booth, *Amongst Those Left: The British Experimental Novel 1940–1980* (e-print: Lulu Press, 2012), p. 487.
39. Established by Malcolm Bradbury and Angus Wilson in 1971.
40. Quin, *Guardian*, August 1973.
41. Quin, interview with Nell Dunn, in Nell Dunn (ed.), *Talking to Women* (London: Silver Press, 2018), p. 185. Page references are given in the text in parentheses.
42. Quin, 'B. B.'s Second Manifesto', in Quin, *The Unmapped Country: Stories and Fragments*, ed. Jennifer Hodgson, pp. 65–8 (pp. 66–7).
43. Letter from Quin to Paddy Kitchen, in Paddy Kitchen, 'Catherine Wheel', p. 54.
44. MSS110, Series 1: boxes 1–16, folders 1–197: 321.1.12, Sward Papers, WUL.
45. Letter in the Creeley Papers, 14/9/65.
46. Ibid.
47. Ibid.
48. Creeley wrote about Quin in *Mabel, A Story, and Other Stories* (London: Marion Boyars, 1976).

> HEARSAY. M's determination at times to be singular, so proposes a sadly endless consequence of herself shall be trailed through minds of her time like roses. She wants to count, and does, as she puts it, count. She is a large, rather sturdy young woman. She does not particularly enjoy this aspect of

herself except that it carries her through, so to speak. She can be, variously, the expected demure young lady, or else the bar-stool swinging drunk broad. It doesn't really seem to matter that much to her.

49. Quin, 'Leaving School', p. 24.
50. Robert Creeley, 'Ann Quin: A Personal Note', 2, unpublished manuscript, Carol Burns Papers.
51. Anthony Blomfield, 'Reasons for Existence', unpublished manuscript, Carol Burns Papers, 3.
52. David R. Slavitt, 'Book Week', *Washington Post*, 13 October 1965, p. 16. All reviews are collected in Quin's scrapbook, LMC 2196, Calder and Boyars MSS.
53. Roland Barthes, *The Pleasure of the Text*, trans. Richard Miller (New York: Hill and Wang, 1975), p. 47.
54. Quin, letter to Carol Burns, 31 March 1962, Carol Burns Papers. I am grateful to Nonia Williams for allowing me quote from Carol Burns's letters.
55. Quin, letter to Burns, 29 January 1963.
56. Giles Gordon, Introduction to *Berg* (Champaign, IL/London/Dublin: Dalkey Archive, 2001), p. ix.
57. 'Down Beside the Sea', *Times Literary Supplement*, 25 June 1964, p. 545.
58. Stevick, 'Voices', pp. 231–2.
59. Ibid., p. 232.
60. Quin, letter to Carol Burns, no day or month, 1961, Carol Burns Papers. *Berg* was translated into French and published by Gallimard in 1967, translated by Anne-Marie Soulac.
61. These were first published in English translation as: Nathalie Sarraute, *Portrait of a Man Unknown*, trans. Maria Jolas (New York: G. Braziller, 1958); *The Age of Suspicion: Essays on the Novel*, trans. Maria Jolas (New York: George Braziller, 1963); *Tropisms*, trans. Maria Jolas (London: John Calder, 1963).
62. Rayner Heppenstall, *The Master Eccentric: The Journals of Rayner Heppenstall*, ed. Jonathan Goodman (London: Allison & Busby, 1986), p. 120.
63. Sarraute, *Age of Suspicion*, p. 88.
64. 'La mort du père', n.d., Olin library archive.
65. Giles Gordon, 'Introduction', in Quin, *Berg* (Chicago and Normal, IL: Dalkey Archive Press, 2001), p. xiii.
66. Marion Boyars, cited in Giles Gordon (ed.), *Beyond the Words: Eleven Writers in Search of a New Fiction* (London: Hutchinson, 1975), p. 251.
67. Patterson, 'Her Body', p. 30.
68. John Fuller, *New Statesman*, 8 January 1965, p. 48.
69. Quin, letter to Alan Burns, September 1961, Carol Burns Papers.
70. Quin, letter to Robert Sward, 31 January 1966, MSS110, Series 1: boxes 1–16, folders 1–197: 321.1.2, Sward Papers, WUL.
71. Ibid.
72. Paddy Kitchen, 'Catherine Wheel: Recollections of Ann Quin', *London Magazine*, 1 June 1979, pp. 50–7 (p. 53).

73. Quin, *Berg*, p. 7. Subsequent references to *Berg* are given in parentheses in the text.
74. Virginia Woolf, 'Modern Fiction', in Virginia Woolf, *Selected Essays*, ed. David Bradshaw (Oxford: Oxford University Press, 2008), pp. 6–12 (p. 8).
75. Martin Levin, *New York Times Book Review*, 31 October 1965, pp. 68–9.
76. David R. Slavitt, 'Book Week', *Washington Post*, 13 October 1965, p. 16.
77. Patterson, 'Her Body',
78. See also Quin's short story, 'Ghostworm' (p. 133): 'Do you still fantasize about killing your father? chop him up into little pieces'. Originally published in *Tak Tak Tak* in 1993, it was republished in *Unmapped Country*.
79. Julia Kristeva, *Powers of Horror: An Essay on Abjection*, trans. Leon S. Roudiez (New York: Columbia University Press, 1982), p. 31.
80. Lorraine Morley, 'The Love Affairs of Ann Quin', *Hungarian Journal of English and American Studies,* 5: 2 (1999), pp. 127–41 (p. 130).
81. Slavitt, 'Book Week', p. 16.
82. Louis Aragon, 'A Man,' *Little Review*, ix, 4 (1923/24), pp. 18–22 (pp. 20–1).
83. Quin, *Three*, p. 61. Subsequent references will be given in the text in parentheses.
84. Quin, letter to Carol Burns, 13 February 1963, Carol Burns Papers. Alan is Carol's husband and the other couple mentioned are Paddy Kitchen and Frank Bowling.
85. Quin, letter to Brocard Sewell, published in Sewell, *Like Black Swans*, p. 183.
86. Quin, letter to Marion Boyars, 13 May 1963, LMC 2196, Series I, box 52: 2, Calder and Boyars MSS.
87. B. S. Johnson, 'Experiment and Espionage', *The Sunday Times*, 5 June 1966, p. 29.
88. Alain Robbe-Grillet, *For a New Novel: Essays on Fiction* (New York: Grove Press, 1965), pp. 138–9.
89. Brian Evenson, 'Introduction', in Ann Quin, *Three* (Chicago and Normal, IL: Dalkey Archive Press, 2001), p. xii.
90. Ronald Hayman observed that Beckett and Sarraute 'infected Ann Quin with her idiosyncratic disdain for inverted commas' (1976), p. 9 in Christine Brooke-Rose, interview with David Hayman and Keith Cohen, *Contemporary Literature*, 17: 1 (1976), pp. 1–23.
91. Sylvia Bruce, on *Three*, unpublished manuscript, Carol Burns Papers, 1.
92. Quin, letter to Carol Burns, 1962, Carol Burns Papers.

    Went to see Bergman's latest THROUGH A GLASS DARKLY – affected me like hell – felt like death when walking out; incest and ALL THAT BUT beautifully photographed and acted; very Ibsenesque – sins of the father etc., family searching for life/God in each other, through each other [. . .] (I) like the way Bergman uses the mythical to get across the anguish of the present day.

93. Evenson, 'Introduction', p. x.
94. John Daniel, *The Spectator,* 10 June 1966.
95. Ibid.
96. Granville Hicks, *Saturday Review*, 3 December 1966, p. 30.

97. Ibid.
98. Daniel Stern, 'What Became of S?', *New York Times Book Review*, 9 October 1966, p. 66.
99. Ibid.
100. Quin, letter to Robert Sward, 23 November 1966, MSS110, Series 1: boxes 1–16, folders 1–197: 321.1.21, Sward Papers, WUL
101. John Calder and Marion Boyars, 'Letter of Recommendation to the Arts Council, re: Ann Quin', 1969, n.d., LMC 2196, Series I, box 52: 3, Calder and Boyars MSS.
102. David Benedictus, 30 April 1969.
103. Lorraine Morley, 'Love Affairs', p. 132.
104. Dulan Barber, 'The Human Sorceress', unpublished manuscript, LMC 2196, box 103: 1–2, Calder and Boyars MSS.
105. Henry Williamson, letter to Carol Burns, 30 July 1964, Carol Burns Papers. According to Williamson, he gave Quin money for this trip.
106. Quin, letter to John Calder, 28 July 1964, LMC 2196, Series II, box 52: 2, Calder and Boyars MSS.
107. All subsequent references to the novel are given in the text in parentheses.
108. Quin, letter to Calder, 4 April 1969, LMC 2196, box 52: 3, Calder and Boyars MSS.
109. Quin, letter to Robert Sward, 17 February 1967, MSS110, Series 1: boxes 1–16, folders 1–197: 321.2.13, Sward Papers, WUL.
110. Evenson, 'Introduction', p. viii.
111. Greece had a military coup known as the Regime of the Colonels in 1967.
112. Williams Korteling, 'Designing Its Own Shadow', p. 122.
113. Morley, 'Love Affairs', p. 133.
114. Quin, letter to Robert Sward, September 1966, MSS110, Series 1: boxes 1–16, folders 1–197: 321.1.16–17, Sward Papers, WUL. See also Diane Sward, letter to Quin, 17 September, 1966, MSS110, Series 1: boxes 1–16, folders 1–197: 386.7.1, Sward Papers, WUL.
115. Quin, letter to Sward, 17 October 1966, MSS110, Series 1: boxes 1–16, folders 1–197: 321.1.18, Sward Papers, WUL.
116. Herbert Marcuse, *Eros and Civilisation: A Philosophical Inquiry into Freud* (Boston, MA: Beacon Press, 1955), p. xxi.
117. Peter Sedgwick, *Nietzsche: The Key Concepts* (London: Routledge, 2009), p. 60. There was a film version of The Performance Group's *Dionysus in '69* based on Euripides' *The Bacchae*. The drive to ecstatic freedom and transgressive rebellion tipped over into excess and bloodshed exemplified in two definitively 'end-of-sixties' events – the Manson murders and the violence at the Altamont Free Festival.
118. Quin, interview with John Hall, 'Landscape with Three-Cornered Dances', *Guardian*, 29 April 1972, p. 8.
119. Jane Miller, *Times Literary Supplement*, 3 March 1969.
120. Creeley Papers, 23/11/67. This is a reference to Quin's half-brother mentioned in the introduction to this chapter.
121. Brian Evenson and Joanna Howard, 'Ann Quin', *Review of Contemporary Fiction*, 23: 2 (2003), pp. 50–75 (p. 50).
122. Robert Nye, piece in memory of Quin, p. 1. Unpublished manuscript, Carol Burns Papers, courtesy of Nonia Williams.

Afterword: Evolution, Batons and Beaks

> We all know that jaded feeling when people and things seem too familiar and we long for something to happen. Then we go on a journey, change our usual surroundings. People and things suddenly acquire a new intensity, appear more 'real'.[1]

Reviewing Ann Quin's *Three* for *The Sunday Times* in 1966, B. S. Johnson paraphrases Nathalie Sarraute's now often-quoted comparison of literary production to a relay race 'in which the baton of each generation's discoveries and advances is handed on to the next'.[2] Sarraute's baton metaphor avoids an insistence on progress or advancement, suggesting rather that the handing over is an act of continuation and inheritance rather one of repudiation and disinheritance. A neat metaphor suggesting aesthetic inheritance rather than complete renewal, Johnson liked it so much that he reused it in the introduction to *Are You Rather Young to Be Writing Your Memoirs?* as well as in many of his public talks. Johnson regarded 'serious' writers as those who sought not only to foster ideas about a 'better' social reality but those who showed, however implicitly, a 'statement of faith' in the 'evolution' of prose form.[3] These five writers, as we have seen, evolved their own writing practices which, in different ways extended the formal possibilities of the novel. In so doing, they offered a significant challenge to the critical narrative proposing that after modernism the experimental tradition in British literature was wholly subsumed by a return to realism. Kavan's expressionistic 'night-time' language, Brigid Brophy's baroquely rococo realism, *Between*'s lipogrammatic multilingualism, the stream of consciousness in Figes's *Winter's Journey* and the 'curled webbed toes' of Quin's Oedipal narrative in *Berg* all pull away from the domestic or marriage plot and in this way, free up their writing to explore what lies beyond the conventions and formulae of the realist script. Writing beyond realism did not simply entail its rejection but was often an engagement with its inherent malleability and vagabond potential.

Concerned about the disappearance of women experimental writers from literary history, Brooke-Rose noted how they have not been treated with the same level of intellectual seriousness as their male counterparts and, as a result, have become 'mysteriously absent' in critical accounts of twentieth-century experimental writing. Acknowledging that at the time she was writing there were only a small number of women experimenters, Brooke-Rose regarded her status as a women experimental writer as rare and unusual as a duck-billed platypus whose beak would one day 'develop into new birds' (*Invisible*, p. 178), thus changing the metaphor from Sarraute's relay race and extending Johnson's reference to writing as an evolutionary process. Brooke-Rose's beak, however oddly shaped, has most definitely evolved; women's experimental writing is thriving. In the British and Irish (North and South) context, Ali Smith, Rachel Cusk, Eimear McBride, Anna Burns, Nicola Barker and Deborah Levy have had substantial successes in what might be called mainstream literary culture, due in no small part to a new literary prize, the Goldsmiths Prize, that specifically rewards experimental writing. The Goldsmiths has arguably nudged its older cousin, the Booker, into less predictable artistic territory, one that recognises and rewards formal innovation as much as originality and relevance of content. The vagabond fictions of these twenty-first century writers might be seen as a contemporary development of a now-traceable lineage of women's experimental writing that stretches internationally from Woolf, Katherine Mansfield, Kate Chopin, Gertrude Stein, Djuna Barnes, through Ivy Compton-Burnett, Marguerite Duras and Nathalie Sarraute to Kathy Acker, Maggie Nelson then Han Kang, Valeria Luiselli and Marie Darrieussecq, to name only a very few from this line of descent.

No longer beholden to either modernism or postmodernism as unavoidable critical coordinates, women experimental writers do not have to contend with the sense of coming after or before any significant literary movement and the discussion of realism as the antithesis to experiment in their writing is discernibly less prevalent. Neither is their work bound into the classification of 'women's writing' insofar as critics have made no claim that their writing is representative of any kind of essential 'womb music' or illustrative of a particular stance on gender or feminism. The landscape of feminist literary criticism has expanded so greatly and in so many different directions that it can now easily accommodate complex discussions about the relationship between aesthetic and ideological concerns. Efforts to pin down or prove any definitive relationship between writing and gender, or to find a specifically female or feminist aesthetic, are now only a very minor chord in feminist literary criticism. The freedom from both rigid periodisation and an essentialist understanding of what constitutes women's writing has released contemporary women experimental writers from past strictures and definitions, ready to pass on all kinds of batons and evolve ever-more innovative beaks.

Notes

1. Brooke-Rose, 'Review of Robert Pinget's *The Inquisitory* and *Degrees* by Michel Butor', *The Sunday Times*, undated galley proofs TXRC98-A40.
2. B. S. Johnson, press clipping, Quin's scrapbook. p. 133. LMC 2196, Series II, box 103: 14–17, Calder and Boyars MSS.
3. B. S. Johnson, 'Introduction to *Aren't You Rather Young to be Writing Your Memoirs?*', in B. S. Johnson, *Well Done God! Selected Prose and Drama of B. S. Johnson*, ed. Jonathan Coe, Philip Tew and Julia Jordan (London: Picador, 2013), pp. 11–31 (p. 16).

Bibliography

Abel, Sam, *Opera in the Flesh: Sexuality in Operatic Performance* (Boulder, CO: Westview Press, 1996).
Abrams, Lynn, 'Liberating the Female Self: Epiphanies, Conflict and Coherence in the Life Stories of Post-war British Women', *Social History*, 39: 1 (2014), pp. 14–35.
Ahmed, Sara, *The Promise of Happiness* (London: Duke University Press, 2010).
Aiston, Sarah, 'A Good Job for a Girl? The Career Biographies of Women Graduates of the University of Liverpool Post-1945,' *Twentieth Century British History*, 15: 4 (2004), pp. 361–87.
Aldiss, Brian, 'Introduction', in Anna Kavan, *Ice* (Bungay, Suffolk: Picador, 1973), pp. 14–21.
Aldiss, Brian, 'Introduction', in Anna Kavan, *My Madness: The Selected Writings of Anna Kavan*, ed. Brian Aldiss (London: Picador, 1990).
Aldiss, Brian, 'Kafka's Sister', in Brian Aldiss, *The Detached Retina: Aspects of SF and Fantasy* (Liverpool: Liverpool University Press, 1995), pp. 137–44.
Allsop, Kenneth, *The Angry Decade: A Survey of the Cultural Revolt of the 1950s* (London: Peter Owen, 1958).
Amis, Kingsley, *Lucky Jim: A Novel* (London: Gollancz, 1953).
Andermahr, Sonya, 'Both/And Aesthetics: Gender, Art, and Language in Brigid Brophy's *In Transit* and Ali Smith's *How to Be Both*', *Contemporary Women's Writing*, 12: 2 (2018), pp. 248–63.
Anon., 'Peter Owen, Publisher – Obituary', *The Telegraph*, 16 May 2016 <https://www.telegraph.co.uk/obituaries/2016/05/31/peter-owen-publisher-obituary> (accessed 25 November 2019).
Anon., 'Sir Michael Levey', *The Telegraph*, 29 December 2008 <http://www.telegraph.co.uk/news/obituaries/4015722/Sir-Michael-Levey.html> (accessed 18 April 2018).
Aragon, Louis, 'A Man', *Little Review*, ix, 4 (1923/4), pp. 18–22.
Auchincloss, Eve, 'Bad Characters', *New York Times Review of Books*, 24 September 1964 <https://www.nybooks.com/articles/1964/09/24/bad-characters> (accessed 18 May 2020).
Austin, Michael (dir.), *Killing Dad: Or How to Love Your Mother*, screenplay by Ann Quin and Michael Austin, British Screen Productions, 1989.
Axelrod, Mark, 'Mozart, Moonshots, and Monkey Business in Brigid Brophy's

Hackenfeller's Ape', *Review of Contemporary Fiction*, 15: 3 (1995), pp. 18–22.

Baker, Niamh, *Happily Ever After? Women's Fiction in Postwar Britain, 1945–1960* (New York: St Martin's Press, 1989).

Bakhtin, Mikhail, *The Dialogic Imagination: Four Essays*, ed. Michael Holquist, trans. Caryl Emerson and Michael Holquist, University of Texas Press Slavic Series, 1 (Austin, TX: University of Texas Press, 1981).

Baldick, Chris, *Criticism and Literary Theory 1890 to the Present* (London: Routledge, 1996).

Barth, John, 'The Literature of Exhaustion', in Malcolm Bradbury (ed.), *The Novel Today: Contemporary Writers on Modern Fiction* (London: Fontana, 1977), pp. 70–83. Originally published in *The Atlantic*, August 1967.

Bartha, Noemi Alice, *Christine Brooke-Rose: The Chameleonic Text Between Self-Reflexivity and Narrative Experiment* (Newcastle upon Tyne: Cambridge Scholars, 2014).

Barthes, Roland, *The Pleasure of the Text*, trans. Richard Miller (New York: Hill and Wang, 1975). Originally published as *Le Plaisir du texte* (Paris: Éditions du Seuil, 1973).

Barthes, Roland, 'The Reality Effect', in Tzvetan Todorov (ed.), *French Literary Theory: A Reader*, trans. R. Carter (Cambridge: Cambridge University Press, 1982), pp. 11–17. Originally published as 'L'Effet de réel', *Communications*, 11 (1968), pp. 84–9.

Barthes, Roland, *S/Z*, trans. Richard Miller (New York: Farrar, Straus and Giroux, 1974). Originally published as *S/Z* (Paris: Éditions du Seuil, 1970).

Beauvoir, Simone de, *The Second Sex*, trans. H. M. Parshley (London: Vintage, 1997). Originally published as *Le Deuxième sexe* (Paris: Éditions Gallimard, 1949).

Beckett, Samuel, 'Dante . . . Bruno. Vico . . . Joyce', in *Disjecta: Miscellaneous Writings and a Dramatic Fragment*, ed. Ruby Cohn (New York: Grove Press, 1984) pp. 19–34. Originally published in *Transition*, 16–17 (June 1929), pp. 242–53.

Belsey, Catherine, 'Constructing the Subject, Deconstructing the Text', in Robyn Warhol and Diane Herndi (eds), *Feminisms: An Anthology of Literary Theory and Criticism* (New Brunswick, NJ: Rutgers University Press, 1991), pp. 657–73.

Belsey, Catherine, *Critical Practice*, 2nd edn (New York: Routledge, 2002 [London: Methuen, 1980]).

Benton, William (ed.), *Britannica Book of the Year* (London: Encyclopaedia Britannica, 1971) <https://archive.org/stream/in.ernet.dli.2015.147390/2015.147390.Britannica-Book-Of-The-Year-1971> (accessed 21 June 2019).

Bergé, Carol, Carol Bergé Papers: Series 1.1.a, box 19, folder 316, Olin Library Collection, Washington University, St Louis.

Bergonzi, Bernard, *The Situation of the Novel* (London: Macmillan, 1970).

Bergson, Henri, *Time and Free Will: An Essay on the Immediate Data of Consciousness*, trans. F. L. Pogson (London: Allen & Unwin, 1910). Originally published as *Essai sur les données immédiates de la conscience* (Paris: F. Alcan, 1889).

Berlant, Lauren and Michael Warner, 'Sex in Public', *Critical Inquiry*, 24: 2 (1998), pp. 547–66.
Berry, Ellen E., *Women's Experimental Writing: Negative Aesthetics and Feminist Critique* (London: Bloomsbury, 2016).
Birch, Sarah, *Christine Brooke-Rose and Contemporary Fiction* (Oxford: Clarendon Press, 1994).
Blackmer, Corinne E. and Patricia Juliana Smith (eds), *En Travesti: Women, Gender Subversion, Opera* (New York: Columbia University Press, 1995).
Blackmer, Corinne E., 'The Finishing Touch and the Tradition of Homoerotic Girls' School Fictions', *Review of Contemporary Fiction*, 15: 3 (1995), pp. 32–9.
Blamires, Harry, *A Short History of English Literature*, 2nd edn (London: Methuen, 1984).
Bluemel, Kirstin (ed.), *Intermodernism: Literary Culture in Mid-Twentieth-Century Britain* (Edinburgh: Edinburgh University Press, 2009).
Booth, Francis, *Amongst Those Left: The British Experimental Novel 1940–1980* (e-print: Lulu Press, 2012).
Booth, Francis, *Stranger Still: The Works of Anna Kavan* (e-print: Lulu Press, 2012).
Borcher, Elisabeth, *The Old Car*, trans. Eva Figes (London: Blackie, 1967).
Boumelha, Penny, 'Realism and the Ends of Feminism', in Susan Sheridan (ed.), *Grafts: Feminist Cultural Criticism* (London: Verso, 1988), pp. 77–91.
Bourke, Angela, Siobhán Marie Kilfeather, Maria Luddy, Margaret MacCurtain, Gerardine Meaney et al. (eds), *The Field Day Anthology of Irish Writing Volumes IV and V: Irish Women's Writing and Traditions* (New York: New York University Press, 2002).
Bourke, Joanna, *Working Class Cultures in Britain 1890–1960: Gender, Class and Ethnicity* (London: Routledge, 1994).
Bowlby, John, *Child Care and the Growth of Love* (Harmondsworth: Penguin, 1953).
Bowlby, Rachel, 'Preface', in Matthew Beaumont (ed.), *Adventures in Realism* (Oxford: Blackwell, 2007), pp. xi–xvii.
Boxall, Peter, *The Value of the Novel* (Cambridge: Cambridge University Press, 2015).
Bradbury, Malcolm, *The Modern British Novel* (London: Penguin, 1994).
Bradbury, Malcolm, *No, Not Bloomsbury* (London: André Deutsch, 1987).
Bradbury, Malcolm (ed.), *The Novel Today: Contemporary Writers on Modern Fiction* (London: Fontana, 1977).
Bradford, Richard, *The Novel Now: Contemporary British Fiction* (Oxford: Blackwell, 2007).
Braine, John, *Room at the Top* (London: John Eyre & Spottiswoode, 1957).
Bray, Joe, Alison Gibbons and Brian McHale (eds) *Routledge Companion to Experimental Literature* (Abingdon: Routledge, 2012).
Brecht, Bertolt, 'From the Popular and the Realistic', trans. John Willett, in Richard Drain (ed.), *Twentieth Century Theatre: A Sourcebook* (London: Routledge, 1995 [1958]), pp. 188–93.
Bristow, Joseph and Trev Lynn Broughton (eds), *The Infernal Desires of Angela Carter: Fiction, Femininity, Feminism* (London: Longman, 1997).

Brooke-Rose, Christine, 'The Baroque Imagination of Robbe-Grillet', *Modern Fiction Studies*, 11: 4 (1965), pp. 405–23.

Brooke-Rose, Christine, *Between* (London: Joseph, 1968).

Brooke-Rose, Christine, *The Christine Brooke-Rose Omnibus: Four Novels – Out, Such, Between, Thru* (Manchester: Carcanet, 1986).

Brooke-Rose, Christine, Christine Brooke-Rose Papers 1893–2005, MS-00532, Harry Ransom Research Center, University of Texas at Austin.

Brooke-Rose, Christine, 'Christine Brooke-Rose: The Texterminator', interview with Tom Boncza-Tomaszewski, *Independent on Sunday*, 27 March 2005 <https://www.independent.co.uk/arts-entertainment/books/features/christine-brooke-rose-the-texterminator-8427.html> (accessed 13 May 2020).

Brooke-Rose, Christine, 'A Conversation with Christine Brooke-Rose', interview with Ellen G. Friedman and Miriam Fuchs, in Ellen G. Friedman and Richard Martin (eds), *Utterly Other Discourse: The Texts of Christine Brooke-Rose* (Chicago and Normal IL: Dalkey Archive Press, 1995), pp. 29–37. Originally published in *Review of Contemporary Fiction*, 9: 3 (1989), pp. 81–90.

Brooke-Rose, Christine, 'A Conversation with Christine Brooke-Rose', interview with Maria del Sapio Garbero, in G. N. Forester and M. J. Nicholls (eds), *Verbivoracious Festschrift Volume 1: Christine Brooke-Rose* (Glentrees, Singapore: Verbivoracious Press, 2014), pp. 144–65.

Brooke-Rose, Christine, *The Dear Deceit* (Great Britain and Glentrees, Singapore: Verbivoracious Press, 2014 [London: Secker & Warburg, 1960]).

Brooke-Rose, Christine, 'The Dissolution of Character in the Novel', in Thomas C. Heller, Morton Sosna and David E. Wellbery (eds), *Reconstructing Individualism: Autonomy, Individuality and the Self in Western Thought* (Stanford, CA: Stanford University Press), pp. 184–96.

Brooke-Rose, Christine, *Go When you See the Green Man Walking* (London: Joseph, 1970).

Brooke-Rose, Christine, *A Grammar of Metaphor* (London: Secker & Warburg, 1958).

Brooke-Rose, Christine, 'Illicitations', *Review of Contemporary Fiction*, 9: 3 (1989), pp. 101–09.

Brooke-Rose, Christine, 'Illiterations', in G. N. Forester and M. J. Nicholls (eds), *Verbivoracious Festschrift Volume 1: Christine Brooke-Rose* (Glentrees, Singapore: Verbivoracious Press, 2014), pp. 41–59. Originally published in Ellen G. Friedman and Miriam Fuchs (eds), *Breaking the Sequence: Women's Experimental Fiction* (Princeton, NJ: Princeton University Press, 1989), pp. 55–71.

Brooke-Rose, Christine, interview with David Hayman and Keith Cohen, *Contemporary Literature*, 17: 1 (1976), pp. 1–23.

Brooke-Rose, Christine, interview with David Seed, *Textual Practice*, 7: 2 (1993), pp. 247–57.

Brooke-Rose, Christine, 'Introduction', in Brigid Brophy, *In Transit: An Heroi-Cyclic Novel* (Chicago and Normal, IL: Dalkey Archive Press, 2002), pp. i–vii.

Brooke-Rose, Christine, *Invisible Author: Last Essays* (Columbus: Ohio State University Press, 2002).

Brooke-Rose, Christine, *The Languages of Love* (London: Secker & Warburg, 1957).
Brooke-Rose, Christine, 'Le devaluation du Livre', *Le Monde*, 24 January 1968, p. 7.
Brooke-Rose, Christine, *Life: End Of* (Manchester: Carcanet, 2006).
Brooke-Rose, Christine, *The Middlemen: A Satire* (London: Secker & Warburg, 1961).
Brooke-Rose, Christine, 'The Nouveau Roman', *Times Literary Supplement*, 7 August 1969, pp. 881–2.
Brooke-Rose, Christine, *Out* (London: Joseph, 1964).
Brooke-Rose, Christine, 'Parallels and Paradoxes', in Anthony Holden and Ursula Owen (eds), *There are Kermodians: A Liber Amicorum for Frank Kermode* (London: Everyman, 1999).
Brooke-Rose, Christine, *Remake* (Manchester: Carcanet, 1996).
Brooke-Rose, Christine, *A Rhetoric of the Unreal: Studies in Narrative and Structure, Especially of the Fantastic* (Cambridge: Cambridge University Press, 1981).
Brooke-Rose, Christine, 'Samuel Beckett and the Anti-Novel', *The London Magazine*, 5: 12 (December 1958), pp. 3–46.
Brooke-Rose, Christine, 'Self-Confrontation and the Writer', *New Literary History*, 9: 1 (1977), pp. 129–36.
Brooke-Rose, Christine, *Stories, Theories and Things* (Cambridge: Cambridge University Press, 1991).
Brooke-Rose, Christine, 'Subscript', interview with Lorna Sage, in Christine Brooke-Rose, *Invisible Author: Last Essays* (Columbus: Ohio State University Press, 2002), pp. 169–80.
Brooke-Rose, Christine, *Such* (London: Joseph, 1966).
Brooke-Rose, Christine, *Thru* (London: Hamilton, 1975).
Brooke-Rose, Christine, 'Woman as Semiotic Object', in *Stories, Theories and Things* (Cambridge: Cambridge University Press, 1991).
Brooke-Rose, Christine, 'A Womb of One's Own', in *Stories, Theories and Things* (Cambridge: Cambridge University Press, 1991).
Brooke-Rose, Christine, 'Women in Their Own Write: A Novel Theory', interview with John Hall, *Guardian*, 16 November 1970, p. 9.
Brooke-Rose, Christine, 'A Writer's Constraints', in Christine Brooke-Rose, *Invisible Author: Last Essays* (Columbus: Ohio State University Press, 2002), pp. 36–52. Originally delivered as James Bryce Memorial lecture, Wolfson Hall, Somerville College, 2 March 1993.
Brooke-Rose, Christine, *A ZBC of Ezra Pound* (London: Faber and Faber, 1971).
Brooke, Stephen, 'Gender and Working Class Identity in Britain in the 1950s', *Journal of Social History*, 34: 4 (2001), pp. 773–95.
Brophy, Brigid, *The Adventures of God in His Search for the Black Girl* (London: Macmillan, 1973).
Brophy, Brigid, *Baroque-'n'-Roll and Other Essays* (London: Hamish Hamilton, 1987).
Brophy, Brigid, *Beardsley and His World* (New York: Harmony Books, 1976).
Brophy, Brigid, *Black and White: A Portrait of Aubrey Beardsley* (London: Jonathan Cape, 1968).

Brophy, Brigid, *Black Ship to Hell* (London: Secker & Warburg, 1962).
Brophy, Brigid, *The Burglar* (London: Cape, 1968).
Brophy, Brigid, *The Crown Princess and Other Stories* (London: Collins, 1953).
Brophy, Brigid, *Don't Never Forget: Collected Views and Reviews* (New York: Holt, Rinehart and Winston, 1966).
Brophy, Brigid, *The Finishing Touch* (London: Secker & Warburg, 1963).
Brophy, Brigid, *Flesh* (London: Faber and Faber, 2013 [London: Secker & Warburg, 1962]).
Brophy, Brigid, 'Foreword', in Elizabeth Smart, *By Grand Central Station I Sat Down and Wept* (London: Panther, 1966).
Brophy, Brigid, *A Guide to Public Lending Right* (Aldershot: Gower, 1983).
Brophy, Brigid, *Hackenfeller's Ape* (London: Virago 1991 [London: Hart Davies, 1953]).
Brophy, Brigid, 'He/She/Hesh', in *Baroque-'n'-Roll and Other Essays* (London: Hamish Hamilton, 1987), pp. 61–7. Originally published as 'Small Boys and Girls', *London Review of Books*, 4: 2, 4 February 1982.
Brophy, Brigid, interview with Leslie Dock, *Contemporary Literature*, 17: 2 (1976), 151–70.
Brophy, Brigid, *In Transit: An Heroi-Cyclic Novel* (London: Macdonald, 1969).
Brophy, Brigid, 'Introduction', in Jane Austen, *Pride and Prejudice* (London: Pan Books, 1967).
Brophy, Brigid, 'James Joyce and the Reader's Understanding', *London Review of Books*, 2: 3 (21 February 1980), pp. 8–9 <http://www.lrb.co.uk/v02/n03/brigid-brophy/james-joyce-and-the-readers-understanding> (accessed 20 April 2019).
Brophy, Brigid, *The King of a Rainy Country* (London: Coelacanth Press, 2012 [London: Secker & Warburg, 1956]).
Brophy, Brigid, 'Letters: Women Painters', *London Review of Books*, 1: 5 (20 December 1979) <https://www.lrb.co.uk/v01/n05/letters> (accessed 20 April 2019).
Brophy, Brigid, *The Longford Threat to Freedom* (London: National Secular Society, 1972). Originally a talk, 3 October 1972, Conway Hall, London.
Brophy, Brigid, *Mozart the Dramatist: A New View of Mozart, His Operas and His Age* (London: Faber and Faber, 1964).
Brophy, Brigid, 'The Nation in the Iron Mask', in *Don't Never Forget: Collected Views and Reviews* (New York: Holt, Rinehart and Winston, 1966), pp. 50–7.
Brophy, Brigid, 'The One-Eyed World of Germaine Greer', *London Review of Books*, 1: 3 (22 November 1979), pp. 1–3 <https://www.lrb.co.uk/v01/n03/brigid-brophy/the-one-eyed-world-of-germaine-greer> (accessed 20 April 2019).
Brophy, Brigid, *Palace without Chairs* (London: Hamilton, 1978).
Brophy, Brigid, *Prancing Novelist: A Defence of Fiction in the Form of a Critical Biography in Praise of Ronald Firbank* (London: Macmillan 1973).
Brophy, Brigid, *The Prince and the Wild Geese* (London: Hamilton, 1983).
Brophy, Brigid, *The Pussy Owl: Superbeast* (London: BBC Books, 1976).
Brophy, Brigid, *Reads: A Collection of Essays* (London: Cardinal, 1989).
Brophy, Brigid, *Religious Education in State Schools* (London: Fabian Society, 1967).

Brophy, Brigid, *The Rights of Animals* (London: Animal Defence and Anti-Vivisection Society, 1969).
Brophy, Brigid, *The Snow Ball* (London: Faber and Faber, 2013 [London: Faber and Faber, 1964]).
Brophy, Brigid, 'The Waste-Disposal Unit', in *Best Short Plays of the World Theatre, 1958–67* (New York: Crown, 1968). Originally for BBC Radio, 1964.
Brophy, Brigid, 'A Woman's Place', *Enquiry*, BBC Two, 27 January 1965, <http://www.bbc.co.uk/archive/marriage/10510.shtml> (accessed 20 April 2019).
Brophy, Brigid, Michael Levey and Charles Osbourne, *Fifty Works of English and American Literature That We Could Do Without* (London: Rapp and Carroll, 1967).
Buckeye, Robert, *Re: Quin* (London: Dalkey Archive Press, 2013).
Burnett, John, *A Social History of Housing 1815–1985*, 2nd edn (London: Methuen, 1986 [Newton Abbott: David and Charles, 1978]).
Burns, Alan, *Babel* (London: Calder and Boyars, 1969).
Burns, Alan, 'Blending Words with Pictures', *Books and Bookmen*, 17: 10 (July 1972).
Burns, Alan, 'The Disintegrating Novel', *Books and Bookmen*, 15: 12 (September 1970), pp. 6–7.
Burns, Alan, 'Essay', in Giles Gordon (ed.), *Beyond the Words: Eleven Writers in Search of a New Fiction* (London: Hutchinson, 1975), pp. 62–8.
Burns, Alan, *Europe After the Rain* (London: John Calder, 1965).
Burns, Alan and B. S. Johnson, *Writers Reading* (London: J. & P. Weldon Ltd, 1969).
Burns, Alan and Charles Sugnet (eds), *The Imagination on Trial: British and American Writers Discuss Their Working Methods* (London: Allison & Busby, 1981).
Burns, Carol, Carol Burns Papers, private collection.
Burroughs, William, *Junkie: Confessions of an Unredeemed Drug Addict* (New York: Penguin, 1977). Originally published as William Lee, *Junkie: Confessions of an Unredeemed Drug Addict* (New York: Ace Books, 1953).
Butler, Judith, *Gender Trouble* (London: Routledge, 1990).
Byatt, A. S., 'An Explosive Embrace', *Times Literary Supplement*, 13 January 1987, p. 269.
Byatt, A. S., 'People in Paper Houses: Attitudes to "Realism" and "Experiment" in English Post-War Fiction', in A. S. Byatt, *Passions of the Mind: Selected Writings* (New York: Turtle Bay Books, 1992), pp. 165–88. Originally published in Malcolm Bradbury and David Palmer (eds), *The Contemporary English Novel* (London: Arnold, 1979), pp. 19–41.
Byrne, Janet, 'Moving Towards Entropy': Anna Kavan's Science Fiction', *Extrapolation*, 23: 1 (1982), pp. 5–11.
Caines, Michael, Blog, *Times Literary Supplement*, 15 May 2015, p. <http.timescolumns.typepad.com/stothard/2015/05/rediscovering-brigid-brophy> (accessed 20 April 2019).
Calder, John, 'Exit Last Exit', *New Statesman*, 1 December 1967.
Calder, John, *Pursuit: The Uncensored Memoirs of John Calder* (London: Calder, 2001).

Calder, John, 'Through That Tunnel', *Review of Contemporary Fiction*, 17: 2 (1997), pp. 179–80.

Calder, John and Marion Boyars, Calder and Boyars MSS, 1939–1980, LMC 2196, Lilly Library, Indiana University, Bloomington, Indiana.

Calinescu, Matei, 'The Idea of the Avant-Garde', in Matei Calinescu, *Five Faces of Modernity: Modernism, Avant-Garde, Decadence, Kitsch, Postmodernism* (Durham, NC: Duke University Press, 1987), pp. 95–148.

Callard, David A., *The Case of Anna Kavan: A Biography* (London: Peter Owen, 1993).

Canepari-Labib, Michela, 'Word-Worlds: The Refusal of Realism and The Critique of Identity in the Fiction of Christine Brooke-Rose' (unpublished doctoral thesis, University of Sussex, 1998).

Canning, Richard and Gerri Kimber (eds), *Brigid Brophy: Avant-Garde Writer, Critic, Activist* (Edinburgh: Edinburgh University Press).

Carter, Angela, 'Notes from the Frontline', in Michelene Wandor (ed.), *On Gender and Writing* (London: Pandora Press, 1983), pp. 66–77.

Carter, Angela, *The Sadeian Woman and the Ideology of Pornography* (London: Virago, 1979).

Carter, Angela, 'Truly It Felt Like Year One', in Sarah Maitland (ed.), *Very Heaven: Looking Back at the 1960s* (London: Virago, 1988), p. 211–12.

Castle, Terry, 'The Carnivalization of Eighteenth-Century English Narrative,' *PMLA*, 99: 5 (1984), pp. 903–16.

Castle, Terry, 'Introduction' and sleeve notes, in Brigid Brophy, *The King of a Rainy Country* (London: Coelacanth Press, 2012).

Cecire, Natalia, 'Experimentalism by Contact', *Diacritics* 43: 1 (2015), pp. 6–35.

Cheyette, Bryan (ed.), *Between 'Race' and Culture: Representations of 'the Jew' in English and American Literature* (Stanford, CA: Stanford University Press, 1996).

Cheyette, Bryan (ed.), *Contemporary Jewish Writing in Britain and Ireland: An Anthology* (Lincoln, NE: University of Nebraska Press, 1998).

Cixous, Hélène, 'The Laugh of the Medusa', trans. Keith Cohen and Paula Cohen, *Signs*, 1: 4 (1976), pp. 875-93.

Clarke, Chris, 'Tracing the Ethical Dimension of Postwar British Experimental Fiction' (unpublished doctoral thesis, University of Southampton, 2015).

Coe, Jonathan, *Like a Fiery Elephant: The Story of B. S. Johnson* (London: Picador, 2004).

Cohen, Paul, 'Happy Birthday Vincennes!: The University of Paris-8 Turns Forty', *History Workshop Journal*, 69 (2010), pp. 206–24.

Cohen, Robert David, Letters, Series 1: Correspondence, boxes 1–16, folders 1–197: 85, Robert Sward Papers, MSS110, 1951–1971, Department of Special Collections, Washington University Libraries, St Louis.

Coleridge, Samuel Taylor, *Selected Poetry*, ed. H. J. Jackson (Oxford: Oxford University Press, 1997).

Connolly, Cyril, 'Comment', in *Horizon: A Review of Literature and Art*, December 1944.

Conradi, Peter, 'Eva Figes', in Jay L. Halio (ed.), *British Novelists Since 1960: Part 1, A–G, Dictionary of Literary Biography*, XIV (Detroit: Gale Research, 1983), pp. 298–302.

Conta, Manfred von, *The Deathbringer: A Novel*, trans. Eva Figes (London: Calder and Boyars).
Coote, Anna and Beatrice Campbell, *Sweet Freedom: The Struggle for Women's Liberation* (London: Picador, 1982).
Creeley, Robert, *Mabel, a Story and Other Stories* (London: Marion Boyars, 1976).
Creeley, Robert, Robert Creeley Papers, MSS031, 1944–1978, Department of Special Collections, Washington University Libraries, St Louis.
Crompton, R., '"Where did all the bright girls go?" Women's Higher Education and Employment Since 1964', in Nicholas Abercrombie and Alan Warde (eds), *Social Change in Contemporary Britain* (Cambridge: Polity Press, 1992), pp. 54–69.
Crosland, Margaret, *Beyond the Lighthouse: English Women Novelists in the Twentieth Century* (London: Constable, 1981).
Crow, Graham, 'The Post-war Development of the Modern Domestic Ideal', in Graham Allan and Graham Crow (eds), *Home and Family: Creating the Domestic Sphere* (Basingstoke: Macmillan, 1989), pp. 14–32.
Cunningham, Valentine, *New Statesman*, 28 March 1975, p. 424.
D'Albia, Carole, *London Life/Look*, 1967, p. 45, Reviews for Winter Journey, press cuttings, 1967–1968, MS 89050/7/5, Eva Figes Archive (1932–2012), British Library, London.
Dallery, Arleen B., 'The Politics of Writing (the) Body: *Écriture Féminine*', in Alison M. Jaggar and Susan Bordo (eds), *Gender/Body/Knowledge: Feminist Reconstructions of Being and Knowing* (New Brunswick, NJ: Rutgers University Press, 1989), pp. 52–67.
Darlington, Joseph, 'Introduction', in Christine Brooke-Rose, *The Dear Deceit* (Great Britain and Glentrees, Singapore: Verbivoracious Press, 2014).
Davies, Rhys, 'Anna Kavan', *Books and Bookmen* (February 1971), pp. 7–9.
Davies, Rhys, 'The Bazooka Girl: A Note on Anna Kavan', *London Magazine*, February 1970, pp. 14–15.
Davies, Rhys, *Honeysuckle Girl* (London: Heinemann, 1975).
Davis, Hugh, *The Making of James Agee* (Knoxville: University of Tennessee Press, 2008).
De Lauretis, Teresa, 'Queer Theory: Lesbian and Gay Sexualities, an Introduction', *differences: A Journal of Feminist Cultural Studies*, 3: 2 (1991), pp. iii–xviii.
De Quincey, Thomas, 'Confessions of an English Opium-Eater', in De Quincey, *Confessions of an English Opium-Eater and Other Writings* ed. Robert Morrison (Oxford: Oxford World's Classics, 2008), pp. 3–80.
DeKoven, Marianne, *A Different Language: Gertrude Stein's Experimental Writing* (Madison: University of Wisconsin Press, 1983).
DeKoven, Marianne, 'Jouissance, Cyborgs, and Companion Species: Feminist Experiment', *PMLA*, 121: 5 (2006), pp. 1690–6.
DeKoven, Marianne, *Utopia Limited: The Sixties and the Emergence of the Postmodern* (Durham, NC: Duke University Press, 2004).
Delaney, Shelagh, *A Taste of Honey* (London: Bloomsbury, 2014).
Derrida, Jacques, 'The Rhetoric of Drugs', trans. Michael Israel, in Jacques Derrida, *Points . . . Interviews, 1974–1994*, ed. Elisabeth Weber, trans. Peggy

Kamuf et al. (Stanford, CA: Stanford University Press, 1995), pp. 228–54. Originally published in *Autrement*, 106 (1989).

Diaz-Dorr, Priscilla, 'Anna Kavan: A Critical Introduction' (unpublished doctoral thesis, University of Tulsa, 1988).

di Leo, Jeffrey R., 'Experimental Writing', *American Book Review*, 37: 5 (2016), pp. 6–7.

Dock, Leslie Ann, 'Brigid Brophy: Author in the Baroque' (unpublished doctoral thesis, 1977).

Dowson, Jane (ed.), *Women's Writing 1945–1960: After the Deluge* (Basingstoke: Palgrave Macmillan, 2003).

Driscoll, Lawrence, 'Planet Heroin: Women and Drugs', in Lawrence Driscoll, *Reconsidering Drugs: Mapping Victorian and Modern Drug Discourses* (London: Palgrave, 2000), pp. 101–27.

Duchamp, Timmel, 'What's the Story: Reading Anna Kavan's *Ice*', *LCRW*, 6 June 2001 <https://smallbeerpress.com/free-stuff-to-read/2001/06/06/whats-the-story-reading-anna-kavans-ice> (accessed 15 April 2019).

Dunn, Nell (ed.), *Talking to Women* (London: MacGibbon & Kee, 1965).

DuPlessis, Rachel Blau, *The Pink Guitar: Writing as Feminist Practice* (London: Routledge, 1990).

DuPlessis, Rachel Blau, *Writing Beyond the Ending: Narrative Strategies of Twentieth-Century Women Writers*, (Bloomington: Indiana University Press, 1985).

Dworkin, Craig, 'The Fate of Echo', in Craig Dworkin and Kenneth Goldsmith (eds), *Against Expression: An Anthology of Conceptual Writing* (Evanston, IL: Northwestern University Press, 2010), pp. xxiii–liv.

Dyhouse, Carol, *Students: A Gendered History* (Abingdon: Routledge, 2005).

Eburne, Jonathan P. and Rita Felski, 'What is an Avant-Garde? Introduction', *New Literary History*, 41: 4 (2010), pp. v–xv.

Eco, Umberto, *The Open Work*, trans. Anna Cancogni (London: Hutchinson Radius, 1989). Originally published as *Opera Aperta* (Milan: Bompinai, 1962).

Edelman, Lee, *No Future: Queer Theory and the Death Drive* (Durham, NC: Duke University Press, 2004).

Ellis, Havelock, *Man and Woman: A Study of Human Secondary Sexual Characters* (London: Walter Scott, 1894).

Ellis, Warren, 'Future Underground', *Brainjuice*, 15 February 2005 <http://www.warrenellis.com/future-underground> (accessed 1 October 2011).

English, James F. (ed.), *A Concise Companion to Contemporary British Fiction* (Oxford: Blackwell, 2006).

Enright, D. J., 'A Writer's Fancy', *London Review of Books*, 2: 3 (21 February 1980), pp. 15–16.

Evenson, Brian, 'Introduction', in Ann Quin, *Three* (Chicago and Normal, IL: Dalkey Archive Press, 2001).

Evenson, Brian and Joanna Howard, 'Ann Quin', *Review of Contemporary Fiction*, 23: 2 (2003), pp. 50–75.

Esty, Jed, 'Realism Wars', *Novel: A Forum on Fiction*, 49: 2 (2016), pp. 316–42.

Fanon, Frantz, *The Wretched of the Earth*, trans. Constance Farrington (London: Penguin, 2001. Originally published as *Les Damnés de la terre* (Paris: François Maspero, 1961).

Faulkner, William, *The Sound and the Fury* (New York: Jonathan Cape and Harrison Smith, 1929).
Federman, Raymond, 'Surfiction – Four Propositions in Form of an Introduction', in Raymond Federman (ed.), *Surfiction: Fiction Now ... and Tomorrow* (Chicago: Swallow Press, 1975), pp. 5–15.
Felski, Rita, *Beyond Feminist Aesthetics: Feminist Literature and Social Change* (Cambridge, MA: Harvard University Press, 1989).
Felski, Rita, *Literature After Feminism* (Chicago: University of Chicago Press, 2003).
Ferris, Natalie, 'The Double Play of Mirrors: Anna Kavan, Autobiography and Self-Portraiture', *Women: A Cultural Review*, 28: 4 (2017), pp. 391–409.
Ferris, Natalie, 'Manna in Mid-Wilderness', in G. N. Forester and M. J. Nichols (eds), *Verbivoracious Festschrift Volume 1: Christine Brooke-Rose* (Glentrees, Singapore: Verbivoracious Press, 2014), pp. 281–8.
Ferris, Natalie, '"I think I preferred it abstract": Christine Brooke-Rose and Visuality in the New Novel', *Textual Practice*, 32: 2 (2018), pp. 225–44.
Field, Michele, 'Eva Figes', *Publishers Weekly*, 231 (16 January 1987), pp. 56–7.
Figes, Eva, 'Accustomed as I am to Public Speaking', *New Humanist*, February 1973.
Figes, Eva, *B* (London: Faber and Faber, 1972).
Figes, Eva, *The Banger* (London: André Deutsch, 1968).
Figes, Eva, 'Battle of the Books', *Guardian*, 9 November 1976, p. 9.
Figes, Eva, 'B. S. Johnson', *Review of Contemporary Fiction*, 5: 2 (1985), pp. 70–1.
Figes, Eva, *Days* (London: Faber, 1974).
Figes, Eva, *Equinox* (Bungay, Suffolk: Panther, 1969 [London: Secker & Warburg, 1966]).
Figes, Eva, Eva Figes Archive (1932–2012), MS 89050, British Library, London.
Figes, Eva, 'Everything Gets Worse', *Guardian*, 5 June 2004 <https://www.theguardian.com/books/2004/jun/05/biography.jonathancoe> (accessed 18 April 2018).
Figes, Eva, *Ghosts* (London: Hamish Hamilton, 1988).
Figes, Eva, 'The Interior Landscape', *The Running Man*, 1: 1 (May–June 1968).
Figes, Eva, interview with Alan Burns, in Alan Burns and Charles Sugnet (eds), *The Imagination on Trial: British and American Writers Discuss Their Working Methods* (London: Allison & Busby, 1981), pp. 31–9.
Figes, Eva, interview with Jan Moir, 'The Feminist That Time Forgot', *Guardian*, 27 October 1993.
Figes, Eva, interview with Laurel Graeber/James McConkey, in James McConkey, 'Get Thee Behind Us, Freud'/ 'New Beginnings in Middle Age', *New York Times*, 25 September 1988, p. 9 <https://www.nytimes.com/1988/09/25/books/get-thee-behind-us-freud.html> (accessed 1 April 2019).
Figes, Eva, interview with Manuel Almagro and Carolina Sánchez-Palencia, *Atlantis*, 22: 1 (2000), pp. 177-86.
Figes, Eva, interview with Olga Kenyon, in Olga Kenyon (ed.), *Women Writers Talk: Interviews with Ten Women Writers* (Oxford: Lennard, 1989), pp. 69–90.

Figes, Eva, interview with Sarah O'Reilly, May 2010–June 2011, *Authors' Lives*, C1276/38, Sound & Moving Image Catalogue, British Library, London.
Figes, Eva, *Journey to Nowhere: One Woman Looks for the Promised Land* (London: Granta, 2008).
Figes, Eva, *The Knot* (London: Sinclair-Stevenson, 1996).
Figes, Eva, *Konek Landing* (London: Faber, 1969).
Figes, Eva, *Light* (London: Hamish Hamilton, 1983).
Figes, Eva, *Little Eden: A Child at War* (London: Faber, 1978).
Figes, Eva, 'The Long Passage to Little England', *The Observer*, 11 June 1978, p. 14.
Figes, Eva, *The Musicians of Bremen: Retold by Eva Figes* (London: Blackie, 1967).
Figes, Eva, *Nelly's Version* (London: Secker & Warburg, 1977).
Figes, Eva, 'The New Humanism', *New Humanist*, December 1972, p. 335.
Figes, Eva, 'Note', in Giles Gordon (ed.), *Beyond the Words: Eleven Writers in Search of a New Fiction* (London: Hutchinson, 1975), pp. 113–14.
Figes, Eva, 'Obbligato, Bedsitter', in Samuel Beckett et al., *Signature Anthology, 20* (London: Calder and Boyars, 1975), pp. 33–47.
Figes, Eva, 'On the Edge', in Julian Evans (ed.), *London Tales* (London: Hamish Hamilton, 1983), pp. 51–9.
Figes, Eva, *Patriarchal Attitudes: Women in Society* (London: Virago, 1978 [London: Faber, 1970]).
Figes, Eva, 'Public Larceny Right', *New Humanist*, 1972.
Figes, Eva, *Scribble Sam* (London: André Deutsch, 1971).
Figes, Eva, *The Seven Ages: A Novel* (London: Hamish Hamilton 1987).
Figes, Eva, *Sex and Subterfuge: Women Writers to 1850* (London: Macmillan, 1982).
Figes, Eva, 'The State of Fiction: A Symposium', *New Review*, 5: 1 (1978), pp. 38–9.
Figes, Eva, *Tales of Innocence and Experience: An Exploration* (London: Bloomsbury, 2003).
Figes, Eva, *The Tenancy* (London: Sinclair-Stevenson, 1993).
Figes, Eva, *Tragedy and Social Evolution* (London: Calder, 1976).
Figes, Eva, *Tree of Knowledge* (London: Sinclair-Stevenson, 1990).
Figes, Eva, *Waking* (London: Hamilton, 1981).
Figes, Eva, 'Why the Euphoria Had to Stop', *Guardian*, 16 May 1978, p. 9.
Figes, Eva, *Winter Journey* (London: Faber, 1967).
Figes, Eva, (ed.), *Women's Letters in Wartime 1450–1945* (London: Pandora, 1993).
Firchow, Peter (ed.), *The Writer's Place: Interviews on the Literary Situation in Contemporary Britain* (Minneapolis: University of Minnesota Press, 1974).
Firestone, Shulamith, *The Dialectic of Sex: The Case for Feminist Revolution* (New York: William Morrow & Company, 1970).
Flood, Alison, 'British Library Acquires Eva Figes Archive', *Guardian*, 12 October 2009 <http://www.guardian.co.uk/books/2009/oct/12/british-library-eva-figes-archive> (accessed 1 October 2018).
Forester, G. N., '*In the Labyrinth*, Translated by Christine Brook-Rose: A Review', in G. N. Forester and M. J. Nicholls (eds), *Verbivoracious Festschrift*

Volume 1: Christine Brooke-Rose (Glentrees, Singapore: Verbivoracious Press, 2014), pp. 86–92.

Forester, G. N. and Nicholls, M. J. (eds), *Verbivoracious Festschrift Volume 1: Christine Brooke-Rose* (Glentrees, Singapore: Verbivoracious Press, 2014).

Fowler, Christopher, 'Invisible Ink No 245: Brigid Brophy', *Independent on Sunday*, 12 October 2014 <https://www.independent.co.uk/arts-entertainment/books/reviews/invisible-ink-no-245-brigid-brophy> (accessed 20 April 2019).

Fox, Margalit, 'Christine Brooke-Rose, Inventive Writer, Dies at 89', *New York Times*, 10 April 2012 <https://www.nytimes.com/2012/04/10/books/christine-brooke-rose-experimental-writer-dies-at-89.html> (accessed 20 April 2019).

Foxcroft, Louise, *The Making of Addiction: The Use and Abuse of Opium in Nineteenth Century-Century Britain* (London: Routledge, 2007).

Freud, Sigmund, 'Mourning and Melancholia', in Sigmund Freud, *On the History of the Psycho-Analytic Movement, Papers on Metapsychology and Other Works*, ed. and trans. James Strachey, *The Standard Edition of the Complete Psychological Works of Sigmund Freud*, 24 vols (London: Vintage, 2001 [London: Hogarth Press, 1917]), XIV (1914–1916), pp. 237–58.

Friedan, Betty, *The Feminine Mystique* (New York: W. W. Norton, 1963).

Friedman, Ellen G., 'The Resisting Author: An Introduction', in Ellen G. Friedman and Richard Martin (eds), *Utterly Other Discourse: The Texts of Christine Brooke-Rose* (Chicago and Normal, IL: Dalkey Archive Press, 1995), pp. 9–18.

Friedman, Ellen G., 'Sexing the Text: Women's Avant-Garde Writing in the Twentieth Century', in Joe Bray, Alison Gibbons and Brian McHale (eds), *The Routledge Companion to Experimental Literature* (Abingdon: Routledge, 2012), pp. 154–67.

Friedman, Ellen G., '"Utterly Other Discourse": The Anticanon of Experimental Women Writers from Dorothy Richardson to Christine Brooke-Rose', *Modern Fiction Studies*, 34: 3 (1988), pp. 353–70.

Friedman, Ellen G., 'Where are the Missing Contents? (Post)Modernism, Gender, and the Canon', *PMLA*, 108: 2 (1993), pp. 240–52.

Friedman, Ellen G. and Miriam Fuchs (eds), *Breaking the Sequence: Women's Experimental Fiction* (Princeton, NJ: Princeton University Press, 1989).

Friedman, Ellen G. and Richard Martin (eds), *Utterly Other Discourse: The Texts of Christine Brooke-Rose* (Chicago and Normal, IL: Dalkey Archive Press, 1995).

Gaedtze, Andrew, *Modernism and the Machinery of Madness* (Cambridge: Cambridge University Press, 2017).

Gallop, Jane, *Feminism and Psychoanalysis: The Daughter's Seduction* (London: Macmillan, 1982).

Ganteau, Jean-Michel, 'In Thy Autonomy is Thy Commitment: Brigid Brophy's *In Transit*', in Jean-Michel Ganteau and Christine Reynier (eds), *Autonomy and Commitment in Twentieth-Century British Literature* (Montpellier: Presses Universitaires de la Méditerranée, 2010), pp. 191–202.

Garman, Emma, 'Feminize Your Canon: Anna Kavan', *The Paris Review*, 10 December 2018 <https://www.theparisreview.org/blog/2018/12/10/feminize-your-canon-anna-kavan> (accessed 20 January 2019).

Garrity, Jane, 'Nocturnal Transgressions in *The House of Sleep*: Anna Kavan's Maternal Registers', *Modern Fiction Studies*, 40: 2 (1994), pp. 253–77.
Gąsiorek, Andrzej, *Post-War British Fiction: Realism and After* (London: Edward Arnold, 1995).
Gass, William H., 'The Concept of Character in Fiction', in Michael J. Hofmann and Patrick D. Murphy (eds), *Essentials of the Theory of Fiction*, 2nd edn (London: Leicester University Press, 1996), pp. 113–121. Originally published in William H. Gass, *Fiction and the Figures of Life* (New York: Alfred Knopf, 1970), pp. 34–54.
Genet, Jean, *Our Lady of the Flowers*, trans. Bernard Frechtman (London: Anthony Blond, 1964).
Gibbons, Alison, *Multimodality, Cognition, and Experimental Literature* (Abingdon: Routledge, 2012).
Gindin, James, *Postwar British Fiction: New Accents and Attitudes* (Berkeley: California University Press, 1962).
Glasgow, Mary M., 'The Concept of the Arts Council', in Milo Keynes (ed.), *Essays on John Maynard Keynes* (Cambridge: Cambridge University Press, 1975), pp. 260–71.
Glynn, Raewyn, 'Anna Kavan on Ice: An Encounter with Anna Kavan's Wartime Writing via New Zealand and the Arctic Imaginary' (unpublished MA dissertation, University of Auckland, 1997).
Goodwin, Craufurd D., *Art and the Market: Roger Fry on Commerce in Art* (Ann Arbor: University of Michigan Press, 1998).
Gordon, Edmund, *The Invention of Angela Carter: A Biography* (Oxford: Oxford University Press, 2017).
Gordon, Giles (ed.), *Beyond the Words: Eleven Writers in Search of a New Fiction* (London: Hutchinson, 1975).
Gordon, Giles, 'Diary: Experimental Slideshows', *London Review of Books*, 15: 19 (7 October 1993) <https://www.lrb.co.uk/the-paper/v15/n19/giles-gordon/diary> (accessed 20 July 2019).
Gordon, Giles, 'Introduction', in Ann Quin, *Berg* (Chicago and Normal, IL: Dalkey Archive Press, 2001).
Gordon, Giles, 'Obituary: Brigid Brophy', *Independent*, 8 August 1995 <http://www.independent.co.uk/news/people/obituary-brigid-brophy-1595286.html> (accessed 20 April 2019).
Gornick, Vivian, 'The Great Depression of Anna Kavan', *Village Voice*, 26: 49 (2–8 December 1981), pp. 49–51.
Gornick, Vivian, *The End of the Novel of Love* (London: Virago, 1999 [Boston, MA: Beacon Press, 1997]).
Gray, Nancy, *Language Unbound: On Experimental Writing by Women* (Urbana: University of Illinois Press, 1992).
Green, André, 'The Dead Mother', in André Green, *On Private Madness* (London: Hogarth Press, 1986), pp. 142–73.
Greene, Gayle, *Changing the Story: Feminist Fiction and the Tradition* (Bloomington, IN: Indiana University Press, 1991).
Greene, Gayle and Coppélia Kahn (eds), *Making a Difference: Feminist Literary Criticism* (London: Methuen, 1985).
Greer, Germaine, *The Female Eunuch* (London: MacGibbon and Kee, 1970).

Greer, Germaine, *The Obstacle Race: The Fortunes of Women Painters and Their Work* (London: Secker & Warburg, 1979).
Groes, Sebastian, *British Fiction of the Sixties: The Making of the Swinging Decade* (London: Bloomsbury, 2016).
Grzimek, Bernard, *He and I and the Elephants*, trans. Eva Figes (London: Thames & Hudson, 1967).
Gutenberg, Andrea, 'Thresholds and Boundaries: Limit Plots in Eva Figes, Penelope Lively and Sara Maitland', in Beate Neumeier (ed.), *Engendering Realism and Postmodernism: Contemporary Writers in Britain* (Amsterdam and New York: Rodopi, 2001), pp. 191–205.
Guy, Adam, '"That's a scientific fact": Christine Brooke-Rose's Experimental Turn', *The Modern Language Review*, 111: 4 (2016), pp. 936–55.
Guy, Josephine, *The British Avant-Garde: The Theory and Politics of Tradition* (London: Harvester Wheatsheaf, 1991).
Hall, John, 'Christine Brooke-Rose', in James Vinson (ed.) *Contemporary Novelists* (London: St James Press, 1972), pp. 182–4.
Halperin, David, *Saint Foucault: Towards a Gay Hagiography* (Oxford: Oxford University Press, 1995).
Hamilton, Ian, interview with Aorewa McLeod, Auckland, 1981, in Raewyn Glynn, 'Anna Kavan on Ice: An Encounter with Anna Kavan's Wartime Writing Via New Zealand and the Arctic Imaginary' (unpublished MA thesis, University of Auckland, 1997), n.p.
Hankin, Kelly, 'Lesbian Locations: The Production of Lesbian Bar Space in "The Killing of Sister George"', *Cinema Journal*, 41: 1 (2001), pp. 3–27.
Hargreaves, Tracy and Alice Ferrebe, 'Introduction: Literature of the 1950s and 1960s', *The Yearbook of English Studies*, 42 (2012), pp. 1–12.
Harrison, Brian, *Seeking a Role: The United Kingdom 1951–1970* (Oxford: Oxford University Press, 2011).
Harrison, Jane Ellen, *Prolegomena to the Study of Greek Religion* (Cambridge: The University Press, 1903).
Hartley, Jenny, *Millions Like Us: British Women's Fiction of the Second World War* (London: Virago, 1997).
Hawkes, John, 'Notes on the Wild Goose Chase', in Marcus Klein (ed.), *The American Novel Since World War II* (Greenwich, CN: Fawcett Premier, 1969), n.p. Originally published in *The Massachusetts Review*, 3: 4 (1962), pp. 784–8.
Hayman, Ronald, *The Novel Today: 1967–1975* (Longman for the British Council, 1976).
Head, Dominic, *The Cambridge Introduction to Modern British Fiction, 1950–2000* (Cambridge: Cambridge University Press, 2002).
Heath, Stephen, *The Nouveau Roman: A Study in the Practice of Writing* (London: Elek, 1972).
Heisenberg, Werner, *Physics and Philosophy: The Revolution in Modern Science* (New York: Harper, 1958).
Heppenstall, Rayner, *The Master Eccentric: The Journals of Rayner Heppenstall*, ed. Jonathan Goodman (London: Allison & Busby, 1986).
Herman, David, *Story Logic: Problems and Possibilities of Narrative* (Lincoln, NE: University of Nebraska Press, 2004).

Hewison, Robert, *Culture and Consensus: England, Art and Politics Since 1940* (Abingdon: Routledge, 2015 [London: Methuen, 1995]).

Hinton, Laura and Cynthia Hogue (eds), *We Who Love to be Astonished: Experimental Women's Writing and Performance Poetics* (Tuscaloosa: University of Alabama Press, 2001).

Hirsch, Marianne, 'The Generation of Postmemory', *Poetics Today*, 29: 1 (2008), pp. 103–28.

Hirsch, Marianne, *The Generation of Postmemory: Writing and Visual Culture After the Holocaust* (New York, Columbia University Press, 2012).

Hocquenghem, Guy, *Homosexual Desire*, trans. Daniella Dangoor (Durham NC: Duke University Press, 1993). Originally published as *Le Désire homosexuel* (Paris: Éditions Universitaires, 1972).

Hodgson, Jennifer, 'Brigid Brophy: In Praise of the Mad Bomber of English Literature' <https://jenniferhodgson.co.uk/writing/brigid-brophy-in-praise-of-the-mad-bomber-of-english-literature> (accessed 8 January 2019). Originally published as 'Afterword', in Brigid Brophy, *The King of a Rainy Country* (London: Coelacanth Press, 2012), pp. 269–73.

Hoepffner, Bernard, 'Translating *In Transit*: Writing – by Proxy', *Review of Contemporary Fiction*, 15: 3 (1995), pp. 54–61.

Holtby, Winifred, 'What We Read and Why We Read It', *The Left Review*, 1: 4 (1935), pp. 112–14.

Hopkins, Chris, 'The Neglect of Brigid Brophy', *Review of Contemporary Fiction*, 15: 3 (1995), pp. 12–17.

Horvath, Brooke, 'Brigid Brophy's It's-All-Right-I'm-Only-Dying Comedy of Modern Manners: Notes on *In Transit*', *Review of Contemporary Fiction*, 15: 3 (1995), pp. 46–53.

Hove, Hannah van, 'Exploring the Realm of the Unconscious in Anna Kavan's *Sleep Has His House*', *Women: A Cultural Review*, 28: 4 (2017), pp. 358–74.

Hubback, Judith, *Wives Who Went to College* (London: Heinemann, 1957).

Humble, Nicola, *The Feminine Middlebrow Novel, 1920s to 1950s: Class, Domesticity, and Bohemianism* (Oxford: Oxford University Press, 2001).

Hutchinson, Robert, *The Politics of the Arts Council* (London: Sinclair Browne, 1982).

Ironside, Virginia, 'Preface', in Anna Kavan, *Julia and the Bazooka* (London: Peter Owen, 2009).

James, David, 'B. S. Johnson Within the Ambit of Modernism', *Critical Engagements: A Journal of Criticism and Theory*, 4: 1–2 (2011), pp. 37–53.

James, David (ed.), *The Cambridge Companion to British Fiction Since 1945* (Cambridge: Cambridge University Press, 2015).

James, David (ed.), *The Legacies of Modernism: Historicising Postwar and Contemporary Fiction* (Cambridge: Cambridge University Press, 2012).

James, David, 'Localizing Late Modernism: Interwar Regionalism and the Genesis of the "Micro Novel"', *Journal of Modern Literature*, 32: 4 (2009), pp. 43–64.

Jameson, Fredric, 'Reflections in Conclusion', in *Aesthetics and Politics, Radical Thinkers* (London: Verso, 2007), pp. 196–213 (p. 211).

Janik, Vicki K., Del Ivan Janik and Emmanuel S. Nelson (eds), *Modern British Women: An A–Z Guide* (London: Greenwood Press, 2002).

Jephcott, Pearl, 'Women, Wife and Worker', Education Commission Report, 1960, London School of Economics, London.
Jephcott, Pearl, Nancy Seear and John H. Smith, *Married Women Working* (London: Allen & Unwin, 1962).
Johnson B. S., 'Introduction to *Aren't You Rather Young to be Writing Your Memoirs?*', in B. S. Johnson, *Well Done God! Selected Prose and Drama of B. S. Johnson*, ed. Jonathan Coe, Philip Tew and Julia Jordan (London: Picador, 2013). Originally published in B. S. Johnson, *Aren't You Rather Young to be Writing Your Memoirs?* (London: Hutchinson, 1973).
Johnson B. S., MS 89001, B. S. Johnson Archive (1933–2004), British Library.
Johnson B. S., *Travelling People* (London: Constable, 1963).
Johnson B. S., 'View/Reviews: 'Telling Stories is Telling Lies . . .', *Vogue*, 1 October 1966, p. 18.
Jones, Stephanie, 'The "Difficult" Relationship: Christine Brooke-Rose, Catholicism and Muriel Spark', *Textual Practice*, 32: 2 (2018), pp. 245–63.
Jordan, Clive, 'Among the Lost Things', *Daily Telegraph*, 25 Feburary 1972, pp. 39–46.
Jordan, Clive, 'Icy Heroin', *New Statesman*, 6 March 1970, pp. 333–4.
Jordan, Julia, 'Autonomous Automata: Opacity and the Fugitive Character in the Modernist Novel and After', in David James (ed.), *The Legacies of Modernism: Historicising Postwar and Contemporary Fiction* (Cambridge: Cambridge University Press, 2011), pp. 96–113.
Jordan, Julia, 'Late Modernism and the Avant-Garde Renaissance', in David James (ed.), *The Cambridge Companion to British Fiction Since 1945* (Cambridge University Press, 2015), pp. 145–59.
Jordan, Julia, 'The Quin Thing', *Times Literary Supplement*, 19 January 2018 <https://www.the-tls.co.uk/articles/the-quin-thing> (accessed 12 May 2019).
Joyce, James, *Finnegans Wake* (London: Faber and Faber, 1939).
Joyce, James, *Letters: Volume III*, ed. Richard Ellman (London: Faber and Faber, 1966).
Joyce, James, *Ulysses* (Paris: Shakespeare, 1922).
Kafka, Franz, 'In the Penal Colony', in Franz Kafka, *The Complete Stories*, ed. Nahum N. Glazer, trans. Willa and Edwin Muir (London: Vintage, 1999), pp. 140–67. Originally published as *In der Strafkolonie* (Leipzig: Kurt Wolff Verlag, 1915).
Kavan, Anna, Anna Kavan Papers, 1867–1991, McFarlin Library, The University of Tulsa.
Kavan, Anna, *Asylum Piece and Other Stories* (London: Peter Owen, 2001 [London: Jonathan Cape, 1940]).
Kavan, Anna, *A Bright Green Field and Other Stories* (London: Peter Owen, 1958).
Kavan, Anna, *Change the Name* (London: Peter Owen, 1993 [London: Jonathan Cape, 1941]).
Kavan, Anna, *A Charmed Circle* (London: Peter Owen, 1994 [London: Jonathan Cape, 1929])
Kavan, Anna, *Guilty* (London: Peter Owen, 2007).
Kavan, Anna, *I am Lazarus* (London: Jonathan Cape, 1945).
Kavan, Anna, *Ice* (London: Peter Owen, 2006 [1967]).
Kavan, Anna, *Julia and the Bazooka* (London: Peter Owen, 2009 [1970]).

Kavan, Anna, *Machines in the Head: Selected Short Writing*, ed. Victoria Walker (London and Chicago: Peter Owen, 2015).

Kavan, Anna, *My Madness: The Selected Writings of Anna Kavan*, ed. Brian Aldiss (London: Picador, 1990).

Kavan, Anna, 'Review: *A Haunted House, and Other Short Stories*, by Virginia Woolf', *Horizon*, April 1944, pp. 283–5 <http://www.unz.org/Pub/Horizon-1944apr-00283> (accessed 26 January 2015).

Kavan, Anna, *A Scarcity of Love* (London: Peter Owen, 1971 [London: Angus Downie, 1956]).

Kavan, Anna, 'Selected Notices: Back to Victoria', *Horizon*, 13: 73, November 1946, pp. 61–6.

Kavan, Anna, *Sleep Has His House* (London: Peter Owen, 1973 [London: Cassell, 1948]).

Kavan, Anna, *Who are You?* (London: Peter Owen, 1975, 2002 [Lowestoft: Scorpion Press, 1963]).

Keenan, Sally, 'Angela Carter's *The Sadeian Woman*: Feminism as Treason', in Joseph Bristow and Trey Lynn Broughton (eds), *The Infernal Desires of Angela Carter: Fiction, Femininity, Feminism* (London: Longman, 1997), pp. 132–48.

Kelly, Richard T., 'The Exquisite Sentences of "Flesh" and "The Finishing Touch" by Brigid Brophy', 29 August 2013 <https://www.faber.co.uk/blog/out-now-the-exquisite-sentences-of-flesh-and-the-finishing-touch-by-brigid-brophy> (accessed 20 April 2019).

Kelly, Richard T., 'Introduction', in Brigid Brophy, *Flesh* (London: Faber and Faber, 2013). Kenyon, Olga (ed.), *Women Writers Talk: Interviews with Ten Women Writers* (Oxford: Lennard, 1989).

Kermode, Frank, *Essays on Fiction, 1971–82* (London: Routledge & Kegan Paul, 1983).

Kermode, Frank, 'Flinch, Wince, Jerk, Shirk', *London Review of Books*, 28: 7 (6 April 2006), p. 17.

Kermode, Frank, 'The House of Fiction: Interviews with Seven Novelists', in Malcolm Bradbury (ed.), *The Novel Today: Contemporary Writers on Modern Fiction* (London: Fontana, 1977), pp. 111–35.

Kermode, Frank, 'Retripotent', *London Review of Books*, 26: 15 (5 August 2004), pp. 11–13.

Keynes, John Maynard, *The Collected Writings of John Maynard Keynes*, ed. Donald Moggridge and Elizabeth Johnson, 30 vols (London: Macmillan Press and Cambridge University Press, 1971–89), XXVIII (London: Macmillan for the Royal Economic Society, 1982).

Kilian, Eveline, 'Discourse Ethics and the Subversion of Gender Norms in Brigid Brophy's *In Transit*', in Susana Onega and Jean-Michel Ganteau (eds), *The Ethical Component in Experimental British Fiction Since the 1960's* (Newcastle: Cambridge Scholars, 2007), pp. 31–49.

Kilian, Eveline, '"My publisher urged me to write an autobiography": Christine Brooke-Rose's Experiment with Life Writing', in Lucia Boldrini and Julia Novak (eds), *Experiments in Life-Writing: Intersections of Auto/Biography and Fiction* (Basingstoke: Palgrave Macmillan, 2017), pp. 79–102.

Kitchen, Paddy, 'Catherine Wheel: Recollections of Ann Quin', *London Magazine*, 1 June 1979, pp. 50–7.

Klein, Viola, *Britain's Married Women Workers* (London: Routledge & Kegan Paul, 1965).
Kristeva, Julia, *Black Sun: Depression and Melancholia*, trans. Leon S. Roudiez (New York: Columbia University Press, 1989). Originally published as *Soleil noir: Dépression et mélancolie* (Paris: Gallimard, 1987).
Kristeva, Julia, 'On the Melancholic Imaginary', trans. Leon S. Roudiez, *New Formations*, 3 (1987), pp. 5–14. Originally published as 'De l'imaginaire mélancolique', *Le Genre humain*, 2: 13 (1985), pp. 65-81.
Kristeva, Julia, *Powers of Horror: An Essay on Abjection*, trans. Leon S. Roudiez (New York: Columbia University Press, 1982). Originally published as *Pouvoirs de l'horreur* (Paris: Éditions du Seuil, 1980).
Kristeva, Julia, 'Women's Time', trans. Alice Jardine and Harry Blake, *Signs*, 7: 1 (1981), pp. 13–35.
Laing, Stuart, 'Novels and the Novel', in Alan Sinfield (ed.), *Society and Literature: 1945–1970* (Abingdon: Routledge, 2013 [London: Methuen, 1983]), pp. 235–59.
Langhamer, Claire, 'Feeling, Women and Work in the Long 1950s', *Women's History Review* 26: 1 (2017), pp. 77–92.
Langhamer, Claire, 'The Meanings of Home in Postwar Britain', *Journal of Contemporary History*, 40: 2 (2005), pp. 341–62.
Latham, Sean, 'Cyril Connolly's *Horizon* (1940–1950) and the End of Modernism', in Peter Brooker and Andrew Thacker (eds), *The Oxford Critical and Cultural History of Modernist Magazines: Volume I, Britain and Ireland, 1880–1955* (Oxford: Oxford University Press, 2009), pp. 856–74.
Lauret, Maria, *Liberating Literature: Feminist Fiction in America* (London: Routledge, 1994).
Lawrence, Karen R., '"Floating on a pinpoint": Travel and Place in Brooke-Rose's *Between*', in Ellen J. Friedman and Richard Martin (eds), *Utterly Other Discourse: The Texts of Christine Brooke-Rose* (Chicago and Normal, IL: Dalkey Archive Press, 1995), pp. 76–96.
Lawrence, Karen R. (ed.), '*In Transit*: From James Joyce to Brigid Brophy', in Karen R. Lawrence (ed.), *Transcultural Joyce* (Cambridge: Cambridge University Press, 1998), pp. 37–45.
Lawrence, Karen R., *Penelope Voyages: Women and Travel in the British Literary Tradition* (Ithaca, NY: Cornell University Press, 1994).
Lawrence, Karen R., *Techniques for Living: Fiction and Theory in the Work of Christine Brooke-Rose* (Columbus: Ohio State University Press, 2010).
Leavis, Q. D., *Fiction and the Reading Public* (London: Pimlico, 2000 [London: Chatto and Windus, 1932]).
Lee, Jennie, 'Theatre and the State', *Hutchinson's Theatre Annual*, 1970–1.
Lee, Patricia, 'Communication Breakdown and the "Twin Genius" of Brophy's *In Transit*', *Review of Contemporary Fiction*, 15: 3 (1995), pp. 62–7.
Lerman, Leo, *The Saturday Review*, 10 August 1946, pp. 9–10.
Lessing, Doris, 'Anna Kavan', in Doris Lessing, *Time Bites: Views and Reviews* (London: Fourth Estate, 2004), p. 142–4.
Levey, Kate, 'Mr. and Mrs. Michael Levey', *Contemporary Women's Writing*, 12: 2 (2018), pp. 142–51.
Levey, Kate, Brigid Brophy Papers, Kate Levey private collection.
Levitt, Morton P, 'Christine Brooke-Rose', in Jay L. Halio (ed.), *British*

Novelists Since 1960: Part 1, A–G, Dictionary of Literary Biography, XIV (Detroit: Gale Research, 1983), pp. 124–9.

Lewis, Jane, *Women in Britain Since 1945: Women, Family, Work and the State in the Post-War Years* (Oxford: Blackwell, 1992).

Lewis, Jeremy, *Cyril Connolly: A Life* (London: Jonathan Cape, 1997).

Little, Judy, *The Experimental Self: Dialogic Subjectivity in Woolf, Pym, and Brooke-Rose* (Carbondale: Southern Illinois University Press, 1996).

Loach, Ken (dir.), *Cathy Come Home*, Jeremy Sandford, BBC Wednesday Play Series, 1965.

Loach, Ken (dir.), *Up the Junction*, screenplay Nell Dunn, BBC Wednesday Play Series, 1965.

Lodge, David, '*Middlemarch* and the Idea of the Classic Realist Text', in Arnold Kettle (ed.), *The Nineteenth-Century Novel: Critical Essays and Documents*, rev edn (London: Heinemann, 1981), pp. 218–38.

Lodge, David, 'The Novelist at the Crossroads', in Malcolm Bradbury (ed.), *The Novel Today: Contemporary Writers on Modern Fiction* (London: Fontana, 1977), pp. 84–110.

Lodge, David, *The Novelist at the Crossroads and Other Essays on Fiction and Criticism* (London: Routledge & Kegan Paul, 1971).

Lodge, David, 'The State of Fiction: A Symposium', *New Review*, 5: 1 (1978), pp. 14–76.

Love, Heather, *Feeling Backward: Loss and the Politics Queer History* (Cambridge MA: Harvard University Press, 2007).

Lucas, John, 'The Sixties: Realism and Experiment', in Laura Marcus and Peter Nicholls (eds), *The Cambridge History of Twentieth-Century English Literature* (Cambridge: Cambridge: University Press, 2004), pp. 545–62.

Lukács, György, 'Realism in the Balance', in *Aesthetics and Politics*, trans. Ronald Taylor (London: New Left, 1977), pp. 28–59. Originally published as 'Es geht um den Realismus', *Das Wort*, 1938.

Lyall, Sarah, 'Brigid Brophy is Dead at 66: Novelist, Critic and Crusader', *New York Times*, 9 August 1995, p. 20 <http://www.nytimes.com/1995/08/09/obituaries/brigid-brophy-is-dead-at-66-novelist-critic-and-crusader.html> (accessed 23 April 2019).

Maack, Annegret, 'Concordia Discors: Brigid Brophy's *In Transit*', *Review of Contemporary Fiction*, 15: 3 (1995), pp. 40–5.

Macaulay, Rose, 'The Future of Fiction', in John Lehmann (ed.), *New Writing and Daylight,* 7 (London: Hogarth Press, 1946), pp. 71–5.

MacCabe, Colin, *James Joyce and the Revolution of the Word* (London: Palgrave, 1979).

MacCabe, Colin, 'Realism and the Cinema: Notes on Some Brechtian Theses', *Screen*, 15: 2 (1974), pp. 7–27.

McCarthy, Helen, 'Women, Marriage and Paid Work in Post-war Britain', *Women's History Review*, 26: 1 (2017), pp. 46–61.

McHale, Brian, '"I draw the line as a rule between one solar system and another": The Postmodernism(s) of Christine Brooke-Rose', in Ellen J. Friedman and Richard Martin (eds), *Utterly Other Discourse: The Texts of Christine Brooke-Rose* (Chicago and Normal, IL: Dalkey Archive Press, 1995), pp. 192–213.

McHale, Brian, *Postmodernist Fiction* (London: Methuen, 1987).

MacKay, Marina, *Modernism and World War II* (Cambridge: Cambridge University Press, 2007).
MacKay, Marina and Lyndsey Stonebridge (eds), *British Fiction After Modernism: The Novel at Mid-Century* (Basingstoke: Palgrave, 2007).
McKay, Robert, 'Brigid Brophy's Pro-Animal Forms', *Contemporary Women's Writing*, 12: 2 (2018), pp. 152–70.
Mackay, Shena, 'Brigid Brophy: A Short Appreciation', *Contemporary Women's Writing*, 12: 2 (2018), pp. 264–7.
Mackrell, Judith, 'Ann Quin', in Jay L. Halio (ed.), *British Novelists Since 1960: Part 1, A–G, Dictionary of Literary Biography*, XIV (Detroit: Gale Research, 1983), pp. 608–14.
Mackrell, Judith, 'B. S. Johnson and the British Experimental Tradition: An Introduction', *Review of Contemporary Fiction*, 5: 2 (1985), pp. 42–64.
McLaughlin, Brian, *Structures of Identity: A Reading of the Self-Provoking Fiction of Christine Brooke-Rose, Bryan Stanley Johnson, Eva Figes, and Paul West* (Michigan: UMI Dissertation Services, 1981).
Maitland, Sara (ed.), *Very Heaven: Looking Back at the 1960s* (London: Virago, 1988).
Mao, Douglas and Rebecca L. Walkowitz, 'The New Modernist Studies', *PMLA*, 123: 3 (2008), pp. 737–48.
Marcus, Frank, *The Killing of Sister George* (New York: Random House, 1965).
Marcus, Laura, 'Feminist Aesthetics and the New Realism', in Isobel Armstrong (ed.), *New Feminist Discourses: Critical Essays on Theories and Texts, Volume 2* (London: Routledge, 1992), pp. 11–25.
Marcuse, Herbert, *Eros and Civilisation: A Philosophical Inquiry into Freud* (Boston, MA: Beacon Press, 1955).
Marwick, Arthur, *British Society Since 1945: The Penguin Social History of Britain*, 4th edn (London: Penguin, 2003).Mellor, Leo, *Reading the Ruins: Modernism, Bombsites and British Culture* (Cambridge: Cambridge University Press, 2011).
Memmi, Albert, *The Colonizer and Colonized* (New York: Orion Press, 1965). Originally published as *Portrait du colonisé, précédé par portrait du colonisateur* (Paris: Éditions Corrêa, Buchet/Chastel, 1957).
Michael, Magali Cornier, *Feminism and the Postmodern Impulse: Post-World War II Fiction* (Albany: State University of New York Press, 1996).
Miller, Casey and Kate Swift, *The Handbook of Non-Sexist Writing for Writers, Editors and Speakers* (London: Women's Press, 1981).
Miller, Tyrus, *Late Modernism: Politics, Fiction, and the Arts between the World Wars* (Berkeley: University of California Press (1999).
Millett, Kate, *Sexual Politics* (New York: Columbia University Press, 1970).
Mitchell, Juliet, 'Women: The Longest Revolution', *New Left Review*, 40 (November–December 1966), pp. 11–37.
Mitchell, Juliet, *Women: The Longest Revolution: Essays in Feminism, Literature and Psychoanalysis* (London: Virago, 1984).
Mitchell, Kaye, 'Post-War Fiction: Realism and Experimentation', in Clare Hanson and Susan Watkins (eds), *The History of British Women's Writing 1945–1975* (London: Macmillan, 2017), pp. 19–36.
Mitchell, Kaye, 'Introduction: The Gender Politics of Experiment', *Contemporary Women's Writing*, 9: 1 (2015), pp. 1–15.

Mitchell, Kaye and Nonia Williams (eds), *British Avant-Garde Fiction of the 1960s* (Edinburgh: Edinburgh University Press, 2019).
Mitchison, Lois, 'Future Shock', *Guardian*, 30 June 1987 <https://static.guim.co.uk/sys-images/Guardian/Pix/pictures/2015/1/6/1420548422496/Lois-Mitchison-30-June-19-001.jpg> (accessed 8 May 2020).
Mitchison, Lois, 'From the Archive, 8 January 1960: The Price of Educating Women', *Guardian,* 8 January 2015 <https://www.theguardian.com/education/2015/jan/08/women-careers-higher-education-archive-1960> (accessed 14 May 2020).
Monsarrat, Nicholas, 'Review of *Flesh*', *New York Times Book Review*, 2 June 1963.
Moore, Steven, 'Brigid Brophy: An Introduction and Checklist', *Review of Contemporary Fiction*, 15: 3 (1995), pp. 7–11.
Morgan, Robin, *Sisterhood is Powerful: An Anthology of Writings from the Women's Liberation Movement* (New York: Random House, 1970).
Morley, Loraine, 'The Love Affairs of Ann Quin', *Hungarian Journal of English and American Studies,* 5: 2 (1999), pp. 127–41.
Motte Jr, Warren F. (ed.), *Oulipo: A Primer of Potential Literature* (Lincoln, NE: University of Nebraska Press, 1986).
Munton, Alan, *English Fiction of the Second World War* (London: Faber and Faber, 1989).
Murdoch, Iris, 'Against Dryness: A Polemical Sketch', in Malcolm Bradbury (ed.), *The Novel Today: Contemporary Writers on Modern Fiction* (London: Fontana, 1977), pp. 23–31. Originally published in *Encounter*, January 1961.
Murdoch, Iris, *Living on Paper: Letters from Iris Murdoch 1934–1995*, ed. Avril Horner and Ann Rowe (London: Chatto and Windus, 2015).
Myrdal, Alva and Viola Klein, *Women's Two Roles: Home and Work* (London: Routledge & Kegan Paul, 1968 [1956]).
Nelson, Victoria, *The Secret Life of Puppets* (Cambridge, MA and London: Harvard University Press, 2001).
Nelson, Victoria, 'Symmes Hole, or the South Polar Romance', *Raritan*, 17: 2 (1997), pp. 136–66.
Neumeier, Beate, 'Reading Matters: "Marginal" British Jewish Writers', in David Brauner and Axel Stähler (eds), *The Edinburgh Companion to Modern Jewish Fiction* (Edinburgh: Edinburgh University Press, 2015), pp. 279–88.
Newman, S. J., 'Brigid Brophy', in Jay L. Halio (ed.), *British Novelists Since 1960: Part 1, A–G, Dictionary of Literary Biography*, XIV (Detroit: Gale Research, 1983), pp. 137–8.
Nicholls, Peter, *Modernisms: A Literary Guide* (London: Macmillan, 1995).
Nicholls, Peter, 'Surrealism in England', in Laura Marcus and Peter Nicholls (eds), *The Cambridge History of Twentieth-Century English Literature* (Cambridge: Cambridge: University Press, 2004), pp. 396–416.
Nin, Anaïs, *The Diary of Anaïs Nin: Volume VI, 1955–1966*, ed. Gunther Stuhlmann (New York: Harcourt Brace Jovanovich, 1976).
Nin, Anaïs, *The Novel of the Future* (New York: Macmillan, 1986 [New York: Macmillan, 1968]).
Nye, Robert, 'Against the Barbarians', *Guardian*, 27 April 1972, p. 15.
Nye, Robert, 'Anna Kavan', in George Woodcock (ed.), *Twentieth-Century Fiction* (London: Macmillan, 1983), pp. 346–8.

Oakley, Ann, *Housewife* (London: Allen Lane, 1974).
Oakley, Ann, *The Sociology of Housework* (New York: Pantheon Books, 1974).
Oates, Joyce Carol, 'Book Review', review of *Asylum Piece* and *Sleep Has His House*, *New York Times*, 1 June 1980, p. 14.
O'Connor, William Van, *The New University Wits and the End of Modernism* (Carbondale: Southern Illinois University Press, 1963).
Olsen, Tillie, 'One Out of Twelve: Writers Who Are Women in Our Century', in *Silences* (New York: Feminist Press, 2003 [New York: Delacorte Press/ Seymour Lawrence, 1978]), pp. 22–46. First published as 'Women Who are Writers in Our Century: One out of Twelve', *College English*, 34: 1 (1972), pp. 6–17. Originally an address at the Modern Language Association Forum on Women Writers in the Twentieth Century, 1971.
Onega, Susana, 'Affective Knowledge, Self-Awareness and the Function of Myth in the Representation and Transmission of Trauma: The Case of Eva Figes' *Konek Landing*', *Journal of Literary Theory*, 6: 1 (2012), pp. 83–102.
Onega, Susana and Jean-Michel Ganteau (eds), *Ethics and Trauma in Contemporary British Fiction* (Amsterdam and New York: Rodopi, 2011).
Orlando: Women's Writing in the British Isles from the Beginnings to the Present <http://orlando.cambridge.org> (accessed 20 April 2019).Osborne, John, *Look Back in Anger: A Play in Three Acts* (London: Faber, 1953).
Owen, Peter, (ed.), *Everything is Nice, and Other Fiction: The Peter Owen 50th Anniversary Anthology* (London: Peter Owen, 2001).
Owen, Peter, 'Introduction', in Anna Kavan, *Asylum Piece and Other Stories* (London: Peter Owen, 2001 [London: Jonathan Cape, 1940]).
Pakenham, Frank, Earl of Longford, *Pornography: The Longford Report* (London: Coronet Press, 1972).
Park, Clara Claiborne, 'Book World', *Washington Post*, 18 August 1974.
Parker, Peter, '"Aggressive, witty, & unrelenting": Brigid Brophy and Ronald Firbank', *Review of Contemporary Fiction*, 15: 3 (1995), pp. 68–78.
Parlati, Marilena, '"Treble Exposure": Fissured Memory in Eva Figes' Fiction', in Helen Thomas (ed.), *Malady and Mortality: Illness, Disease and Death in Literary and Visual Culture* (Cambridge: Cambridge Scholars, 2016), pp. 129–43.
Patterson, Ian, 'Her Body or the Sea', *London Review of Books*, 40: 12 (21 June 2018) <https://www.lrb.co.uk/v40/n12/ian-patterson/her-body-or-the-sea> (accessed 21 May 2019).
Pellicer-Ortín, Silvia, 'The Ethical Clock of Trauma in Eva Figes' *Winter Journey*', in Susana Onega and Jean-Michel Ganteau (eds), *Ethics and Trauma in Contemporary British Fiction* (Amsterdam and New York: Rodopi, 2011), pp 37–60.
Pellicer-Ortín, Silvia, *Eva Figes's Writings: A Journey Through Trauma* (Cambridge: Cambridge Scholars, 2015).
Pellicer-Ortín, Silvia, 'Intertextuality and the Working Through of Trauma in Eva Figes', in Rafael Galán Moya (ed.), *Tales of Innocence and Experience* (Cadiz: Servicio de Publicaciones de la Universidad de Cádiz, 2010), pp. 96–105.
Pellicer-Ortín, Silvia, 'Testimony and the Representation of Trauma in Eva Figes' *Journey to Nowhere*', *Atlantis: Journal of the Spanish Association of Anglo-American Studies*, 33: 1 (2011), pp. 69–84.

Perec, Georges, *La Disparition* (Paris: Denoël, 1969).
Phelps, Robert, '*In Transit*, a Novel by Brigid Brophy, Reviewed', *Life*, 13 February 1970, p. 10.
Philips, Deborah, *Women's Fiction: From 1945 to Today: Writing Romance* (London: Continuum, 2006).
Piette, Adam, *The Literary Cold War: 1945 to Vietnam* (Edinburgh: Edinburgh University Press, 2009).
Plain, Gill (ed.), *British Literature in Transition, 1940–1960: Post-war* (Cambridge: Cambridge University Press, 2018).
Plain, Gill, *Literature of the 1940s: War, Postwar and 'Peace'*, The Edinburgh History of Twentieth-Century Literature, V (Edinburgh: Edinburgh University Press, 2013).
Plain, Gill, *Present*, 2nd edn, 2 vols (London: Eurospan, 1972).
Pound, Ezra, *The Selected Letters of Ezra Pound, 1907–1941*, ed. D. D. Paige (New York: New Directions, 1970 [New York: Harcourt Brace Jovanovich, 1950]).
Powell, Anthony, *A Dance to the Music of Time* (London: Heinemann, 1951–75).
Pugh, Martin, *Women and the Women's Movement in Britain, Since 1914*, 2nd edn (London: Palgrave, 2000 [Basingstoke: Macmillan, 1992]).
Quin, Ann, *Berg* (Chicago and Normal, IL: Dalkey Archive Press, 2001 [London: John Calder, 1964]).
Quin, Ann, 'Every Cripple Has His Own Way of Walking', *Nova*, December 1966, pp. 127–35.
Quin, Ann, 'Eyes that Watch behind the Wind', in Samuel Beckett et al., *A Signature Anthology*, 20 (London: Calder and Boyars, 1975), pp. 131–49.
Quin, Ann, 'From *The Unmapped Country*: An Unfinished Novel', in Giles Gordon (ed.), *Beyond the Words: Eleven Writers in Search of a New Fiction* (London: Hutchinson, 1975), pp. 252–74.
Quin, Ann, 'Ghostworm', in Keith Jafrate et al. (eds), *Tak Tak Tak*: No. 6 (London: Art Data, 1993), pp. 61-89.
Quin, Ann, interview with Nell Dunn, in Nell Dunn (ed.), *Talking to Women* (London: Silver Press, 2018 [MacGibbon & Kee, 1965]).
Quin, Ann, 'Leaving School – XI', *London Magazine* 6: 4 (July 1966), pp. 63–8.
Quin, Ann, 'Motherlogue', *The Transatlantic Review*, 32 (1969), pp. 101–5.
Quin, Ann, *Passages* (Chicago and Normal, IL: Dalkey Archive Press, 2003 [London: Calder and Boyars, 1969]).
Quin, Ann, 'Reads from *Three*', *Extensions of Poetry* <https://duende.band camp.com/album/ann-quin-reads-from-three> (accessed 1 May 2019).
Quin, Ann, *Three* (Chicago and Normal, IL: Dalkey Archive Press, 2001 [London: Calder and Boyars, 1966]).
Quin, Ann, *Tripticks* (Chicago and Normal, IL: Dalkey Archive Press, 2002 [London: Calder and Boyars, 1972]).
Quin, Ann, *The Unmapped Country: Stories and Fragments*, ed. Jennifer Hodgson (Sheffield, London and New Haven, CT: And Other Stories, 2018).
Quin, Ann and Robert Sward, 'Living in the Present', *Ambit*, 34 (1968), pp. 20–1.
Raban, Jonathan, 'Family Scrapbook', *New Statesman*, 5 September 1969, p. 315.

Rabinowitz, Rubin, *The Reaction against Experiment in the English Novel, 1950–60* (New York: Columbia University Press, 1967).
Rabinowitz, Rubin, 'The Reaction against Modernism: Amis, Snow, Wilson', in John Richetti, John Bender, Deirdre David and Michael Seidel (eds), *The Columbia History of the British Novel* (New York: Columbia University Press, 1994), pp. 895–927.
Radway, Janice, *A Feeling for Books: Book-of-the-Month Club, Literary Taste and Middle-Class Desire* (Chapel Hill: University of North Caroline Press, 1997).
Rao, Eleonora, '"The Black Sun": Anna Kavan's Narratives of Abjection', *Textus*, 4 (1991), pp. 119–46.
Rasp, Renate, *A Family Failure: A Novel*, trans. Eva Figes (London: Calder and Boyars).
Raven, Simon, 'Brophy and Brigid', *The Spectator*, 25 November 1966, p. 21.
Reed, Jeremy, 'A Stranger on Earth, by Doris Lessing: Ice in an Outlaw's Heart', *Independent*, 7 July 2006 <https://www.independent.co.uk/arts-entertainment/books/reviews/a-stranger-on-earth-by-doris-lessing-6096149.html> (accessed 18 May 2020).
Reed, Jeremy, *A Stranger on Earth: The Life and Work of Anna Kavan* (London: Peter Owen, 2006).
Reese, Sam, 'Renaissance Women: Brigid Brophy, Mary McCarthy, and the Public Intellectual', *Contemporary Women's Writing* 12: 2 (2018), pp. 207–21.
Resnais, Alain (dir.), *L'année dernière à Marienbad*, screenplay Alain Robbe-Grillet, 1961.
Reyes, Heather, 'The British and Their "Fixions," The French and Their Factions', in Ellen G. Friedman and Richard Martin (eds), *Utterly Other Discourse* (Chicago and Normal, IL: Dalkey Archive Press, 1995), pp. 52–63.
Reyes, Heather, 'Delectable Metarealism/Ethical Experiments: Re-reading Christine Brooke-Rose' (unpublished doctoral thesis, Birkbeck, University of London, 1998).
Reynolds, Paige, 'Colleen Modernism: Modernism's Afterlife in Irish Women's Writing', *Éire-Ireland: A Journal of Irish Studies*, 44: 3 (2009), pp. 94–117.
Robbe-Grillet, Alain, *For a New Novel: Essays on Fiction* (New York: Grove Press, 1965). Originally published as *Pour un nouveau roman* (Paris: Les Éditions de Minuit, 1963).
Robbe-Grillet, Alain, *La Jalousie* (Paris: Les Éditions de Minuet, 1957).
Robbe-Grillet, Alain, *Snapshots and Towards a New Novel*, trans. Barbara Wright (London: Calder and Boyars, 1965). Originally published as *Instantanés* (Paris Les Éditions de Minuit, 1962) and *Pour un nouveau roman* (Paris: Les Éditions de Minuit, 1963).
Robinson, Jill, 'Anna Kavan Transformed Her Pain to Art', *New York Times Book Review*, 11 May 1975, pp. 47–8.
Rolleston Report, Ministry of Health, Departmental Committee on Morphine and Heroin Addiction (London: HMSO, 1926).
Rose, Jacqueline, 'This is not a Biography', *London Review of Books*, 24: 16 (22 August 2002), pp. 12–15 <https://www.lrb.co.uk/v24/n16/jacqueline-rose/this-is-not-a-biography> (accessed 12 April 2019).

Rowbotham, Sheila, *A Century of Women: The History of Women in Britain and the United States* (London: Penguin, 1999).

Rowbotham, Sheila, *The Past is Before Us: Feminism in Action Since the 1960s* (London: Pandora, 1989).

Rowbotham, Sheila, *Promise of a Dream: Remembering the Sixties* (London: Allen Lane, 2000).

Royal Pharmaceutical Society Museum, 'Drugs for Pleasure, Drugs for Pain? Developing Treatments with Controlled Drugs Part Two: Opium, Morphine, & Heroin' (2011) <https://www.rpharms.com/museum-pdfs/controlled-drugs---opium--morphine-and-heroin.pdf> (accessed 1 October 2016).

Rubenstein, Roberta, 'The Feminist Novel in the Wake of Virginia Woolf', in Brian W. Shaffer (ed.), *A Companion to the British and Irish Novel, 1945–2000* (Oxford: Blackwell, 2005), pp. 45–64.

Ryle, Martin and Julia Jordan (eds), *B. S. Johnson and Postwar Literature: Possibilities of the Avant-Garde* (London: Palgrave, 2014).

Sage, Lorna, *Moments of Truth: Twelve Twentieth-Century Women Writers* (London: Fourth Estate, 2001).

Sage, Lorna, 'A Place for Displacement', *Times Literary Supplement*, 12 August 1994, p. 21.

Sage, Lorna, 'Review of Amalgamemnon', *The Observer*, 18 November 1984, p. 29.

Sand, George, *Little Fadette*, trans. Eva Figes (London: Blackie, 1967).

Sarraute, Nathalie, *The Age of Suspicion: Essays on The Novel*, trans. Maria Jolas (New York: George Braziller, 1963). Originally published as *L'Ère du soupçon* (Paris: Gallimard, 1956).

Sarraute, Nathalie, *Portrait of a Man Unknown*, trans. Maria Jolas (New York: G. Braziller, 1958). Originally published as *Portrait d'un inconnu* (Paris: Robert Marin, 1948).

Sarraute, Nathalie, *Tropisms*, trans. Maria Jolas (London: John Calder, 1963). Originally published as *Tropismes* (Paris: Denoël, 1939).

Sartre, Jean-Paul, *Being and Nothingness: An Essay on Phenomenological Ontology*, trans. Sarah Richmond (London: Routledge). Originally published as *L'Être et le néant* (Paris: Gallimard, 1943).

Schabert, Ina, 'Translation Trouble: Gender Indeterminacy in English Novels and Their French Versions', *Translation and Literature*, 19: 1 (2010) pp. 72–92.

Scholes, Robert, *The Fabulators* (New York: Oxford University Press, 1967).

Sedgwick, Eve Kosofsky, *Epistemology of the Closet* (Berkeley: University of California Press, 1990).

Sedgwick, Eve Kosofsky, *Tendencies* (Durham, NC: Duke University Press, 1993).

Sedgwick, Peter, *Nietzsche: The Key Concepts* (London: Routledge, 2009).

Sewell, Brocard, *Like Black Swans: Some People and Themes* (Padstow: Tabb House, 1982).

Shelden, Michael, *Friends of Promise: Cyril Connolly and the World of Horizon* (London: Hamish Hamilton, 1989).

Shenker, Israel, 'Brigid Brophy Puns in Response to Questionnaire', *New York Times*, 27 February 1970, p. 28 <https://www.nytimes.com/1970/02/27/

archives/brigid-brophy-puns-in-response-to-questionnaire> (accessed 10 April 2019).

Showalter, Elaine, *A Literature of Their Own: British Women Novelists: From Bronte to Lessing*, rev. edn (Princeton, NJ: Princeton University Press, 1999 [1977]).

Shrapnel, Norman, 'Between Prophecy and Fantasy', *Guardian*, 13 November 1964.

Sloan, Mary Margaret (ed.), *Moving Borders: Three Decades of Innovative Writing by Women* (Jersey City: Talisman House, 1998).

Smith, Ali, *The Accidental* (London: Hamish Hamilton, 2005).

Smith, Ali, 'The Armchair, the World', *Times Literary Supplement*, 24 March 2006, p. 21.

Smith, Ali, sleeve notes, Brigid Brophy, *The King of a Rainy Country* (London: Coelacanth Press, 2012).

Smith, Patricia Juliana, 'Desperately Seeking Susan[na]: Closeted Quests and Mozartean Gender Bending in Brigid Brophy's *The King of a Rainy Country*', *Review of Contemporary Fiction*, 15: 3 (1995), pp. 23–31.

Snow, C. P., *The Two Cultures* (Cambridge: Cambridge University Press, 1993). Originally published as *The Rede Lecture, 1959: The Two Cultures and the Scientific Revolution* (Cambridge, Cambridge University Press, 1959).

Sontag, Susan, 'Notes on "Camp"', *Partisan Review*, 31: 4 (1964), pp. 515–30.

Spark, Muriel, *The Comforters* (London: Macmillan, 1957).

Spark, Muriel, *Loitering with Intent* (London: Bodley Head, 1981).

Spender, Dale, *Man Made Language* (London: Routledge & Kegan Paul, 1980).

Stade, George and Karen Karbiener (eds), *Encyclopedia of British Writers: 1800 to the Present*, 2nd edn, 2 vols (London: Eurospan, 2005–9).

Stavans, Anat and Charlotte Hoffmann (eds), *Multilingualism* (Cambridge: Cambridge University Press, 2015).

Stein, Thomas Michael, 'Inscribing the Holocaust into the Modern Gothic Novel: Eva Figes' *The Tenancy*', in Ulrike Behlau and Bernhard Reitz (eds), *Jewish Women's Writing of the 1990s and Beyond in Great Britain and the United States* (Trier, Germany: Wissenschaftlicher Verlag Trier, 2004), pp. 153–61.

Stevenson, Randall, *The British Novel Since the Thirties: An Introduction* (London: Batsford Ltd, 1986).

Stevenson, Randall, *Modernist Fiction: An Introduction,* (New York and London: Harvester Wheatsheaf, 1992).

Stevenson, Sheryl, 'Language and Gender in Transit: Feminist Extensions of Bakhtin', in Dale M. Bauer and Susan Jaret McKinstry (eds), *Feminism, Bakhtin, and the Dialogic* (Albany, NY: State University of New York Press, 1991), pp. 181–98.

Stevenson, Sheryl, 'The Never-Last Word: Parody, Ideology, and the Open Work' (thesis, University of Maryland, 1986).

Stevick, Philip (ed.), *Anti-Story: An Anthology of Experimental Fiction* (New York: The Free Press, 1971).

Stevick, Philip, 'Voices in the Head: Style and Consciousness in the Fiction of Ann Quin', in Ellen G. Friedman and Miriam Fuchs (eds), *Breaking the Sequence: Women's Experimental Fiction* (Princeton, NJ: Princeton University Press, 1989), pp. 231–9.

Stonebridge, Lyndsey, *The Writing of Anxiety: Imagining Wartime in Mid-Century British Culture* (Basingstoke: Palgrave Macmillan, 2007).

Stringer, Jenny (ed.), *The Oxford Companion of Twentieth-Century Literature in English* (Oxford: Oxford University Press, 1996).

Stuby, Anna Maria, 'Eva Figes's Novels', in Beate Neumeier (ed.), *Engendering Realism and Postmodernism: Contemporary Women Writers in Britain* (Amsterdam: Rodopi, 2001), pp. 105–16.

Stuby, Anna Maria, '"A piece of shrapnel lodges in my flesh, and when it moves, I write": The Fiction of Eva Figes', in Anna Maria Stuby and Irmgard Maassen (eds), *(Sub)Versions of Realism: Recent Women's Fiction in Britain* (Heidelberg: Universitätsverlag C. Winter, 1997), pp. 113–27.

Stuhlmann, Gunther, 'Anna Kavan Revisited, the Web of Unreality', *Anaïs: An International Journal*, 3 (1985), pp. 55–62.

Sturm, Jennifer, 'Anna Kavan', *The Literary Encyclopedia*, 30 October 2007 <http://www.litencyc.com/php/speople.php?rec=true&UID=2441> (accessed 16 January 2018).

Sturm, Jennifer (ed.), *Anna Kavan's New Zealand: A Pacific Interlude in a Turbulent Life* (Auckland: Vintage, 2009).

Sturm, Jennifer, 'Fictionalising the Facts: An Exploration of the "Place" of Aotearoa/ New Zealand in the Post-War Autobiographical Fiction of Anna Kavan' (unpublished doctoral dissertation, University of Auckland, 2006).

Sturm, Jennifer, 'Introduction', in Anna Kavan, *Guilty* (London: Peter Owen, 2007).

Sukenick, Ronald, *In Form: Digressions on the Act of Fiction* (Carbondale: Southern Illinois University Press, 1985).

Suleiman, Susan Rubin, *Subversive Intent: Gender, Politics, and the Avant-Garde* (Cambridge, MA: Harvard University Press, 1990).

Sward, Robert, Robert Sward Papers, MSS110, 1951–1971, Department of Special Collections, Washington University Libraries, St Louis.

Sweeney, Carole, 'Cadaverized Girls: The Writing of Anna Kavan', *Textual Practice*, 31: 2 (2017), pp. 1–22.

Sweeney, Carole, 'The Dissenting Feminist', in Richard Canning and Gerri Kimber (eds), *Brigid Brophy: Avant-Garde Writer, Critic, Activist* (Edinburgh University Press, 2020) pp. 220–34.

Sweeney, Carole, '"Groping inside language": Translation, Humour and Experiment in Christine Brooke-Rose's *Between* and Brigid Brophy's *In Transit*', *Textual Practice*, 32: 2 (2018), pp. 301–16.

Sweeney, Carole, '"Keeping the ruins private": Anna Kavan and Heroin Addiction', *Women: A Cultural Review*, 28: 4 (2017), pp. 312–26.

Sweeney, Carole, '"Why this rather than that?": The Delightful Perversity of Brigid Brophy', *Contemporary Women's Writing*, 12: 2 (2018), pp. 233–47.

Szreter, Simon and Kate Fisher (eds), *Sex Before the Sexual Revolution: Intimate life in England, 1918–1963* (Cambridge: Cambridge University Press, 2010).

Taylor, D. J., *After the War: The Novel and English Society Since 1945* (London: Chatto & Windus, 1993).

Tew, Philip, *The Contemporary British Novel* (London: Continuum, 2004).

Thane, Pat, 'Women Since 1945', in Paul Johnson (ed.), *Twentieth-Century Britain: Economic, Social, and Cultural Change* (London: Longman, 1994), pp. 392–411.

Thomas, Nick, 'Will the Real 1950s Please Stand Up? Views of a Contradictory Decade', *Cultural and Social History*, 5: 2 (2008), pp. 227–35.
Todd, Janet, *Feminist Literary History* (Cambridge: Polity Press, 1988).
Tofantšuk, Julia, *Construction of Identity in the Fiction of Contemporary British Women Writers: Jeanette Winterson, Meera Syal and Eva Figes* (Tallinn: Tallinn University Press, 2007).
Tofantšuk, Julia, 'Time, Space and (Her)Story in the Fiction of Eva Figes', in Ann Heilmann and Mark Llewellyn (eds), *Metafiction and Metahistory in Contemporary Women's Writing* (Basingstoke: Palgrave Macmillan, 2007), pp. 59–72.
Trilling, Lionel, *The Liberal Imagination: Essays on Literature and Society* (New York: Viking Press, 1950).
Tucker, Eva, 'Eva Figes Obituary', *Guardian*, 7 September 2012 <https://www.theguardian.com/ books/2012/sep/07/eva-figes> (accessed 12 April 2018).
Upchurch, Anna, 'John Maynard Keynes, the Bloomsbury Group and the Origins of the Arts Council Movement,' *International Journal of Cultural Policy*, 10: 2 (2004), pp. 203–17.
Usandizaga, Aranzazu, 'Childhood and Self in Eva Figes' *Little Eden*', in James Olney (ed.), *Studies in Autobiography* (Oxford: Oxford University Press, 1988), pp. 207–14.
Valman, Nadia (ed.), *Jewish Women Writers in Britain* (Detroit: Wayne State University Press, 2014).
Venuti, Lawrence, 'Translation, Empiricism, Ethics', *Profession*, 10 (2010), pp. 72–81.
Verdon, Cheryl, 'Forgotten Words: Trauma, Memory and Herstory in Eva Figes's Fiction', in Nadia Valman (ed.), *Jewish Women Writers in Britain* (Detroit: Wayne State Univeristy Press, 2014), pp. 116–34.
Vichnar, David, 'The Avant Postman: James Joyce, the Avant Garde and Postmodernism' (unpublished doctoral thesis, Université de la Sorbonne Nouvelle, 2013).
Vincent-Arnaud, Nathalie, '"A fading syllable drifting in mist": Leaving Behind Otherness, or the Linguistic Reconstruction of the Self in Eva Figes's Autobiographical Writing', *Interstudia*, 1 (2008), pp. 28–34.
Vinson, James (ed.), *Contemporary Novelists* (London: St James Press, 1972).
Walker, Victoria, 'The Fiction of Anna Kavan (1901–1968)' (unpublished doctoral thesis, Queen Mary, University of London, 2012).
Walker, Victoria, 'Hearts and Minds: War Neurosis and the Politics of Madness in Anna Kavan's *I am Lazarus*', *Women: A Cultural Review*, 28: 4 (2017), pp. 375–90.
Walker, Victoria, 'An Introduction to Anna Kavan: New Readings', *Women: A Cultural Review*, 28: 4 (2017), pp. 285–94.
Walker, Victoria, 'Ornithology and Ontology: The Existential Birdcall in Jean Rhys's *Wide Sargasso Sea* and Anna Kavan's *Who are You?*', *Women: A Cultural Review*, 23: 4 (2012), pp. 490–509.
Walser, Martin, *The Gadarene Club*, trans. Eva Figes (London: Longmans, 1960).
Ward, Geoff, 'The Wibberlee Wobberlee Walk: Lowry, Hamilton, Kavan and the Addictions of 1940s Fiction', in Rod Mengham and N. H. Reeve

(eds), *The Fiction of the 1940s: Stories of Survival* (Basingstoke: Palgrave Macmillan, 2001), pp. 26–45.

Wardle, Irving, 'Twilight in St Petersburg', *The Observer*, 3 September 1967, p. 23.

Warnock, Mary, 'A Hard Time for Satire, *The Listener*, 6 December 1973, pp. 785–6.

Wasson, Sara, *Urban Gothic of the Second World War: Dark London* (Basingstoke: Palgrave Macmillan, 2010).

Watkins, Peter, *The War Game*, directed by Peter Watkins, BBC Wednesday Play Series, 1965.

Waugh, Evelyn, *Brideshead Revisited* (London: Chapman and Hall, 1945).

Waugh, Patricia, 'Feminism and Writing: The Politics of Culture', in Laura Marcus and Peter Nicholls (eds), *The Cambridge History of Twentieth Century Literature* (Cambridge: Cambridge: University Press, 2004), pp. 600–17.

Waugh, Patricia, *Feminist Fictions: Revisiting the Postmodern* (London: Routledge, 1989).

Waugh, Patricia, *Harvest of the Sixties: English Literature and its Background, 1960 to 1990* (Oxford: Oxford University Press, 1995).

Waugh, Patricia, 'The Woman Writer and the Continuities of Feminism', in James F. English (ed.), *A Concise Companion to Contemporary British Fiction* (Oxford: Blackwell, 2006), pp. 188–209.

Webb, Bill, 'Winning Work of Fiction', *Guardian*, 25 November 1967, p. 3.

Wells, Juliette, 'Eva Figes', in Merrit Moseley (ed.), *British and Irish Novelists Since 1960* (Detroit: Thomson Gale, 2003), pp. 130–8.

Wheeler, Kathleen, *A Critical Guide to Twentieth-Century Women Novelists* (Oxford: Blackwell, 1997).

White, Glyn, *Reading the Graphic Surface: The Presence of the Book in Prose Fiction* (Manchester: Manchester University Press, 2005).

Whitehead, Peter (dir.), *Wholly Communion*, Lorrimer Films, 1965.

Williams, Nonia, '"Infuriating" Experiments?', in Kaye Mitchell and Nonia Williams (eds), *British Avant-Garde Fiction of the 1960s* (Edinburgh: Edinburgh University Press, 2019), pp. 193–214.

Williams Korteling, Nonia, 'Designing Its Own Shadow: Reading Ann Quin' (unpublished dissertation, University of East Anglia, 2013).

Williams, Raymond, 'The Arts Council', *The Political Quarterly*, 50: 2 (1979), pp. 157–71.

Williams, Raymond, *The Long Revolution* (Harmondsworth: Penguin, 1965 [London: Chatto & Windus, 1961]).

Williams, Raymond, 'Middlemen: The Arts Council', in Raymond Williams, *What I Came to Say*, ed. Neil Belton, Frances Mulhern and Jenny Taylor (London: Hutchinson Radius, 1989), pp. 98–107.

Williams, Raymond, 'Realism and the Contemporary Novel', *Universities and Left Review*, 4 (Summer 1948), pp. 22–4.

Williamson, Henry, *Tarka the Otter: His Joyful Water-Life and Death in the Country of the Two Rivers* (London: Chiswick Press, 1927).

Wilson, Colin, 'Introduction', in Brocard Sewell, *Like Black Swans: Some People and Themes* (Padstow: Tabb House, 1982).

Wilson, Elizabeth, *Only Halfway to Paradise: Women in Postwar Britain, 1945–1968* (London: Tavistock Publications, 1980).
Wilson, Janet, 'A Pacific Sojourn: Anna Kavan and the New Zealand Connection, 1941-2', *Women: A Cultural Review*, 28: 4 (2017), pp. 343–57.
Wilson, Leigh, 'Anna Kavan's *Ice* and Alan Burns' *Europe After the Rain*: Repetition with a Difference', *Women: A Cultural Review*, 28: 4 (2017), p. 328.
Wittig, Monique, 'The Mark of Gender', in Nancy K. Miller (ed.), *The Poetics of Gender* (New York: Columbia University Press, 1986), pp. 63–73.
Witts, Richard, *Artist Unknown: An Alternative History of the Arts Council* (London: Little Brown, 1998).
Wolfe, Gary K., *Evaporating Genres: Essays on Fantastic Literature* (Middletown, CT: Wesleyan University Press, 2011).
Wolff, Janet, 'Eddie Cochran, Donna Anna and the Dark Sister', in Janet Wolff, *Resident Alien: Feminist Cultural Criticism* (New Haven, CT: Yale University Press, 1995), pp. 23–40.
Woodburn, John, *The Saturday Review*, 23 August 1947, Anna Kavan Papers, 1867–1991, McFarlin Library, The University of Tulsa.
Woodcock, George (ed.), *Twentieth-Century Fiction* (London: Palgrave Macmillan, 1983).
Woolf, Virginia, *The Common Reader: Volume 1*, rev. edn, ed. Andrew McNeillie (London: Vintage, 1984, 2003 [London: Hogarth Press, 1925]).
Woolf, Virginia, *The Diary of Virginia Woolf: Volume 3, 1925–1930*, ed. Anne Olivier Bell and Andrew McNeillie (London: Hogarth Press, 1980).
Woolf, Virginia, 'Middlebrow', in *The Death of the Moth and Other Essays* (New York: Harcourt Brace Jovanovich, 1974 [London: Hogarth Press, 1942]), pp. 180–4.
Woolf, Virginia, 'Mr. Bennett and Mrs. Brown', in *Collected Essays: Volume I*, ed. Leonard Woolf (London: Hogarth Press, 1966), pp. 319–37. Originally published as 'Character in Fiction', *The Criterion*, 2: 8 (July 1924), pp. 409–30.
Woolf, Virginia, *Orlando: A Biography* (New York: Harcourt Brace 1928 [London: Hogarth Press, 1928]).
Woolf, Virginia, 'Professions for Women', in *The Death of the Moth and Other Essays* (New York: Harcourt Brace Jovanovich, 1974 [London: Hogarth Press, 1942]), pp. 236–42. Originally an address to National Society for Women's Service, 21 January 1931.
Woolf, Virginia, *A Room of One's Own* (London: Hogarth Press, 1929).
Woolf, Virginia, *A Writer's Diary: Being Extracts from the Diary of Virginia Woolf*, ed. Leonard Woolf (London: Harcourt, 1953).
Young, Elizabeth, *Pandora's Handbag: Adventures in the Book World – Selected Prose Past and Present* (London: Serpent's Tail, 2001).
Yudkin, Simon and Anthea Holme, *Working Mothers and Their Children: A Study for the Council for Children's Welfare* (London: Joseph, 1963).
Zambreno, Kate, 'Anna Kavan: Context No. 18', Dalkeyarchive.com <http://www.dalkeyarchive.com/anna-kavan> (accessed 11 June 2014).

Index

Agee, James, *Let Us Now Praise Famous Men*, 44
Aldiss, Brian, 32, 40, 61, 66n
   The Detached Retina: Aspects of SF and Fantasy, 32, 66n
Allsop, Kenneth, 186
Amis, Kingsley, 13, 76, 90, 144
   Lucky Jim, 90
   on modernism, 119–20
Angry Young Men, 13
Apartheid, 138
   Pass laws, Bantu Act, 138
Arts Council, 157n, 169–70, 200n, 207, 211, 233
Austen, Jane, 82, 109

Baldick, Chris, 13, 15
Ballard, J. G., 62, 66n, 169
Barnes, Djuna, 21, 76
Barth, John, 250n
   'The Literature of Exhaustion', 168
Barthes, Roland, 16, 128, 131–2, 143, 217
   atopia, 131
   reality effect, 16
   'The Death of the Author', 128, 134
   The Pleasure of the Text, 143, 217
BBC, 11, 25n, 104, 112n, 114n, 156n
   Bookmark, 156n
   Brigid Brophy, 'A Woman's Place', 104
   Samira Ahmed, 25n
   Third Programme, 11
   Wednesday Play, 112n, 114n
Beardsley, Aubrey, 76, 81, 85, 94, 114n
de Beauvoir, Simone, 21, 105, 174, 250 n
Beckett, Samuel, 66n, 67n, 121, 126–7, 136, 173, 189, 219

Happy Days, 173
The Unnamable, 189
Watt, 126–7
Bergonzi, Bernard, 12–13, 25n
   The Situation of the Novel, 12
Berry, Ellen E., 17, 27 n, 251n
Birch, Sarah, 118, 123, 144
Bletchley Park, 21, 121–2, 155n
   CXMS, 122
   Ultra, 155n
Black Mountain Poets, 7, 226
Bluth, Karl Theodor, 44, 58, 60–1
   existential psychiatry, 44
   heroin, 58, 60–1
Booth, Francis, 32
Boxall, Peter, *The Value of the Novel*, 4, 251n
Boyars, Marion, 219, 233, 242n
Bradbury, Malcolm, 11–12, 14, 16, 251n
   modernism, 11–12
   'No, Not Bloomsbury', 11
   The Novel Today: Contemporary Writers on Modern Fiction, 14, 16
   The Modern British Novel, 251n
Brain Committee, 57
Braine, John, 13, 90, 97, 220
Brecht, Bertolt, 16, 27n, 251n
   on realism, 16, 27n
   Fredric Jameson, 28n
Brighton, 207, 208–9, 213
Brooke-Rose, Christine, 118–61
   A Grammar of Metaphor, 131
   A Rhetoric of the Unreal, 253n
   'A Womb of One's Own', 151
   A ZBC of Ezra Pound, 148
   Between, 126, 142–150
   father, 122–3

illness, 123
'Illiterations', 20, 149, 152
Invisible Author: Last Essays, 1, 128, 129–130, 252n
Out, 126–7, 133–142
Remake, 133
Stories, Theories, and Things, 125, 143, 152, 253n
The Dear Deceit, 123, 124
The Languages of Love, 123–4, 126
The Middlemen: A Satire, 123–4
Thru, 134
Women's Auxiliary Air Force, 121–2, 155n
Brophy, Brigid, 73–117
and Maureen Duffy, 6, 85, 169
Animal Rights Movement, 74, 77, 105
'Baroque method', 98
Baroque 'n' Roll, 77
Black and White: A Portrait of Aubrey Beardsley, 94, *114n*
Black Ship to Hell, 74
Don't Never Forget, 112n
Fifty Works of English and American Literature that We Could Do Without, 82
Flesh, 91–5
Hackenfeller's Ape, 80, 81, 88, 254n
In Transit, 7, 75–7, 79, 85, 88, 98–104, 106
Ireland, 79
and Maureen Duffy, 6, 85, 169
National Anti-Vivisection Society, 74
on Germaine Greer, 106–7
on Jane Austen, 82, 109, 112n
Prancing Novelist: In Praise of Ronald Firbank, 77, 81, 85
The Burglar, 74, 81, 83
The Finishing Touch, 81, 83
The King of a Rainy Country, 7, 80, 83, 86–91
'The Nation in the Iron Mask', 82
The Snowball, 112n, 96–9
'The Waste Disposal Unit', 82
Burns, Alan, 62, 77, 167–9, 209, 211, 225
Burns, Carol, 168, 217, 225, 241n, 242n
Burroughs, William, 169, 200n, 219
Junkie: Confessions of an Unredeemed Drug Addict, 255n
Butler, Judith, 103
Gender Trouble, 103 , 255n

Butor, Michel, 129
Byatt, A. S., 255n

Calder, John, 142, 169–70, 199n, 209–13, 218–9, 233
Callard, David, 33, 55
Canning, Richard and Gerri Kimber, *Brigid Brophy: Avant-Garde Writer, Critic, Activist*, 26n, 276n
Carter, Angela, 1, 6, 19–20, 66n, 109, 256n
The Sadeian Woman and the Ideology of Pornography, 19–20, 109
Castle, Terry, 83, 97, 112n, 115n, 256n
Cheyette, Brian, 194, 198n
Cixous, Hélène, 18, 95, 126, 132, 151
'Le Rire de la méduse', 18, 150
Clarke, Chris, 256n
Coe, Jonathan, 126, 167
Coleridge, Samuel Taylor
'Khubla Khan', 56–7, 133
Cold War, 62, 65, 71n
Creeley, Robert, 77, 210–2, 216–7, 219, 242n, 257n
Compton-Burnett, Ivy, 5, 21, 76, 247
Connolly, Cyril, 11, 44, 69n
Cross dressing, 87, 100–4, 217–9, 231
Berg, 217–9
hosenrolle, 87
In Transit, 100–4
Three, 231
travesti, 87
Cuban Missile Crisis, 62
Cunningham, Valentine, 41

Dangerous Drugs Act, 57
Davies, Rhys, 38, 40, 56
De Lauretis, Teresa, 88
'Queer theory', 88
Delaney, Shelagh, 26n, 90
Derrida, Jacques, 61, 120, 132
'The Rhetoric of Drugs', 61
Dick, Kay, 44
Divorce Reform Act, 10
Dock, Leslie Ann, 81, 98, 108
Driscoll, Lawrence, 55
Drugs, 38, 43, 55–61, 68N, 70n, 210, 239
cocaine, 55
heroin, 38, 43, 55–61, 68n, 70n
LSD and peyote, 210, 239
morphine, 55, 57
Duffy, Maureen, 6, 85, 169

Dunn, Nell, 114n, 214
  Talking to Women, 214
  Up The Junction, 268n
DuPlessis, Rachel Blau, 19

Eco, Umberto, 152, 158n
Edelman, Lee, 88
  Queer Theory and The Death Drive, 88
Edmonds, Stuart, 43
Écriture féminine, 6, 18, 20, 144, 150
Ellis, Havelock, 176
Equal Pay Act, 2

Fanon, Frantz, 138, 258n
  Les Damnés de la terre, 138
Faulkner, William, 187
Felski, Rita, 6, 18–20, 22, 29n
  Beyond Feminist Aesthetics: Feminist Literature and Social Change, 18–20, 22
Feminism, 2, 17–23, 74, 103–9, 125, 149–53, 165, 174–9, 216, 247
  1960s, 2–3, 17
  Ann Quin, 216
  Brigid Brophy, 7, 104–9
  Christine Brooke-Rose, 21, 125, 149–53
  Education, 10, 24n, 178
  Eva Figes, 165, 174–9
  French feminism, 21
Ferris, Natalie, 67n, 68n, 139
Figes, Eva, 162–204
  Equinox, 166, 180–6
  Jewishness, 162–5, 180, 185, 191–7, 198n
  Journey to Nowhere, 166, 193
  Konek Landing, 166, 178, 185, 191–7
  Little Eden: A Child at War, 163
  Nelly's Version, 165
  Patriarchal Attitudes: Women in Society, 2, 165, 175–9, 183
  Sex and Subterfuge: Women Writers to 1850, 165
  Tragedy and Social Evolution, 165
  Waking, 165
  Winter Journey, 165–6, 186–91
Firbank, Ronald, 76–8, 81, 85–6
Firestone, Shulamith, 175
  The Dialectic of Sex: The Case for Feminist Revolution, 175
Friedan, Betty, 105
  The Feminine Mystique, 105, 261n

Friedman, Ellen G., 121
Friedman, Ellen G. and Miriam Fuchs, 3, 5, 22, 162, 198n
Friedman, Ellen G. and Richard Martin, *Utterly Other Discourse* 252n
Freud, Sigmund, 74, 93–4, 176, 217
  'Mourning and Melancholia', 46, 261n
  decathexis, 46
  Oedipus Complex, 217

Garrity, Jane, 35, 40, 52, 58, 262n
Genet, Jean, 56, 95
Goldsmiths Prize, 247
Gordon, Giles, 11, 75, 211, 219, 222
  Beyond The Words: Eleven Writers in Search of a New Fiction, 211, 262n
Gornick, Vivian, 32, 40, 42, 57, 262n
Greene, Gayle, 17
Gąsiorek, Andrzej, 14, 16
Grass, Günter, 171
Green, André, 49
  'The Dead Mother', 51–3
  On Private Madness, 262n
Greer, Germaine, 2, 106–7, 116n
  The Female Eunuch, 198n, 262n, 263n
Gruppe 47, 199n
Guy, Adam 127, 156n

Hamilton, Ian, 44, 78–9
Harrison, Jane, 234–5
  Prolegomena to the Study of Greek Religion, 234–5
Heppenstall, Rayner, 168, 218, 263n
Hirsch, Marianne, 164, 264n
Hocquenghem, Guy, 88
Hodgson, Jennifer, 111n, 114n, 240n, 264n
Horizon, 45–5, 69n

International Poetry Incarnation, 210

James, David, 14–5, 26n, 27n, 264n
Jameson, Fredric, *Aesthetics and Politics*, 264n
Jarry, Alfred, 100, 225
  Ubu Roi, 225
Jewishness
  in Brophy, 92
  in Figes, 162–5, 180, 185, 191–7, 198n

Holocaust, 162–4
Kristallnacht, 162
Law on Tenancies, 194
Tales of Innocence and Experience: An Exploration, 165
Johnson, B. S., 31, 77, 130, 136, 166–71, 211, 226, 246
Jones, Stephanie, 265n
Jordan, Clive, 56
Jordan, Julia, 70n
Joyce, James, 3, 12–3, 15, 77–8, 107, 119, 173, 192, 222, 265n

Kavan, Anna, 31–72
  A Scarcity of Love, 51–2, 54, 56–7
  Asylum Piece, 46–52
  Guilty, 36
  heroin, 38, 43, 55–61, 68n, 70n
  I Am Lazarus, 31, 44
  Ice, 61–66
  Julia and The Bazooka, 53, 55, 58–61
  New Zealand, 44, 61, 66
  Sleep Has His House, 43, 46
  as Ferguson, Helen, 33, 35–6, 45
  A Charmed Circle, 35
  Let Me Alone, 38
Kafka, Franz, 32, 47–8, 61, 63, 66n, 172, 192, 265n, 266n
Kelly, Richard T., 93, 105
Kermode, Frank, 27n, 143, 157n, 160n, 170–1
Kitchen, Paddy, 220, 244n
Kristeva, Julia, 20, 22, 132, 151, 224
  abjection, 224
  Black Sun, 34, 41, 49–50, 52, 62
  'Women's Time', 151

Labour Party, 9–10, 24n, 169–70
Lady Chatterley Trial, 99
Langhamer, Claire, 9
Lauret, Maria, 17
Lawrence, Karen, 2, 77, 120, 139, 145
Lessing, Doris, 26n, 35, 61, 81
Levey, Kate, 74, 80
Levey, Sir Michael, 80, 109
Loach, Ken,
  Cathy Come Home, 268n
  Up The Junction, 268n
Lodge, David, 16, 268n,
  'The Novelist at the Crossroads', 26n
  'The State of Fiction', 16, 268n

Love, Heather, *Feeling Backward: Loss and the Politics of Queer History*, 113n
Lukács, György, 'Realism in the Balance,' 28n, 268n

MacCabe, Colin, 78, 107
McHale, Brian, 100, 136, 148, 161n
  Postmodernist Fiction, 100, 268n
MacKay, Marina and Lyndsey Stonebridge, *British Fiction After Modernism: The Novel at Mid-Century*, 14–15, 269n
Marcus, Laura, 15, 269n
Marcuse, Herbert, *Eros and Civilisation*, 238–9
Married Women's Property Act, 10
Marriot, Raymond, 38
Marwick, Arthur, 8n, 9, 269n
Memmi, Albert
  The Colonizer and the Colonized Portrait du colonisé, précédé du portrait du colonisateur 139, 159n, 269n
Mental Health Act, 212
Miller, Casey and Kate Swift, *The Handbook of Non-Sexist Writing*, 105–6
Miller, Tyrus, 4, 269n
Millett, Kate, 106
Mitchell, Juliet, 22, 108
Mitchell, Kaye, 20
Mitchell, Kaye and Nonia Williams, 26n, 240n
Mitchison, Lois, 178, 2022n
Modernism, 1, 3–4, 11–17, 23, 33, 70n, 119, 246–7
Movement poets, 13
Mozart, 81, 87, 96–7
Murdoch, Iris, 15, 77, 81, 83, 91, 124, 157n
  'Against Dryness; A Polemical Sketch', 15
  and Brigid Brophy, 77
Mythology, 234, 238, 245
  Bacchae
  Dionysus, 234, 238, 245n
  Pueblo, 234–5

National Women's Liberation Conference, 11
Nelson, Victoria, 58
Nicholls, Peter, 270n
Nin, Anaïs, 37, 47, 55, 67n, 269n

Nouveau roman, 7, 32, 119, 125, 128–31, 199n, 217–21, 226
Nuremberg Trials, 161n
Nye, Robert, 32, 56, 162, 187, 189, 239, 270n

Oakley, Anne, 184
Oates, Joyce Carol, 46
Onega, Susana, 196
Osborne, John, 13, 90, 217, 220
OULIPO, 7, 121, 143
Owen, Peter, 31, 61

Patterson, Ian, 206, 271n
Perec, Georges, 143
 La Disparition, 143
Peterkiewicz, Jerzy, 122
Pinget, Robert, 129
Plain, Gill, 25n, 272n
Poststructuralism, 76, 121, 143
Postmodernism 4, 20, 23, 77, 100, 131, 174, 247
Pound, Ezra, 121, 130, 147
Profumo Affair, 82
Psychoanalysis, 50, 55, 57–8, 82, 109
Public Lending Right, 74, 76, 105, 169

Quin, Ann, 205–45
 Berg, 206, 209, 210–12, 216–25
 Drugs: Peyote and LSD, 239
 Mental illness, 209, 211–13
 New Mexico, 210
 Passages, 233–40
 Robert Creeley, 210–212, 216, 219, 242n
 Three, 225–32
 Tripticks, 206
Queneau, Raymond, 77
De Quincey, Thomas, 56–7, 60

Rabinowitz, Rubin, 12
 The Reaction against Experiment in the English Novel, 1950–60, 12
Realism, 3–5, 12–23, 27n, 28n, 33, 36, 76, 81, 85, 120, 128–31, 167–8, 172–3, 246–7
Reed, Jeremy, 33, 55
Resnais, Alain, 230
Reyes, Heather, 119, 158n, 273n
 L'Année dernière à Marienbad, 230
Robbe-Grillet, Alain, 120, 128, 141, 218–9, 227, 230
 For A New Novel: Essays on Fiction, 120–1, 130–1

La Jalousie, 91, 124, 138
Dans Le Labyrinthe, 128
Rose, Jacqueline, 40
Rowbotham, Sheila, 90, 201n
 Promise of a dream: remembering the Sixties 274n

Sage, Lorna, 120, 124, 131–2, 139, 149, 158n, 274n
 Moments of Truth: Twelve Twentieth-Century Women Writers 156n
Sarraute, Natalie, 16, 21, 121, 128–9, 131, 217–18, 244n, 246
 The Age of Suspicion: Essays on The Novel, 16, 128–9
 Portrait of a Man Unknown, 218
 Tropisms, 218
Sartre, Jean Paul, 27, 139, 159n, 219, 274n
Scholes, Robert, 26n, 274n
Sedgwick, Eve Kosofsky, 93, 113n
Sexual violence, 63–5, 215, 228–9, 237–8
 Ice, 63–5
 Passages, 237–8
 Three, 215, 228–9
 Who are You?, 65
Showalter, Elaine, 19
 A Literature of Their Own: British Women Novelists: From Bronte to Lessing, 19
Sillitoe, Alan, 97, 169
Smith, Ali, 86, 133n, 118, 153n, 226, 247
Snow, C. P. 15, 27n, 127, 156n
 The Two Cultures, 127
Sontag, Susan, 76
Spark, Muriel, 5, 6, 8n, 83, 90, 123, 155n, 275n
 The Comforters 81
Spender, Dale, *Manmade Language* 116n, 275n
Stein, Gertrude, 3, 21, 100
Stevenson, Randall, 14
Stevick, Philip, 206, 212, 218
Stonebridge, Lyndsey and Marina McKay, 15, 26n, 276n
Structuralism, 149
Stevenson, Randall, 14, 26n, 275n
Sturm, Jennifer, 33, 36, 44, 276n
Suleiman, Susan, 28n, 276n
Sward, Robert, 211
Sweeney, Carole, 68n, 276n

Themerson, Stefan, 168
Todd, Janet, 22, 105
Translation, 77, 87, 95, 102–3, 115n, 128, 143–8, 157n, 161n, 165

Valman, Nadia, 198n
  Jewish Women Writers in Britain, 277n
Venuti, Lawrence, 146
Vincennes, L'Université de Paris, 120–1, 125, 133, 150, 156n

Wain, John, 12
War, 9, 11, 177, 187
  rationing, 177
  reconstruction, 9
  VE Day, 187
Waugh, Patricia, 2, 8n, 104, 114n, 176, 278n
Walker, Victoria, 33, 36, 38, 45, 58
Wasson, Sara, 31

Williams, Nonia, 26n, 236, 240n, 241n
Williams, Raymond, 13, 26n, 278n
Williams, William Carlos, 205
Wilson, Leigh, 63, 67n, 71n, 279n
Williamson, Henry, 211–12, 242n
Wittig, Monique, 39, 279n
Women's Auxiliary Air Force, 9, 121–2, 155n
Women's Liberation Movement, 104
Woolf, Virginia, 1, 3, 13, 15, 17–18, 32, 45–6, 85–6, 103, 133, 150, 172–3, 231
  'Modern Fiction', 221
  'Mr. Bennett and Mrs. Brown', 85
  A Room of One's Own, 1, 20, 107, 173
Writers Reading Group, 166–71, 211

Young, Elizabeth, 56, 58

Zambreno, Kate, 69n

EU representative:
Easy Access System Europe
Mustamäe tee 50, 10621 Tallinn, Estonia
Gpsr.requests@easproject.com

www.ingramcontent.com/pod-product-compliance
Lightning Source LLC
Chambersburg PA
CBHW071829230426
43672CB00013B/2798